THE CONTESTED TERRAIN

The Contested Terrain

Perspectives on Education in India

Edited by

SABYASACHI BHATTACHARYA

Orient Longman

ORIENT LONGMAN LIMITED

Registered Office
3-6-272 Himayatnagar, Hyderabad 500 029 (A.P.), India

Other Offices
Bangalore, Bhopal, Bhubaneshwar, Calcutta, Chennai, Ernakulam, Guwahati, Hyderabad, Jaipur, Lucknow, Mumbai, New Delhi, Patna

First Published 1998

Edited by Sabyasachi Bhattacharya
with the assistance of
Joseph Bara, ERRU, Jawaharlal Nehru University

ISBN 81 250 1429 2

Typeset by
Scribe Consultants
New Delhi 110 029

Printed in India at
Baba Barkha Nath Printers
New Delhi 110 015

Published by
Orient Longman Limited
1/24 Asaf Ali Road
New Delhi 110 002

Contents

Acknowledgements

I would like to thank all the authors for their contributions to this volume and for their participation at the Conferences organized at the Educational Records Research Unit, Jawaharlal Nehru University, on March 19–20 and September 26–27, 1997. Acknowledgements are due to the Ministry of Human Resource Development, Government of India, for the grant of Rs 100,000 and to the Indian Council of Historical Research for the grant of Rs 20,000 towards funding these conferences. I am grateful to the members of the ERRU Advisory Board, Dr. Chitra Naik, Professor Amrik Singh, Professor S.C. Shukla, and Professor Tapas Majumdar for their support and advice. The conferences at ERRU owed a great deal to the organizational efficiency of Mr. Joseph Bara who also corrected the proofs of this book expeditiously. I shall be failing in my duty if I do not thank the staff of the ERRU for their supportive role. Finally, I would like to thank Hemlata Shankar of Orient Longman for seeing this volume though press with a rare kind of professional competence and commitment.

SABYASACHI BHATTACHARYA

Notes on the Contributors

PROMESH ACHARYA has taught at the Indian Institute of Management of Calcutta and has conducted several research projects on education in India sponsored by UNESCO, UNDP, Indian Council of Social Science Research etc.; he is widely known as the author of a book on indigenous education in Bengal entitled *Banglar Deshaja Sikshadhara*.

AMRIK SINGH, former Vice-Chancellor of Punjabi University, Patiala, has also played an important role as Secretary of the Association of Indian Universities; he has published his memoirs of Vice-Chancellorship, numerous essays on educational ideas and institutions, *Higher Education in India* and *Redeeming Higher Educational Policy*.

SUMANTA BANERJEE, a journalist and author was associated as Senior Fellow with the National Institute of Adult Education, New Delhi; author of *The Parlour and the Streets: Elite and Popular Culture in 19th Century Calcutta*, he has also published a number of articles on the social history of Bengal in scholarly journals.

JOSEPH BARA, Editor at Educational Records Research Unit, Jawaharlal Nehru University coordinates its research and publication programmes; he has contributed articles and reviews on the subjects of popular education and caste, tribe and class in modern Indian education in scholarly journals; at present he is working on The Evolution of the National Education Movement in India 1880–1905.

APARNA BASU who retired as Professor of history at Delhi University recently, has published *Growth of Education and*

Political Development of India 1898–1920, Essays in the History of Indian Education, apart from several works in the area of gender studies; she is Vice-Pesident of All India Women's Conference and editorial advisor to several gender studies journals within India and abroad.

SABYASACHI BHATTACHARYA, formerly Vice-Chancellor at Visva-Bharati University at Santiniketan, is Professor at the Centre for Historical Studies, J.N.U.; his publications include *The Financial Foundations of the British Raj* and, in the area of history of ideas, he has edited *The Common Pursuit*, on Tagore's educational ideas, and *The Mahatma and the Poet: Debates between Gandhi and Tagore, 1915–1941*.

NARESH P. BHOKTA did his doctoral research at the Central Institute of Education, Delhi University on the issue of language and mass education in colonial India; at present he is Lecturer at the Department of Education, Gorakhpur University, Uttar Pradesh.

UMA DAS GUPTA is at present Regional Director, United Sates Educational Foundation in India in Calcutta; she has published *Rise of an Indian Public: Impact of Official Policy 1870–80* and her post-doctoral research is on the history of Rabindranath Tagore's educational institutions at Santiniketan and Sriniketan, 1901–41.

V.N. DATTA, Emeritus Professor of History at Kurukshetra University; has published a number of books on the nationalist movement; among his other publications are: *Sati: A Historical, Social and Philosophical Enquiry into The Hindu Rite of Widow Burning* and *Maulana Azad*.

JOSEPH DI BONA who has researched Indian education since his visit to Sevagram in 1954 has authored *One Teacher, One School, Change and Conflict in the Indian University* and *Critical Perspectives on Indian Education* as well as numerous research papers.

S. IRFAN HABIB is a Scientist in the History of Science Division at the National Institute of Science, Technology and

Development Studies, New Delhi; the area of his special interest is culture and science in modern India on which he has published a number of essays in academic journals.

HETUKAR JHA, Professor of Sociology, Patna University has published numerous research papers and books on the Sociology of rural India, and rural education and culture in historical perspective; he is currently engaged in studies of folklores and genealogical records of north Bihar.

DEEPAK KUMAR who worked in the History of Science Division in the National Institute of Science, Technology and Development Studies, New Delhi has recently joined JNU as an Associate Professor at Zakir Husain Centre for Educational Studies; he is the author of *The Science and the Raj* and the editor of *Science and Empire* and *Technology and the Raj*.

NITA KUMAR, currently Fellow at the Centre for Studies in Social Sciences at Calcutta is the author of *Lessons from School: Essays on the History of Education in Banaras* and *The Artisans of Banaras*; she has also edited *Women as Subjects*.

B.M. SANKHDHER, a Research Officer with the Educational Records Research Unit, JNU has worked on a number of research volumes on the history of education in modern India; his doctoral thesis has been published under the title *Press, Politics and Public Opinion in India: Dynamics of Social Transformation*; his publications include *Rammohan Roy: An Apostle of Indian Awakening: Some Contemporary Estimates*, *Pioneers of Freedom and Social Change in India*, etc.

S.Y. SHAH, currently Director of Adult, Continuing Education and Extension Unit at JNU earlier served at the National Institute of Adult Education and the Planning Commission; his publications include *Higher Education and Politics in Colonial India*, *Indian Adult Education: A Historical Perspective* and *Source Book on Adult Education*.

S.C. SHUKLA retired as Professor of Education, Central Institute of Education at Delhi University; his publications include *Elementary Education in British India* and *The*

Context of Education in Developing Societies and he was the founder editor of the *Journal of Higher Education* of the University Grants Commission.

R.P. SINGH retired as Professor of Education at the National Council of Educational Research and Training New Delhi; he was Fullbright Fellow on higher education and Joint Secretary at the Ministry of Human Resource Development, Government of India; he has published a number of books and articles on various aspects of education in India.

GOURI SRIVASTAVA is Reader in Education in the Department of Women's Studies, National Council of Educational Research and Training, New Delhi; since completing her M. Phil at JNU and Ph.D. at Delhi University she has published widely in academic journals.

TAN CHUNG was Reader in Chinese at Delhi University from 1971 to 1978 and Professor of Chinese from 1978 to 1994 at JNU; since then he has served as Professor Consultant at Indira Gandhi National Centre for the Arts; his publications include *China and the Brave New World: A Study of the Origin of the Opium War 1840–42* and *Triton and Dragon: Studies on Nineteenth Century China and Imperialism*.

B.R. TOMLINSON, Professor at the Department of History, Strathclyde University, Glasgow is the author of *Indian National Congress and the Raj, 1929–1942: The Penultimate Phase* and *Political Economy of the Raj 1914–1947: The Economics of Decolonisation in India*.

INTRODUCTION

The Contested Terrain of Education

SABYASACHI BHATTACHARYA

This collection of essays aims at providing a comparative and historical perspective on education in modern India. Contributions from some of the leading experts in this area of research—and in some neighbouring areas—have been organized in terms of the following thematic framework: the volume begins with a consideration of the nationalist paradigm, with its many variants, in the educational discourse of the late 19th and early 20th centuries. In this first section we perceive that the educational ideas of Indian nationalists were unlike the philosophy of 'national education' in many other countries where it developed as an instrument of ideologization by the rulers of the new nation states, e.g. Bonapartist France or Bismarckian Germany or post-Risorgimento Italy. A challenge to the colonial approach to education and a critique of state policies characterize nationalist thinking in India from the very beginning. This contestation was, however, marked by an ambivalence. To the beneficiaries of 'English education' in the colonial regime, education was a means of economic advancement, chiefly through employment in the service of the state and its allied agencies. Hence, the ambivalence. And differing appreciation of 'English education' as a conduit to the European world of ideas also accounted for that ambivalence.

Needless to say inequality was inherent in the distribution of educational opportunities and the material benefits that access to education secured. This inequality exacerbated pre-existing inequalities in our society. Hence a second area of contestation: between egalitarian thinking on education and vested interests, between attempts to bring to an end unequal access to education and efforts to preserve it, between the privileged and the disprivileged. This struggle found its way into the educational discourse in a variety of forms: the issue of 'popular education', the denial of parity to the vernacular school system as compared to schools for 'English education', abortive educational efforts among peasants and labouring classes, etc. These issues are addressed in Section II of this volume.

While some historians of education have adopted a somewhat reductionist view of nationalist ideology of education—a point on which a number of the essays in the following pages have critical things to say—an attempt is made in Section III to explore the diversities within the nationalist fold. This is done through the study of the individualities in the approach of some leading thinkers such as Mahatma Gandhi, Rabindranath Tagore and Abul Kalam Azad.

As one would expect, in their proclaimed objective of de-colonizing the educational system, the intellectual leaders of the nationalist school had to negotiate a space for the reception of science and technology from the West (since the production of that species of knowledge was not yet attainable in India). Except for moments of rejection of that gift from the West—a notable moment was the composition of *Hind Swaraj*—its reception, however critical a reception, was inevitably on the agenda. This theme is addressed in Section IV. Now, in the European context the infusion of science and technology into the educational agenda had not been problematic in the same way as it was in India. That infusion was partly demand-led in industrializing societies and, on the supply side, science and technology was an organic growth within the European socio-cultural framework. In India there was no such organic relationship between science-technology education and indigenous society, nor the kind of industrialization that would create demand for it. Given the limited extent to which science and technology could be transmitted, a number of issues came up. How could this knowledge be transmitted through the vernacular medium? How could science be internalized in a culture that no longer participated in the production of scientific knowledge? In the context of the preference of the privileged upper castes for a liberal education that was appropriate for non-manual work, to whom and how was technology to be transmitted? These are some of the questions discussed in the fourth section.

Finally, Section V opens up some much debated issues with essays in cross-cultural comparative studies. These essays also have a bearing on the long-run developments in the Indian educational system leading up to the status of education in our own times. What for instance is the meaning read today in the old contest between indigenistic, nationally oriented education and the universalizing orientation which has been strengthened today by an international communication revolution? Now that the policy of the Mao era (1949–76) of assuring government employment to graduates has been reversed in China in favour of a 'market approach', how will the debate on marketization in India be resolved in the sphere of education? Has post-colonial India measured up to the demands of globalization in terms of her educational system? These are some of the questions which arise out of the empirical studies and analyses in the last section.

☆ ☆ ☆

While this volume has been organized thematically into the five sections outlined above, the integrative element is provided by the design of the conference at which the essays in this anthology were presented. The conference was designed to explore education as a terrain of contestation between ideologies, interests and powers. Needless to say, not all participants shared my own perspective; indeed, in inviting them care was taken to draw in participants with diverse perspectives. This helped towards sharpening the questions.

Let us first spell out the questions, as I see them, in generalized terms before we turn to the specificities of the

Indian context. When we look upon education as part of a certain social formation, i.e. the totality of the socio-economic and political order, the question that unavoidably comes up is, what role does education play in preserving that order, in ensuring the hegemonic position of certain social groups (be it classes or status groups or a foreign ruling race), and by what means does education bring it about? To rephrase Jeremy Bentham's well-known statement on the 'agenda of the state', what is the hidden agenda behind education as a social enterprise, as a system maintenance mechanism in a given social formation? As soon as you face this question you are into an area of contestation between the hegemonized and the hegemons, between ideologies promoting system stability and adversarial ideologies, between those who possess the power to provide and control education and those who are the recipients. In this problematique one can appropriately place the contraposition of the colonial state versus the subject race, the colonial versus nationalist ideological positions, the decision-makers in education policy versus the recipients of education who are denied a subject role. This set of contrapositions is essentially what the contestation is about in the nationalist educational discourse. At the same time, the same problematique also accommodates a different kind of contestation: that between the privileged within Indian society (upper caste, 'English educated', professional occupational groups) and the disprivileged (tribal groups, so-called backward castes or *dalits*, products of vernacular education at best, and more often than not engaged in manual labour). The contest between nationalism in education with the colonial state is inseparably intertwined historically with the contest for hegemony within our society.

In suggesting this approach, it is my contention that in the light of generic questions arising out of it we may arrive at a common interpretative framework in order to elicit the general significance of the emprically rich essays in the following pages, essays elucidating particular segments of the educational discourse in colonial India.

In relation to education in capitalist society Pierre Bourdieu has offered a conceptual framework which emphasises the role of education as a means of "reproduction of knowledge" for the common masses; this essentially is a means of reproducing or preserving the capitalist society. This education for the masses is distinguished by him from the "production of knowledge" which is the outcome of education of a higher order.[1] By an extension of that argument I may suggest that in the imperial scheme, the *production* of knowledge is a function attributed to the metropolitan country ruling the Empire, while the *reproduction* of that knowledge, its transmission and replication, is the function assigned to the education system for the colonized people. It can be further argued that the colonial system of education can be viewed as a means of the preservation and reproduction of colonial authority, not only *cognitive* authority but also *political* authority, among the "natives" of the colonized country. Likewise, we may argue that what we have said about the colonial-metropolitan relationship could be hypothesized in respect of the concentration of the competence in the production of knowledge in the sphere of the socially and educationally privileged, and the reinforcement of the cognitive authority and hegemony of that stratum. This is a somewhat schematic statement but it serves for the present in explicating the two terrains of contestation I mentioned earlier, i.e. the fight on two fronts, against challenges to hegemony within colonial India society and against colonialism without. The empirical studies available in this volume allow us to test the hypotheses posited above. Let us turn now to these studies.

☆ ☆ ☆

Two sets of essays in Section I and II explore the issues contested at the interface between the evolving paradigms of colonial, national and popular education.

Sumanta Bannerjee examines the ideas and activities of the middle class social reformers in 19th century Bengal engaged in educating the labouring poor. Case studies of two such experiments have been offered: a school for peasant boys set up in 1863–64 and an educational enterprise among industrial workers in Calcutta, along with a broadsheet published for their benefit, from 1874.[2] The first experiment, launched by a middle-class social reform association patronized by the local *zamindar* lasted about a year, and the second which was the creation of a dedicated philanthropist Sashipada Banerjee, lasted for about a decade. Shortlived as they were—comparable to the unsustainability of literacy programmes in our days, Banerjee observes—these are interesting instances of the middle class or the *bhadralok* trying to expand the ambit of education to include the labouring poor. But what kind of education was it and what kind of purpose did it serve? Banerjee regards these as pioneering attempts to introduce what we call today functional literacy and also as attempts to evolve a limited kind of education which would function as "socializing mechanisms so that the labourers were mentally oriented towards the type of work that they were expected to do." It was essentially a strategy for building a better qualified labour force and hence emphasis in the teaching programme on "deference and loyalty to superiors, and individual enterprise and perserverence for self-advancement.... Both the experiments turned out to be instruments to facilitate the integration of labourers into the logic of the prevalent economic system and bring about conformity to it, instead of helping them to deal critically with reality and alter the existing circumstances."

Poromesh Acharya in his essay on the law and politics of primary education in Bengal clearly shows that "the attitudes of Hindu *bhadraloks* of Bengal towards the primary education of the mass of the people were not really very sympathetic."[3] Even at the all-India level, the Indian National Congress did not pass a resolution to demand free and compulsory primary education till 1904, i.e. only after Curzon took the initiative to accept that as a duty of the state. Acharya argues that the middle class beneficiaries of 'English education' at high schools and colleges fought hard against extension of compulsory primary education because that would have meant corresponding reduction in government funding for higher education. Efforts in the late 1920's to enact a law to tax the rural wealthy to fund schools for the poor were opposed by middle class associations and proto-political groups: they "almost in unison opposed fresh taxation in the form of education cess for expanding primary education facilities." The opposition of the landlords was particularly strong throughout the first half of the 20th century. These and other evidence cited in his essay leads Acharya to emphasize in his narration of events from 1920's till today, "the apathy of the Indian elite or dominant classes towards the education of the mass of the people."

An extremely interesting kind of evidence is provided by Naresh Prasad Bhokta in his paper on the marginalisation of folk languages in northern India in the last decades of the 19th and the early years of the 20th century.[4] It seems that privileging the English language vis-a-vis the socalled vernacular languages was accompanied by a process of disprivileging folk languages or dialects vis-a-vis Sanskritised, chaste Hindi or *shisht bhasha*. The *lok bhasha*, i.e. the languages o the common people, like Maithli, Bhojpuri, Awadhi, Brajbhasha, etc. had developed to a high form in course of the *Bhakti* movement in the period between the fourteenth and the seventeenth centuries. But from the late nineteenth century the schools run by the missionaries, the government and the local 'English educated' gentry gradually replaced the *lok bhasha*—earlier used, at least in primary schools—with the *khari boli* or *shisht bhasha*. Thus the "middle class tried to foster its separate cultural identity." The exclusion of the *lok bhasha* from the *pathshalas* (primary schools) adversely affected the participation of lower caste students. This applies with equal force in the case of tribal groups of Chhotanagpur and Santal Parganas. G.A. Grierson, the author of the monumental *Linguistic Survey of India* (1903–1928) was a lone dissenter in the ranks of the bureaucracy and his protestations were brushed aside by a government which was all for standardization of text-books in *shisht* Hindi. Bhokta's essay provides significant evidence of the consequences of a cultural hegemony in the sphere of school education.

Joseph Bara addresses the same question in a more general perspective. Preservation of traditional social hierarchy and denial of educational equity to the under-privileged castes and tribal groups remained the over-riding facts of the educational scene in the colonial period.[5] In his view, the scene immediately preceding the colonial period is characterized by greater educational equity than the colonial period; be that as it may, Joseph Bara demonstrates that efforts like Gokhale's Elementary Education Bill (1911) notwithstanding, the Indian elite did not put education for the masses very high on their agenda; nor was this objective pursued with the same political will which was displayed in the constitutional and political struggle. He concludes that the Indian middle class "had firmly entrenched itself into the bureaucracy and the social system in general and it could not compromise with any educational measure that it feared could destabilize their established social position." While this accords with the judgement of other scholars in the area of educational research, e.g. Krishna Kumar,[6] the picture is fuzzy so far as the pre-colonial past is concerned.

Eighteenth century India, in the opinion of Dharampal,[7] was endowed with institutions of popular education, an indigenous tradition that was lost in course of the nineteenth century under the Macaulay dispensation. Joseph Di Bona[8] also tends to present the indigenous system of schooling at the popular level in a very favourable light compared to the system introduced under British rule. Kazi Shahidullah has praised the *pathshalas* or indigenous schools, "secular educational institutions imparting practical instruction in accordance with the requirements of the local community" in early 19th century Bengal; he has shown how governmental intervention undermined this system.[9] The well-known sociologist Hetukar Jha in his essay in this volume records that a network of similar schools in early 19th century Bihar was "an institutionalized part of rural life.... The children of the peasantry belonging to different castes and communities were equipped with enough competence in such schools for carrying on their occupational obligations."[10] He cites James Ray Hagen's research in support of his argument that while some of these indigenous schools were annexed to the system created under British rule in the 1870's the rest of them declined precipitately for want of funding. The resumption of revenue free land by the British government denied funds for these schools while the caste associations of Bhumihar Brahmans and Kayasthas abandoned indigenous schools in favour of 'English education' to secure government jobs from about the end of the 19th century.

While it is true that the network of indigenous schools does appear to be very widespread, we have no quantitative data on their reach and the level of literacy in pre-colonial times; moreover what was the content of the education they imparted? In Shahidullah's opinion: "children were given an education not to enlarge their mind.... They were taught simply because they needed to learn how to address the landlord and village elders, and how to protect themselves against dishonest reckoning of the moneylenders the shopkeepers, and the landlord's steward."[11] Poromesh Acharya's extensive research into the indigenous schooling system led him to the conclusion that, in Bengal, it "served the practical needs of daily life" and it "contributed in perpetuating the hierarchical social structure and Brahminic hegemony over society."[12] We have to await further research but it is advisable to be cautious against idealization of the indigenous schooling for the 'masses' in pre-colonial or early colonial times.

At the same time, it is difficult to agree with Nigel Crook when be reduces transmission of knowledge through the indigenous system for the people to mere 'memory access', as in a computer, as distinct from 'cognitive competence'. Since Crook's book is the latest in the field and is likely to be influential, the point calls for some elaboration'.[13] Like Bourdieu, Nigel Crook makes a distinction between knowledge production capacity and mere reproduction of knowledge. "Cognitive competence is the storage of programmes (K).

Knowledge of facts is the storage of raw data to which these programmes can be applied (M). More precisely, I would add, cognitive competence is the storage of programmes to write programmes (K_1), as well as the storage of programmes to analyse raw data (K_2).... The rich and powerful (whom initially we take the liberty to assume to have acquired K_1, K_2, and M) devise an educational policy for their society. The expansion of M is beneficial to their social structure and is fairly harmless without K. The expansion of K_2, and *a fortiori* of K_1, is potentially harmful to the reproduction of society (since it creates the ability to challenge the rich and the powerful themselves) but their lethal nature is somewhat mitigated if there is little M to work on." (p. 4) The rich and the powerful "withhold K_1 and K_2" to perpetuate their own hegemony; they may be compelled to transmit part of what they have and withhold if external challenge to the society so demands. Such a transmission of K-type knowledge involves them in a dilemma.

I think there are some problems with this model. The conceptual distinction made between M (= information, 'knowledge of facts'), and K (= cognitive competence) divisible into K_1 (cognitive strategies) and K_2 (intellectual skills to process information) is useful. So far so good. It is age old wisdom that $M \neq K$; that M is not equal to K should not however lead us to extend the computer-derived analogy (data and programming) too far, as I think Crook does. Secondly, the model, in positing effective exclusion (as distinct from intended exclusion) of the hegemonised from transmission of K-type competence and knowledge is possibly erroneous. I will take the second point first.

The Crook model does not seem to fit all classes of knowledge. Consider for instance bits of knowledge accumulating in the 'M' sector as a result of praxis, the application of prior 'M' resources in practice by people who are 'excluded' from access to the 'K' sector. The artisan's or the skilled worker's knowledge accumulating in praxis is different in nature from another kind of knowledge, say the grammarian's knowledge or the theologian's knowledge i.e.

knowledge in the hands of people to whom the 'K' sector is accessible. But it will be absurd to deny that both are kinds of knowledge. (Consider, for example, technological advancement built upon artisans' knowledge and practice). The implication of Crook's model is to deny it. Or, more accurately, if there is any difference in the epistemological status of the two, he does not state it. In fact Crook admits it in an oblique fashion that his model of K would deny a place to the category of knowledge I have exemplified with an artisan: "we are postulating a working hypothesis that knowledge of the 'K' type *tends* to be concentrated in the rich and powerful in the stable state." (p. 5) It is curious that elsewhere Crook says: "It is as dangerous to *assume* creative competence in the subalterns as it is to *deny* it," (p. 25) Deny it he does in the postulate identifying 'K' as an exclusive attribute of the "rich and powerful." Crook's intellectual stance vis-a-vis the 'subaltern class's' knowledge and practices clearly privileges the knowledge system of the hegemonic class.

The other problem with the model is that it leaves out the feedback loops in mapping the flow of M and K. Or, to put it in a stronger statement, he makes an unreal distinction between information and judgement, between M and K. A distinction between M and K sectors is no doubt conceptually valid. In human society, however, cognitive competence or K is the outcome of accumulation of M, unlike the intelligent machines from which the computer analogy is derived by Crook. The computer is programmed externally by man (and even self-programming of the machine is itself the consequence of an externally planted programme). Who programmes the programmer when we are considering not a machine but a human social system? None externally, at least not *ab initio*; for it is the result of feedback loops between M and K. Crook could not have been unaware of that, but in the model he presents the feedback circuitry is not given attention; as a result one gets a picture of a static machine which, as in initial condition, is endowed with a M sector and a K sector. In reality in human social systems K grows out of M so to speak. That is not to say that: $M_1 + M_2 + M_3 \ldots M_n = K$. But the aggregation and synergistic interaction within M leads to K. Only the K type judgement or cognitive competence can recognize and accumulate M or data, and accumulation of data enables K type judgements to be made. In writing history there is a pretty common example of this in our effort to judge the "factness" of facts, to apply judgement to data.

If this point about the feedback process between M and K sectors is conceded an interesting logical consequence follows. Nigel Crook's thesis on the control of K sector and exclusion of subaltern classes from K-type exercises is irretrievably damaged. What happens to the hegemons doling out bits of 'M' judiciously, to keep the system going but carefully keeping K type cognitive competence to itself in order to preserve its own hegemony? They might find critical cognitive competence growing despite their effort to "control the expansion" of knowledge among the disprivileged and the hegemonised. Thus, in the ultimate analysis, no knowledge is "safe" for the system the hegemons wish to preserve. Rationed supply of 'M' in Crook's model has the potential to lead to K-type competence, damaging to homeostasis. At the same time a modicum of 'M' is necessary to make the system a going concern. This is the essential contradiction that faces the masters of the system of "controlling knowledge".

Crook does identify a dilemma of this kind but, as we have seen, to him the dilemma arises as a result of *external* challenge. The scenario fits some historical situations, but neglects the *internal* dynamics of the so-called stable system and this is because of his separation of "knowledge of fact" from "knowledge of how" (p. 3). This separation, it has been argued above, is alright as an *analytical* distinction but it is inapplicable to the *process* of knowledge formation and transmission.

Finally, it must be recognized that Nigel Crook's is an excellent exposition of the thesis that educational and other knowledge transmission institutions are ideological apparatuses of the hegemones in society and allows "the rich and the powerful to reproduce their position". It is a thesis in itself unexceptionable. And what I have said in criticism of its exposition by Crook means to suggest not the rejection of the theoretical approach but to demand its refinement, i.e. to point to the need for more room in that model for real historical processes as distinct from linear relationships between theoretical constructs.

If, as I have argued earlier, the contest was not only between "the rich and the powerful" natives and the natives hegemonized, but also between the colonial rulers and the colonized,—an aspect Crook altogether ignores—what form did that other contest assume? The more purely ideological form is examined in S.C. Shukla, V.N. Datta, Gauri Srivastava and B.M. Sankhdher. Nationalism in its programmatic form and in institution building has been studied by Amrik Singh, Aparna Basu, Uma Dasgupta and Nita Kumar.

When we look back upon personalities like Abul Kalam Azad (in V.N. Datta's essay), Mahatma Gandhi (Amrik Singh, B.M. Sankhdher) or Rabindranath Tagore one cannot fail to be impressed with the ideals which inspired them, and, at the same time, the ambivalences and limitations of the nationalist agenda of action cannot be denied. V.N. Datta cites Maulana Azad's speech in Lok Sabha at a time when he was assailed by latter-day politicians: "Forty years ago, when nobody had even heard of my friends sitting around here, I decided to dedicate my life to the service of my country. I am talking of 1907 when I was 18 or 19 years of age and joined the Revolutionary Party of Bengal.... When a man expels personal interest from his life, he is free and detached. Do you know what it means to be free and detached. You do not know."[14] Azad spoke here for a generation of intellectual leaders who did indeed dedicate their life to a cause which was, in their light, above and beyond personal and material interests. In contrast, look at the equally honest and perspicacious statement of G.L. Mehta: "does not the coward lurk in me—does not the lover of ease and comfort, the talker and not the doer, prompt me to give intellectual justification for my inability to sacrifice? ... Is it not one's duty as an Indian to see that the challenge of the government meets with a universal response .... Alas! only if I had got some strength of character, some overpowering moral conviction, that would conquer my hesitation, incapacity to sacrifice ..."[15] Amrik Singh cites this letter, written during the Non-cooperation Movement, to illustrate "the dilemma confronting the Indian middle class."[16] I contrapose these two passages to point to the need to look at, to use a cliche, 'both sides of the question' so that we might steer clear of stereotypical eulogy on the one hand and denigration on the other.

I think that collectively these essays, written from different perspectives, help us to arrive at such a balanced evaluation. These essays indicate that while the significance of the nationalist agenda 'decolonizing' education is recognized, an uncritical attitude towards the heroic age of nationalist struggle is now a thing of the past. It is recognized that, as Aparna Basu puts it perceptively, it was appropriate that "education was a central concern in the nationalist quest for self-identity, for it was in education that the cultural agenda of colonization had been most succinctly expressed."[17] However, the essays in the following pages also reflect a very critical stance towards nationalist initiatives and institutions in the sphere of education. (A cynic might say that this is what calls for an explanation: are not the critics the successors to the pre-independence nationalist intelligentsia as well as the beneficiaries of what they had wrought?) What are the main strands of criticism?

A great deal of criticism is focused upon the role of the "middle classes". This is a recurrent theme. Amrik Singh insightfully examines the limited success of that great spurt in nationalist educational activities, the boycott during the Non-cooperation Movement of 1920–22. He points to the fact that Mahatma Gandhi's calls for boycott of schools and colleges did *not* bring about a "spectacular decline in the number of students" from 1919 to 1922. As for the alternative institutions created under nationalist auspices, "none of these institutions flourished in any significant way.... When Gandhi launched his non-cooperation movement he had no alternative except to seek to mobilize the middle class. But this itself was the cause of weakness..." Likewise, R.P. Singh in his narration of British educational policy in the nineteenth century concludes that the beneficiaries of the nineteenth century educational system were "basically pragmatists: they have had their educational preferences and economic goals in tune with time", guided by "instincts of survival".[18]

Aparna Basu in her detailed study of the National Education movement in Bengal in 1905–11 shows that British officials were apprehensive of the National Schools, about forty in number, as "nurseries of sedition".[19] But this fear exaggerates the long-term effects of that kind of institutional enterprise. The National Schools—with the exception of the Technical Institute—declined and disappeared within a decade: their students were acceptable to "neither the government nor European merchant houses" and thus their student intake fell with the dissipation of the initial euphoria of 1905–07. The commitment of an ambivalent *bhadralok* class did not last long.

S.C. Shukla in course of his discursive reflections on nationalism and education, draws upon his vast experience and earlier writings, beginning from his unpublished Ph.D. thesis of 1958.[20] "The point of these discursive statements", he remarks, "for the present discussion is that there are many discourses in the educational area which were embedded—and perhaps have even existed in actual fact—of which most scholars at least are not aware. So also, the educational ideas of the socialist, working class, peasant movements and those self-proclaimed 'nationalists' of the Hindu Mahasabha... The definitional problem of what constitutes nationalist educational through is, therefore, a complex one." In the interest of accuracy one must note that diversities within the nationalist discourse on education have been recognized even in the commonly used text-books, e.g. the work of J.P. Naik and Syed Nurrullah, first published in 1945.[21] However, there is perhaps an urgent need to re-examine the diversities in the political agenda, the search for cultural identity and the 'technology of education' within the discourse of National Education. This has to be done through empirical research. One of the best examples of that kind of research is Nita Kumar's essay in this volume, 'Why does national education fail?'[22] This case study of new educational institutions in Banaras from the 1880's to 1930's, involves detailed examination of the agents involved in actually creating and running institutions—"the local social and economic leaders of small towns, those in trade, banking, the professions and service, groups neither under-privileged nor national level thinkers," and yet part of "a quasi-nationalist quest for... the construction of a new, modern self by building educational institutions." Nita Kumar points out that her evidence suggest that various "occupational, regional or caste groups" did not feel a need to give up their identities, on the contrary each defended by means of education "its identity, its self-hood." Thus, educational institutions like that built by the Khatris of Banaras, while being part of an all-national effort to create a space outside of the State-sponsored educational system, simultaneously promoted and consolidated a group identity of a caste. As regards the failure of many such institutions, Nita Kumar suggests that it was mainly at the level of "the technology of education... physical space, curricula, and rituals" of schooling; "the failure of the middle level nationalists and Indianists and progressivists in cities like Banaras was a pedagogic and technical one, not a political one."

Another limitation of the institutional initiatives to offer an alternative to the colonial educational system is brought out by Uma Das Gupta in her essay on Tagore's Visva-Bharati. "Sriniketan and Santineketan contributed to a significant change in middle class Indian taste... to the cultural enrichment of the elite. But the village hardly changed."[23] Thus Sriniketan, founded to be a change-agent in rural reconstructions, failed; as for Santiniketan where the school and departments of higher studies were located, that too "fell well behind the founder's goal of creating an Indian who would become the social conscience and cultural leader in that age." There have been many appreciative commentaries on Tagore's educational philosophy, from Sarvepalli

Radhakrishnan's during Tagore's life-time till today;[24] but the institutional form of his educational ideas left the poet himself deeply dissatisfied. It is not surprising that to the middle classes the aesthetic excellence attained at Tagore's schools of science and art and artisenal production mattered more than the message of social responsibility which Tagore put highest on his agenda. I have argued elsewhere that Tagore, self-critical as always, realized how circumscribed and limited was the social impact of his intervention in education and thus he turned to the concept of *loka-shiksha* or popular education through non-formal means.[25]

Gauri Srivastava has shown in her paper that while educated men did a great deal to spread education among women, their project was cast, judging by the evidence produced here, in a highly male-centered frame of mind. The objective was stated to be, as B.M. Malabari put it, "improvement of the home" by making women fit for their role as mothers and wives; "an educated man cannot share his life with an illiterate life", said the poet Narmada; Kashibai Kanitkar took to educating herself because her husband disliked her "ordinary looks" and thought that only if she were educated "it would be possible to live with her...."[26] These are some of Gauri Srivastava's evidence which suggest a somewhat instrumentalist view of education for women—they were to be educated to make them better marriage partners and mothers. Since Srivastava has not problematized the issue in her narrative of educational initiatives targeted towards women, we cannot go deeper into the complexity of the gender question in this context. However, there is plenty of evidence in the recent research of many other scholars indicating the consequences of gender discrimination in the sphere of educational efforts of the late 19th and early 20th centuries.

Finally, one may note a fissure within the group of nationalist thinkers in terms of attitude to Western civilization. From *Hind Swaraj* to *The Discovery of India*, from the first decade of this century to Independence, from Mahatma Gandhi to Jawaharlal Nehru, there was a continuing debate on this issue. This has not been sufficiently explored in this volume. The most significant example of this aspect of the cultural discourse of the early 20th century was the long debate between Mahatma Gandhi and Rabindranath Tagore. Tagore pointed to the assimilation of many cultures in Indian civilization through the ages, and to the need to view Western civilization—in particular its gift of science and technology—as a part of an universal human heritage, and thus to redefine India's cultural personality.[27] Mahatma Gandhi's approach in *Hind Swaraj* (1909): "I believe that the civilization India has evolved is not to be beaten in the world. Nothing can equal the seeds sown by our ancestors... India remains immovable and that is her glory... India has nothing to learn from anybody else and this is as it should be."[28] Gandhi seems to have evolved a different intellectual stance by 1921 in course of his debates with Tagore. Witness, that memorable statement: "I do not want my house to be walled in all sides and my windows to be stuffed. I want the culture of all the lands to be blown about my house as freely as possible. But I refuse to be blown off my feet."[29]

One aspect of the above debate is addressed in a set of essays by Deepak Kumar, B.R. Tomlinson and S. Irfan Habib in this volume. How was a space for science and technology to be negotiated within the framework of a colonial culture which did not have a participatory role in the production of knowledge in that sphere, and in a colonial economy that did not generate the kind of synergistic relationship between industry and science-technology which characterized developed countries of the West?

As regards the reception of Western science "the dilemma faced by the Indian educationists was pretty real," writes Deepak Kumar. "Total acceptance of the Western episteme was not held desirable, while its rejection was almost impossible. There were no clear-cut solutions."[30] Hence an intellectual ambivalence and self-contradictions. There were some who aimed at a "synthesis". And there were some who accepted the superiority of Western science; the influence of Comtean Positivism was a factor,[31] and so was the rationalist criticism of elements in traditional Indian culture.[32] Deepak Kumar rejects Krishna Kumar's characterization of this attitude as "paternalistic in the style of English administrators", indistinguishable from the attitude of "every English officer in India". [30] Deepak Kumar's view is that "this similarity is superficial. The diagnosis (by the colonial bureaucracy and Indian science educationists like M.L. Sircar) might be the same, but their motives and methods differed and their prescriptions differed even more. The colonialist and the nationalist discourse cannot be painted with the same broad brush."[34] The second major conclusion Deepak Kumar arrives at is as follows: Science was generally recognized as a priority in the thinking of the nationalist agenda of education in Bengal, but in fact "the educational *juggernaut* remained the way it was.... In a homogeneous and free country like Japan it was possible to take the new knowledge to every section of society. In contrast the Indian policy was that light must reach the mountain tops, before it can pierce to the levels and the depths. It remained a pious hope and could never become a reality." As to why and how this happened, S. Irfan Habib's essay provides valuable evidence. His argument is that in colonial policy, science education was conceived in a model which "did not involve any participatory element from (or role of) the local population which was supposed to receive the scientific wisdom from above" in a passive manner.[35] One way of breaking this pattern, restricting science knowledge to the English educated upper strata, was to spread scientific works in vernacular languages, in the form of translations and also original writings. An effort made in this direction by Master Ramchandra and Munshi Zakaullah in the last half of the 19th century in Delhi has been studied by Habib. He shows that "the dependence of the intellectuals on the colonial state's initiative for the implementation of their programme made this design a self-defeating exercise since it was distinctly different in its assumptions and purposes from the colonial educational policy."

B.R. Tomlinson in his paper in this volume proposes to examine Indian receptiveness to technical education between 1880 and 1914.[36] He examines "the mixture of political, philanthropic and educational motives" in the founding of two non-government institutions, Bengal Technical Institute (1906) which later became the Jadavpur University, and the Indian Institute of Science (1911) in Bangalore, as well as some other educational initiatives including those by the government. Tomlinson finds that science and technology was valued "as a badge of modernity" by the Indian intellectuals and educators but there was a stress on "high culture over artisanal skills", a higher value attributed to "the theoretical over the practical", and hence an impediment to the internalization of technology. In brief, gentlemen would not soil their hands in manual work. Hence a scarcity of 'suitable boys', i.e. the technically trained. To what extent we can accept a supply-side explanation of retardation of Indian economic growth, in terms of non-availability of human capital, is not examined by Tomlinson; while he does not accept a totally culturalist explanation, he raises important questions about the culture of the high caste, 'English-educated' *babus*' preference for non-maual occupations and their distance from the artisan's shop or the factory floor.

When we turn to the contemporary scene, in the essays in the last section, we can observe continuities which suggest that the fifty years since 1947 have not taken us very far from the pre-independence period and its concerns. The concern of those days with 'popular education', or lack of it, match with India's present day engagement with adult literacy.[37] Likewise indigenism versus universalism in education,[38] and search for roots of education in a country's civilization[39] fall in a recursive pattern, though the context of the discourse has changed today. The change which leaps to the eye is that the world has, so to speak, shrunk and global patterns push us into patterns of thought and action which are much less local or national in origin than they ever were. S.Y. Shah has elaborated on the permeation of ideas and action programmes from overseas in India. Joseph Di Bona: "As the world becomes more closely integrated financially, industrially and in terms of communication and media, there appears to be a greater need for national systems of education to reflect the global tendency..." Tan Chung feels the need to look at Chinese education today "through the prism of India." With globalization, a cross-cultural comparative approach seems inherent in these scholars' analyses of the contemporary educational scene. While that has lessons for us we must also look back upon India's own historical experience. As Di Bona has said in his insightful reflective essay in the following pages: "It seems appropriate to look carefully at this storehouse of experience" so that we may try to "combine the best of the past with the future needs of society."[40] Our interrogation of the past and the contestations in the terrain of education from diverse perspectives in this volume will hopefully push forward such an endeavour.

Notes

1. Pierre Bourdieu, 'Cultural reproduction and social reproduction' in R. Brown (ed.) *Knowledge, education and cultural change: Papers in the sociology of education* (London, 1973); P. Bourdieu and J.C. Passeron, *Reproduction in education, society and culture* (London, 1977).
2. Sumanta Banerjee, 'Education of the labouring poor in 19th century Bengal: Two experiments', *infra* Section II. A school for peasants' children at the initiative of members of the intelligentsia of Bengal was a rare instance in 1863–64; when Rabindranath Tagore established a school of that kind at Sriniketan, with the assistance of L.K. Elmhirst, in 1922 it was the unique instance of such initiative in Bengal; *vide* S. Bhattacharya 'Introduction' pp. 13–38, in Sabyasachi Bhattacharya and A. Mukhopadhyay (eds.) *The Common Pursuit* (Visva Bharati, Calcutta, 1995), on Tagore's educational thinking on rural schooling system.
3. Poromesh Acharya, 'Law and politics of primary education in Bengal', *infra*, Section II.
4. N.P. Bhokta, 'Marginalisation of popular languages and growth of sectarian education in colonial India', *infra*, Section II.
5. Joseph Bara, 'Colonialism and educational fragmentation in India', *infra*, Section II.
6. Krishna Kumar, *Political agenda of education: a study of colonialist and nationalist ideas* (Delhi, 1991).

7. Dharampal, *The beautiful tree: indigenous education in the 18th century* (Delhi, 1983).
8. Joseph Di Bona, *One teacher, one school* (Delhi, 1983).
9. Kazi Shahidullah, 'The purpose and impact of government policy on *pathshala gurumahashays*', in N. Crook (ed.), *The transmission of knowledge in South Asia* (Delhi, 1966), pp. 119–134.
10. Hetakar Jha, 'Decline of vernacular education in Bihar in the 19th century', *infra*, Section II; an eminent sociologist, Dr. Jha is known for his work on caste mobility in Bihar and his observations here on Bhumihar and Kayastha castes vis-a-vis the rest is of special significance. James Ray Hagen's Ph.D. thesis cited by him, is entitled 'Indigenous Society, the political economy and colonial education in Patna district: 1811–1951' (Ph.D. thesis, University of Virginia, 1981).
11. K. Shahidullah, *op. cit.*, p. 132.
12. Poromesh Acharya, 'Indigenous education and Bhahminical hegemony in Bengal', in N. Crook (ed.) *op. cit.*, 116; also see Acharya, *Banglar deshaja shikshadhara* (Calcutta, 1989).
13. Nigel Crook, 'The control and expansion of knowledge' in Crook (ed.) *The transmission of knowledge in South Asia* (Delhi, 1996).
14. Abul Kalam Azad's speech in the Lok Sabha, 20 May 1954, cited in V.N. Datta, 'Maulana Azad's perception of Muslim education', *infra*, Section III.
15. G.L. Mehta to S.A. Barelvi, Jan. 1922, cited in Amrik Singh, 'Education and the national movement', *infra*, Section I.
16. Amrik Singh, *op. cit.*, On the 'middle class' as a category in historiography, Sabyasachi Bhattacharya 'Notes on the role of the intelligentsia in colonial society: India from the mid-nineteenth century', *Studies in History*, Jan-June 1979, pp. 89–104.
17. Aparna Basu, 'National education in Bengal, 1905–1912', *infra*, Section I.
18. R.P. Singh, 'British educational policy in 19th century India: a nationalist critique', *infra*, Section I.
19. Aparna Basu, *op. cit.*
20. S.C. Shukla, 'Nationalist educational thought: continuity and change', *infra*, Section I.
21. J.P. Naik and S. Nurullah, *A students' history of education in India, 1800–1973* (Delhi, 1945, 6th ed. 1974).

22. Nita Kumar, 'Why does nationalist education fail? The case of Banaras, 1880's to the 1930's,' *infra*, Section I.
23. Uma Das Gupta, 'Rabindranath Tagore's educational experiment at Santiniketan and Sriniketan, 1901–1941', *infra*, Section III.
24. S. Radhakrishnan, *The philosophy of Rabindranath Tagore* (reprint, Baroda, 1961); L.K. Elmhirst, *Rabindranath Tagore: A pioneer in education* (London, 1961); H.B. Mukherjee, *Education for fulness* (Bombay, 1962); Mohit Chakraborti, *Tagore and Education for rural change* (Calcutta, 1993).
25. Sabyasachi Bhattacharya, 'Introduction' in Bhattacharya and A. Mukhopadhyay, *op. cit.* (1995), pp. 13–38.
26. Gauri Srivastava, 'The contribution of the male intelligentsia in promoting women's education in Bombay Presidency', *infra*, Section III.
27. Sabyasachi Bhattacharya (ed.), *The Mahatma and the Poet: letters and debates between Gandhi and Tagore, 1915–1941* (Delhi, 1997), editor's Introduction, pp. 1–37.
28. M.K. Gandhi, *Hind Swaraj, Collected Works of Mahatma Gandhi* (Delhi, 1963), Vol. X, pp. 36–37.
29. M.K. Gandhi, 'The great sentinel', *Young India*, 1 June 1921. An evaluation of Mahatma Gandhi's views on culture vis-a-vis education is the subject of M. Sankhdher, 'Mahatma Gandhi, British colonialism and India's movement for national education', *infra*, Section III.
30. Deepak Kumar, 'Educational ideas of the Indian men of science: Bengal, 1850–1920', *infra*, Section IV.
31. While Positivism did encourage a kind of radical nationalism, as suggested by Kumar, its multivocal nature in Bengal, also engendering a species of conservatism, should be considered; this was my argument in S. Bhattacharya, 'Positivism in 19th century Bengal' in R.S. Sharma (ed.), *Indian Society: Historical Probings: In Memory of D.D. Kosambi* (Delhi, 1974).
32. Kumar observes that M.L. Sircar looked to modern science "as a cure for defects in the Hindu mind", Kumar, *op. cit.*
33. Krishna Kumar, 'Colonial citizen as an educational ideal', *Economic and Political Weekly*, 28 Jan. 1989, cited by Deepak Kumar.
34. Deepak Kumar, *op. cit.*
35. S. Irfan Habib, 'Teaching science through the local language: an aborted pedagogical project', *infra*, Section IV.

36. B.R. Tomlinson, "Searching for a 'suitable boy': technical education in colonial India, 1880–1914", *infra*, Section IV.
37. S.Y. Shah, 'International cooperation in Indian adult education: Indo-British scenario 1970–1990', *infra*, Section V.
38. Joseph Di Bona, 'Going back to the educational future', *infra*, Section V.
39. Tan Chung, 'Education in China through Indian eyes', *infra*, Section V.
40. Joseph Di Bona, *op. cit.*

Section I: The Concept of National Education

Nationalist Educational Thought: Continuity and Change

SURESHCHANDRA SHUKLA

The exploration of nationalist educational thought commenced with a counterposure of national to colonial.[1] One also had to interrogate the dichotomy,[2] as there were many strands in either which coincided with the assumed opposite. (Saying "assumed" does not in any way imply a denial of the basic opposition between colonial and national on both educational and broader fronts.) We are now also extending our discussion to the contemporary relevance of nationalist thought on education, a difficult and perhaps even problematic enterprise. For relevance is not independent of both context and goals; both vary over time and also with different elements in society at the same time. Even to the extent a national goal can be defined, one notices changes in its variation over time: for instance, from the early years when we were laying the basis of society and economy in independent India, through the "socialistic", "self-reliant" economy of the next three or more decades, to the not-quite-unanimously agreed liberalization and internationalization of the economy and corresponding shifts in social, political, educational and cultural policies. Understandably, it is possible to draw on many different sources in the nationalist educational discourse to take off for the varying goals of contemporary times.

It is customary to begin a consideration of nationalist thought with a look at the pre-independence period. There are, however, important ideas and policies of the period following independence which deserve our consideration; they are integrally related, and are temporal and logical outcomes of nationalist thought.

India as Nation

The "nation" in our country is itself a widely discussed, if not actually contested entity or category—both post-and pre-independence. Some of us have lived through times when two nations were emphatically, and ultimately successfully asserted. The third "separate" entity-in-the-making—dalits (scheduled castes of yesteryear and the Constitution)—did not or could not quite materalize then, and has not so far asserted nationhood, though (now Babasaheb) Ambedkar's assertive separation from the Hindu fold, later formalized for some dalits by conversion to Buddhism (which many would assert is only a form of Hindusim) has now been emphatically documented in academic and theoretical terms,[3] as much as it is presented in political domains by dalit spokespersons themselves.

Many linguistic-cultural units of India, the Tamils most conspicuous among them, have asserted a separate nationhood for themselves, both before and after independence. Some in the north-east and north-west are continuing to do so, though possibly less stridently. It is arguable that the civilizational state that is India according to some, and India the multinational state in pre-independence Marxist thought of one variety, could, under particular historical circumstances, have developed more like a Europe of many nations, each with its own language and culture, and possibly come together more like today's European Union.

The point of these discursive statements for the present discussion is that there are many aspects in the educational area—embedded and perhaps even existing in actual fact—of which most scholars, at least, are not aware. This applies also to the educational ideas of the socialist and working class/peasant movements, and those of the self-proclaimed nationalists of the Hindu Mahasabha and their successors, the RSS and the BJP. The definitional problem of what constitutes nationalist educational thought is, therefore, complex. The entire exercise is beyond the competence available. A treatment of what is identified as "mainstream" nationalist thought has to be received with an awareness of its limited character, although influential in shaping contemporary Indian education. It must also be borne in mind that the policies and practices emerging from such a discussion are made operational through the consciousness and purposes of only an expressive and assertive part of India's people: north Indian, largely upper-caste Hindus, with a substantial sprinkling of Muslims, Parsis, western Indians, south Indians and, of course, Bengalis, who are very well represented and much in the lead.

As students of the history of the national movement well know, the non-brahmins of Madras Presidency developed somewhat separately (and laid the foundations of what is, there, a strong reservation movement since the Justice Party of the 1920s). There were many other similarly differentiated streams in different periods and parts of the country which have in many aspects shared—but in many others demarcated themselves from—mainstream nationalist educational thought and movements. We append herewith[4] an earlier attempt at representing this mainstream from the perspective of a possible alternative development without much recognition of the variety within national educational thought to which reference has been made above. However, it is even more naive and simplistic today than it was then, not to recognize the great diversity in Indian thought, practice and experimentation over the last century and a quarter. Both actual developments in Indian society, and the work of historians and social scientists have helped to open the possibility of a fuller and, hopefully, richer account. Greater respect has also developed for the oral accounts of the participants themselves in the events over these years. Some material of this kind, particularly on Gandhi's thought and work has also become available. (See notes 7–10 below as examples.)

Impact of the Early Independence Period

Paradoxically but understandably, the advent of independence brought about simultaneously, very explicit, if not always very effective, action following from the viewpoints and controversies in the national movement of the pre-independence period. On the other hand, a very unhistorical approach was also apparent in the understanding of education.

Ever since Gokhale introduced his bill in the Viceroy's (Governor-General's) Legislative Council early in the century, mass education was initially visualized as universal primary education of children in the school ages. Subsequently, in the late 1930s, mass literacy campaigns were also undertaken under the Congress ministries in the provinces.[5] An early, urgent task which the government leaders of free India set for themselves was the completion of this work; alas, it has not yet been accomplished.[6]

Some of the early discussions on this matter are interesting. The various sources of Gandhi's ideas on basic education have been noted in an earlier paper (note 4). These include the Gandhian vision of Sarvodaya society, Congress ministers' need for an economical scheme, and the desire of humanistic educators like Zakir Hussain and Saiyidain for liberation of the child from the tyranny of textbooks, rote memory and examinations, and his enrichment by reality and action. Our hypothesis is that the B.G. Kher committee set up by the Central Advisory Board of Education was able to work out a scheme for the universalization of elementary education in ten years, which was then put into article 45 of the Constitution as "education up to the age of 14", and that this relied on the self-sufficiency aspect of Gandhi's experiments with basic education at Wardha.[7] The scheme appeared to show that the recovery of the cost of materials and teachers' salaries was possible, particularly in the senior basic schools.

However, in the discussions of the first two

post-independence decades, there is already a tension between the economic productivity of working children and their educational possibilities. There was also the question of the low salaries of teachers, and the claims of rival objectives in childrens' education: intellectual development, manual and social skills, values and culture. Thus the scarcity of resources for education led in the direction of accepting less than 7 or 8, even just 5 years of schooling. The conventional wisdom on early infancy suggested an emphasis on the five years from 6 to 11, i.e., lower primary education. This was supported by what Zakir Hussain called the ideology of early socialization in the Anglo-Saxon world. To this (which, incidentally, would mean lower economic production by the younger children), he counterposed the experience of the Scandinavian countries and Russia, where schooling commenced at 6 or even 7, not 5, and continued till 13 or 14. This took advantage of the natural maturation of the early years, and used the firmer absorption of concepts, world views and skills in early adolescence for a more lasting impact.

My own teacher, the late Professor Ananthnath Basu was among the small minority of educationalists who supported Zakir Hussain's view. Although the discussion remained inconclusive, the idea lost out in practice while winning a victory of sorts in theory. It had strong opponents, not only from the deep-rooted traditions borrowed from the Anglo-Saxon world, but also in the need and capacity of the middle classes to send their children to school early. Even practical exigencies from the more earthy countryside were urged against Zakir Hussain's view. The chief (and earlier education) minister of U.P., Sampurnanand, argued in the Central Advisory Board of Education that parents, particularly rural parents, would need older boys to help out on the farm or domestic craft, and could spare only smaller children. (Incidentally, although the national movement had a strong urge towards the participation and "uplift" of women, much of the discussion was about boys. It is apparent, however, that older girls, too, would be handicapped, for they needed to start helping out in the home.)

So, while Mr. Hussain's plea for the later years led to the use of the words "up to the age of 14" in the relevant section of the Constitution, the realization that finances might permit only five years of schooling and that many children could start at 5 or 6, led to not specifying the age of commencement. Again, despite some evidence on the productivity of older children, and the realization that smaller children would predominate, work-centred basic education was attempted but not insisted upon rigidly. Gandhians, on the other hand, who were seen as dogmatically committed to work as the core of schooling and education, insisted that Gandhi was very particular about developing the mind,[8] and that it was Kher who was particular about the skills of the finger,[9] even though he was viewed as a less dogmatic person committed to sarvodaya society. There are other, similar, contemporary accounts.

We must view this whole discussion against the background of the national outcry when, in 1944, the Central Advisory Board of Education approved the report of the Sargent Committee. He was an English educationist and administrator who had come out as Educational Adviser to the Government of India. His report laid down the principle that elementary schooling would spread as well-prepared teachers became available. By his reckoning this would take 40 years, i.e., not till 1984. The national movement was against this imperial stance.

The antagonists and the nature of the divide were the same as those in the years before and immediately following Curzon at the turn of the century. At that time, the rulers were even more emphatic on "quality" in higher education. They tended to be restrictive and gradualist, as against the expansionist nationalist approach (see below).

There were other oppositions to the Sargent report, too. Gandhi, always politically suspect, was also non-conformist in the extreme in social conceptions such as sarvodaya society. His views on basic education, with extreme versions making work in the productive mode the primary core, also came under keen and not always friendly scrutiny at the hands of

Sargent. He understood activity-centred and similar education well enough, but his committee's interrogation of Zakir Hussian was not too friendly. Himself no great orthodox Gandhian in social or even pedagogical matters,[10] Hussian was called upon to explain the self-sufficiency aspect of the basic education scheme. Some differences persisted, so that the Sargent report, while generally accepting work and activity, tended to water down the concept.

As can be seen in retrospect, the country ultimately had to follow both the time schedule and the pedagogical formulations of the Sargent Committee. Although partly the work of Zakir Hussain as well, it was at that time in no mood to take it lying down. There was a real feeling of national urgency, which was related to national pride and dignity, as well as equity for all citizens with regard to basic education and the constitutional directive of education up to the age of 14. With hindsight, one can see many unrealistic assumptions and the neglect of underlying realities. For example, the ridiculous salary of Rs 15 per month for teachers was mentioned in one of the reports. The impact of poverty and hunger was overlooked, as was the lack of economic motivation for literacy or schooling in view of the kind of work the children could actually look forward to. These factors persist even today, notwithstanding all the economic development of the last half-century.

We mentioned the costs of basic education. In practice, its economic self-sufficiency was not realized. Many, like R.V. Parulekar of Bombay and his disciple J.P. Naik, were inclined to argue that for early universalization, simple non-basic education would lead to more rapid results. When the Rajagopalachari government of Madras sought the assistance of Parulekar in the early 50s in devising a basic scheme for the universalization of elementary education, he just cut the childrens' school day in half, expecting teachers to work two shifts per day. The crafts and productive subjects were supposed to be taken care of by the parents during the time the child was not at school. The scheme was immediately unpopular with teachers for the extra work they had to do in reality if not on paper. It was much more unpopular with non-brahmin legislators, even those of the Congress and their constitutents. Rajagopalachari's government fell and K. Kamaraj took over. The former's scheme was accused, not inaccurately, of perpetuating a situation in which old caste-occupation distinctions would be perpetuated, even strengthened, through basic education. It was followed by an upsurge among largely rural non-brahmin leaderships under Congress wings. Kamaraj went from village to village mobilizing them to ask for school buildings, food for children and vigilance over errant teachers.[11] As noted earlier, school-meal schemes did not do equally well in all states, in terms of school enrolment, attendance, retention and achievement.[12] The costs of this kind of effort (which was notable for its absence from the earlier nationalist discourse) were high, as a recent paper by Binod Khadria has shown.[13] Sensing these realities would not have been difficult for the keen, but perhaps the class positions of the nationalist leadership were not helpful.

J.P. Naik, in his long stewardship of the nation's most forward-looking thrust in mass education, particularly at the elementary level, clearly never committed the universalization effort to basic education. The Education Commission report of 1964–66 fails to mention the word "basic" even once. As he explained when questioned, it had become a fairly controversial concept on many grounds other than those we have already noticed.

Ahistoricity

Immediately after independence, nationalist thought was the basis in education, although contemporary Western thought and practice was freely drawn upon. Looking back at one's own history and drawing lessons from it was, thus, only summarily attempted in the rush of urgent national tasks. The author's own very respected teacher, a reputable historian of education, found no time to found a school to study the history of education,[14] while working as member-secretary of the Secondary Education Commission (1953) and in other committees. J.P. Naik himself, a very considerable scholar in the field, was in 1961 unable to accept an analysis that characterized the first decade and a half of independence by the dominance of the rural and upper middle classes,[15] although only eighteen years later, from his vantage point as Member-Secretary of the Indian Council of Social Science Research, he developed his empirical coefficient of inequality.

The pioneer generation was not alone in not accounting for history. Even today, leading scholars attribute such virtues as relevance and child friendliness to the pre-British indigenous school; they would ideally want these in contemporary education.[16] Selective (or no) reading of our own history has more pervasive influences. Thus, the report of the (Yashpal) National Advisory Committee on Curriculum Load, *Learning Without Burden,* takes legitimate inspiration from R.K. Narayan's intervention in the Rajya Sabha in defence of children, but omits altogether to remember Nehru's speech in parliament calling for the designing of a schoolbag which would keep their hands free.

The leadership of independent India had many tasks to accomplish, including the building of infrastructure for industry and irrigation. This required secondary, higher and technical education, a need that coincided with the interests and tendencies of the dominant middle classes, initially urban and "upper caste" but increasingly, under the "democratic" pressure of the ballot box, also rural and middle class/caste groups. It took an occasional reminder from outside observers such as Alva Myrdal in her foundation day address at the Central Institute of Education in 1961, that education was not only a democratic but also in the (not so) long run an economic requirement. The relatively weak push for elementary education and literacy in actual practice and policy reflected a lack of clarity in pre-independence nationalist educational thought about economic and related issues. These were that mass education had a certain minimum cost, that poverty to the point of absolute hunger meant, if not socio-economic restructuring on a large scale, at least substantial palliative measures such as school meals and community participation. The latter was itself a mixed bag on account of the disproportionate influence and sexist male domination of landed rural communities, even after such land reforms as might prove possible.

The lack of awareness of such issues and the euphoria of independence was persistent and not fully corrected by the National Policy of Education (1986), let alone the Education Commission (1964–66) or its predecessors.[17] We might also note that this lack of historical consciousness and the overlooking of the political and socio-economic dimensions of educational policies and processes, was also reflected in the structuring of educational studies themselves, with the history of education being neglected or pursued in sterile, formal, constitutional terms. The sociology, economics and politics of education also developed very late, and even then in an unanalytical framework that did not question the existing structures of power and hierarchy.[18] This is, however, a separate subject; it is mentioned primarily in terms of being a sequel to nationalist thought in education, which tended to ignore or overlook social differentiation and conflict and even obvious matters like hunger and poverty as factors relevant to education. We turn now to a few major questions on which nationalist educational thought actually concentrated, namely, language and culture, higher education, technical and vocational education, and control of education.[19]

Language and Culture

It has been a staple of discussions on British educational policy in India that, by imposing the use of English as the medium of the highest education, cultural as well political domination was secured. It is apposite in this connection to note that, even as late as the parliamentary enquiry of 1833, Mill of the India Office pointed out that a post as high as member of the Board of Revenue could be satisfactorily filled without a knowledge of the English language.[20] The Macaulay-Bentinck decision in favour of English should not, therefore, be viewed as merely a device to prepare clerical workers. The shift to English has to be seen as part of the orientation towards political and cultural domination which accompanied the changeover in the economic relationship from one of extracting revenue and tribute, to industrial Britain using the colonized country as a market for goods manufactured in the home country and as a source of raw materials. Simultaneously, cultural (and, for some, religious) evangelism pervaded thinking in the ruling country. Some, like Hodgson,[21] who had not yet fallen in line with such thought, still argued for the use of "vernacular" languages. They tried to minimize the problems in their use by arguing, for example, that the Bengal Presidency had fewer languages than was the case, listing Assamese and Oriya as mere dialects of Bengali!

On the part of the Empire, the process set in motion with the foundation of the Hindu (later Presidency) College in Calcutta, and culminating in the 1835 decision on educational language, should be seen as part of a larger trend which followed the change in the official court language from Persian in the 1830s. During the second half of the century, the move towards art and related education was also guided in part by the urge to create tastes similar to those of the British. It was also linked to the more "practical" consideration of resuscitating the local arts and crafts deemed necessary for the revival of the rural economy. In actual fact, of course, the excessive revenue demands of the government and the neglect of irrigation had led to famines, as has been well documented by nationalist economic hisorians.

After Gandhi, the enshrinement of Indian languages at the apex of the educational structure was a proclaimed goal, along with a lighter emphasis on Hindi as the "national language". In retrospect, it is easy to see that there was some ambivalence about this and a reluctance to force the issue. It appears to have been accepted tacitly that, on the one hand, the privileged position which English gave to the elite using it would be hard to take away, even as the technical problems in transferring modern knowledge to the Indian languages were seen as substantial though, in principle, negotiable. On the other hand, it could not have escaped the notice of any that the multiplicity of major languages in the country would offer problems in the adoption of any one as the national language. Some ambivalence, some doublespeak, some doublethink appear to have characterized nationalist educational thought on this matter. Although not all preferred modern Westernized modes of thought and living, English was the preferred language of all during most of this period.

Technical and Vocational Education

There has been virtual unanimity in nationalist thought on the need for technical and vocational education for national advance, particularly since the defeat by Japan of Russia in 1905, which was attributed to Japan's technical prowess based on its education and training network. The setting up in the first decade of this century of the Bengal National Council of Technical Education (which later gave birth to Jadavpur University), and the development of engineering, mining and metallurgy education at Banaras Hindu University in the next decade by an otherwise not very modern-minded Madan Mohan Malaviya, represent the trend. Indian nationalist opinion was not very strong or vocal on lower-level technical and vocational education. The British repeatedly attributed this to the reluctance of the Indian middle class to dirty their hands, overlooking the reality of their own preference for Anglo-Indian lads for this kind of work, or the dead-end nature of such training with only a modest prospect of upward mobility. The latter is a handicap from which vocational education suffers all over the world, even today.

It might be useful to note here that the policy of the Empire was, quite understandably, not very forward-looking in respect of technical education in India. The small amount of engineering employment which the railways, irrigation and roads could provide, was sought to be offered to British expatriates trained at the Royal Indian Engineering College founded in 1871 at Cooper's Hill in the U.K., because such an establishment would, hopefully, fulfil the needs of other parts of the Empire as well. Thus, the development of technical education in India was discouraged by the fact that 40 to 50 engineers were brought in every year with guaranteed employment. All through the last quarter of the 19th century, the Indian railways always had a surplus of engineers. There was an allotted employment for the four Indian colleges: Roorkee (8–9), and one each to Sibpur, Guindy and Poona. The rest of the local output was employed at the overseer level.

Higher Education and Universities

In the 1880s, provision was made for elections to Indian university senates, and the expansion of colleges was given a strong fillip by the Indian leadership. Simultaneously, British officers of the Indian Education Service developed a plan for a teaching university at Calcutta, to be led by scientifically trained British personnel from Presidency College, and separate from the existing Calcutta University. Gurudas Banerji and later, much more prominently, Asutosh Mukerji took the view that education must "both rise and spread". They felt that nuclei of advanced teaching and research should develop in the university, even as it followed a forward policy of affiliating colleges in large numbers. This policy was actually carried out by Asutosh Mukerji when he was vice-chancellor of Calcutta University in the early years of the 20th century. Meanwhile, the imperial policy of restricting all higher education in the name of quality was officially proclaimed by the Indian Universities Commission set up by Curzon, and also in pronouncements on Indian educational policy. It could be they did not foresee a Raman or a Bose.

This was the general stance of the early nationalist movement, and scientific research developed at centres like the Indian Institute of Science set up by J.N. Tata (with encouragement from the government) at Bangalore, the Indian Association for the Cultivation of Science and Technological Education at Calcutta (set up by the Bengal National Council of Education), and Banaras Hindu University. However, the national political movement took a radical turn under the leadership of Gandhi in the 1920s. Higher education and research became important again only in the middle 1930s and later, due to the modern socialistic ideas of Nehru and (the somewhat forgotten) Subhash Bose. The Gandhian strand in the national movement did not take a strong negative position on higher scientific education and research. Its general social perspective was, however, indifferent to it, concentrating much more on mass education, as already discussed. Both strands were also keen on addressing more immediate questions such as the struggle for freedom against imperialism and national unity against communal division.

This latter had an important educational correlate—the image of India, its historical past, and its vision of the future. National schools and universities were started after Gandhi called for a boycott of "satanic" education. Jamia Millia, Kashi Vidyapeeth, Gujarat Vidyapeeth and a number of other institutions got separate curriculums. Much of their view of India's past glorified the ancient and, in varying degrees, sought to present a harmonious medieval period, in contrast to the more "Hindu" views of the Arya Samaj, etc.

The national integrationist or tolerant position did not have a wide impact on common schools; essentially, the national movement was too preoccupied with the tasks of political mobilization and constitutional negotiation to pay much systematic attention to education, apart from an occasional thought or idea developed by a committed educationalist and implemented in an institution or chain of institutions. Neither was the national movement a unified, systematic, mass or cadre-based movement, like the communist movements in some countries or the religious/ particularist movements in our own, such as the Arya Samaj, Rashtriya Swayamsevak Sangh, Jamat-i-Islami, Tabligh, etc., which carried out educational work and systematic propaganda as in the communist parlance.

There is also a more basic consideration militating against major changes in the educational structure or content of a country or society, which some, including this author, have discussed elsewhere.[22] Each educational system has a built-in inertia, the tendency to remain more or less the same in essential style and even content. Teachers tend to teach in the manner they were taught, even what they were taught. Textbooks might be rewritten, but not only is their dissemination from centre to periphery slow, it often does not reach the majority of schools. Also, the overall ideological/ cultural climate, and the nature of family and peer-group socialization all tend to pull in the direction of what already exists. This phenomenon has been called the genetic imprint of an educational system. Thus, the directions of national integration, pluralism, tolerance, equity and justice, or even "socialistic" orientations, were proclaimed as important to the national movement, but their reflection in educational thought or practice has been modest, to put it mildly.

The ideas of science, especially its rationality, technical applications and push towards a modern life, appear to have made greater impact. However, the search for an "Indian" identity, itself a much contested thing (with its Hindu and "secular"/multicultural/integrationist versions in contest for the whole of the last century), has tended to turn into particularistic directions, notwithstanding the more universalistic aspirations of the national movement. This has found its due reflection in education. Still, the liberal traditions of the past retain a lot of meaning; they can and should be recaptured, but with very determined, well-planned, organized effort.

Conclusion

Each of the foreging themes deserve full treatment in whole papers and treatises, some of which have, in fact, been written. The essential purpose of this paper is twofold. One is to draw attention to the *pedagogic* dimensions of national or nationalist educational thought. One sees less of this aspect than the political and cultural aspects or substance of nationalist educational thought in the focus of historians and political scientists. In exploring these pedagogic elements, we have come across ideas similar to the progressive, child-centred orientations that characterize the whole movement of educational thought and practice in the Western world and even in non-Western countries as they develop into modern nation states with more participatory, democratic politics, industrial economies, and a more urban lifestyle based on science and industry.

Some of the more enlightened British educational officials did make some beginnings in this direction, but like everything else they did, these efforts were coupled with a strongly authoritarian, paternalistic style, tending to exclude the large, rising nationalist intelligentsia. The major advances in a progressive direction came when this intelligentsia teamed up with the national political movement for freedom and independence. Nothing distinctive may have come from this were it not for the leader of the independence struggle, Gandhi. His social vision was a utopian sarvodaya, but it struck a strong sympathetic cord with the mass of Indian people, not only because of nationalist aspiration and the desire to be different, if only to assert an identity, but because their poverty and the very rudimentary pre-industrial economic milieu of much of India made the sarvodaya vision appear eminently fair and realistic. Thus, Gandhi's ideas of self-sufficiency in basic education tied in with the work-, child-, life- and community-centred perspectives of Western pedagogical theory, which was largely Anglo-Saxon but had a critical element contributed by the German-trained Zakir Hussain, who had known the German *arbeitschule.* In higher education, too, the universal trend in the direction of research and technical education was taken up by the national movement and its leaders. While, in the name of "quality", the British rulers tended to *restrict* expansion, the Indian leadership *linked* expansion to it (Ironically, the post-independence leadership, too, tends to decry expansion, student activism, etc., the same qualities its predecessors had upheld.)

The other main thrust of this paper has been to draw attention to the somewhat limited middle-class perspectives of the national movement and a tendency to oversimplify the problem of national unity by overlooking regional and caste/class diversity within India. This has understandably appeared to privilege the dominant/visible upper-caste/north Indian/Hindu perspectives, even as a substantial set of diverging perspectives from the "lower" castes (e.g., those of Phule and Ambedkar), and from other regions and religious communities, were recognized and sought to be integrated. That task has remained substantially unaccomplished, as the history of the half-century since independence bears witness.

On the contrary, questions emerge as to whether the large variety of linguistic, ethnic and religious entities are capable of welding into as unified a nation as the constitutional political unity of the Union suggests or requires. One form of unification began under British rule, particularly from 1835, when English was ordained as the language of higher education. There emerged a relatively like-minded English-using intelligentsia constituting 3 to 7 per cent of the population which is closely integrated with the world economy and techno-structure, particularly bearing in mind the millions of expatriates in the Indian diaspora, a substantial proportion of whom are in the developed West. It is at least as close to the techno-economic magnets outside as to the country and its populace. The mobilizing ideas of the nationalist period form a sort of basic substratum for educated Indians. But their legacy is not entirely univocal, leading instead in both particularistic and universalistic (or pluralistic) directions. The recent influences of new communications and computer technology add a modern dimension at the level of skill, and enhance the feeling of belonging with the rest of the world (at least its more prosperous and powerful part). Meanwhile, the legacy of the national movement, which responded to the poorer, exploited sections of society, is tending to get lost in the educational enterprise.

In fact, the basic threads as well as the lacunae, conflicts and contradictions within nationalist educational thought require deep, sustained enquiry to apprehend today's reality. Some insight may be gained from the Nehru-Azad-Radhakrishnan divergences. (Patel had a very different orientation and took little direct part in educational work as such.) All of them showed much deference to Gandhi and meticulous courtesy to each other, and were committed to observing the code of unity for a secular democratic republic. But it is well-known that the man who was rashtrapati (as the Congress president was called) from the mid-1940s until partition was obliged to ruminate in frustration as education minister, while the main business of government was handled by Nehru and Patel, and even the ceremonial headship of state was offered to Rajendra Prasad, who could only elucidate some of his opinions in speeches and addresses (e.g., on the Hindu Code Bill).

The point of recalling these varying emphases and tilts is that, while Nehru espoused straight, "socialist", scientific, modern practices and institutions, the corpus of "Oriental" and traditional medical, legal and trading skills (not to mention the ritual, sacerdotal and not-very-scientific part of India's original learning, very much alive and in practice then and, perhaps, even now to a lesser extent) were ignored and not incorporated in the educational system, except marginally as low-profile, ayurvedic, Unani or Oriental departments and colleges.[23] We did not go even so far as Sri Lanka, which got influenced by Buddhist clergy under the Bandarnaike regime to open two Sinhala universities. Azad could, perhaps, have provided the educational leadership to fill this gap.

On the other hand, we find S. Gopal documenting in his rather explicit biography of his father Radhakrishnan, his own and, presumably, his father's criticism of the isolated and not-so-effective Azad as minister of education for not implementing ideas which Radhakrishnan had commended for attention and action, presumably with the agreement of Nehru, however mild and respectful. It is possible to view these three as Nehru the wholesale modernizer, Azad the syncretic synthesiser of many Indian traditions into some kind of modernity, and Radhakrishnan the Oxbridge-educated, brahminical Indian modern. With a different balance between them, India's educational system, and the character of modern

India *vis a vis* secularity and modernity could have been very different. I have discussed some of this elsewhere.[24]

This interplay of personalities and outlooks also illustrates the more general difference between Western educational development, with modernity built into a continuous cultural tradition, and that of a non-Western colonized country, whose experience is of break, schism and/or dominance.[25] By ignoring the indigenous educational legacy, our post-independence leadership appears to have adopted the same stance as the Anglicists in the controversy at the time of Macaulay and Bentinck.

Apart from this, there is also the residue of the resistance of the students and peasant classes during the national movement for independence. The expansion and quantum of education, the linking of educational activity to ongoing socio-political and economic activities and employment needs of young people, these were all seen as broadly irrelevant to post-independence educational development and reconstruction. Thus, although one heard an occasional address such as Govind Ballabh Pant's at Gorakhpur University on its foundation, which called for vast expansion of higher education, the general policy stances of governments after independence have been to restrict in the name of quality. Student participation in governance, autonomy and similar ideas have also been seen as something to cope with rather than carry out. What peasants and workers could contribute in terms of reorienting the content of education was poorly enough articulated by their own movements; they have made virtually no impression on educational policy and action. When one compares this with the West, east Asia, Korea, Japan, China, etc., there is a distinct "counterpopulism", if one may coin a term to describe the enclave mentality which has influenced higher education, particularly, and most education, in general. The influences noted above were not the most dominant in nationalist *thought* on education, although they had wide influence in the national movement itself, the former being a little more brahminical than the reality of the latter.

Our view of their relevance today is a function of our positions on a wider set of social and political questions.

A discussion of nationalist educational thought can be unending. But I will close the present contribution to it by referring again, in a little more detail to a continuing controversy or dilemma. There has been much criticism in recent years of the lack of emphasis on mass education in independent India, compared to the rapid growth in higher education. Often, the country has been criticized for trying, as it were, to build a house from top downwards. Two sets of factors need to be underlined here. First, the simile is inappropriate, for an educational system draws its essential knowledge as much, if not more, from the staple content at the higher reaches (filtering it down to the secondary and elementary stages), as from the skills and knowledge at the lower reaches. In any case, parallels are imperfect as reasoning. It was a clear aspiration of the leadership of the national movement to build a nation that was "powerful", industrially and militarily, notwithstanding the highly visible Gandhian influence. Subjectively, the education of the masses was strongly desired, but it was visualized more as a basis for a strong nation than as a basic democratic imperative.

If we take a comparative look at other under-developed and/or colonized/semi-colonized countries, few, with the exception of China and Mexico, could claim as strong and continuous a tradition of higher learning. Fewer still had as stratified a society (caste, etc.). Nor could many claim the dubious benefit of an intelligentsia of comparable magnitude nurtured in the language and culture of the ruling power. In India, the objective and subjective possibilities of an elitist, "strong" national development have merged with the class interests of the empowered, who, in the peculiar logic of ballot-box democracy, were impelled to take the direction that was taken. This is unlike China, for instance, where a single-party communist regime had other priorities as well as possibilities.

It is within the limitations just outlined that nationalist thought and action, both pre- and post-independence, espoused mass education. As for the question of language (see earlier), there was some doublethink, doublespeak and indecision, all combining in reluctance and hesitation on determined action for mass education and its opposite—higher, technical and scientific education. In this the post-independence leadership acted little differently from what could have been foreseen from pre-independence thought and action.

Notes

1. Conference on "colonialism, education and nationalism in India", Educational Records Research Unit, Delhi, Jawaharlal Nehru University, March 1996.
2. S. Shukla, "National and colonial in Indian education—interrogating the dichotomy", paper in *ibid.*
3. Kancha Iliah, *Why I am not a Hindu*, Calcutta, Samya Publications, 1996.
4. S. Shukla, "Indian educational thought and experiments" in *Comparative Education*, Carfax Publishing, Oxfordshire, 1983. Originally prepared for a seminar on alternatives in education at the Indian Institute of Advanced Study, Simla, 1978, and the Indian Council of Social Science Research (see proceedings of the conference on "colonialism, education and nationalism in India", March 1996, ERRU, JNU).
5. The slogan "each one, teach one" coined by Frank Laubach caught the fancy of Congress ministries, and students were sought to be mobilized for literacy campaigns and demonstrations on Literacy Day. I have discussed this in a couple of articles elsewhere.
6. Most educational thinking has, unfortunately, overlooked some crucial factors, either out of the persistence of thought patterns developed during the colonial period under the pressure of the rulers and other reactionary groups to emphasize the impossibility of universalization, or because it is seen as a defeatist response to India's contemporary problems. It could also be encouraged by the unwillingness to recognize the unpleasant reality that independent India has a socio-economic structure to which poverty and hunger are endemic. This is a reflection of the privileged character of the middle classes from

which our intellectuals are drawn; they are loth to recognize the consequences of their privilege. This could well be an illustration of a proposition in the sociology of knowledge.

7. D.P. Nayar (see below), however, is disinclined to agree (personal conversation).
8. D.P. Nayar (personal conversation), has cited, from a writing of B.G. Kher, a sentence Gandhi added in his own hand to his article: "The result would have been of no value if it did not also mean education, i.e., improvement of the mind" (Nayar, *op.cit.*, p. 176). This is after Nayar's own sentence, "So far about its economic aspect...."
9. D.P. Nayar, his sister Dr. Sushila Nayar and brother Pyarelal were devoted Gandhians who worked in Sevagram. He worked for a long period in the Planning Commission, rising to the level of Adviser, after his earlier stint in the basic school at Wardha. Nayar does not feel that B.G. Kher was keen to recover the costs of schooling through the work of children. Kher was inclined to emphasise "skills of the finger", meaning that the educational value of craft was important. D.P. Nayar's own work at the school showed that the product of children in grade 8 exceeded costs in value. D.P. Nayar, *Towards a National System of Education*, New Delhi, Mittal Publications, 1989, pp. 177, 181.

   Here, accounts of those with some first-hand experience of the period or location might be useful. Dr. Salamatullah joined the Teacher's Training Institute set up by Dr. Zakir Hussain in Jamia Millia after the formulation of the basic scheme. He was attracted to Gandhi's ideas in general, even during his student days at Aligarh. He speaks of a discussion with Gandhi in which he expressed his disappointment with the wage of two annas a day for the tanners in the magarwadi at Wardha. Gandhi replied that this was double the wage drawn outside. Basic education was designed by him for this kind of situation. The Teacher's Training Institute struggled along with (often very few) students of varying educational qualification, as low as the 4th grade. One year, no students joined, and the young teacher-educator suggested they wind up to Zakir Hussain. Only a bad tradesman shuts shop he was told! If there were no students, the faculty should write about basic education. The Institute acquired stability only after independence, when the government sent it displaced persons from Punjab. They were mostly educated women who had horrific images of Muslims and were apprehensive of what would befall them here. When they left, they spoke touchingly and emotionally of sharing the warmth of feeling and understanding of the other culture. Basic education thus carried the message of national unity, a major objective of the national movement that was, unfortunately, not effectively pursued in education.

Devi Prasad, a practicing artist, joined the Sevagram basic school in 1944 after artistic training at Santiniketan on clay sculpture on the potter's wheel. He speaks of the essential unity of the ideas of Tagore and Gandhi on education, but grants the former a greater emphasis on creativity and commitment to productive work, both because this was closer to the life of the common working people, and because the tangible, commensurable quality of the end product made it that much more possible to be sure learning and education had taken place. And yet, he recounts the occasion when he wished the children could all go and spend time together enjoying the Sharad Purnima moon and was held up by a committed colleague who said the time could be more usefully spent spinning. Ashadevi advised him to write to Gandhi for his opinion. The latter wrote back to say that what Nandalal Bose had taught Devi Prasad was what he should do. Gandhi had a basic orientation, an open mind and a pragmatic approach. He also relied on the opinions and judgement of those who specialized in the field. Devi Prasad also dissented from this author's suspicion that schooling and education might have occupied a marginal place in Gandhi's concerns in the midst of his many large preoccupations. Yet some biographers of Gandhi have paid very little attention to basic education. Thus, Martin Green's *Gandhi—Voice of the New Age Revolution* (New York, Continuum, 1993), which claims exclusive attention to personal and intimate (including, according to the author, intellectual) details, contains only one reference to basic education in its 400 pages. His earlier work comparing Gandhi and Tolstoy again has only one possible reference to education by mentioning Zakir Hussain. Rajmohan Gandhi's biography does not do very much more.

10. In one of his addresses to the Hindustani Talimi conference as president, he speaks of four stages in work: selecting what to do, planning, execution, and evaluation. Three of these, he

claims, are intellectual, while one is manual. Not only does he emphasize the cognitive aspects of basic education, he goes on in the same address to say that, in this sense, even reading poetry is work.

11. Mani Shankar Aiyar in *Sunday* and *National Herald*, around 1993 or 1994.
12. S.C. Mittal, R.R. Saxena *et al.*, *Impact of Mid-day Meals Programme on Enrolment and Retention at Primary Stage*, Delhi, NCERT, mimeo, 1984. Prodipto Roy and Radhanath Rath, *School Land in Orissa*, Delhi, Council for Social Development, 1972.
13. Binod Khadria, "Child labour reform through a fiscal instrument", *Economic and Political Weekly*, Bombay, July 27, 1996, pp. 2009–10.
14. A.N. Basu (ed.), *Adam's Reports on Indigenous Instruction in Bengal, Bihar and Orissa*, Calcutta University Press, 1935, from which Joseph Di Bona has abstracted *One Teacher, One School*, Delhi, Impex Biblica, 1983; *Indian Education in Parliamentary Papers*, Asia Publishing House, Bombay, 1952.
15. See S. Nurullah and J.P. Naik, *A Student's History of Education in India*, Macmillan, Bombay, 1963. This author was commissioned to add the chapter on 1947–61, but his draft was totally revised by J.P. Naik. In his enthusiam for the new, he was unwilling to accept my implicit or explicit social criticism of the new state's policy, at least then, when he had just joined the government as Adviser with the responsibility of universalizing primary education.
16. See also Krishna Kumar, *The Political Agenda of Education*, Sage Publications, Delhi, 1991, p. 72 and elsewhere.
17. See, for example, the reports of the (Radhakrishnan) University Education Commission, 1948–49, or those of the Secondary Education Commission, 1953, headed by Lakshmanswami Mudaliar.
18. The entire work of sociologists relating caste and caste associations to education and school management lacked awareness of power dimensions until Harold Gould's paper on the subject in Rudolph and Rudolph (eds.), *op. cit.*
19. My doctoral dissertation, *Educational Development in British India*, Delhi University, 1958 (unpublished), which some well-published scholars in the field have seen but found too low-key in its first-order inferences to ever cite, brings together

most of the facts we note later in this paper. Some of the ideas have also been discussed in my paper, "Public educational systems in colonial contexts—the case of India's transition from indigenous to modern ideas and institutions in the nineteenth century", *Journal of Education*, **165**(4), Boston, Fall, 1983. It is an editorially-revised, shortened version of my contribution "Education in relation to some ideas and concepts during the later nineteenth century" in Bisheshwar Prasad (ed.), *Ideas in History*, Asia Publishing House, Bombay, 1970. However, as the vicissitudes in the field of the history of ideas shows, such historically unrooted or ahistorical explorations lead nowhere.

20. A.N. Basu, 1952, *op. cit.*
21. A.C. Boman Behram, *Educational Controversies in India.*
22. In my "Reconsidering educational theory" (paper to the NCERT seminar, 1963, mimeo) and "Educational techniques and educational planning", *Educational Sciences*, Pergamon Press, Vol. II, No. 1, October 1967, I have drawn attention to the phenomenon of inertia in education. Susan and Lloyd Rudolph in *Politics and Education in India*, OUP, 1972, have spoken of the "genetic imprint" of an educational system.
23. Philip Foster, "The vocational school fallacy", *Comparative Education Review*, Chicago, later 1950's.
24. S. Shukla, "Secular and non-secular elements in Indian education", *Teacher Today*, Bikaner, April-June, 1974. Originally at the secularism seminar, IIAS, Simla, 1973.
25. S. Shukla, "Educational transitions in southern Asia", paper for the inaugural symposium, Comparative Education Centre, University of Hongkong, May, 1995, in *IASSI Quarterly*, April-June 1995, Vol. 132, No. 4. Also in *Economic and Political Weekly*, Bombay, 1 June 1996. Some part of this basic position appears in S. Shukla, "Comparative education: Indian perspective", a revised version of the presidential address at the first conference of the Comparative Education Society of India, Pune, 1981.

National Education in Bengal: 1905–1912

Aparna Basu

The idea of national education like that of the nation is a comparatively recent historical innovation. Before the emergence of the nation state, education in Europe, supported by the church and private agencies, was confined to the clergy and the aristocracy. With the emergence of the idea of nationalism after the French Revolution, it was argued that to promote national unity all children should have a uniform system of education which required centralized control. Napoleon was the first ruler in Europe to advocate a system of national education and vested the control at all levels from the primary to the university in the hands of the *University de France.* After its defeat by Prussia in 1870, the teaching of patriotism became very important in France. In Prussia and later in a united Germany under Bismarck, education was used to foster loyalty to the state, a trend which reached its apogee in Nazi Germany, Fascist Italy, Soviet Russia and in Japan before World War II. In democratic countries, a national system developed usually in response to demands for universal compulsory education.

Before the British came to India emperors, nawabs, zamindars patronized learning by granting *inam* land to *maktabs*, *madarsas*, *tols* and *pathshalas* or maintaining scholars at the court. Those were the government schools or colleges or a uniform system of education. There was a widespread network of village elementary schools and schools of higher learning, Hindu and Islamic, in which there was a great deal of flexibility and teachers developed the curriculum. The East India Company was also initially reluctant to accept any responsibility for the education of its Indian subjects. It was only with growing pressure from the Evangelicals, Utilitarians and Liberals in the early nineteenth century and its own need for English educated Indians in the lower ranges of its civil service, that the Company agreed in 1813 to promote education by setting aside an amount of one lakh rupees a year. Bentinck's famous Resolution announced that in future government funds would be used for English education. Even then schools were run not by the government but by Christian missionaries, official and non-official Englishmen and by Indians. Wood's Despatch of 1854 stated for the first time that there would be Department of Education in each Presidency headed by a civil servant of the Company, a model government school in each district which would be subject to constant and careful inspection and that the government would establish universities in Calcutta, Bombay and Madras.

In the West, the nations that wanted to assert their political unity, like Germany or Italy had the necessary linguistic, educational and professional skills. They did not have to equip themselves culturally by appropriating what was alien to them. The Eastern type nationalism was accompanied by an effort to re-equip the nation culturally to transform it. But this could not be done by simply imitating the alien culture, for then the nation would lose its own identity. The search, consequently, was for a regeneration of national culture, adapted to the requirement of certain global standards of progress and civilization set by the advanced nations of Western Europe. But at the same time, these countries wanted to retain their identities.

In India, the idea of national education emerged not to promote loyalty to the state, as in Europe, but in opposition to the system of education introduced by the colonial masters. To begin with, this system was enthusiastically welcomed by the elite of Calcutta, Bombay and Madras not only because it was an avenue to employment but also because it was seen as a crucial agent of social transformation. Rammohan Roy, one of the first to support English education did so because be saw it as a weapon to fight the abuses and perversions that had crept into our religious beliefs and social practices and as a means of removing irrational superstitions and outmoded rituals and thus pave the way for modernization. As Gopal Krishna Gokhale said, Western education would liberate the Indian mind from 'the thraldom of old world ideas'.

From the initial, almost blind admiration for English education in the generation called Young Bengal, there was a growing disenchantment in the closing years of the nineteenth century with a system that denationalized the youth and produced only clerks and lawyers. A number of educational movements were started to replace the existing system.

One school of thought felt that the prevailing system ignored religious education. To remedy this, the Arya Samaj opened the Dayanand Anglo-Vedic (DAV) schools and colleges and the gurukul at Kangri, where the emphasis was on Sanskrit and Hindu learning, particularly in the gurukul. The Central Hindu college started by Annie Besant also stressed India's ancient heritage and the study of Hinduism. The seminary at Deoband imparted Islamic learning, while the khalsa colleges taught the tenets of Sikhism.

In Maharashtra, the teacher Chiplunkar was transferred from the Poona government high school to the relative Siberia of a small Ratnagiri school for the political views he expressed in *Nibandhmala*. He resigned in disgust and, in 1880, started the New English School. He was soon joined by four young men full of nationalist sentiments. Tilak, Agarkar, Karandikar and Namjoshi, all chitapavan brahmins and graduates of Bombay University. The men behind the New English School and the Deccan Education Society (DES), which was founded in 1884, believed that the degraded condition of their country could be lifted only by the right kind of education.

Gokhale, too, joined the society, and the story of the conflict between him and Tilak, which finally led to Tilak's resignation from the DES, reflected their differing political and educational philosophies. Tilak was more for the teaching of

Hindu ideals and for independence from government control. The fact that DES's college was named after the retiring governor of Bombay, Sir James Fergusson, who laid the foundation stone, and that it accepted government aid for its school and college, showed that the DES required government patronage and support. In 1987, it agreed to the conditions imposed on it by the Director of Public Instruction (DPI) and promised to keep a more vigilant control over the politics of its employees.

What distinguished the DES in its early years was the spirit of self-sacrifice and dedication of its life-members, directors and teachers. They were interested in spreading education, making it available to as many people as possible. The fees were low, teachers accepted minimum salaries, and Fergusson College became a byword for efficient education; students flocked to it. Tilak was not against English teaching; he was of the view that the English language was "like the milk of the tigress, a strong diet" and if young men were brought up on it, India's liberation could not be long delayed. The Deccan Education Society, the DAV college and the Central Hindu College all began as a result of the impetus given to private education by the report of the Indian Education Commission of 1884.

Gokhale was intimately connected with the DES. He became its chief, and the most eloquent spokesman of the opponents of Curzon's university reforms. Since these reforms were aimed mainly at Calcutta University and private colleges affiliated to it, the outcry against them was loudest in Bengal. We have to look only at the contemporary native newspapers to get an idea of how severely Curzon was attacked. As Vincent Chirol observes, "the least that Curzon was charged with was a deliberate attempt to throttle higher education in India." Dr. Gurudas Bannerjee added a note of dissent to the above-mentioned report, criticizing the attempt to place education under government control. Gokhale said that the Universities Bill would make universities a department of the state. It was feared that, by stricter conditions of affiliation, higher fees, etc., the government aimed to restrict the spread of higher education. One of the staunchest opponents of the report was Satish Chandra Mukherji, editor of *Dawn*. In July, 1902, in protest, he founded the Dawn Society. Its office was located in the Metropolitan Institution, a large, privately managed college. The criticism of Curzon's education policy continued till the Universities Act of 1904. After this act was passed, Annie Besant, in an article published in the Dawn Society's magazine (January 1906, Part II), urged educated Indians to take the question of education in their own hands, as the University Act had rendered higher education very costly and shut the doors to universities to poor students.

In 1905, the partition of Bengal was announced and led to the swadeshi movement. A group of students of Calcutta University wanted to boycott the impending examination. Their leaders were members of the Dawn Society who lived in the same mess as its founder, Satish Chandra Mukherji. The steward of the mess was Brahmabandhab Upadhyaya, editor of *Sandhya*. All these students belonged to the bhadralok class. The Calcutta students took public views on the ideas of of swadeshi and boycott at several meetings in July-August, 1905 (*Sanjibani*, August 3, 1905, editorial titled "West Bengal Partition and Student Community"). Students and leaders in various district and mofussil towns picketed shops selling foreign cloth, preached swadeshi, attended political meetings, and marched in procession shouting "bande mataram".

The Bengal government issued a circular on October 10 condemning the use of students for political purposes as a subversion of discipline and injurious in the highest degree to their interests (see circular issued by R.W. Carlyle, chief secretary to the government of Bengal, 10-10-1905, Home, *Pol. A.*, August, 1906, Proc. 261–71). It requested district magistrates and collectors to report to heads of schools and colleges any students who took part in boycotting, picketing or other action connected with the swadeshi movement. These heads were warned that unless they took action, their grants-in-aid and the privilege of competing for government scholarship examinations would be withdrawn, as would their recognition by the university. This circular was published in the *Statesman* of 22-10-1905, *Amrita Bazar Patrika* of 23-10-1905, and the *Bengalee* of 24-10-1905. The Carlyle circular was unreservedly condemned by the Bengali press. The *Amrita Bazar Patrika* called it an "anti-swadeshi circular" (Oct. 25, 26, 30 and Nov. 2). Leaders of the anti-partition movement such as Bipin Chandra Pal and Surendranath Banerjee held meetings and wrote articles on establishing a national university. Students were asked not to bow before the Carlyle circular, and continue to work for swadeshi and boycott.

With all this encouragement from Calcutta, the students of the Rangpur zila school decided to disobey the order issued by their district magistrate. They attended public meetings shouting "bande mataram", and pledged themselves to oppose partition by all possible means. They were fined five rupees each and not allowed to attend till the fines were paid. When news of the Rangpur incident reached Calcutta, a student's meeting was held at College Square and a decision was taken to establish a society to fight the Carlyle circular. Representatives of this group rushed to Rangpur, where the agitation, as elsewhere, was being led by local pleaders and barristers. It was decided to help the expelled students by starting a "national" school. Such a school was started in November 1905; it was the first national school in East Bengal. Students in other schools, too, had defied authority and been expelled. Other national schools were started to accommodate them at Dacca and Dinajpur. Some students joined who had failed in examinations or were unable to follow the curricula prescribed in the government schools.

The Mymensingh national school was started in 1906 as a result of a visit by B.C. Pal and Arobindo Ghose, who urged students to boycott the government zila school. Some dismissed teachers also started national schools. Some schools, such as those in Uthari and Amrajhuri, declared themselves "national" because they had had government grants withdrawn on political grounds. Others at Bhola and Habibganj went "national" when Calcutta University withdrew recognition. A national school was started at Taraganj because there was a man in the village who had nothing else to do! The demand for education in Bengal and East Bengal was so great that it was the easiest thing to start a new school; it was also fairly profitable. Most national schools were founded between 1906 and 1908.

In 1907 there was a secondary-level national school, and by 1909 there were approximately 40 national schools in the two Bengals. The number of pupils varied with time but, at a rough estimate, there were 2,500 to 3,000 boys in these schools. The more important schools were usually situated at district or sub-divisional headquarters such as Dacca, Chittaganj or Comicha. Most of these were secondary schools (high to middle), but there were a few primary schools, e.g., the Pabna national school. In Babarganj, Dacca and Faridpur, three districts where English education had spread very rapidly, there were national schools in small villages, too. There were also a few girl's schools, e.g., those at Mymensingh and Naogaon (Rajshahi).

It was in these circumstances that Asutosh Chaudhury issued a manifesto calling for the boycott of Calcutta University to the leading citizens of Calcutta. A meeting was held at the Bengal landholder's association under the presidency of Raja Peary Mohun Mukherjee. It was attended by Guru Das Banerjee, Bipin Chandra Pal, Surendranath Banerji, Tarak Nath Palit, Bhupendra Nath Basu, C.R. Das and, in fact, all the leading public men of Calcutta of that time. A decision was taken to establish a Jatiya Shiksha Parishad or National Council of Education (NCE) with the object of imparting education—literary as well as scientific and technical—on national lines and exclusively under national control, *not in opposition to, but standing apart from*, the existing systems of primary, secondary and university education. Among the aims were

1. education through the vernacular medium with English as a compulsory subject;
2. preparation of suitable textbooks, especially in the vernaculars;
3. promoting physical and moral education, providing for

denominational religious education, and inspiring students with a genuine love for, and a real desire to serve their country;
4. attaching special importance to a knowledge of the literature, history and philosophy of the country, and incorporating the best Oriental ideals of life and thought and the best available ideals of the West;
5. imparting scientific, professional and technical education to develop the material resources of the country;
6. including the ayurvedic and hakimi systems in medical education.

While most of the nationalist leaders of Bengal realized the inadequacy of the prevailing system of English education, not all were in favour of boycotting Calcutta University. The existing system was condemned as too academic and literary. A group headed by Tarak Nath Palit, Bhupendra Nath Basu, Nagendra Nath Ghosh, Nilratan Sircar and others wanted simply to supplement the existing system by a regular arrangement for technical education. Accordingly, Palit started the Society for the Promotion of Technical Education, which set up the Bengal Technical Institute in July, 1906.

The curricula of the Bengal National College started by the NCE included lessons in politics, religion and economics. Stress was also laid on physical and technical education. Apart from this, there was not much difference between its courses and those of Calcutta University. The NCE also organized a system of grants-in-aid, scholarships and stipends. To begin with, money came from zamindars like Subodh Chandra Mullick and the rajas of Gouripur and Mymensingh. Nine of the more important schools were affiliated to the NCE and received grants varying from Rs 125 (Dacca) to Rs 25 (Kamaragram).

The smaller schools (pathshalas) received grants from local organizations such as the Swadesh Bandhad Samiti of Bakarganj or the Sebak Samiti of Comicha. The NCE often gave grants to these local associations for onward disbursement. They were distinctly political in aim, and the NCE often extracted a vow of swadeshi from teachers before sanctioning a grant. Financial help was also given, in some cases, by local zamindars, pleaders and mukhtars, who were almost invariably the chief supporters of these schools. Teachers and pupils also collected funds at theatrical performances held at river ghats and railway stations, and by other means.

Behind the rise of these national schools there was an avowedly anti-government feeling created by the partition of Bengal. They therefore became centres of political activity. Teachers were often leaders of the district who had been dismissed from aided or recognized schools by their school committees. As noted, some of them even started their own national schools. The position of these teachers was not very happy financially, since they had to depend for their pay on alms collected in public places by their pupils.

The schoolhouses were also used as rendezvous points by extremist politicians. Meetings were addressed by Bipin Chandra Pal, Surendra Nath Banerjee, Subodh Chandra Mullick, Arobindo Ghosh and others, and attended by students and teachers. The national schools were often closely connected with the national "volunteer" movement, in whose ranks many pupils were enrolled. The captain-general of the volunteers was Pulin Bihari Das, a member of the Anusilan Samiti and also the founder of the Dacca national school. The student volunteers were used to maintain order at national meetings and fairs, to assist at boycotts and pickets, and later even for organized gang raids, dacoities and murders. Many of the national schools taught the use of lathis, swords and daggers, and were closely linked with secret revolutionary societies such as the Anusilan Samiti of Dacca and the Swadesh Bandhab Samiti of Bakarganj. The Rangpur school was associated with Prafulla Chaki, the man who helped Khudiram Bose. The teachers and students of national schools read and distributed newspapers such as *Juganta* and *Sandhya*. Some of the students of the Dacca national school were involved in the Barra dacoity case. Two students of the national college at Giridih were members of the secret society of Basin Ghosh (Home Pol. Deposit No. 17, May, 1908). The pattern of political teaching was about the same in all the national schools: singing, patriotic songs, poems, lathi drills, and the reading and distribution of anti-government newspapers and literature.

The government had hardly any local powers to control schools that did not accept financial aid and were not recognized by the universities. Only in extreme cases, if a school stored arms or manufactured bombs, could the government force it to close down by applying the Criminal Law Amendment Act, enforceable against dangerous associations. Craddock, chief commissioner of the Central Provinces suggested that in order to control such schools, a system of licensing should be introduced. No school could be opened without a licence, to be renewed annually and cancelled if the management was found to be inculcating subversive doctrines. "We must strike at these evils at their roots, and protect the young from the danger that threatens them, instead of standing with folded hands watching nurseries of sedition growing up round about us," he said. He wanted the government to take stern measures to check the "manufacture of rebels" which was going on in schools all over the country. If no action was taken, "in the next generation our officials will be contaminated. Even now our ministerial officials are infected" (Pol. Deposit Confidential, June, 1908, Proc. 20).

The home department of the government of India did not, however, consider Craddock's proposals practicable or necessary. On the contrary, it felt that such measures would only "intensify and spread the very sentiments against which they were aimed" (letter from Sir Harold Stuart to Craddock, *ibid.*). According to Henry Sharp, the DPI of Bengal, the most effective way of meeting the problem was

1. to improve government secondary schools;
2. to increase aid to private schools and improve them;
3. to increase the facility for technical education in schools by organizing artisan classes, etc.;
4. to show tacit disapproval of the national schools by

refusing transfers from these schools to government, board or aided schools

(*Pol. A.*, March, 1909, No. 10–11 (notes), Sharp, 22.10.1908).

By 1913 the government was thinking of passing a bill requiring all schools and teachers to be registered but, at the last minute, the proposal was dropped because of the outbreak of the first world war. Meanwhile, the national schools themselves started dying out. The signs had already begun in 1910, when 4 schools closed down, bringing the total to 7 from the original 13 in Bengal (excluding East Bengal). By 1910 there was also no great popular support for them. The total number of pupils, excluding Calcutta, was 453, and including Calcutta it was 600 to 650. Four of the schools were national in name only, and in no way different from ordinary schools.

By 1913 according to Sharp (*Pol. B.*, Nov., 1914, Proc. 235), the national schools were a spent force. Two of the politically most active, those at Rangpur and Dinajpur, disappeared. There were only 16 national schools in 1912 and 15 in 1913 in reunited Bengal; Assam, Bihar and Orissa had never had any national schools. Only a few of these now received aid from the National Council of Education, grants from individual and district associations became rare, and door-to-door collections (mushitibhikshas) were abandoned. Fees were the only source of income, but they yielded little. The number of pupils in 1913 was 800, down from 1,000 the previous year. A large number of applications were received from the pupils of national schools seeking transfer to recognized schools. Hornell, the DPI of Bengal, thought that the movement had been considerably crippled and would shortly come to a standstill.

The NCE and SPTE had started as separate bodies in 1906. They merged in 1910, with the arts and pure science departments becoming the Bengal National College, and the technical and applied science departments the Bengal Technical Institute. In a few years, however, the Bengal National College found itself with empty branches and ceased to exist. By 1916-17, not one student cared to acquire a literary or scientific education on national lines. But the Bengal Technical Institute continued to thrive.

The demand for national education was not confined to Bengal. At the Indian National Congress session in Bengal in 1916, a resolution moved by Hirendra Nath Dutta, secretary of the NCE, was adopted unanimously. It said that in the opinion of the Congress, "the time had arrived for people all over the country earnestly to take up the question of national education for both boys and girls, and organize a system of education—literary, scientific and technical—suited to the requirements of the country, on national lines and under national control." In moving the resolution, Dutta said that swadeshi was a three-faced goddess, the three aspects being political, industrial, and last but not least, educational. He went on to say that people had not fully recognized the role of education in national regeneration. The idea of national education was being spread by district and provincial conferences, in Satara, Poona and other places in Maharashtra. Tilak made strong pleas for national education as the means of creating patriotic young men. Lajpatrai, too, was an enthusiastic advocate of national education.

As political passions subsided with the reversal of the partition of Bengal in 1911, so did the enthusiasm for national education. Though the government did not adopt a repressive policy of closing down the schools, it was not going to stand by a passive spectator either. It used pressure on Bash Behari Ghose, president of the NCE, to ensure that anti-British propaganda was not carried on in the national schools (*Pol. A.*, March, 1911, Proc. 5–7). As a result, the secretaries of the NCE issued circulars asking the national schools not to engage in political activity. But once the political content was removed, there was little to distinguish the national schools. The curriculum was the same as in government schools, except for a few additional books. Nor were the teachers better qualified. The zila government schools were much better from the academic point of view. Moreover, education in India has always been an avenue to employment, and prospects for this were bleak for national school graduates, as neither the government nor European merchant houses would accept them. The national schools also faced financial problems as donations started dwindling, since they got no government grants and fees were too low. Further, the education imparted in them was not of a high standard. As a result, their products did not even command much public respect. As Dr. S.C. Roy painfully recorded, "They (the public) would not recognize them as educated and sometimes would even deny them the privileges of educated men. This was also very greatly instrumental in ultimately detracting from the attractions of the national schools and colleges." The only attractive courses not offered elsewhere were the technical ones. This is why the Technical Institute survived.

How far was the Bengal national education movement the forerunner of Gandhi's ideas on education? His experiments began in South Africa with the foundation of the Phoenix settlement in Natal in 1904, i.e., before the partition of Bengal. A distinguishing feature of Gandhian education is the importance given to manual work. Both in his school at Tolstoy Farm in South Africa as well as in his Basic Education Scheme, education through craft was stressed. He used to say, "there is no point in developing the brain only. One has to develop one's brain through one's hands. If I were a poet, I would write a beautiful poem on the possibilities of the five fingers of this hand ... Books are never sufficiently interesting to hold the interest of the mind. The mind begins to wander. Only manual work brings you back to reality." By contrast, manual work was not a part of the curriculum of the national schools of Bengal, as the pupils and teachers were bhadralok who were divorced from manual work. Another difference is that in the Gandhian scheme of education, the mother tongue is the medium of instruction at all levels, and there is compulsory teaching of Hindi. At the national schools of Bengal the medium was, in fact, Bengali at the primary and secondary levels, but English was given great importance.

Like the leaders of the swadeshi movement, Gandhi, too, wanted students to work for the country's freedom from foreign rule. The objective of his education, however, was not only swaraj but also sarvodaya, a new social-economic order. His education principles can be seen in *Hind Swaraj,* the social manifesto written in 1909, in which he enumerated an 18-point programme for the economic, social and political reconstruction of Indian society. He envisioned true education coming about primarily through a particular pattern of life in a community, and not merely through formal instruction in schools. Schools were there to prepare citizens for a new, non-violent society, and to teach children to live on the basis of cooperation, truth and non-violence.

It was very difficult for educational institutions which were anti-establishment to flourish under colonial rule. Private education survived only at apolitical institutions such as the gurukuls, Vishwabharati, Dakshinasti, and the theosophical schools at Adaiyar and Banaras. The Gujarat and Kashi vidyapiths survived despite being political, because by 1921, under Dyaseley, education was a "transferred subject" and there was less official pressure. The national schools in Bengal were distinctly political in aim, and the men behind them were agitators rather than educationists. Once the political emphoria subsided, the impetus was lost. At the height of the movement, there were about 40 national schools with 2,500–3,000 pupils. They did play a part in sustaining the swadeshi movement and arousing patriotic sentiments.

Education and the National Movement

AMRIK SINGH

I

Before approaching the theme in hand, there are two contextual problems which need to be dealt with. The first one is: what precisely is meant by the national movement. Quite some people would argue that the national movement can be traced back to 1885, when the Indian National Congress was founded, if not earlier. Even if one chooses to avoid a debate on this problem, there was the agitation following the partition of Bengal in 1905 which convulsed at least that state, if not the rest of India. Even if the earlier two decades had no impact on education, the Swadeshi movement which flared up in Bengal after the decision to divide the province had an unmistakeable educational dimension. What became Jadavpur University had its origin in that agitation. For my part, I will confine myself to the emergence of Gandhi as a political leader and the Non-Cooperation movement which he launched on behalf of the Congress, which assumed mass dimensions in the years 1920–1922.

Having delineated the precise period when the national (non-cooperation) movement changed the character and temper of Indian politics irretrievably, it is also necessary to provide a second dimension to the context. This is the situation on the educational front as it had evolved during the preceding couple of decades. In 1912, for instance, Gokhale had moved his resolution for compulsory primary education for everybody. It had not been accepted then. Consequently, the situation of school education continued to be what it was. That is, only a very small proportion of children went to school and the rest of them remained illiterate. There was hardly any move to promote vocational or technical education. In any case, the outbreak of World War I made it difficult to find any additional funds.

Two relevant developments might, however, be noted. One was the establishment of Banaras Hindu University in 1916. The proposal to set up this university had been under consideration for quite some time. Once arguments in regard to what kind of a university it should be—whether it should be affiliating in character or not, what kind of control the government should have over it, and so on—had been settled, a bill was passed even during the war period.

The second major development was the appointment of a commission for Calcutta University. It was headed by Sir Michael Sadler, whom Curzon had tried to lure to India at the beginning of the century. He did not come then and went on to become the vice-chancellor of Leeds University. When he did come here some years later, he had usefully acquired a much wider range of experience.

Sadler's commission strongly disfavoured the system of affiliating universities that do little more than examine students. The system had been taken over in 1857 from the manner in which the University of London was organized. A year later, in 1858 to be precise, London abandoned this system. It is a comment on our situation that even a century-and-a-half later, we are still struck with the original London model.[1] In the wake of this recommendation, Allahabad, which used to be an affiliating university, changed its character and essentially became a unitary university. Lucknow, too, was founded in the post-Sadler era as a unitary university. Dacca University, which had been under consideration for over a decade, was also given a unitary character. It should not be necessary to refer to Banaras, because this university was conceived as a unitary university and continues to be one.

The second major recommendation made by the commission was to raise the age of entry into university, specifically from matriculation to intermediate. It would be difficult to maintain that this new idea was adopted everywhere. Funds of the required magnitude were not available, so it could not be introduced throughout the country. U.P. took to it in a marked way, however, and intermediate colleges continue to dot the landscape in that state even today. Unsuccessful attempts were made in the late 50s to persuade the state to give up this pattern. In the 70s, twelve years of schooling, which correspond to the intermediate examination, was enforced as a national policy, and by now almost every state has fallen in line. In a sense, thus, U.P.'s refusal to conform to the interim pattern of the 50s was vindicated.

The commission made a number of other recommendations, but these need not be gone into. The ones referred to are those that had a long range impact. What needs to be underlined is the fact that, when the national movement took on a mass character under the leadership of Gandhi, the situation was more or less what it had been at the beginning of the century.

II

It is not necessary to go into the details of how Gandhi captured the leadership of the Indian National Congress and converted this body, "a shambling debating society which could be easily swayed by canny manoeuvres," into "a potentially formidable national organization and fighting force," to quote Judith Brown.[2] Till then, as the *Amrita Bazar Patrika* put it in January, 1915, the Congress was a white elephant which cost at least one lakh rupees annually, and did "nothing but make some speeches and pass a few stereotyped resolutions."[3]

The character change the Congress underwent was entirely owing to one man, Gandhi, and there is ample material available for those interested in knowing more about it. For our purposes, what needs to be underlined is, once his dominance became accepted, he insisted repeatedly that, as a part of the Non-Cooperation movement, Indians should give up what he called their "three infatuations."[4] These were schools either run or aided by the government, practice in law courts, and membership of legislatures. Gandhi argued that non- cooperation meant refusal to do anything which would enable the government administration to continue to run. That meant a refusal to obey laws or pay taxes, take employment under the government, whether in the civil or military arena, accept titles or honorary positions, boycott the courts and the legislatures, and withdraw children from schools and colleges run or aided by the government. According to Gandhi, only this kind of total non- cooperation would work. It was such a drastic programme of action that to implement it in full would have been extraordinary. The fact that this did not happen does not indicate that Gandhi was half-hearted. It only shows that people lacked the commitment and courage to do what was expected.

It may not be out of place to mention one thing in passing. Till the tragedy of Jallianwala Bagh, Gandhi was very loyal to the British empire. He had genuine faith in the sense of fairness of the British. His two-decade-long battle in South Africa, where he evolved the technique of satyagraha, was based on this assumption. Once the April 1919 incident took place, however, and the government tried to cover its tracks in a shamefaced manner, Gandhi lost faith in the proverbial sense of justice of the British. The Hunter Committee which inquired into that incident was split along racial lines. Not a single Indian member voted the same way as the English members. The announcement of the Montagu-Chelmsford reforms at the end of 1919 did excite him briefly, but he soon returned to the conviction, formed earlier, that the British were being unjust.

It was against this background that the Khilafat movement began to gather force. For a variety of reasons which it is not possible to go into here, he got involved in it. This combination of Hindu and Muslim indignation, connected with two separate issues, queered the pitch to such an extent that, when the Indian National Congress held a special meeting on September, 1920, at Calcutta, Gandhi's line of non-cooperation came to be acepted. This was confirmed at the regular session at Nagpur three months later. After that, there was never any doubt about the ascendancy of Gandhi in Indian politics. He emerged as the dominant figure in the Congress, and for the next two years steered the non-cooperation movement through a variety of situations till it was called off at the beginning of 1922.

One thing that was achieved in these two years was that, for the first time, the national movement assumed a mass character. There was widespread political awakening in the country. The countryside, which had remained untouched so far, participated in the national struggle in a massive way. Gone was the era when resolutions were adopted, and that was the end of it. If anything was sought to be achieved, delegations would go to London and lobby for their demands. No one ever thought of anything like self-rule except in name. Less than a decade earlier, a home rule league had been established, but it had limited popular roots. Everything was urban and elitist. Gandhi changed all that and, in the course of time, built up a national movement unlike that in any other colonized country.

All this was happening on the political plane. In respect of education, his basically subversive ideas have already been referred to. That he attached extraordinary importance to the boycott of educational institutions should be evident from the following instance. His answer to the question of why the agitation against the partition of Bengal had failed was twofold: (1) the students had not been withdrawn from classes, and (2) the leaders continued to send their children to colleges.[5] He felt so strongly about it that he used the word "sinful" about children going to schools run or aided by the government.[6]

He maintained that, while education was compulsory, there was no compulsion to attend a particular school. "In my view," he said, "the most important education is to learn to be a man. Submission to slavery is not being a man." Therefore, he insisted time and again upon boycotting these schools. On one occasion, when asked how to celebrate Diwali, he replied that the first thing to do was withdraw the children from the schools. In fact, he went so far as to ask the young "to cease to procreate for the time being." He added, "I render this advice even to the newly married."[7]

Most people would regard such statements as unbalanced, but to describe Gandhi as unbalanced would be utterly wrong. He was so determined to not cooperate with the British that he did not favour any half measures. He wanted the boycott to be complete and unconditional. Not only did he insist upon this, he referred again and again to all such things, including the boycott of courts. It was because of this unwavering commitment to his non-violent brand of revolution that he talked in this vein and people listened to him. More than that, they even followed him to the extent of doing quite a few of the things that he wanted of them.

Perhaps his biggest achievement during those two years was removing fear of the British from the minds of his countrymen. There were failures and setbacks but, qualitatively speaking, the situation underwent a change the like of which had not been witnessed in prior years.

III

It is now time to go over things in a more orderly manner. Throughout 1919, it was the Jallianwala Bagh tragedy which occupied the attention of the country, and also of Gandhi. Once he started projecting the new hypothesis of non-cooperation with the British, the tempo of political activity began to pick up. In September, 1920, a special session of the Congress was convened at Calcutta. At this session, there was quite some opposition, but the majority went with Gandhi and his new strategy was approved. One reason why Gandhi was able to get the support of the majority was that, by then, the Khilafat movement had picked up considerable momentum. For instance, in the summer of 1920, there had been a joint Hindu-Muslim meeting at Allahabad, which had witnessed turbulent scenes of raw emotion and unrestrained criticism of the British government. Gandhi had exercised a distinctly moderating influence.

By then, he had more or less formuled the doctrine of non-cooperation. It was, in a sense, a further refinement of the kind of satyagraha he had successfully practised during his years in South Africa. However, there was one important difference with the situation in India. In South Africa, he had been able to mobilize almost the entire Indian community. To start with, only 150 men and women had sought imprisonment in pursuance of satyagraha, but later, nearly 40,000 courted jail and 10,000 were actually imprisoned.[8] This was about one quarter of the small population of Indians in South Africa at that time. In India, however, many millions had to be mobilized. Gandhi was able to do it to some extent, but not as much as he wanted.

In one respect, the South African experience set a precedent which helped Gandhi develop the new technique of non-cooperation. He saw that people like Smuts and Herzog had given up their legal practice and enlisted in the army. He also knew that, during the war, Boer mothers did not permit their children to speak a single word of English. Even when the Boers had been defeated in the battlefield, they refused to cooperate with the government till a new constitution that was acceptable to them had been adopted by the British parliament and implemented. It was this example of total non-cooperation which Gandhi had at the back of his mind. Apart from other things, this is what persuaded him to present his programme at Calcutta. It called for title holders to return their titles, lawyers to stop going to courts, and students to stop going to schools and colleges that were funded by the government. In response to criticism, he conceded that the boycott of schools and courts would create problems. But then, he affirmed, when the nation was at war, whether violent or non-violent, it was "an indispensable condition that it stop its schools and courts."

In fact, it was at this session of the Congress that he went so far as to say that swaraj could be won within one year, provided people genuinely and honestly followed the line of non-cooperation suggested by him. People laughed and even ridiculed the whole notion, but Gandhi was dead serious. It was a precondition, he said, that all he suggested be followed in full and with utter sincerity. Swaraj, of course, did not come so quickly, and the result was that large numbers felt a kind of anti-climax at the end of the year. By then, he had also called off the Bardoli satyagraha that the Congress was getting ready to launch. What persuaded Gandhi to say the British could be made to leave in one year? One explanation is that he wanted people to act with more determination than they actually had. In one of his letters of April, 1920, Dr. M.A. Ansari had previsaged this. He had said that neither the talukdars and other gentry spawned during the British period nor the title holders would non-cooperate. Only a few government servants might give up their jobs and, as to the police and army, perhaps none.[9]

In the opinion of J.P. Naik in his *History of Education in India*, no other item of boycott had so much success as the boycott of schools and colleges. Statistically, there was no spectacular decline in the number of students during those years. According to data analysed by B.R. Nanda, the number of students in the arts colleges fell by about 4,000 from 1919-20 to 1920-21. In the subsequent year, 1921-22, there was a further fall of 3,000. Similarly, at the secondary school level, the numbers fell by 30,000 in the first year and another 1,000 or so in the following year. Instead, what were called "national" schools and colleges were established, and as many as 80,000 students got enrolled in them. There were over 1,200 such institutions.[10] They were established in all kinds of places and at different levels. In the different volumes of Gandhi's *Collected Works*, something like a dozen addresses and speeches delivered on these occasions are included.

Madan Mohan Malviya did not agree with this approach. Banaras Hindu University had been founded only a few years earlier, and he did not want that institution to be hurt in any way. It was in these circumstances that, at the initiative of Dr. Bhagwan Das, an eminent scholar, the Kashi Vidyapith was established. From the very large number of institutions established at that time, this and the Gujarat Vidyapith are the only ones that have managed to survive with a certain degree of success. The rest had to be closed sooner or later for want of funds and students. The dilemma confronting the Indian middle class which patronized these insitutions was best expressed by G.L. Mehta in January 1922. He was studying at the London School of Economics and wrote to his friend S.A. Barelvi of the *Bombay Chronicle* as follows:[11]

> ... I have never concealed my total disagreement with the policy of civil disobedience, but does not the coward lurk in me—does not the lover of ease and comfort, the talker and not the doer, prompt me to give intellectual justification for my inability to sacrifice? ... Is it not one's duty as an Indian to see that the challenge of the government meets with a universal response, and prisons are filled till they are overfull? Sitting as I am miles away, I can literally think of nothing else. Alas! if only I had some strength of character, some over-powering moral conviction that would conquer my hesitation, incapacity to sacrifice, and take me to jail. You call me exceptionally gifted ... What use am I to the country? It is character that is needed in our country, and not ability or brains.

That Gandhi had a different perception of things should be clear from what he said on November 15, 1920, when the Gujarat Vidyapith was established:

> I have done a good many things in my life; some of them I feel proud of, though some others I regret. A few of them were very responsible undertakings. But I should like to state here—I am sure I am guilty of no exaggeration—nothing I have done so far can stand comparison with what we are about to do today.[12]

On this occasion, he was elected the first chancellor of the Vidyapith, which he continued to be till the day of his death.

During the next three decades, the Vidyapith had to suffer all kinds of setbacks. For instance, it was closed down in 1930, when the second non-cooperation movement was launched, and remained closed for the next five years. It was closed again from 1940 to 1942. It began to flourish (if one can use that word) rather than merely survive, only after India became independent. Earlier, it had not been allowed to function properly by the British government. Funding was scarce and the inflow of students was meagre. In 1963, the UGC recognized it as a "deemed university". Since then, the financial situation has eased a great deal. To some extent, the same can be said about the Kashi Vidyapith, which also became a "deemed university" at about the same time, and was subsequently made a state university.

Why none of these institutions flourished in any significant way is explained in the letter of G.L. Mehta quoted above. The Indian middle class, a product of the British impact on India, had become a kind of curious hybrid during the preceding century or so. When Gandhi launched his non-cooperation movement, he had no alternative except to seek to mobilize this class. But Gandhi himself noted their weakness:

> Councillors want their (railway) fares and extras, the ministers their salaries, the lawyers their fees, the suitors (in the courts) their decrees, the parents such education for their boys as would give them status in the present life, the millionaires want facilities for multiplying their millions, and the rest their unmanly peace.[13]

This was written in the aftermath of the first non-cooperation movement, when it was clear to Gandhi that the middle class was not prepared to make all the sacrifices he wanted of them. In this connection, B.R. Nanda's comment is most telling:

> Gandhi's ultimate aim was the politicization of the masses, but the programme he placed before the country in 1920 largely depended for its success on the responsibilities of the middle class.[14]

This indeed was the paradox of the Indian national scene.

Not only did it remain unresolved during the three decades of Gandhi's political dominance, it is the middle class which eventually inherited the mantle of political power in 1947. What it has done to the country is there for everybody to see and does not call for any detailed comment.

IV

The narrative would remain incomplete unless a reference to the events at Aligarh is also made. Perhaps nowhere else did the situation become so explosive as at Aligarh. This was for two reasons, both of them important. One was the sustained pro-British atmosphere that characterized the working of the MAO school and then the MAO college. Second, there was the cavalier treatment of Turkey by the British government.

The enterprise at Aligarh was established after Syed Ahmed's long visit to England when his son went to study at Cambridge. It was the Oxford-Cambridge model which gripped his imagination, and his institution at Aligarh was set up on those lines. Right till the establishment of the university in 1920, the heads of both institutions were Englishmen. Opinion in regard to them was divided, but what they did ensure was that the bulk of those who joined remained pro-British. Since most students were eventually going into middle- and lower-level government jobs, this was not difficult. Altogether, the tone of life at Aligarh was fervently pro-British. Even those who succeeded Syed Ahmed maintained the tradition.

However, things began to change even before World War I because of the unsympathetic attitude of the British government towards Turkey. Once Turkey, an ally of Germany during the war, was defeated, the Ottoman Empire was dismembered. More particularly, those countries of the Middle East which had been under Ottoman rule were detached and relaunched under different auspices.

All this caused a commotion in India. While even the Mughals had refused to recognize the Caliph as someone to whom they owed their loyalty, things began to change in the 19th century. Muslims in India began to look upon Turkey as a surviving symbol of former Islamic glory and power. What happened to it therefore exercised an emotional hold on the Muslims. With every setback that Turkey received in the later part of the 19th century, this identification became stronger. By the time the war ended, it had become a situation of complete identification between the Muslims in India and the fate of Turkey.

These pressures had been manifesting themselves for quite some time. Two people emerged on the Muslim horizon and exercised profound influence upon the new generation in Aligarh. One of them, who had nothing to do with Aligarh, was Maulana Azad; the other was Maulana Mohammad Ali who had been a student of Aligarh and had close emotional and cultural links with it. Now, however, he adopted an attitude of defiance. As the political temper in the country began to rise, so did that at Aligarh.

On November 28, 1917, Gandhi paid a visit to Aligarh. The students were so excited by this visit that they unhorsed the carriage in which he was riding and hauled it through the streets themselves. The British principal did not allow a meeting in the union room, but one was held elsewhere. Gandhi visited Aligarh again in the company of the Ali brothers on October 11, 1920. The general sentiment was that the college should sever its connection with the government. This was not acceptable to those in control of things, and the syndicate of the college decided against it by 48 votes to 10.[15] A few days after Gandhi's visit, the students passed a resolution against continued affiliation with Allahabad, and gave a fortnight's ultimatum to the college to this effect. They stopped attending classes, and the principal wrote to the parents asking them to recall their children. There was unrelieved tension that year.

It was Zakir Husain who led the agitation. He was on the staff of MAO college, and when he was accused of hypocrisy at a public meeting, he resigned his job on the spot. Noting the respect in which he was held by everybody, the authorities tried to tempt him back by offering him a deputy collectorship in the state administration. He rejected them with disdain.[16]

Discussions regarding the university status of MAO college had been in progress for about a decade. In the surcharged atmosphere, the government tried to bargain with the college authorities. Zakir Husain felt that university status was not to be all and end-all of everything. Between him and the public leadership of Mohammad Ali, things came to a crisis point by the end of the month. The authorities took steps to forcibly evict the latter from the premises he had occupied. Not only did he walk out, so did 225 other students. Two buildings had been rented in advance, and a new campus was set up. This is how Jamia Millia Islamia was established.

When, a quarter of century later, the silver jubilee of Jamia was celebrated in 1946, this is what Zakir Husain said with special reference to the support of the Shaikh-ul-Hind:[17]

> I remember the time when, in the Aligarh mosque, a saintly soul was seated, leaning against a wall. He could not even address the gathering as he was so weak, and his message was read by his student Maulana Shabir Ahmed Usmani. Gentlemen, please remember that the wall against which he was leaning was not just made of bricks and stones. It was of solid faith, and as a result of that faith, a mighty national wall of the past had been erected. On that day, no foundation stone of any big building was laid, nor was there inauguration of any construction. No announcement of any donation was made and yet this caravan had set out without any of the required needs. It was bargaining immediate loss against immediate gains. It preferred lasting value to fleeting things ... It was in this atmosphere that Jamia came into existence on 29 October 1920.

It was an act of faith by a whole new generation of students for which there were very few parallels during the Non-Cooperation movement.

What happened at Ahmedabad a few weeks later was equally momentous, but there was one difference. Aligarh was an act of defiance against established authority. The MAO college had been in existence for about four decades. In all that time it was a bastion of conservatism, and invariably had a pro-British stance. With the winds of change blowing fiercely through the Muslim community, the old order was sought to be subverted, even if not in the literal sense of the word. A new beginning was made and, unlike most other institutions except those referred to in Ahmedabad and Banaras, this act of defiance was to yield extraordinary results.

In the following few years, Jamia went through all kinds of trials and tribulations, first at Aligarh and then at Delhi, where it was moved by Hakim Ajmal Khan, its first chancellor. After his death in 1927, Dr. M.A. Ansari continued to guide and support it. Zakir Husain and some of his colleagues, like M. Mujeeb and Abid Hussain, had joined Jamia by then. With their hard work and dedication, they were able to build it up and bring it to a level of achievement whereby, even before the British left, it began to attract patronage from the public as also some visiting dignitaries.

Whatever might be said about the subsequent history of Jamia, it was the combined work of Gandhi and Zakir Husain which led to the formulation of what came to be called the basic system of education. This happened around the time when Congress ministries were formed in some of the provinces. To talk about it would be to go beyond the self-imposed limits of our chronology. What seems to be generally acknowledged is that the one man who made a difference was Zakir Husain. It was the commitment and dedication of this talented man that enabled the Jamia experiment to succeed, whereas the rest had fallen by the wayside. When a man with talent and dedication undertakes to do a job, he always succeeds; it is as simple as that.

Notes

1. For details, see Eric Ashby, *Universities: British, Indian, African,* Harvard, 1966, particularly, pp. 54–64.
2. Judith Brown, *Gandhi,* Yale, 1989, p. 156.

3. Quoted by B.R. Nanda, *Gandhi: Pan-Islamism, Nationalism and Imperialism*, Oxford, 1989, p. 189.
4. Gandhi, *Collected Works*, Vol. XVIII, p. 207.
5. *Ibid*., p. 302.
6. *Ibid*., p. 306.
7. *Ibid*., p. 347.
8. B.R. Nanda, *op. cit*., p. 405.
9. Quoted by B.R. Nanda, *op. cit*., p. 216.
10. B.R. Nanda, *op. cit*., p. 260.
11. Quoted by B.R. Nanda, *op. cit*., p. 261.
12. Gandhi, *Collected Works*, Vol. XVIII, p. 463.
13. Gandhi, *ibid*., Vol. XXIII, p. 53.
14. B.R. Nanda, *op. cit*., p. 404.
15. Mushirul Hassan, *A Nationalist Conscience: M.A. Ansari, the Congress and the Raj*, Manohar, 1987, p. 100.
16. B. Sheikh Ali, *Zakir Husain*, Vikas, 1991, p. 120.
17. Quoted by B. Sheikh Ali, *op. cit*., p. 121.

Why Does Nationalist Education Fail? The Case of Banaras from the 1880s to the 1930s

NITA KUMAR

Nationalism and Education

Nationalism, among other things, is a new perspective on the self. There are many pre-nationalist definitions of the self in Banaras. Most prominently, it is defined by lineage or sub-caste, by occupational group, and by some notion of a "tradition" that dictates norms and practices. There are, likewise, various definitions of the term nationalist. One might expect or wish that, both academically and politically, nationalism would mean a belief in the idea of a nation. No doubt the various nationalisms that grow in soils like that of Banaras are progressively striving towards that. But from the 1880s to the 1930s they are varied, although they have the following set of features in common:

1. Many social practices are condemned because they are seen as mechanical and/or not reflective of progress, e.g., certain rituals, obscenities and consumption of liquor. The effort is to redefine a new "us" that is more alert, proud and culturally competitive in a world of nations.
2. Economic progress is to be striven for, but it should include symbolic progress, a recognition of being at the helm and an inner feeling of self-satisfaction. This is to be achieved, as all good things have been achieved throughout history, by recognizing the course of change,

and being pliable enough to bend with it like bamboo stalks in flood waters, when stiffer flora is uprooted.[1]

3. For these purposes, one needs new institutions like schools, community and meeting halls, newspapers and journals, new rituals, and new symbols.

It is a challenging exercise to place oneself at the turn of the century. What kind of blueprint would an ordinary person who is not a philosopher or visionary draw up for his new self? To answer this, one must take seriously the meaning of choice and the limitations on action. This, in turn, means understanding how everyone is an actor in history, some minuscule, others gigantic. Why this is not always obvious is because first, the action takes place in the realm of the mundane. Routine, everyday life, such as with women, is something history has hardly begun to appreciate as real or problematic. Second, there is no continuity between act and outcome. The agent thinks and chooses within limits, but the factors that go into the actual processes in which he or she plays a part are manifold and quite beyond their own world of action. The factors include technology, demography, other agents with their wills, chance and circumstance. The result is almost never what is planned by the actors. We historians, looking at the past with the benefit of hindsight, might well be tempted to suppose that the actors did not act at all but were manipulated or victimized. Instead, we must ask ourselves: what else or what better would *we* have done?

The subjects of my study are actors of the middle range, the local social and economic leaders of small towns, those in trade, banking, the professions and service, groups neither underpriviliged nor national-level thinkers. They are actors, yes, but actors moulded by their history and production relations. They are, at every stage, calculating, worrying about, and constructing their futures. They do this on a threefold basis:

1. an assessment of what is rational and essential for them;
2. an assessment of what is usable from their past; and
3. on the technology available to them.

To be given the space and epithet of actor does not also

mean to be acknowledged a successful one. This judgement is passed by those more fortunately located, that is, by us, who have strict criteria of "success". The actors themselves are, typically, modest enough to leave their own judgments on their very limited success for posterity to read. Since historians inevitably take sides, it is best to clarify here that, when I speak openly about "failure", I do so because of my privileged vision, because my subjects have thus passed judgement on themselves, and also because the fact of failure does not prove detrimental to their status as agents and actors, a status with its accompanying ideologies that I am more interested in than success or failure *per se*.

We are looking today at the case of education, a natural step from nationalist consciousness. When the people of Banaras began to condemn certain practices of the past, tried to envision a future more intelligent and commendable, and planned the institutions and rituals to make this a reality, the first area of life which they chose to operate on was education. In our present discourse, this means, of course, colonial education. Discourses on nationalism and education had many crucial links, as they have today. All nationalist, reform-minded, progressive people were educated. The school was the natural centre for influencing young minds and hearts. Those who did not believe in education were obviously backward and unsuccessful. Our past glories were all based on excellence in education. Western states were great nations because of their reformed education systems.

So the people of Banaras launched on a quasi-nationalist quest for improvement, self-satisfaction, and the construction of a new, modern self by building educational institutions. They worked on the three criteria mentioned above.

The Reproduction of Identity

In Banaras, as far as I am aware, there was no call for throwing over completely one's own identity, even if we presume, going by the secondary literature, that there was such a call in Bengal. Every occupational, regional, or caste group rallied into an association with the declared purpose of defending its identity, its "self-hood", now threatened in assorted ways. Those who joined later, did so with the clear understanding that it was their "identity" which delayed this necessary step.

The terms identity and self-hood need to be qualified in two ways. First, each group had an agenda: to define itself for an "other" in dimensions that were meaningful to a public audience. There is nothing either natural or unnatural about this definition of self-hood. There had been responses, counter-responses, definitions, defences and constructions of identity at various levels before colonialism and nationalism. However, now it became a wave in which every component drop participated. Every self-identified social group had to declare "what" they were, where they came from, how they declined, what they stood for, what they must preserve, and what they must change.

A more serious qualification concerns the actual people encompassed by the self-identification of a group. There are spokesmen more articulate than others, and there are leaders both natural and not so natural. Correspondingly, there are those who either do not speak or are silenced, there are the meditative or passive, there are those "behind" the times, and those engaged in active resistance through non-participation. We can be certain that at least two kinds of people are being excluded from the present discussion. One is those, such as women, who were never given the status of real human beings with their own rights; they were only useful as symbols. The other kind are those who did not participate in the agenda of self-identification in the form being undertaken, or else raised their voices in ways which are not known to us; they remain unrepresented forever.

These qualifications made, we are confronted, between the 1890s and the 1930s, with a city in which every "touchable" male belongs or is exhorted to belong to a reformist organization whose pronouncements concern the issues of identity, and whose agenda has at its forefront the setting up of a school for its members.

The Case of the Khatris

I take up the case of the khatris because they were in our period, and continue to be today, dominant among the silk merchants of Banaras. With these secure occupational rootings, they represent, together with the agrawalas, Gujarati vaishyas and marwaris, a caste cluster which had an unconventional view of nationalism and a complex attitude to education.

The khatris had their caste history written, their journal started, and their association subscribed to, all in the 1930s. The immediate stimulus was probably the 1901 census which degraded them to vaishyas, when there was no confusion whatever about their being kshatriyas, albeit equally occupied in trading and administration. As expatriates from Punjab, they were totally in trading in cities like Banaras.[2] Before their new educational agenda was voiced, the system patronized by them had two overlapping dimensions, described by me elsewhere as "vocational" and "ethical". The khatri boy learnt mahajani accounts, book keeping, and the Munda or Kaithi script from an accountant at home, in the company of other boys, or at a school for a few hours every day. With his father or other senior male family members, he learnt the ethics of the business, from how to recognize, in certain intangible ways, the quality of the product and how to deal with artisans and employees, to how to be a proper citizen, spend wisely and ethically, and live life in a holistic, rounded way.

Motivated by the concept of a good *rais*, the khatris were active patrons of the brahmins, Sanskrit learning, vedas, rituals, cows and scholars. The *Khatri Hitkari* was started in 1906 by Balmukund Verma, who said, "Our efforts will be to remove our jati's shortcomings. Let us see how far our brothers listen and help themselves. How good it would be if, instead of putting their dear children into dalali and kothis, they gave attention to their studies. Khatri brothers should open a school for khatri and saraswat boys in this city of learning."[3,4]

While this hope lay dormant, the khatri elite came to the service of Hindi literature and journalism as first generation

"Hindiwallas", their premier claim, perhaps, to nationalism. Shyam Sundar Das was the founder of the Nagari Pracharini Sabha, and Samkatha Prasad Khatri was the founder of the Carmichael Library. Ram Krishna Verma was the editor of *Bharat Jiwan* and an influential owner of a press. Devaki Nandan Khatri was a renowned novelist.[5]

The *Khatri Hitaishi* and *Khatri Hitkari* tell us what khatris worried about regarding their identity. They called themselves a caste (jati) and worried about (1) "pind gati pragati" or how to keep the substance pure, and (2) "samskar gati pragati" or progress in politics, science, literature, and public life by borrowing from the best in other cultures while keeping the jati's social basis undisturbed.[6]

Simultaneously, in magazines and occasional publications, there were calls directed at more precise ends: respecting elders; worshipping scholars, guests and cows; unselfishness, service and demonstration of love to all; removal of child marriage and marriage rituals such as obscene songs, dowry and gauna; discouragement of drinking and gambling; permission for foreign travel; and a provincial association for schools, libraries and reading rooms. At a larger level, there were ongoing discussions of the Aryan, Hindu/sanatani or Indian ways of life as opposed to the Western, Christian or British.

The problem was not peculiar to the khatris, but shared by all those occupationally secure in Banaras: how to maintain the essential aspects of one's identity while showing enough wisdom to move with the times and take advantage of the offerings of science, Western knowledge and the English language in colonial education. The Saraswat Khatri Vidyalaya was set up in 1917 with the explicit aim of preserving the strengths of the community, while providing the content and much of the style of Western education. This had already been done by several other communities: the Central Hindu School for merchants, chiefly the agrawalas; the Harishchandra School, also for the agrawalas; the Hewitt Kshatriya School for the thakurs; and the Anglo-Bengali and Bengalitola schools for the Bengalis. These schools differed from each other only in the self-declared identities of their founders. The new khatri school was different from them only in its notion of being for the khatris and, by virtue of that declaration, somehow magically able to preserve "essential khatri qualities" and "khatri culture" for its young men.

The Uses of the Past

The articulation of the question "who are we?" was never made in a very grand manner by any of the newly awakened groups of Banaras; the answers were typically modest, too. They called the valued dimensions of their practices and ideology, dharma, sabhyata, gyan and samskara (duty, culture, knowledge and tradition). The values to which these were opposed had the prefix pashchimi or pashchatya (Western).

It was Annie Besant, not local caste associations, representatives of brahmin scholars or ritual specialists, who first identified "we" with Hindu. "Some of us," she wrote, "resolved to take practical steps to build up in Hindu India a national system of education, which would give Hindu boys all that was best in Hindu learning, hand in hand with religious and moral education based on the Hindu shastras."[7] She used the interesting term "religio-secular", meaning "Hinduism (religion) + Western science and knowledge (secularism)". There was more than one problem with this formulation and the experiment based upon it called Central Hindu School, founded in 1898. Of these, I will discuss only one in this section: the non- flexibility of the vision of the past that it encompassed.

Besant wrote often about her vision of India's past: "That high ideal of life which the sages of India are known to have lived in the dim past and left vestiges thereof in their sublime and evergreen literature ... Hindu life and thought ... as it must have been in times when it had freshness, courage, hope and joy; had free life, free thought, free action and aspiration; when it knew how to welcome the world and be welcomed by it; was a full-grown nation, able to repel an enemy and make treaties of peace ..."[8]

By calling her Hinduism "non-sectarian", Besant was, in fact, rejecting whatever systems of practice encompassed this new ism. She was rejecting local ways and choices as implicitly backward, silencing differences, and robbing idioms of meaning. As late as 1932, Bhagwan Das, her staunchest supporter, could not use the words Hindu or Hinduism unreflectively. He would call the religion vedism or vaidic dharma, sanatan dharma, Arya dharma, or manav dharma (vedic law, Aryan law, eternal law, human law), and add that it was "now commonly called Hinduism."[9]

With an agenda as large as hers, that of creating a modern Hindu nation, there were bound to be difficulties. At the beginning of the process of setting up the school, she called a meeting of Banaras pundits and "laid the needs of Hindu youth before them and urged them to render help."[10] They did not cooperate, and there were a few murmurs of doubt against Besant in the papers.[11]

We could, of course, take the view that, like many reformers and nationalists, she suffered unwarranted opposition from a group solidly entrenched in the old hierarchy, too narrow in their vision to desire a change that benefitted a larger public, and too orthodox in their stubborn adherence to the *status quo* to warrant continued respect as leaders of the tradition. After all, in her dreams of Hindu nationalism, Besant seems more attractive than the pundits of Banaras, who did not seem to move a finger or lay a single brick towards building the nation.

But alternate interpretations are possible. For instance, some pundits were unconvinced that Besant had, in fact, repudiated Christianity. They saw her as wedded to British/Western civilizational ideals, such as those of the gentlemen who wore hats, rode horses and kept their elbows off the dining table. That she was a colonialist was also clear to them, being so certain that her definitions of Hinduism were the most comprehensive, holding the richest promise for the future, and to which all Indians must naturally subscribe. Cultural imperialism was as, if not more, familiar to the pundits as any other kind, given that the world they had to lose was a cultural one. She was surprised when the sanatan dharma series published by her was received critically by the pundits with whom she had shared the draft effort.[12]

We know of Besant's views of Hinduism not only from her writings but from the practices she introduced in her school. In the effort to Hinduize or Indianize her boarders, she introduced innovative rituals that reflected nothing in the home culture of the students: rituals regarding dressing, eating, greeting and meditating.[13] She either could not or did not wish to comprehend that, notwithstanding her claims for her version of Hinduism being all-encompassing, it was, in fact, selective and reductive. In her choices, Besant sacrificed most of the practical aspects of the system, those aspects that her boarders must have actually encountered at home: body language; attitudes towards space, time, cosmology and cosmogony; concepts of life, death, work and leisure, to say nothing of science. Not a single Hindu pundit of her time, and none today for that matter, would claim that Hinduism does not include its own sciences of physiology, psychology, medicine, architecture, the arts, sex, diet, and so on.

By labelling her boarder's practices a religion, and contrasting it to secular life and science, she robbed religion of its potency. From a matter of life it became a matter of culture. From something that was lived, it became something to merely celebrate. It remained neither a value system or lifestyle, nor, in an educational context, an intellectual challenge. It became a matter of certain rituals, of some scriptures to be read from, of exemplary tales of rather hilarious past times. It had to be defended and preserved, a kind of precious possession to stick to loyally in spite of the needs announced loudly by a changing world. However, the practices of Besant are important not only because they are so well documented. They are also representative of, and in Banaras they were a model for, all the local nationalist experiments made.

Resources

Let us come back to my proposal to place oneself at the turn of the century and address the task of how to create a nationalist system of education. What are the resources available to the educator to build new citizens in a new nation? The following come to mind.

Physical Space

In the discussions of neither nationalist nor indigenous education in India is there a recognition of the space within which students learn as having relevance in teaching them crucial ideas regarding hierarchy, authority and the self. Well before the period we are looking at, a special school building, different from that of indigenous schools, was regarded as indispensable to proper education. The first new schools in Banaras, Jai Narain Ghoshal and Cutting Memorial, were like that. One may say that the ideal type was well established by the time of the founding of the Central Hindu School.

With her plan of a new Hindu nationalism, Besant may have been expected to be more inventive about physical space. She was not. When Arundale came out to Central Hindu in 1903, he was astonished by the size and aspect of the school: "A quadrangle-shaped boarding house somewhat like the colleges at Oxford or Cambridge, a large hall with a big stone platform extending from it, large classrooms, and in front of the main entrance, a fine field for hockey, football, lawn tennis, etc."[14] An alumnus rhapsodized that the building was "a presage that the Hindus are again to become a nation," but was quick to explain that what was Hindu was the spirit within, not, self-evidently, the "fine set of buildings, shapely masses of brick, mortar and stones."[15]

In this matter, some other nationalists showed more perspicacity, as the numerous gurukuls show. However, all the new schools, especially the Vidyapiths and DAV schools, relied on the bottomline of a four-walled classroom. The symbolic significance of this is not our glorious past or our burgeoning nation, however these are defined. Rather, if there is a symbolic meaning, such a classroom represents a foreign authority, using the design to confine and control. The older fluidity of space and continuity between outside and inside was lost. The concept of the relativity of space, and its contextuality of use according to need, was replaced by one of non-flexibility, specialization, and a separation between outdoors and indoors.

The repercussions of all the multi-vocal symbolism residing in the various uses of physical space are not for us to go into here, nor am I laying down the law regarding the only possible choice of space deployment to achieve a nationalistic spirit. I am suggesting that physical space is a crucial item in the repertoire of the educationist; what is done with space has an impact on what one wishes to achieve. Those in search of a nationalistic outcome, however, did not consider this possibility, and used space unreflectively.

The Syllabus

In most cases, the syllabus was framed by a governing or affiliating body and could not be varied by choice. The framer was conscious that the power to name and categorize was the power to control. Over the last decades of the 19th century, the colonial state in India acquired a monopolistic control over the power to decide what was knowledge, what were the key concepts to pass on to future generations, and what could not be any of these things. There was no question in the British mind as to what education should consist of. They silenced all public dialogue regarding which aspects of the curriculum were relevant or desirable, and gradually transformed into a singular, legitimacy-appropriating system, what was a mosaic of coexisting indigenous systems of education, each institution of which was appropriate for a certain profession and therefore valued only by its members, although tolerated by all. In such a situation, the two sides, British and Indian, were seen as obviously unequal in terms of quality as well as motivation. The British view was neutral and benevolent, while the Indian view was variously, political, religious, communal and motivated. Indeed, given the monopoly over curricula claimed by the state, the opposition to them had no choice but to be political.

All the schools of Banaras were resigned to accepting the government curricula. One exception was the Agrawal

Mahajani School, whose curriculum focussed on book keeping and Indian arithmetic. It drew a gratifying number of students only decades after its foundation, when it also introduced English and Western subjects.[16] For all the other schools, the solution was to increase the required subjects with the *addition* of desired subjects. Annie Besant admitted that the syllabus of the Hindu School was more difficult than in England, and boasted that she had made it singular (in weight) by adding religious and moral instruction. Other schools introduced, in the name of nationalism, scriptures, vedic shlokas, Sanskrit, moral science, art, music, and domestic subjects like cooking, knitting and sewing for girls.

All educators accepted this double load as the necessary price of aiming for the religion-plus-science formula, and seemed to believe that they could make the students carry it by simply instituting it. In the beginning, there were some calls of frustration. Schools complained that if they had to teach the government syllabus, they had no time to give religious instruction.[17] With time, the problem became too familiar to arouse an outcry, but the effort remained institutionalized with no comment on its efficacy. Annie Besant, in all her complaints against the government, missionaries, pundits and so on, never once mentioned the problem from the student's point of view. It was as if it were a choice simply for the educators: whether to have lessons in religion or not.

The problem of an overweighted curriculum causes permanent damage to the learning and creative abilities of students, and is a little-explored form of violence. More pernicious was the definition of the desired subjects as "optional". Loud were the cries and prolific the writing of various activists against the uselessness of Western learning, except for science and mathematics. In fact, however, the actions of these activists legitimized Western learning and marginalized Indian knowledge. The knowledge which was compulsory was rendered "sacred", and that which was optional became marginalized. The additional subjects of Indian languages, and Indian mathematics, art, music, etc., were received less than seriously, partly because they were additional to an already complete syllabus that ate up all the energies of students and teachers, and partly because they were unofficial and unrecognized, secondary and illegitimate.

Everyday School Routines

Every little detail of a student's activities in school, an educator will tell you, contributes to the messages he learns. These range from the deployment of furniture in the classroom; the nature of the spaces otherwise; the periods of transition and movement in the morning, at break time, at the end, and between classes; the dress codes; the forms of greeting and other uses of language; and special school days and activities.

When an educator wished to use a school or, more modestly, a classroom for the purpose of instilling nationalism in the students, there was a wide-open terrain in front of him. He was in a position to manufacture every little ritual of school life. He could delve into various traditions, use the past of his society and the present of the Western model. What he could not do was copy if he wished to eschew the rigidity, hierarchy and placidity, perhaps, of his own society, and the authoritarianism and different cultural content of the West. Every educator, in fact, searched for a synthesis, and each was critical of the others for balancing the various strains to a different degree. But all, khatri, agrawal, ansari and pundit, understood the power of naming, that of bestowing meaning.

The case of morning assembly at Central Hindu School is telling. It consisted of hymns and readings from the Gita and Mahabharata. Then followed the principal's talk on the subject of the students' conduct in life. "This feature of the curriculum is regarded by the authorities as of the greatest importance."[18] The principal was a Briton who considered "proper conduct" to be not the practices derived from the student's own culture, but those that he had himself been socialized into, exactly like Besant herself, including the appropriate codes for dress, behaviour, speech and ethics.[19] The significance of this lies in that Besant and others like her did not even realize that readings from the vedic hymns, Ramayana and Mahabharata were being consistently marginalized by the principal's talk that followed.

Conclusion

The political-cultural goal of nationalism was refined progressively and articulated with increasing sophistication. However, to make education a cooperative enterprise in the nationalistic venture and, in fact, its bulwark, a certain amount of pedagogic acumen, of observation and thought regarding educational resources and professionalism was necessary. The grand objectives of revolutionizing society, regenerating the Hindus, and building a new nation and faith in it, failed and was destined to fail for certain reasons.

First, there was the problem of donors and endowments. The statement of ideology that would appeal to a marwari seth was not likely to find favour with a thakur grandee. All the educationists in Banaras, in their search for the funds needed for new, impressive campuses, ended up relying on the lowest common denominator. They taught a version of Hinduism, tradition and Indian culture that was pitifully inadequate compared to the lived-in reality of the student's home cultures. Even those who gave donations did not accept, in principle or in practice, the definitions of self espoused by the educational ideologists.

But my main argument is that the experiments were destined to fail because of the special power of ritual. All the rituals tried in the new Indian schools failed before the changing evaluation of the prestige of English education, the image of an educated, modern person, and the need for self-questioning and reform. Moreover, these Indianizing rituals were defeated by other, more powerful rituals. "Any type of teaching must, to a large extent, produce a need for its own product."[20] This has to be done with a particular deployment of resources. The resources of education, as I have argued in this paper, are physical space, curricula and school routines. Those who wanted reform and nationalism did see through the mask of science, universalism and secularism worn by British authority, but they did not proceed to attack it on its own terms, which would have been to develop symbols and forms to match the others in potency.

This argument is opposed to Michael Apple and other sociologists of education, who would have us pay more attention to the "why", not the "how to" of schooling, and to the political, not the technical issues. In the case of Indian education, far too much attention has been paid to the political issues, and not enough to the technical ones. The failure of middle-level nationalists, Indianists and progressivists in cities like Banaras was pedagogic and technical, not political. They simply did not evolve a pedagogy to match their intentions. Their nationalism was dead on the mark, but their technical expertise next to nil. They were ideologues, nationalists, reformers, political activists, journalists, orators, and fund-raisers. What they were not is educators. The questions that faced them were answered on an ideological and political basis, not ever along the lines: will it suit the children, will it work in the classroom, is it a workable pedagogic methodology, how does it fit into the classroom, and most of all, what does it mean for the child? The question, in short, was always what is good for our politics, not what is good for the children. It was based on a deep misunderstanding of the educational process. Because, for intentions to be translated into reality through the classroom, the techniques applied must be constantly modified according to the interaction with the students. Of such techniques we have no records.

Notes

1. "Hamari jati men vidvan kyon nain hote", *Khatri Hitkari*, 31 December 1906.
2. "Jatiyan, sabhayen aur samsthayen", *Khatri Hitaishi*, November 1938.
3. "Hamari dasha", *Khatri Hitkari*, February 1907.
4. "Vidyalaya ki avashyakta", *Khatri Hitkari*, March 1907.

5. N. Kumar, "Changing education and the stubborn work concept in the silk industry", *Purushartha*, **14**, 1991, pp. 315–38.
6. "Khatriyon ki jati sampati kya hai?", *Khatri Hitaishi,* golden jubilee souvenir.
7. *Central Hindu College* (*CHC*) *Magazine*, 1 March 1904.
8. *Ibid.*, 1 July 1904.
9. Bhagwan Das, *The Essential Unity of all Religions*, Banaras, Kashi Vidyapith, 1939, pp. xi, xxvi.
10. *CHC Magazine*, 1 January 1904.
11. Baladev Upadhyaya, *Varanasi ki panditya parampara,* Banaras, Vishwavidyalaya Prakashan, 1983.
12. *CHC Magazine*, 1 January 1904.
13. G.S. Arundale, "Ten years in the Central Hindu College, Banaras City", *CHC Magazine*, 1 January 1913.
14. *Ibid.*, p. 12.
15. *CHC Magazine*, 1 July 1904.
16. Annual reports of *Sri Kashi Agrawal Samaj* and *Ardhashati Itihas.*
17. Report of the Committee on Primary Education, United Provinces, Allahabad, 1913; Education File 1083, U.P. state archives, 1925.
18. *CHC Magazine,* 1 January 1904.
19. All Arundale's reminiscenses in the college magazine testify to this; see *CHC Magazine*, 1 January 1913.
20. Pierre Bourdieu and J.C. Paseron, *Reproduction in Education, Society and Culture,* London, Sage, 1977, p. 197.

British Educational Policy in 19th Century India: A Nationalist Critique

R.P. SINGH

No educational analysis of 19th century India can be attempted without first offering a prefatory note about the various strands which constitute its background. This is because first, it is the most documented century in our history. Second, there are numerous players who demand our individual attention. Third, one can trace from here the beginnings of a "modern" India, in which one witnesses, on the one hand, crumbling social edifices and structures and the replacement of age-old economic laws and financial institutions by a newer set, and, on the other hand, the gradual emergence of a colonial power the like of which India had never seen before. For our purpose, the picture is completed by adding that a new educational policy was being formulated in stages by an alien government from across the seas to supplant a system of education which had served the country down the ages.

For the first time, we find numerous controversies arising in the field of education. Indians are suddenly agitated over the content and medium of instruction, and argue heatedly about the variety and form of education. Previously, the two distinctly different peoples of India, Muslims and Hindus, had no history of conflict regarding either the medium of instruction in the madrasas or the curriculum. Both communities had to master Persian and Arabic, the languages of the cultured and the learned. Hindu students outnumbered Muslims in these institutions, nor were they unwelcome as teachers, since the brahmins were adept in both teaching and learning these languages. Until the oft-quoted minutes of T.B. Macaulay, we have no policy notes or debates, and certainly no historical parallels. Also, until we were told that we had an "indigenous" education, no one had either heard or thought of qualifying Indian education by any such term.

We should not forget that, when discussing 19th century India, there was actually no such entity. Despite the geographical unity of the subcontinent, we are still both politically and socially a very diverse people. Nineteenth-century India saw a foreign mercantile company struggle and assume a permanent political role through a series of diplomatic coups and battles, financing and commanding one set of Indian soldiers to outmanoeuver other sets belonging to "native" rulers. The British crown and parliament took over the reins of power from the East India Company in 1857, professing to be more forgiving, understanding and generous towards the "subject" people. In fact, neither in policy nor institutions can we discern any major shift. Only, what was till then one country culturally, was gradually transformed into a political reality.

Most educational critiques of 19th century India seem to overlook a few ground realities.

1. Colonies are not set up for philanthropic purposes.
2. Education cannot precede political considerations or rise above social concerns.
3. The controversies that appear to dominate the educational scene are, in fact, clashes between interest groups, with the interest of the masses serving only as an excuse to fulfill the elite's unstated motives. In other words, there is a difference between the content and the form of the debates.
4. The most important point to note is that education in those times did not have the same purpose as today. Very few needed education to take up jobs. Even the

> nobility had very limited use for education. Not only were the lower castes barred from education, so were women of all classes. In brief, very few needed it, and for them the existing system was adequate to meet requirements.

Two more points need special consideration. A policy is merely a set of guidelines laid down to give directions when required. The presence of a policy does not necessarily result in a matching performance. The Sharda Act was pursued more in its breach than in practice. The famous Charter Act of 1813 said that not less than one lakh rupees should be made available to educate the natives; in reality, the first instalment of that money was drawn in 1823, a full decade later. It is therefore imperative to take stock carefully of the impact of a policy.

Additionally, education can be perceived very differently by different people. For example, Christian missionaries equated illiteracy with moral inadequacy; for them education meant helping people see the light through mass conversion. Traditionally dominant castes and the newly-emerged middle class had a very different purpose for education. For them "modern" education meant learning the languages of the rulers to create bridges of communication and avenues for seeking favours. Others discovered in education the tools of economic growth and power.

To summarize, what I am trying to say is that the analysis of educational policies in 19th century India must be attempted with a good deal of caution. It should also be kept in mind that the jurisdiction of the raj was limited to areas where the British ruled directly; it excluded vast tracts of the subcontinent that made up the "native" states. In this paper, we will be examining the following:

1. The nature and composition of Indan society.
2. The intentions behind the educational policies.
3. The nature and meaning of the controversies regarding education.
4. The revenues and infrastructure for education.
5. Indian and European models of education.

We will conclude with a critique of national policies and performance.

Nature and Composition of 19th Century Indian Society

Jawaharlal Nehru observed contradictions at every turn in the record of British rule in India: "The British became dominant in India and the foremost power in the world because they were the heralds of the new-age, big-machine industrial civilization". While they represented a new historic force, "their outlook and objectives were reactionary."[1] He further remarks, "individual Englishmen, educationists, orientalists, journalists, missionaries and others played an important part in bringing Western culture to India, and in their attempts to do so, often came into conflict with their own government."[2]

If there are so many contradictions in British attitudes and practices, the ambivalence is equally obvious in the characteristics of the Indian people and their society. Raja Ram Mohan Roy was no less observant to record, "I regret to say that the present system of religion adhered to by the Hindus is not well calculated to promote their political interests. The distinction of caste, introducing innumerable divisions and sub-divisions among them, has entirely deprived them of patriotic feeling, and the multitude of religious rites and ceremonies and laws of purification has totally disqualified them from undertaking any difficult enterprise. It is, I think, necessary that some change should take place in their religion."[3]

Apart from religious obscurantism, child marriage, infanticide, rampant female illiteracy, the harsh conditions of widows, the dominance of a few over the rest, there were other features that prevented Hindu society from waking up out of its centuries-old stupor and sloth. The Indian Famine Commission of 1880 mentioned in its report: "At the root of much poverty of the people of India, and the risks to which they are exposed in seasons of scarcity, lies the unfortunate circumstances that agriculture forms almost the sole occupation of the population."[4]

The 19th century was marked by famines and riots. Their devastative effects[5] are listed in Table 1. The social and religious divisions of Indian society intensified in the 19th century.[6] The British played only a marginal role in all this because the Indians required no help in worrying their existing wounds. These social divisions soon became a political agenda whose climax was the division of the subcontinent.

TABLE 1 Famines and riots in the 19th century

Year	*Famine deaths*	*Riots*
1782	—	Sylhet, Assam
1809	—	Banaras
1800–25	1,000,000	—
1825–50	400,000	—
1850–75	5,000,000	—
1851, 1874, 1893	—	Bombay
1875–1900	15,000,000	—
1884	—	Moplah
1886	—	Etawah and Delhi
1897	—	Chitpur

The major stumbling block in putting up a real challenge to the emerging British rule in the country was a feeling among Muslims that (1) Hindus were outstripping them in every walk of life; (2) Hindus were reviving themselves through their religion; and (3) some day, being in the majority, Hindus would rule over them. The last thought forced them to become openly hostile to the Hindus, and in order to attract the attention of the rulers, they brought only those facts to the latters' notice as suited their own interests.

Muslim jealousy of Hindus has attracted the attention of historians, but why the Muslims did not lead in education after a rule of over seven hundred years has not been analyzed. The reason could be that Muslims have class and caste divisions nearly as well-marked as Hindus. The upper classes, called ashrafs, consisted mainly of people of foreign origin. They had contempt for the local converts, ajlafs and astrafs, who constituted the majority. Moin Shakir says, "The people (ajlafs) were hated and treated with contempt by their rulers. Often they were equated with animals. It was justified because of their low lineage and progeny. The people were deliberately kept uneducated." He cites Barani to endorse this point: "Since education makes low-born Muslims efficient and capable, so that they are able to challenge and suppress their betters, the state should prevent Muslim boys of lower orders from obtaining education, and anyone who ventures to teach them should be punished and exiled from the city." If Barani is not taken as representative, Akbar (the Great) told Abul Fazl that education might cause disturbance and sedition in society, and therefore its spread should be made selective.[7]

As much in politics as in crime, Hindus and Muslims have seldom remained within the bounds of their religions. For, ignoring the right of the masses to education, both have shown preference for a "secular" social order. It is therefore interesting to observe that on every occasion possible, Muslims have tended to raise the bogey of their educational backwardness. They have demanded immediate rectification of this social lacuna without bothering to acknowledge that Hindus had nothing to do with it, that they had themselves ruled the country for such a long stretch of time.

Indeed, it is possible to establish that, except for the Muslims, all other religious groups that have ruled in India, howsoever briefly, have never ever been equalled by their subject. I think this point should not be overlooked in our study of education; reality should not be overshadowed by a blatant untruth. Delhi, which was the capital of the Mughal empire for so long, returned the following statistics in the 1911 census:[8] "Of the different religions, the Sikhs seem to be the most enlightened, as 38 per cent are literate ... Christians come next with 32 per cent but, of course, education is an initial step to conversion. Of the Jains, a small and wealthy community, 29 per cent are literate; of the Hindus 4.7 per cent, and the Mohammedans 5.5 per cent..." Since the Sikhs ruled in the Punjab and their rule came to an end by 1850, we should have noticed some disadvantage to them in the Delhi area compared to the Muslims. Even the local Christian converts seem to have been better off than Muslims.

We must go a little deeper into the nature of the problems Muslims face *vis-a-vis* education. Apart from the fact that elite Muslims were not particularly keen to educate their lower classes, another reason has been recorded in an analysis of education patterns in Thane district: "The Mohammedans had their own educational needs as distinct from those of the Hindus. Being intensely religious, they desired to acquire the ability to read the Koran written in Arabic."[9]

A third reason is that the Devanagari script began to replace Persian around 1837. It was made mandatory in the Patna and Bhagalpur divisions in 1880, having been introduced earlier as an experiment by the lieutenant governor. Muslims agitated against this replacement; they called it "cheap sentimentalism", and said that it sacrificed the norms of administrative efficiency.[10] But the fact appears to be that the whole community had "sunk with the empire", says J.N. Farquhar.[11]

We have supporting evidence to endorse Farquhar. Even in Persian and Arabic schools in the year 1850, the statistics shown in Table 2 present a none-too-happy picture of the state of Muslim education in north-west U.P.[12] Although technically, the Mughals still governed the country, one finds 5,526 Hindu *vs* 4,528 Muslim students in areas as close to the capital Delhi as Agra and Aligarh. One hardly stretches the point by saying that in Hindu schools, the number of Muslim students was either nil or negligible. Even among teachers of Arabic and Persian, one finds more than 200 Hindus out of a total of 1,445.[13] Needless to say, such could not have been the case for Muslims in Sanskrit schools.

TABLE 2 Castes attending Arabic and Persian schools

District	*Brahmins*	*Rajputs*	*Kayasthas*	*Banias*	*Others*	*Muslims*	*Total*
Agra	88	63	212	81	79	565	1,088
Aligarh	49	74	544	158	104	812	1,741
Bareilly	95	37	886	71	143	848	2,080
Etawah	53	14	182	27	24	130	430
Farrukhabad	91	43	793	40	87	925	1,979
Manipuri	15	25	377	14	41	189	661
Mathura	70	47	174	80	17	266	654
Shahjahanpur	39	59	471	10	49	793	1,421
Total	500	362	3,629	481	544	4,528	10,054

That learning is a matter of tradition has been ably brought out by C.W. Leitner. He says in his report, that the effort to get educated, whether in Persian or English, "is first, a tradition of brahmins, khatris, suds and the kayastha castes, and secondly, an attempt to secure a monopoly of appointments which may give them both political power and social prestige over those higher than themselves in the Indian scale."[14] Such a tradition would make a particular class of people adept in the art of changing their role models. In the case of India, and particularly among the Hindus, Karen Leonard talks of the cultural attributes of the twelve sub-castes of north-Indian kayasthas, all said to be descended from the mythical Chitra Gupta, the record-keeper of Yama, the god of death. According to her, "Boys were well educated in Persian and Urdu ... Kayasthas wore the customary court dress and could converse fluently in Persian and Urdu, following the conversational and social mannerisms appropriate to Mughal court society. Kayasthas often took personal names customarily used by Muslims, as in Jehangir Prasad."[15] Numerous other names in the same genre can easily be cited.

It is perhaps in the same tradition that, during the days of the East India Company, the Kayastha Mahasabha, headquartered in Patna, submitted a memorandum to the British crown to allow them to possess the exclusive right to learn the English language. In other words, for those who change so easily with the times, there are always some role models available in all societies. The phrase "colonial citizen as educational ideal"[16] therefore carries no particular message, either of discovery or innovation, except a deep-seated desire on the part of some to survive under all conditions.

By contrast, the Muslims did not show a corresponding ability to change; they only put a lot of pressure on the alien rulers to accord them a higher status than the Hindus. "The condition of the Mahomedan population of India as regards education has of late been frequently pressed upon the attention of the government of India. From statistics recently submitted to the Governor-General in council, it is evident that in no part of the country, except perhaps in the North-Western Provinces and the Punjab, do the Mahomedans adequately, or in proportion to the rest of the community, avail themselves of the educational advantages that the government offers."[17] W.W. Hunter wrote, "They (Muslims) know as an absolute truth that the Arabic grammar, law, rhetoric and logic comprise all that is worth knowing upon earth. They have learned that the most extensive kingdoms in the world are Arabia, then England, France and Russia, and the largest town, next to Mecca and Medina and Cairo, is London ... The English are infidels and will find themselves in a very hot place in the next world."[18]

In brief, until Sir Syed Ahmed Khan took concrete measures to revive Muslim education and learning, they had shown a peculiar unwillingness to come forward to learn the Western sciences and the English language. While formulating his two-nation theory, Sir Syed asserted, "we have our own language, literature, history and religion to study, and unless we are altogether devoid of ordinary feelings of humanity, we cannot but desire that our children should possess some knowledge at least of these subjects. I must confess that I cannot help sympathizing with them in their contempt for a Muhammadan youth calling himself an educated gentleman who does not possess a decent knowledge of his religion and of Urdu and Persian literature."[19]

Intentions behind Educational Policies

Some other major reasons why Western education did not spread in colonial India as quickly as one would have wished also need mention. In his book *Discovery of India*, Nehru observed that "even the British Government, in spite of its dislike of education, was compelled by circumstances to arrange for the training and production of clerks for its growing establishment."[20] Education was offered to Indians despite feeling that "to educate natives is our high road back to Europe."[21] The British had learnt a lesson in America and had no wish to repeat it. Rawlinson once cryptically remarked that empires were not founded for philanthropic purposes. It is clear that education was provided to Indians for far more compelling reasons than altruism. Of course, there were dissenting voices like that of Sir Charles Metcalf, who condemned such apprehensions as "unworthy of a liberal government." "The world is governed by an irrestible power," he said, "which giveth and taketh away dominion, and vain would be the impotent prudence of man against the operations of its almighty influence."[22] Charles Trevelyan remarked, "If we perform our duty in this respect, the gratitude of India, and the admiration of the world, will accompany our name through all ages, whatever may be the revolution of futurity."[23] Lord Moira said in 1815 that "imparting education to natives is our moral duty, and it is for the credit of the British name that this beneficial revolution should rise under British sway."[24]

These lofty ideals had, in reality, a much more mundane face than is acknowledged. The directors of the East India Company were constantly pressing their Indian governments to drastically reduce the costs of administration. The problem of education became closely linked with the problem of providing trained Indians for government service.[25]

We all know that north India came under the Company's rule around the first decade of the 19th century, and Punjab only after the third battle of the Sikhs. Interestingly, the provincial government of the North-West Province (now Uttar Pradesh and Delhi) decided to open schools in which instruction was in the local vernaculars, not English. The reason for the departure in practice is recorded thus:

> In estimating the progress which has been made in the educational department in these provinces, as well as informing schemes for its future management, it must never be forgotten how much less encouragement there exists here for the study of English than is the case in the lower provinces and in the presidencies of Madras and Bombay. There are here very few European residents, except a few European merchants transacting their business in the English method. There is no supreme court where justice is administered in English, no English bar or attorneys, no European sea-borne commerce with its shipping and English sailors and constant influx of foreign articles and commodities. Even in the public service, the posts are very few in which knowledge of the English language is necessary for a discharge of their functions.[26]

This is the most elaborate explanation of why the English language and English institutions were supported either by the Company or the local people. Also to be noted is the fact that it contains no frills or innuendoes, or the vague futuristic idealism so characteristic of missives arriving from the London headquarters of the Company. It is a very prosaic note with a bland message.

Controversies

Perhaps too much has been read into the controversies which originated in Calcutta, the capital of the East India Company. What is generally overlooked is that, like a very reluctant bride, the British were forced by circumstances into a mismatched matrimony. They had no educational model from back home to offer, and absolutely no intention to spend money on the unrewarding enterprise of educating the natives. The casual observations on education of stray idealists and administrators have been mistaken for policy statements.

As for the few Indians who were apparently enthusiastic about Western learning and science, unwarranted claims have been made. There were other, more numerous, saner, practical people as well, but because of a quirk of reasoning and circumstances, they have been neglected in favour of these enthusiasts. There are ideological parallels between today's India and what happened around 150 years ago in Calcutta. The "secularists" of today use an almost identical idiom to that once employed by persons like Raja Ram Mohan Roy. At that time, too, people like Raja Radhakant Deb were condemned for being orthodox and enamoured of their religion. To illustrate the point, Raja Ram Mohan Roy has been praised sky high for opposing the setting up of a Sanskrit college, and for calling Sanskrit a language "best calculated to keep people ignorant" in a letter which is regarded by the majority of Indian historians as indicative of the beginnings of the Indian renaissance. What has been ignored is a statement of Raja Radhakant Deb which is neither derogatory of Sanskrit nor very appreciative of English: "Under the happiest reigns of Hindu and Muhammadan princes, the knowledge which was employed for the happiness of the State was always drawn, not from the vernacular, but from a foreign source. Certain it is, that there is now no one that presents claims equal to English."[27]

Recall that the Indian elite had a long tradition of accepting the contemporary court language and culture. Persons who changed lifestyles without batting an eyelid did not need legal or logical persuasion to discover light and wisdom in European sciences and manners. I feel the entire list of controversies has been kept alive without serious analysis of the traditions of a practical, worldly-wise people. It deserves to be consigned to a corner where overused knick-knacks are stored.

India also had two more small colonial pockets governed by the French and the Portuguese. They serve as parallel examples to extend the argument just advanced. There, too, French and Portuguese were learnt by those who needed these languages for mundane reasons. Why should we drag the name of Macaulay into the discussion, as if without him the Indians would not have learnt English. There is enough evidence to suggest that, long before either Raja Ram Mohan Roy wrote his famous memorandum or Macaulay his minutes, the Indians had learnt the value of English as a means of communication and power.[28]

Today, 50 years after India gained independence, we have English schools dotted all over the subcontinent. This is happening despite government efforts to promote Hindi and the regional languages. We should appreciate the real reasons why a people would ignore government fiats on certain issues. There is enough evidence to suggest that "modern" education and the spread of Christianity had a cause-and-effect relationship, but there is hardly any explanation why a majority of Hindus did not accept the idea of conversion despite all the inherent drawbacks in not converting. We have a parallel in the 800 years of Muslim rule: all the crusading zeal of the Muslim ulemas failed to succeed in making India an Islamic country. I have already given a table to show that in Arabic and Persian schools, Hindu students outnumbered their Muslim counterparts, as they also did in Christian mission schools and colleges. Hindu students now outnumber Christian students and outsmart them, too, in academic performance.

Let us understand the fact that in India, we have always had a small section of the Hindu population which has changed loyalties, educational models, mores and culture as and when it suited them. In most cases, they anticipated future prospects, even as, today, they sense where the green pastures lie. Controversies in education are merely meant to divert attention from harsh realities. The three major controversies of the 19th century are (1) Anglicists *vs* Orientalists, (2) the filter-down theory, and (3) the Macaulay minutes.

I have already given my opinion about all three. Now let me give at least one piece of evidence to endorse my view. If we ask what impact the Anglicists had on India, the reply is, very little. Even without their efforts we would be more or less the way we are. R.C. Majumdar makes an assessment of Raja Ram Mohan Roy's efforts to modernize India thus: "There is hardly anything to his credit which changed the foundation of the Bang Samaj. The story of his impact is writ large in blazing letters upon the illuminated gates of two thousand Durga Puja pandals in Calcutta; loudspeakers and dhak or trumpets proclaim in deafening noise, year after year, the failure of Ram Mohan Roy to make the slightest impression from his point of view on 99.9 per cent of the vast Hindu samaj, either in the 19th or in the 20th century."[29]

The concept of "down filtration" has taken such deep roots in the psyche of scholars that even in 1995, J.K. Galbraith talked of "the trickle-down theory". This invited a justifiably pungent comment from Lal Krishna Advani: "It means feeding horses with oatmeal so that sparrows can feed on their dung."[30] The entire theory is based on the assumption that the Indian upper castes and classes have a philanthropic commitment towards their poor, ignorant compatriots. There is no evidence to support this view; India's charitable institutions exist on the belief that those who founded them will one day get special privileges from the Almighty. The poor and ignorant do not figure in their consideration.

As far as Macaulay's minutes are concerned, Arthur Mayhew summarized the entire debate thus: "Macaulay was not the prime mover, his intervention was late, and the forces which he represented would probably have been successful without his singular, tactless and blundering championship."[31] As far as their impact is concerned, Lord Curzon observed, "The vernaculars are the living languages of this great continent. English is the vehicle of learning and advancement to the small minority, but for the vast bulk, it is a foreign tongue which they do not speak and rarely hear."[32]

Revenues and Infrastructure for Education

We come now to the brass tacks. How much money was the East India Company willing to spare for education? What were the facilities needed to translate policy into ground reality? These were real issues. India already had a system of education. Was the company willing to leave it alone? If not, were they in a position to offer an alternative? Or did they want a compromise between existing institutions and any new ones they were willing to set up? What role were they willing to permit the missionaries in any system they introduced? Were missionaries to be partners furthering the company's mercantilism and profits, or just a kind of civilizing institution to convert the "heathens". Should they invite the "natives" to join in the effort and on what conditions?

In his *Observations* of 1792, Charles Grant clearly stated, "The communication of our light and knowledge would prove the best remedy for their disorders."[33] His idea of an enlightened India was a Christian India. In this opinion, India's slavery and moral inadequacy were put at par. Leitner, in his survey of education in the Punjab, stated that, compared with the Indians, "even Englishmen and Germans are not quite on a par as regards acquiring knowledge for its own sake ... In India, whereas khatris, kayasthas and Hindus generally value knowledge in proportion to its 'loaves and fishes', the brahmins study for study's sake; the Sikhs in order to maintain the special characteristics which have raised them physically and nationally over their fellow Hindus; and Muhammadans, in order to cultivate their intellects and to gain a passport to paradise by means of their cherished learning, which makes men equal."[34] As regards religions or caste-wise typology of schools in Punjab, he gave the following findings.[35]

1. A maktab was a Persian school for Muslims.
2. A madrasa was an Arabic school where Persian was also taught. It was a "place of lessons".
3. A pathshala was a Sanskrit elementary school.
4. A gurmukh school was for Sikhs alone.

5. Traders were taught Lande and Sarati in a mahajani school.

The first government surveys on education were those of Sir Thomas Munro for Madras, Mountstuart Elphinstone for Bombay and Lord William Bentinck for Bengal. They found 12,500 schools in Madras presidency for a population of 12,850,000, and 1,705 schools with 35,143 students for 4,681,735 people in Bombay presidency.[36] In Bengal, Adam conducted three surveys, the last in 1835. His third report is for the five thanas of Daulatbazar (Murshidabad). Nanglia (Birbhum), Culna (Burdwan), Jehanabad (South Behar) and Bhawara (Tirhut). The results are summarized in Table 3. From these figures, the total percentage of children receiving education both in schools and homes works out to 6, 8, 16, 5.8 and 2.5 for the thanas, respectively.[37] I would like to mention that if the percentage of literacy varied, so did other factors. For example, the predominance of brahmins in the system was absolutely unchallenged in Bombay, but in Bengal the kayasthas put up a stiff resistance. Women's education, however, is uniformly rare. Accordingly, the recommendations of the surveyors were not the same for each region.

TABLE 3 Education in Bengal in 1835

No. of children 5–14	*Thana*	*Number of families*		*Domestic instruction*	
		Hindu	*Muslim*	*Hindu*	*Muslim*
10,428	Daulatbazar	7,058	5,774	201	53
8,929	Nanglia	7,597	612	197	10
18,176	Culna	19,047	4,287	414	61
15,595	Jehanabad	12,549	2,404	295	65
13,409	Bhawara	11,946	1,194	223	12

Since Adam's scheme for reform is familiar, I will take it up as a "model" for adoption. In his letter to Lord William Bentinck, Adam urged, "To whatever extent [native Indian institutions of education] exist, and in whatever condition they may be found, they present the only true and sure foundations on which any scheme of general or national education can be established."[38] Sir Charles Metcalfe said in September, 1815, in response to an apprehension that imparting education to the natives may mean undermining British dominion: "My own opinion is that the more blessings we confer on them the better hold we shall have on their affection, and in consequence the greater duration and strength to our empire."[39] As chairman of the General Committee of Public Instruction, Macaulay regarded Adam's scheme as "hopeless". He was unwilling to support the native schools, and was unsure it would make the present breed of elementary teachers any more efficient.[40] The Hunter Commission of 1882 recommended (para 8), "It is desirable that the whole population of India should be literate. In order to ensure general literacy, full and adequate educational facilities should be provided. Special funds should be granted and set apart for education of backward communities, the distribution of these funds being left to the discretion of local administrations on whom complete powers for spending this money should be devolved."

Though most contemporary in their idiom, these recommendations were given a go by, or else why would Gandhi raise the issue in October 1931 at London: "I say, without fear of my figures being challenged successfully, that today India is more illiterate than it was fifty or a hundred years ago."[41] Whether or not this statement ever found any statistical endorsement is not for me to go into. The fact remains that when the British left India, it was no more literate, or her education any less caste-based, than what they discovered through Adam, Munro and Elphinstone in the early part of the 19th century.

In fact, what the history of education in India records are two basic facts. First, the British did not support or promote indigenous education, but neither did they discourage it directly. The conditions created by their mercantilism were such that indigenous schools gradually became dysfunctional.[42] Second, what the British did encourage was government schools to which a teacher-training diploma or degree was essential for appointment, and where English was a subject, not a medium of instruction. Thereby we had three types of schools offering "modern" education: (1) government schools, (2) grant-in-aided schools, and (3) privately financed schools where English was both a subject and the medium of instruction.

The idea of grant-in-aid was one of the most economical systems evolved by the British. Without much investment, they could both control and supervise schools run by the natives.[43] In its 1904 resolution on educational policy, the government accepted the recommendation made by the Hunter Commission of 1882 on the control of education. This called for the progressive devolution of primary, secondary and collegiate education on private enterprise. Section 4 of the report of the Commission discusses the five grant-in-aid systems then existing: (1) the system of salary grants in Madras, (2) the payment-by-results system in Bombay and Madras, (3) the combined system in Bengal, C.P. and Hyderabad, (4) the fixed period system in Bengal (mostly), and (5) the capitation-grant system in some girl's schools of Bengal.

In his magnanimity, His Majesty at the Delhi durbar gave Rs 50 lakhs from imperial funds for popular education. "It is my wish that there may be spread over the land a network of schools and colleges," he said.[44] However, although the government declared in its Indian education policy resolution of 1913 (p. 9) that the breaking down of illiteracy must have a predominant claim on public funds, it refused the principle of compulsory education.

In brief, I have attempted to show that the policies, periodic declarations and resolutions of the government did not match the ground reality in terms of performance. The reason was that its typically mercantile laws and innovations aimed at saving revenues, not spending money on such a non-profit enterprise as education then was. It did create an infrastructure to supervise and control education and introduced grants-in-aid, but located thousands of miles away from the country under its charge, the government found it only morally, not financially, rewarding to educate the Indians. It entrusted the task to its own representatives, Christian missionaries and the natives. After all, pious wishes and the occasional voices of concern did not cost the British a penny. They could afford to be liberal. Indeed, rather than promoting education, they saw to it that education beyond their supervision ceased to sustain itself.

Indian and European Models

Educational records of the 19th century use the term "model" in two senses only. One for those schools where trainee teachers were taught, and the other for "schools established by government as models" to raise the level of the indigenous schools in the area.[45] These records also attempt to define "good" education and "higher classes".[46] "The great problem of a sufficiently cheap system of vernacular education, through the direct instrumentality of government remained the subject of discussion and reports till 1860."[47] That is, cheap education was good education, provided the results were good, the curriculum was monitored, and the teaching was supervised and evaluated.

The fact of the matter is that until 1872, England had no experience of mass education. They had three universities: two for their elite and one to examine their workers' attainments in higher education and their colonial effort as well. Sir C.P. Snow, in his Rede lectures in 1959 observed, "The curious thing was that in Germany, in the 1820s and 1840s, long before serious industrialization had started there, it was possible to get a good university education in applied science. Then they (Germans) came to England, met no competition at all, brought in other Germans, and made fortunes exactly as though they were dealing with a rich, illiterate, colonial territory."[48]

I have no wish to go into details but merely state that in the 19th century, England itself was not a rich, highly educated, progressive nation in the modern sense. Furthermore, as it grew in prosperity, social advancement and literacy, its colonies suffered in inverse ratio in all these respects. It is more than obvious that one could not expect much from its government, its people or its policies.

Summation

It is known that the entire subcontinent came under the sway of the British at different points of time. Thus, they ruled over the Punjab for less than 90 years, over Bengal for over two centuries and over Madras a little more than that. In our academic discussions, we generally overlook these significant details. Until we have the Indian National Congress in 1885, there was neither a national forum nor a national debate, although the use of term "national" was fairly common. The introduction of the railways, posts, telegraph, printing press, etc., brought about significant changes in Indian social and political attitudes. We generally have, in the 19th century, Bengali, Maharashtrian or Madrasi critiques; there was no national critique as such.[49] If the grants-in-aid system varied in the three presidencies, so did the character of the people and their response towards British rule. Even in matters educational, it is difficult to pinpoint a "nationalist" critique, because the term "nation" was used rather loosely then.

Still, India was in the process of getting a "modern" system of education with an emphasis on evaluation and coverage. In the bargain, it had to bid goodbye to its traditional, "indigenous" system. If, at one time, India learnt Persian without demur to establish channels of communication and culture with its rulers, it was now the turn of the English language and Christian culture. However, these are all, in reality, superficial reactions, because when all is said and done, we continue to retain intact the core of our culture. Child marriages may not be as common, gender bias so prominent, or caste barriers so insurmountable as before, but they have not yet vanished. Similarly, Hindus have remained as traditional in religious practice and superstition as ever. Being basically pragmatists, they have changed their educational preferences and economic goals in tune with time. And for that they have never waited for a debate to take place or an official note to be approved. Indian instincts for survival are too strong to await an appreciative nod. They are there to take note of.

Notes

1. Jawaharlal Nehru, *The Discovery of India*, Meridian Books, 1956, p. 312.
2. *Ibid.*, p. 313.
3. B.P. Barua (ed.), *Raja Ram Mohan Roy and the New Learning*. Orient Longman, 1988, p. 87.
4. R. Palme Dutt, *British Rule in India*, People's Publishing House, Bombay, 1947, p. 106.
5. Figures from the Royal commissions cited by Rajani Palme Dutt, *ibid.*, p. 113.
6. Rafiq Zakaria, *Rise of Muslims in Indian Politics*, Somaiya, 1970, pp. 278–309.
7. Moin Shakir, *Khilafat to Partition*, Kalamkar Prakashan, New Delhi, 1970. p. 5.
8. *Gazetteer of Delhi District*, Part A, 1912, p. 203.
9. N.R. Parasnis, *The History and Survey of Education in Thana District*, University of Bombay, 1967, p. 51.
10. Rafiq Zakaria, *op. cit.*, p. 296.
11. J.N. Farquhar, *Modern Religious Movements in India*, Munshiram Manohar Lal, Delhi, 1967, p. 91.
12. *Report on Indigenous Education and Vernacular Schools in Agra, Aligarh, Bareilly, Etawah, Farukhabad, Mainpuri, Mathura and Shahajanpur for 1850–51*, Agra, Secundara Press, 1852, p. 176.
13. *Ibid.*, p. 173.
14. C.W. Leitner, *History of Indigenous Education in the Panjab since Annexation*, Government Printing House, Calcutta, 1882, p. 17.
15. Karen Isaksen Leonard, *Social History of an Indian Caste*, Berkeley, 1978, pp. 12–14.
16. Krishna Kumar, *Political Agenda of Education*, Sage, New Delhi, 1991, pp. 23–47.
17. *Selection from Educational Records*. Vol. 1, National Archives, 1960 (*Educational Reports*, 1859–71) p. 561.

18. W.W. Hunter, *Indian Musalman*, Indological Book House, 1969 (reprint), p. 167.
19. A.G. Noorani, *Badruddin Tyabji*, Publications Division, Government of India, 1969, p. 83.
20. *Ibid.*, p. 313.
21. Percival Griffiths, *The British Impact on India*, MacDonald, London, 1952, p. 245.
22. Charles Trevelyan, *On the Education of the People of India*, Longman, London, 1838, pp. 189–194.
23. *Ibid.*, p. 193.
24. H. Sharp, *Selections from Educational Records*, Vol. I, p. 29.
25. C.H. Phillips, *The East India Company*, Oxford, 1961, p. 306.
26. J.A. Richey, *Selections from Educational Records*, Vol. II, Calcutta, pp. 228–9.
27. Shyamlendu Sen Gupta, *A Conservative Hindu of Colonial India—Raja Radhakant Deb and His Milieu*, Navrang, New Delhi, 1990, p. 54.
28. R.C. Majumdar, *Glimpses of Bengal in the 19th Century*, Firma K.L. Mukhopadyaya, Calcutta, 1960, pp. 33. He says, "In the first place, English education was not introduced by the British rulers, and they did not encourage it till the new policy was inaugurated in 1835."
29. R.C. Majumdar, *On Raja Ram Mohan Roy*, Asiatic Society, Calcutta, 1972, pp. 20–52.
30. *Times of India*, February 26, 1995.
31. R.P. Singh, *Education in an Imperial Colony*, National Publishing House, Delhi, 1979, p. 116. See also R.P. Singh, "The language issue and Macaulay's infamous minutes", *Progress of Education*, Pune, September, 1964 (Vol. XXXIX, No. 2), pp. 52–55,
32. Sir John A.R. Marriot, *The English in India*, Oxford, 1932, p. 207.
33. B.P. Barua, *Raj Ram Mohan Roy and the New Learning, op. cit.*, p. 30.
34. C.W. Leitner, *History of Indigenous Education in the Panjab, op. cit.*, p. 84.
35. *Ibid.*, p. 10.
36. Sir Philip Hartog, *Some Aspects of Indian Education—Past and Present*, Oxford University Press, 1939, p. 11.
37. Joseph di Bona, *One Teacher, One School*, Biblica Impex, New Delhi, 1983, p. 26.

38. Memorandum B: The reports of William Adam on vernacular education in Bengal and Bihar 1835–38, and the legend of the 100,000 schools, p. 87.
39. *Ibid.*, p. 90.
40. *Ibid.*, p. 90.
41. R.P. Singh, *Education and the Indian National Congress (1885–1947)*, Scenario Publications (India), New Delhi, 1996, p. 139.
42. Joseph de Bona, *One Teacher, One School*, *op. cit.*, p. 4.
43. *Report of the Board of Education for the Year 1845*, Bombay, No. VI, p. 81, carries rules and regulations of the educational establishments under the Board of Education. See, especially, the clauses concerning the establishment of new schools.
44. P.J. Hartog committee report, *Survey of Indian Educational Policy down to the Reforms*, Government of India Press, Delhi, 1929, p. 11.
45. *Selections from Educational Records*, Vol. I, 1859–91, *op. cit.*, p. 125, p. 193, etc.
46. *Ibid.*, p. 47, p. 190, etc.
47. *Ibid.*, p. 190.
48. R.P. Singh, *Education in an Imperial Colony*, *op. cit.*, p. 53.
49. G. Parameswaran Pillai, *Representative Indians*, 2nd edition, Thacker, London, 1902 (see introduction by Sir Richard Temple).

SECTION II: CONTINUITY AND CHANGE IN POPULAR EDUCATION

Colonialism and Educational Fragmentation in India

JOSEPH BARA

This essay surveys the broad educational trends in India since pre-colonial times. It presents a critique of the over-generalized views on the educational changes of recent times, and concentrates on the attempts at educational equity, with special reference to the area of popular education. Using the comparative approach, the essay juxtaposes the colonial situation with the pre-colonial one and, briefly, that of Britain. It argues that the traditional forces against educational equity centering around caste, though vigorous and resilient, were somewhat relaxed during the pre-colonial period and conceded discernible growth and expansion to popular education. The colonial situation, however, so reactivated these forces that post-colonial, nationalistic efforts at educational reconstruction have found it hard to override them.

I

Education in India under colonialism was a battleground for protracted cultural conflict between imperialists and nationalists. The initiative to replace indigenous education with Western education started in the mid-nineteenth century, when free-trade imperialism wanted an expedient tool to educate Indians in a manner appropriate to their position, and as a system of "development". As part of this policy, imperialist ideologues not only denigrated indigenous education, they also attempted to bury it. By contrast, Western education, as enunciated by the resolution of William Bentinck in 1835, was projected as the panacea to Indian backwardness. It was to serve as the base for a "national education", promising "extension, not the monopoly of learning; to rouse the mind and elevate the character of the whole people, not keep them in slavish submission to a particular sect."[1]

The "filtration" method adopted by the government in the 1835 resolution hardly filtered education down to the common people over the next one hundred years. Nevertheless, the colonialists insisted that the Western system stood for the standardization of knowledge and the democratization of education. These contrasting perceptions of the Western system being progressive and the indigenous one as retrograde, were reiterated in 1930 by the Indian Statutory Commission while reviewing British educational policies in India. Not denying the traditions and achievements of ancient learning, the Commission noted that education in India at the beginning of the nineteenth century was "at a very low ebb," with no printed books either in the classical languages or the vernaculars. It found the indigenous village schools "too antiquated ... to cope with more than a fraction of the vast child population."[2]

The apparently positive impact of British educational policy has immensely influenced the historiography of educational development in modern India. The influence was so great that even the advanced stage of Indian nationalism at the dawn of independence was not able to shake it off. More known for politically volatile situations, the period since 1930 witnessed the most radical educational nationalism. There was verbal criticism of the colonial system and defence of indigenous educational traditions, including a constructive rehabilitation of those traditions from the viewpoint of people's education. This had two important expressions. First, Gandhi joined issue with Philip Hartog, chairman of the auxiliary committee on education of the Indian Statutory Commission, and others on the contemporary state of literacy in India as a result of British rule. He said that indigenous popular education was like a "beautiful tree" which made India more literate. Second, Gandhi articulated his conception of "basic education" in the Wardha conclave of educationists, and held wide discussions on it with fellow nationalists at the Haripura session of the Indian National Congress in 1938.

However, underneath the euphoria of educational nationalism, there persisted an ambivalence which found reflection in the works of R.V. Parulekar, R.P. Paranjape, A.N. Basu, J.P. Naik and S. Nurullah on popular education during pre-British and colonial times.[3] Being nationalists did not deter these authors from appreciating that Western education initiated the process of "democratization", "secularization" and "modernization" in India.[4] On the other hand, seen unmistakably is the lack of a proper appreciation of the indigenous system deeper than nationalist political outbursts. As regards "democratization", which is used simply to connote equitable distribution of educational opportunities, one argument goes as follows:

> Even the most violent critic of the British Government will admit that modern educational institutions in India have been a great contribution of the British people towards the uplift of the country. But even a great blessing may have its defects. A white elephant may be a valuable gift or a source of anxiety, according to the resources of the presentee. The modern primary schools have been valuable institutions from the education viewpoint, but they have hindered rather than helped the spread of literacy, with the result that, in this respect the country has made no advance since the days of Adam. It is even held that India is, at present, less literate on good foundations. The wholesale replacement of indigenous schools by schools conducted or aided by the Education Department was not a wise step.[5]

Nationalist historiography of this kind is often found squabbling over minor historical details of the imperialist viewpoint, not challenging the general paradigm which posited that the colonial pattern of education, imposed from above, was an autonomous engine of progress. Though the fervour of nationalism compelled these authors to uphold indigenous education, the relationship between the latter and Western education was depicted as "small brother" *vs* "big brother". Thus the decline of the indigenous system was caused by its being bullied by the elder brother. In terms of quality, the superiority of Western education was unquestionable as it was "revolutionary" in nature, hence "a great blessing in disguise," whereas indigenous education was only a filler. It was not perceived that colonial educational was "education controlled from without for the aims and profit of a foreigner rather than for the nation."[6] The result was a tendency to waver between condemnation of Western education and appreciation of indigenous education.

One of the most perceptive nationalist educationists, J.P. Naik, depicts this dilemma well. In his editorial introduction to Parulekar and Paranjape's *Literacy in India in Pre-British Days*, he found it "interesting" that the view of the British system of education as being a boon to India had not yet been challenged.[7] Earlier, as co-author of *History of Education in Modern India*, he forthrightly saw enough potential for educational growth in indigenous systems.[8] But instead of pursuing this twin issue, Naik, like other nationalist authors, ultimately ended up underlining the "revolutionary" nature of Western education. Such a shaky theoretical plank may easily make one fall in line with the colonialist stand that their education, though sound in principle, could have occasional aberrations, "like some harmful byproduct of a useful chemical process."[9]

Radical educational nationalism sprouted studies on pre-colonial indigenous education. It went even further back into the past, inspiring a number of works on the state of education in India during the medieval and ancient periods.[10] Despite theoretical weaknesses, the patriotic sentiments in these books created a new sense of respect for Indian ideas in popular education. They added a new dimension to the earlier phase of educational nationalism initiated by G.K. Gokhale for educating the masses. Other than this, there is not much in these studies, either on the state of pre-colonial Indian education or the fundamental weaknesses of Western education for the nation.

The legacy of such literature on educational nationalism worldwide is the rise of a silent educational movement among many developing countries, in which indigenism is an important plank of post-colonial educational reconstruction. The movement was consummated in the international Commission on the Development of Education set up by UNESCO in 1971. This forum agreed that the "educational roots" of the new nations were "fertile for thought and enrich present-day education with unduly neglected values and experience," provided one avoided "falling into the trap of retrospective idealizations" of the days of acrimonious nationalist movements.[11]

This evolving perspective inspired the works of S.C. Shukla forty years back and, more recently, those of Kazi Shahidullah. In reviewing developments in popular education during the late nineteenth and early twentieth centuries, these studies go beyond the cliché of the "good old days", and find inadequacies in the British system.[12] They describe the integration of indigenous popular education with the official system as one aspect of what has recently been explained as the imperialist "political agenda of education".

Dharampal and Joseph Di Bona, on the other hand, concentrate on the pre-colonial condition of the indigenous system in its "contextual perspective".[13] Using the comparative approach, Dharampal argues that Indian education, when seen side by side with contemporary British education, was not as archaic and static as made out by the imperialists. Di Bona underscores the positive aspects of the system by pointing out its purposiveness, secular character and self-sufficiency, rooted in the cultural setting of rural India. He goes on to argue that the British system generated and promoted new class interests.

While Dharampal and Di Bona provide useful theoretical models to help us understand indigenous popular education, they present too general a picture of its actual state, and romanticize the subject without elaborating on the educational fluidity of pre-colonial India. In the absence of adequate background knowledge, it is presumptuous to gauge the potential of India taking the Japanese or Israeli route to educational growth in a non-colonial situation, as Di Bona argues. In the Indian situation, the power of knowledge has traditionally been used by the higher classes to subjugate the lower classes; depriving the latter of the opportunities of knowledge was an adjunct strategy. P. Radhakrishnan[14] believes in the continuity of pre-colonial indigenous popular education, while Krishna Kumar[15] explains how colonial education raised a reincarnated literati out of the erstwhile higher classes. Hints of this sort on the state of pre-colonial and colonial education leave scope for a deeper probe. Radhakrishnan, for instance, omits mentioning the salutary effects of pre-colonial Islam, such as promoting the writing of books, and spreading the study of Persian, Urdu and Hindustani. As regards the colonial period, recent works by David Leliveld and Christopher Ronald King reveal that the linguistic controversies in north India were essentially a creation of the higher classes.[16]

These instances show that social forces have been at work to shape the system of education both before and during the colonial period. Taking our cue from Dharampal and Di Bona, that popular education was growing spontaneously during the pre-colonial period, an attempt is made in this essay to survey its features and juxtapose them with developments in the colonial period. An examination of the continuity and changes in the two periods should enable us to test the generalization that colonialism was synonymous with revolutionary changes in Indian education.

We shall make special reference to Bengal, where English education was most advanced. It is also there that nationalist historiography often locates the greatest flowering of popular education on the eve of British rule. Most authors, including Dharampal and Di Bona, have naively tended to treat popular education independently of higher education in the pre-colonial set-up. The present essay, on the contrary, emphasizes that popular education was remote-controlled continuously through subtle means by the higher classes at the helm of higher education. Typical of pre-colonial society, traditional forces centering on caste were still vigorous and resilient. However, they relaxed enough to concede discernible growth and expansion of popular education. Colonialism so reactivated these forces that they retained an indirect but intense and often overt control over popular education. So much so, that even post-colonial nationalistic efforts at educational reconstruction are finding it hard to override them. The Kothari commission of 1964 found the socio-educational distance between high and low "large, tending to widen," and being made more complicated by the "undemocratic institution of caste."[17]

II

A recapitulation of certain broad features of the preceding situation should help us appreciate the educational dynamism of the pre-colonial period better. Since ancient times, the segmentation of Indian society on caste lines was constantly manipulated by the higher castes, led by the brahmins, to reserve the domain of higher learning exclusively for themselves. They saw in knowledge the power of "moral ascendancy over other castes."[18] Scientific developments, though secular in nature, were often coated with what D.P. Chattopadhyaya calls "ritual techniques".[19] Sanskrit, the language of literary composition, was not allowed to descend to the lower castes. In order to maintain a monopoly on knowledge, the brahmins used the oral tradition to communicate and preserve it. A popular Sanskrit couplet says, "The man who keeps his knowledge in a book and his money with other persons, has neither knowledge nor money at a time of emergency."[20] The brahmins were therefore living books, and whatever communication of knowledge took place was mediated through *paribrajakas* (wanderers) exclusively in the oral method under their direct influence.[21]

Interestingly, this was true when the art of writing was quite common in government and commerce, as is evident in Kautilya's *Arthasastra*, composed in the fourth century B.C.[22] At this time, Ashoka, the Mauryan emperor made extensive use of writing to communicate his *dhamma* to the masses. Just as his Buddhist principles bypassed the brahmins and directly approached the common man in a missionary spirit, they also promoted popular education a good deal. The employment of link languages like Prakrit for the discourse of knowledge was another important legacy of Buddhism.

The decline of Buddhism and the simultaneous revival of brahminism largely restored the earlier situation. For instance, in the university of Nalanda, which was supposed to be open to all, the learned brahmins resorted to strong "gate-keeping" measures to maintain their hegemony over higher education.[23] As for technical education, it was shaped by strong trade guilds, often stunting its growth. By the twelfth century, Indian scientific knowledge and literature, available exclusively in Sanskrit, were, according to the Arab traveller Alberuni, sealed to the vaishyas.[24] Moreover, the eagerness to share knowledge with foreigners, as recorded by Chinese travellers in the heyday of Buddhism, was replaced by stand-offishness. This coincides with the popular Sanskrit prose of the Budhist period being reduced to mnemonic verse style to facilitate oral traditions.[25] These regressive developments were legitimized by the political system, particularly the rise of feudalism, in which empires got parcelled out into feudatories, and local rulers desperately needed the support of the priestly class. The rehabilitation of Sanskrit in this manner is in contrast with the Western experience, where classical Greek and Latin declined with the onset of feudalism.

The advent of Islam caused dislocations to the above scenario. Culturally, it was efflorescent during the eighteenth century, qualifying it as the "Indian century of Islam" in the Muslim world.[26] The gradual break-up of the Moghul empire proved to be a blessing in disguise. The ulema, cornerstones of Muslim culture, were forced to follow an independent course outside state patronage. A similar voluntary urge had already started in Hinduism with the Muslim invasion.[27] By the eighteenth century, education began to depend upon private initiative and private encouragement sustained by local grants and presents.[28] Other factors, such as the resurgence of regional powers and the influx of learned men from Iran, revived some old centres of learning or gave rise to new ones. There was a proliferation of personal libraries and literary societies. In the absence of printing, books were not cheaply available, but this gap was filled by professional amanuenses, making calligraphy greatly valued.[29] So popular were these handwritten books and so established had the amanuenses become, that printing technology was initially resisted.[30]

The medieval period initiated mutual interest among Hindus and Muslims in each other's learning. Muslim interest in Sanskrit started with the need to know better the new subject race. This gave a jolt to the brahmins' grip over knowledge. Islam introduced new books for education that had far-reaching ramifications. It not only introduced "other" views on brahminical knowledge, but also weakened the sanctity of the oral method.[31] The Hindus, on their part, took to the study of Persian and Arabic for positions in the new government. While high-caste Hindus, particularly the brahmins, looked down on Persian education, the kayasthas, traditionally a caste of writers, readily adopted it.[32] The relative openness of the Muslim system allowed interested Hindus to pursue this education.

Emperor Akbar's policy of religious tolerance, one of the four pillars of the Moghul empire according to historian Percival Spear, proved most congenial to it, since Hindus now felt they were partners.[33] Besides Akbar's personal encouragement, his Hindu courtiers exhorted their co-religionists to study Persian. Since the higher-caste Hindus enjoyed religious and moral security in the joint family system, they did not hesitate to do so; by now they had realized that Persian education was not antagonistic to their beliefs and sentiments.[34] When William Adam carried out his survey on indigenous popular education in Bengal, he found almost as many Hindus proficient in Persian as "educated Englishmen of their mother tongue."[35]

Continuous interaction between the Hindu and Islamic systems gave impetus to scientific knowledge in areas like astronomy, music, fine arts, etc. So pervasive was the yearning for scientific knowledge that the fanatical Moghul ruler Aurangzeb (1656–1707) rebuked his tutor for not teaching him geography, history and other "rational" subjects.[36] Some scientific developments, particularly their applications during the later phase of medieval India, even found an outlet to the great market for science in the West.[37]

Meanwhile, irregular and inadequate patronage of Sanskrit knowledge left it somewhat stagnant, and many of its chief promoters, the brahmins, reduced to the status of "ramblers" roaming about the city streets. For their livelihood, many of them had to become fortune tellers, and remain satisfied with being "consulted and believed by the poor."[38] In contrast to Sanskrit, Persian, vernaculars like Bengali, and hybrids like Hindi and Urdu developed and became conspicuously popular. The new vernaculars became the vehicles for age-old popular vocational education catering to the needs of the agricultural and commercial sectors. To this Akbar added a humanitarian aspect by insisting that all his subjects should get educated on matters of daily social life.[39]

The system, of course, was not impeccable. Growing agrarian crises made the masses unmindful of elementary education, howsoever useful it was. Common Muslims preferred maktabs, which imparted a primitive kind of religious education; Muslim openness hardly broke the monopoly of their nobility over higher education. Among the Hindus, Persian and Arabic education bred a special class that could not be pulled down even by Aurangzeb's pro-Muslim recruitment policy for civilian posts in government.[40]

Nevertheless, the overall Indian knowledge system was not so static as to be called "a pound wrapped in a napkin," as T.B. Macaulay said derogatorily.[41] It was operating in and catering to a semi-feudal society; the changes taking place have to be appreciated in that context. "Like a stream which does not rise higher than its source," popular education "could not go beyond the demand for education in the community."[42] Despite this, it did progress with spontaneity; early nineteenth-century British surveyors found it "still vigorous even though at a very low ebb."[43] If it had developed normally as part of this phase of Indian history, the country would probably not have needed such a thing as a "national literacy mission" to impart the three Rs.

Before a critical appraisal of how potent the pre-colonial system was, a look at the contemporary British scenario shows that, despite certain advantages over India, educational advancement in Britain was not so striking. Dharampal has ably argued that reassertive aristocracy was an important factor in shaping educational developments in Britain between the mid-sixteenth and late-eighteenth centuries. While higher education grew phenomenally to benefit the aristocratic classes, elementary education for the masses did not keep pace with it. In a society where literacy had become an integral part of education,[44] and printing had progressed tremendously since the fifteenth century, half the English population could not write, and only two out of three were able to read till the early nineteenth century.[45] It was not simply a case of disinterest among the common people, since many illiterates evinced keen interest in printed matter for messages that concerned them.[46] It was, rather, a fallout of the rigid class interests of the aristocracy. In contemporary India, this mindset helped create the "racial gulf" that Percival Spear explains in *The Nabobs*. Various British experiments in popular education—the Sunday schools of the late eighteenth century, and the Lancastrian system of the early nineteenth century that taught the three Rs and some morals—were termed "destructive to the nation."[47] Pedagogically speaking, the Lancastrian system that helped expand popular education and paved the way for a national education, was of Indian origin.

The rigid anti-poor attitude of the British aristocracy synchronized with the French Revolution and its aftermath surcharged with democratic ideals. This typifies the paradox of British society, in which education became the "harbour for medieval ideas of a rigidly-moulded social order in the modern world."[48] The ruling classes saw any scheme for popular education as jeopardizing the *status quo*. The nineteenth-century movement for national education, "an educational system maintained and directed by the state,"[49] therefore became a protracted battle between the working and ruling classes. E.P. Thompson traces the origin of the movement to the early nineteenth century, in the consciousness of the working class that emanated "out of their own experience and with the help of their hard-won and erratic education."[50] Thus, the "age of reason" in the West became a case of no reason for the smooth growth of popular education.

As regards the eighteenth century, Indian nationalists have been preoccupied since the 1930s with whether or not the masses were technically more literate. The basic problem in India, as in Britain and maybe elsewhere, is the deprivation of knowledge, which was seen as a power that could cause turbulence to the existing social order. If that is the crux of the matter, then the crucial questions regarding pre-colonial educational democratization in India are: (1) what was the nature of education among the higher classes? and (2) was popular education changing itself in any manner into a vehicle of knowledge so as to attract the privileged classes? To answer these, we will need to take a closer look into the content of knowledge and the employment of the media.

From various available data, it is descernible that the period saw a continued swing in favour of Persian education for reasons of social position. It became increasingly popular among the higher Hindu classes, brahmins as well as kayasthas. K.K. Dutta, quoting from contemporary sources, narrates interesting instances of learned Hindus switching to Persian from Sanskrit during the mid-eighteenth century.[51] The popularity of Persian even in the Hindu heartlands is corroborated by Percival Spear: "[In Persian], educated Hindus and Muslims had thus a common language, a common taste in art and literature, a common etiquette. Persian would carry you from Peshawar to Madura, from Mughul court to raja's durbar, and into the camp of the militant champions of Hinduism themselves, the Marathas."[52] Not only was it used in government offices and courts or for literary tastes, it was also becoming the medium of private business transactions, and communications through correspondence and even newspapers. While tracing the background of British Orientalism, David Kopf finds in Bengal a section of "Persianized Hindus" among the high castes who shared a common culture with the Muslim elite, although this did not mean submergence of their Hindu identity.[53] This led Adam, to whom anything beyond vernacular education was of peripheral interest, to believe that "the Persian language therefore must be pronounced to have a strong hold on native society."[54] This view looks realistic, for as late as the middle of the nineteenth century, when the popularity of English education becomes evident, the rejuvenation of Persian from its deathbed was still feared by the Anglicists. While dealing routinely with the language question in his office in 1836, Macaulay said, "to teach [Indians] Persian would be to set up a rival and, as I apprehend, a very unworthy rival, to the English language."[55] Thus, despite an "artificial" origin as a way to a position in government, Persian education had put down roots in Indian society. One section of higher-class Hindus, the brahmins in particular, still banked on Sanskrit learning, in an attitude of wait-and-see, and also as a reaction against the ongoing cultural impact of Muslim rule. The revival of Sanskrit education during this period in, for example, west India, where thousands of learned brahmins converged annually at Poona to receive a "dakshina" grant from the Peshwa was, among other reasons, part of this hope.[56]

However, education in spoken and classical Persian, Arabic and Sanskrit were all the concerns of the upper classes of Indian society. Despite being on the threshold of achieving status as a national language, Persian kept the common men completely outside its pale. This is worth noting in view of two facts: (1) the practice of teaching it gratuitously despite there being a market for it, and (2) growing demand for it from thriving local trade, thanks mainly to the European companies in various parts of the country. A language aligned with the aristocracy is not likely to percolate down to the masses with natural flow. The historical experience of India shows, rather pessimistically, that the language and education of the privileged are "opposite" those of the unprivileged. Seen under this backdrop, pre-colonial India presents a distinctive linguistic bridge between the classical languages and the vernaculars.

Adam points out an interesting emergent combination of Bengali and Persian in elementary education.[57] Bengali was simultaneously under the "great influence" of Persian on its vocabulary and Sanskrit on its literary composition.[58] Marriages of this kind were not stray phenomena. The Indian Education Commission of 1882 found that Urdu was already being preferred along with Persian in numerous Persian schools of Punjab before the advent of the British.[59] The proximity of Persian and Urdu is also common in the North-Western Provinces, according to the data of H.S. Reid and J. Thornton. By the middle of the nineteenth century, Persian instruction had gone mofussil. In all the districts of the North-Western Provinces except Mathura, centres of Persian instruction outnumbered those of other types of indigenous instruction. Again, instruction in a combination of Persian and Urdu was quite popular, almost comparable to the combination of Sanskrit and Nagari.[60] Persian instruction was, of course, not to reach the common people, but popular Urdu literature received a fillip through the proxy of Persian education. When the government wanted to develop textbooks for its popular education schemes based on the ingredients of indigenous education, the Urdu language naturally emerged as a favourite choice, along with Hindustani.[61] Persian was universally attractive at this stage, and its combination with local languages on a modest scale can be seen even in the Bombay district of Dharwar and the presidency of Madras.[62]

The contiguity of the hybrids and vernaculars with the classical languages—the languages of authority—during the pre-colonial period was important, socially in general, and educationally in particular. It allowed knowledge to filter down to the common people. In large parts of north India, Hindustani and Urdu emerged not only as popular languages, but were also turning into literary languages. At their own pace, some of the vernaculars were also developing literatures. According to the doyen of Indian linguistics, G.A. Grierson, even the then less-known patois of Bihari, that he considered the people's language for a large part of central India, was tagging along in this trend.[63]

One special feature of the literary development of the period was a serious attempt at prose writing,[64] while the construction of a popular literature included the writing down of orally-preserved, traditional ballads. More significantly, classical literature was contributing amicably to the enrichment of popular literature. In Bengal, many Sanskrit works were being transliterated or adapted in the Bengali language.[65] About the reincarnation of Marathi, surveyor T.B. Jervis has the following to report: "The Hindus have also a variety of works in the vernacular language, either commentaries or translations of the poorans, tales, dramas, and scientific works, or short and interesting histories originally written in the Maratha language."[66] By the time of the Education Commission of 1882, Hindi had became the door through which the Hindu populations far and wide could have access to the original religious books in Sanskrit.[67] For the downward flow of the quantities of literature available in Persian and Arabic, Urdu was a similar gateway. In the southern Tamil regions, the brahmins were still strong, but "they had nothing like the monopoly over literacy and learning held by brahmins further north."[68]

Historically, when literature in popular languages grows by drawing substance from classical languages, it implies unprecedented yielding on the part of the higher classes. But the concessions were not unqualified. In Bengal, for instance, lower castes were admitted on a limited scale to Sanskrit education, but this was marred by allowing them to study only "grammar and toxicology, poetical and dramatic literature, rhetoric, astrology and medicine." Subjects like "law, the writings of the six schools of philosophy, and the sacred mythological poems" continued as "the peculiar inheritance of the brahmin caste."[69] In Madras, disciplines like theology, metaphysics, ethics and law were mainly limited to the brahmins, but secular subjects like astronomy and medicine were studied by a variety of scholars.[70]

While higher education continued to be in the grip of the brahmins even though Sanskrit had lost its earlier grandeur, the relationship between the growth of popular literature and that of popular education needs a critical look. Available data on pre-colonial popular education shows beyond dispute the existence of literary content. It was probably rare earlier, as the system was content with education in the three Rs. In Adam's own admission, the phenomenon was contrary to his previous belief.[71] It is difficult to trace the origin of this process. In all probability, the literary content was introduced by a small group of brahmins driven to embark on popular education by compulsion of livelihood rather than choice.

The decline of the Moghul empire put a brake on Persianization. A popular dictum said, "Behold the vagaries of Fate, he is educated in Persian and still sells oil."[72] Meanwhile, brisk local trade and the proliferation of landlords created a market for professional agents, accountants and record keepers trained in the indigenous manner. Adding some rudimentary Sanskrit to the rather terse popular education would serve two purposes to the brahmins. First, it would make the system more appealing with some literature, though actual Sanskritic pursuits would be carried on in the family. Second, it would be an orientation for those interested in higher Sanskritic studies in the institutions of higher education called *tols*.

These two objectives also determined the nature of the literary content. In the Bengal region, where books were more in use, all except one of the books in the list were grammatical works. These, Adam opines, were the "remains of a former superior system of popular instruction."[73] Such "relics" were also found entrenched in the regions of the North-Western Provinces, where "even the humblest village school taught some Sanskrit grammar, without which no one could lay claim to any pretension of education."[74] In the context of pre-colonial India, this preponderance of grammatical works smacks of the traditional discrimination against non-brahmins. Also, the absence of science and other secular subjects, of which higher learning was not bereft, shows the superciliousness of the teachers, the majority of whom were brahmins.[75] Besides these shortcomings, the downward flow of knowledge was further hampered by the literary style employed. This is seen better in the Telugu and Kannada centres of instructions in the Bellary district of Madras, where verse compositions and a dialect "quite distinct from that of conversation and business" were used, though the alphabets of the two were the same.[76] Profuse use of the verse style as an aid to memory and to make the students learn verbatim, meant making idle "the external senses for the reception of knowledge."[77] It also made all-important the few teachers who knew the hidden meaning in the verses. As for the Persian elementary schools, grammar and the Koran formed the core subjects, but the presence of subjects like history and Arabic arithmetic, and the systematic use of books, greatly added to their relative merit.[78]

Notwithstanding these handicaps, eighteenth-century Bengal did see some popular literature written by men belonging to the lower strata.[79] One is, however, not sure whether it had any definite bearing on popular education. Adam's report, at least, does not record the names associated with this literature as mentioned by K.K. Dutta.

The scenario in Arabic and Persian learning was no better. Data from Jervis and Adam indicate conclusively that the link language Urdu had a rich literature comprising "a great variety of tales and poetry translated from the Persian ... or originally composed."[80] Despite this and other advantages, Urdu was not employed in popular education, even in regions inhabited by Urdu-speaking, lower-class Bengali Muslims, who disliked the Bengali language. Adam's observation is quite telling in this regard:

> Although Urdu is more copious and expressive, more cultivated and refined than either [Hindi or Bengali], and possesses a richer and more comprehensive literature, Urdu schoolbooks are wholly unknown. It is the language of conversation in the daily intercourse of life and in the business world, and it is the language also of oral instruction for the explanation of Persian and Arabic, but is never taught or learned for its own sake or for what it contains.[81]

Cynical about this state of affairs, Reid in the North-Western Provinces felt that a "long time will elapse before purely Urdu schools are set on foot."[82] In fact, the hurdles were not overcome till the spontaneous desire for literacy acquired sufficient momentum. It was not till the turn of the nineteenth century that the expanding maktabs, to which the common Muslims clung for elementary instruction, employed Urdu "everywhere", along with a little Persian and parts of the Koran. Bengali, too, earlier detested by the Muslims, became acceptable in maktab education.[83]

Eighteenth-century Indian society was fluid. It was marked by pulls and pushes among the various social groups for new sources of livelihood to acquire a social position or to refurbish an already acquired position. Indigenous popular education became expedient. The trend was boosted by expanding landlords and growing local trade, thanks to the European trading companies. Blocking the new entrants from the lower social strata from partaking of the benefits of this education became a common strategy of the higher classes. The application of this strategy varied with time and region. It ranged from blunt discouragement to the use of constitutional means.

In the course of his survey, Adam came across a "strange instance of narrow mindedness" of both the Hindu and Muslim higher classes, who wanted the outright abolition of some schools where the children of ahus, guddees, etc., were being instructed.[84] In neighbouring Bihar, the language and script were manipulated to stop the common people from getting educated. This continued into the late nineteenth century: witness Grierson's abortive attempt to get the common man's Bihari language and Kaithi script adopted in popular education. Among the opponents were the kayasthas, who decried Bihari as "the language of the poor low castes, domes and dusadhs." They were joined by high-class Muslims in opposing the introduction of Kaithi in the law courts.[85] The same classes who had reaped the benefits of Persian education to acquire a social position resisted the British government's move in the last quarter of the nineteenth century to substitute the archaic Persian script by Kaithi or Devnagari in the courts and offices of Bihar. They not only hurried a memorandum to the Indian government against the move, but also managed to voice their concern in the House of Lords in England.[86] W.D. Arnold, Director of Public Instruction in Punjab, reported a similar case in the 1850s. The government there found Urdu "the nearest approach that exists to a common vernacular," and wanted to use it as the medium of instruction in the popular schools, replacing Persian. Though the meaning of most Persian books was incomprehensible to a vast majority, the move was "diametrically opposed by a whole people weddded to a system," on the grounds that Urdu was "utterly inconsistent with and indeed apposed to the ideas of erudition and learning."[87]

Beneath these over-reactions was an undercurrent of class interests. The higher classes feared the loss of their age-old hold over government machinery and, thereby, the mechanism of social control over the masses. A close observer of these developments, Radhika Prusunno Mookerjee, an assistant inspector of schools in central Bihar, puts it forthrightly: "There have gathered, however, in and about the courts in Bihar, a body of ministerial officers, pleaders, mukhtars and tauters, who have hitherto monopolized all power of a character which is foreign to the generality of suitors, and this powerful interest has hitherto opposed successfully much needed reforms in the administration of the country."[88] Anyway, some of these classes were known to treat elements of village accounts as trade secrets; they did not want them brought under the purview of popular education.[89] This kind of blocking by the higher classes was combined with a close, opportunistic vigil on the movement of the educational weather-cock.

Under these circumstances, there could not be any meaningful expansion of popular education to benefit the lower classes of pre-colonial society. All the more so when there was mass poverty and the system of popular education itself was getting monetized. Earlier, the centres of instruction were self-supporting and located on rent-free land. The teacher took up his profession "with the certainty of dying in harness," whereas in a broken community, he taught as a stop-gap, always on the lookout for a more lucrative career.[90] To the majority of poor cultivators, sending their children to these centres was a source of double strain: it caused them economic loss, especially in the busy period of cultivation, and they also had to pay the teacher. Even for those who sacrificed in the hope of a better future, the "lottery of life" offered them only blanks.[91] By the 1830s, Adam did not discover in the Bihar districts "any instance in which instruction was given without compensation."[92] As an interesting corollary, the teachers of indigenous education in Punjab refused to cooperate with the government's attempt to improve the system from 1865 to 1869 unless they were promised "full advantages" at par with those of teachers in neighbouring government schools.[93] The readiness to pay for education on the part of those ambitious enough and in a position to do so proliferated makeshift tuition centres throughout the country. The bulk of the impoverished masses, however, could not afford these centres. The result was that even indigenous popular education tended to be the domain of the upper classes. By 1865, an inspector of schools involved in extending indigenous popular education among the masses of Bengal found the system usurped and adapted by these classes: "The pathshalas are not and cannot be schools for the masses *exclusively*; [rather] they are primarily preparatory schools for children of the higher and middle ranks."[94]

The attitudes of the higher class would not change easily; they have still not vanished. But the cumulative result of social and political changes, particularly the social reform movements that began in the medieval period, was steadily relaxing caste rigidites. When it came to popular education, the higher classes had to forget their inhibitions and share space with the shudras. According to Adam, even the outcastes, whose shadows alone were supposed to be bad omens, were drawn into the wave of popular education, not only as students, but also as teachers.[95] This is indicative of the whittled-down psyche of the upper class. A number of nineteenth-century intelligentsia testified to this effect before the Indian Education Commission of 1882. One of them, Rajendralala Mitra, cited cases of employment of pods (one of the lowest castes in Bengal) by high-caste men, including his own father, as court assistants and estate record keepers. Earlier, in 1868, he was emphatic that, besides the constraints of time and money, there was nothing that prevented the lower castes from availing of the indigenous and other existing schools.[96]

This kind of caste liberalism has been corroborated by the best critics of the caste system, the Christian missionaries. They found the upper castes not exactly opposed but "indifferent" to the education of the masses.[97] R.V. Parulekar is, therefore, not off the mark in his "nationalistic" outburst when he says that "neither the custom, nor the tradition, nor the unwillingness of the high castes," but "appalling poverty" stood in the way of mass education in pre-colonial India.[98] In Bombay province, outcastes like the maharas and mangs, absent from the system earlier, were found represented in 1840s data from the Poona and Ahmednagar collectorates.[99] The trend was so set in Bombay that, in spite of the British government's firm policy of Western-oriented education and its planting of vernacular "opposition" schools to throttle the indigenous system, the number of children attending the latter type of schools increased appreciably between 1842 and 1847.[100] As part of this trend in central Bihar, Grierson witnessed a "villager's son pure and simple" joining elementary instruction in the indigenous system.[101]

Apart from the general relaxation of social rigidities, the

predominantly elementary and vocational nature of indigenous instruction, just enough to ready the recipient for a job, leaving perfection to subsequent apprenticeship, made the higher castes less concerned with the limited entry of the lower castes into the system. This enabled the lower classes actively participating in an educational system managed by the higher classes without any compulsion whatsoever.

When the British government, as part of its anti-landlord attitude, especially in the post-Mutiny period, took steps to reorganize indigenous popular education in Bengal to overcome the hurdle of poverty, the enthusiasm of the common people was overwhelming. Bhudev Mookerjee, an additional inspector of schools involved in these plans, reported the following with regard to a model centre he established: "The pathshala meets twice every day in the morning and evening, and it is increasing in numbers so fast, that unless some provision is made for their better accommodation, admission must be refused to fresh candidates."[102] A general craze for education created by colonialism might have some role here. Basically, however, it was the pre-colonial quest of the lower classes to look for a better life through the pathway of indigenous popular education. The latter retained relevance at the grassroots level till the late nineteenth-century.

The kunbis (cultivating classes) of western India were next only to the brahmins in this education, and exemplified the pre-colonial aspiration for it. Thanks to the rise of a general desire for literacy towards the end of the nineteenth-century, the cultivating classes, which formed about 75 per cent of the total population according to the nationalist Poona Sarvajanik Sabha, were "not averse to simple education if only the agency is elastic enough to adjust itself to their needs."[103] The "encroachment of the dumb animals on the skirts of learning," as the missionary James Long said of the lower-class cultivators, is rightly described as a "spontaneous movement."[104]

Their spontaneity, however, had to be sustained by a process of upward social mobility. But here, society was too conditioned to allow popular education to be an open passport for moving up. This kind of movement would involve changing a hereditary occupation for a socially more dignified one. It would mean encroaching on the monopoly of others, inviting resistance. It would also mean a dislocation in the existing system of economic interdependence, and necessitate a number of fresh social adjustments. Essentially a medieval feature of society, blocks to mobility persisted till the early British period. An important feature of social mobility was, in fact, a reverse trend, with agriculture always being a refuge for spillovers from other, unpromising occupations.[105] Among those unable to rise were handcraftsmen and workers in small-scale industries, made up mostly of the lower castes. These local producers depended on advance financing from the traders through whom their products were sold. With the flourishing local trade, the actual mobility took place among a small group of fortunate artisans, manufacturers and shopkeepers.[106]

Irrespective of the restricted upward social mobility, there existed thorough social intercourse between the different social groups—high and low—within conventional norms. This is what sustained the idea of social mobility in pre-colonial Indian society and enabled its tempo to increase in times of political change. Mountstuart Elphinstone noted this in his communication on the subject of "native education" to a select committee of the House of Commons in 1832:

> Notwithstanding the institution of castes, there is no country where men rise with more ease from the lowest rank to the highest. The first nabab (now king) of Oude, was a petty merchant; the first peishwa, a village accountant; the ancestors of Holcar were goatherds and those of Sindhia slaves. All these and many other instances took place within the last century. Promotions from among the common people to all the ranks of civil and military employment, short of sovereignty, are of daily occurrence under native states, and this keeps up the spirit of the people, and in that respect partially

> supplies the place of popular institutions. The free intercourse of the different ranks also keeps up a sort of circulation and diffusion of such knowledge and such sentiments as exist in the society.[107]

The overall social liberalism and resultant flexibility in popular education made Elphinstone believe that the contemporary situation in his own country was "contrary", the people being sharply divided into two groups, of which "one is torpid and inactive, while all the sense and power seems concentrated in the other."[108] John Duer Broughton, in his *Selections from the Popular Poetry of the Hindus* (London, 1814), testifies to the keen interest and full participation of brahmin *sipahis*, who "soon lose many of their earlier prejudices ... are generally well-versed in the common principles and ceremonies of their religion and the historical legends connected with it, are ready to share them, and inquisitive for such popular knowledge on the British culture."[109] Thus, the generally literate culture, relative liberalism with regard to caste, and economic expediency of indigenous popular education, all cumulatively sensitized the lower-class populations to this education and motivated them to move up.

How the time-tested system of popular education effectively served pre-colonial society is evident from various accounts, right from official British interest on educational matters during the early nineteenth century, when the system possessed vitality, to the end of the century, when it became inert.[110] Thomas Munro, statesman and governor of Madras, says it best:

> The state of education here exhibited, low as it compared with that of our own country, is higher than it was in most of the European countries at no very distant period. It has, no doubt, been better in earlier times, but for the last century it does not appear to have undergone any other change than what arose from the number of schools diminishing in one place and increasing in another, in consequence of the shifting of populations from war or other causes.[111]

It was the permanency and potency of the system, not just the operational or financial pragmatism of the colonial state, that attracted individual humanitarian workers, their like-minded friends in the colonial administrative establishment, some noted local intelligentsia, and Christian missionaries during the nineteenth-century in their attempts to reform Indian society through the existing infrastructure. Adam and Bhudev did not hesitate to appoint brahmin leadership in the event of government initiative and sponsorship.[112] Radical utilitarians and missionaries, on the other hand, were unsparingly critical of the role of the caste system and brahmin teachers. While the spirit of the indigenous system was, by and large, accepted, the teachers were the target of the choicest derogatory remarks. To the missionary Alexander Duff, they were "dregs", while the scientist Mahendralal Sarkar called them "objects of dread than of respect and love ... [with] very low morals." Even Bhudev, while implementing the government's improvement scheme, found that the gurus (teachers) and not the pathshalas were "objects of slight and derision." Lal Behari Dey went to the extent of wanting them to be "sent away to do duties more suited to their capacities, like selling oil in the bazar, or tending cows in the field."[113]

Contrary to the assertions of the Westernizers, the pre-colonial system was not devoid of value-based morals. They were nurtured and practised by the general literate population mainly in the family, and passed on from generation to generation.[114] Such a transmission of culture in pre-modern societies, we are told by historian Edward Thompson, is independent of literacy.[115] Bhudev, who firmly believed in the redeeming features of Hindu values, must have seen an indigenous education system already so inclined when he wanted to spread those values through it. Perhaps the most candid admission of the existence of sound moral teachings is recorded by such a devout Westernizer as Elphinstone, when he favoured rehabilitation of those values and morals at the cost of the stability of the empire:

> I do not perceive anything that we can do to improve the morals of the people except by improving their education ... Books are scarce and the common ones probably ill-chosen, but there exist in the Hindu languages many tales and fables that would be generally read and that would circulate sound morals. There must be religious books tending more directly to the same end. If many of these were printed and distributed cheaply or gratuitously, the effect would without doubt be great and beneficial ... We might silently omit all precepts of questionable morality, but the slightest infusion of controversy would insure failure of the design.[116]

III

Before the results of the general quest for literacy and literate culture coupled with restricted social mobility could be seen, there was a swift turn of events in the mid-nineteenth century in favour of Western education. Apart from effecting structural changes in Indian society, this directed the minds and tastes of the Indian people to free-trade imperialism, with Westernization of Indian education as a pervasive measure. Particularly, higher education in this scheme played the role of a blinker in the way the curriculum and textbooks of the popular schools were recast.[117] Neither Bentinck's resolution nor its preparatory, Macaulay's minutes, show any sign of British politico-commercial objectives. But C.E. Trevelyan, another noted protagonist of Western education, was explicit:

> Trained by us to happiness and independence and endowed with our learning and our political institutions, India will remain the proudest monument of British benevolence, and we shall long continue to reap, in the affectionate attachment of the people, and in a great commercial intercourse with their splendid country, the fruit of that liberal and enlightened policy suggested to us by this line of conduct.[118]

A matter of whisper-talk among the imperialists for some time, this design was openly but still reticently admitted in the educational despatch of 1854, reiterating and elaborating British policy for Western education.[119]

Resource-wise, there was the enormity of the task of setting up a Western educational network in a colonial state. Moreover, the sentiments of the Indian population on local questions had to be accommodated in any educational modality for the stability of the empire. This gave two broad features to the action policy to be followed. First, one had to promote a class of "interpreters" or English-educated Indians to catalyse the spread of Western knowledge to the masses. Second, the existing indigenous education had to be integrated with the proposed Western scheme, instead of closing it outright, as Macaulay and others who abhorred Oriental knowledge might have wished.

Amidst suspicion, the British were emboldened by the discernible quest of a group of urban Indians for Western knowledge in preference to Oriental knowledge: "The steamboats passing up and down the Ganges are boarded by native boys begging, not for money, but for books."[120] To a British educationist with vast experience in the department of public instruction, Bengal, in particular, was a "land of promise". "In no country of the world," he remarked, "are young children more pleasing in appearance, more intelligent in countenance, and more eager for knowledge."[121] Traditionally interested in any new learning, the Bengalis rewarded British optimism and responded enthusiastically to Western education. Concrete manifestations of their eagerness included the establishment of the Hindu College in 1817, the Calcutta School Book Society in 1817, and the Calcutta School Society in 1818. For his initiative and drive, David Hare, a watch-maker by profession, had the rare privilege of being accepted as a *jatbhye* or kindred soul by higher-class Bengali society, including its orthodox elements.[122] All this convinced ardent supporters of Western education to act confidently, as did Macaulay in summing up the Anglicists' points in his minutes of 1835.

True to the spirit of free-trade colonialism, the main concern was the spread of Western knowledge, particularly the accompanying values, among the common population. This was sought to be achieved through the mediation of a handful of English-educated Indians and the vernaculars, bypassing the existing institutional infrastructure of popular education. This weakness was realized by Bentinck's successor Auckland, who said, "It is not to be implied from this that, in my view, elementary education for the mass of the people is a thing necessarily to be neglected, or postponed for an indefinite period." But like many well-disposed British civil servants, he shrugged off the whole issue. In the same vein, William Adam's "valuable and intelligent" suggestions for the improvement of vernacular education were scuttled on the plea that "the period has not yet arrived when the government can join in these attempts with reasonable hope of practical good."[123] Though stray experiments were carried out by some enthusiastic officials like Thomas Munro in Madras, Henry Hardinge in Bengal and James Thomason in the North-Western Provinces, it was only with the 1854 despatch that the British government came up with a policy for mass education.[124]

In fact, the government's proposal to spread popular education was illogical within a colonial situation. Both financially and administratively, it would be too taxing to the colonial state, while its political return was quite uncertain. During a review of the role of Western education in the mutiny of 1857, the policy makers were convinced that a network of popular education could not guarantee a general population with "plastic docility", as it supposedly did in Bengal.[125] Rather, some colonial administrators sensed a greater risk to the empire in Bihar. There the moulvis and pundits, as religious leaders and teachers in the indigenous popular schools, took the establishment of official vernacular schools as "an unjustified invasion" on their rights, and believed that these schools were agents for the conversion of the Indian people to Christianity.[126] The inspector of Bihar district reported in 1855 that "the presentiment is strong and by no means transitory ... the conviction is shared alike by all classes and all sects and I do not think it is in the power of government to remove it. This uneasy feeling is ready to display itself on the most trivial occasion."[127]

The enthusiasm to "civilize" the masses was not fazed by such apprehensions from the field, which were dubbed "exaggerated".[128] But they did influence the actual modality of British educational policy. By now, with the government's inability and the ineptitude of the English-educated Indian middle class for undertaking the education of the masses, the only takers for the job were Christian missionaries. They were assigned this responsibility, but restrictedly, and whatever government money they got under the policy of grants-in-aid was not always based on pure merit. Thus, reasons fundamental to colonialism and immediate political considerations precluded meaningful popular education, reducing the policy enunciated in the despatch of 1854 to a political stunt. In the absence of political will, the best Christian missionary spirit, the benevolence of individual civil servants, or the reforming zeal of enlightened Indians would yield only limited success. For instance, Vidyasagar and Bhudev were left in the lurch by insensitive government machinery while implementing their respective schemes, and the successful experiment of James Thomason between 1843 and 1853 in the North-Western Provinces declined after his death.

Unlike the area of popular education, matters in higher education, which catered to a very small population, were quite smooth. It grew phenomenally after the establishment of the first universities at Calcutta, Bombay and Madras in 1857, following the colonial government's decision in the despatch of 1854. Though the caste system had no place in British educational policy,[129] higher education became, in practice, the domain of the same high castes who had dominated the pre-colonial scenario.[130] Stray recruitment of some low-caste people was driven more by British liberalism (part of the contradictory nature of the colonial system) rather than accommodation on the part of the higher castes.

In Bengal, many of the high-caste English-educated were the new "absentee" landlords, to whom colonial Western education was basically a means, or rather, a "hallmark", according to J.H. Broomfield, to a new social status. They became bhadralok in the local parlance.[131] The Sedition Commission formed in 1919 to examine the rise of revolutionary movements in India found in Bengal a concrete nexus between landed property and English education.[132] The status attached to Western education and the new, easy livelihood it brought created an insatiable craving for it. The system of indigenous learning, till now the bastion of social position, was steadily integrated with mainstream Western education as a supplement to it. This was done with the active cooperation of the upper classes. In effect, the whole thing was a transfer of old wine into a new bottle. Private enterprise, too, contributed to the expansion of higher education. But this stunted the growth of popular education and created a widening gulf between the English-educated middle class and the masses, contrary to the expectations expressed in Bentinck's resolution of 1835. In this regard, the Bengal situation attracted the special attention of the despatch of 1854.[133]

While indifference and a non-committal attitude marked the policy of the colonial government to popular education, the Western-educated middle class turned their backs on the question. Some sections of it even grew hostile to the idea of a stepped-up policy to coordinate popular education with Western higher education. One such instance arose in Bengal between 1867 and 1871. The colonial government had proposed an educational cess to finance popular education and, subsequently, moved to transfer a part of the grants earmarked for higher education.[134] Concerned by the threat to their social position, the new middle class went back to the traditions of caste. In the town of Chanda in the Central Provinces, the dominant brahmins refused outright to share space in a government school with the lower-caste dhers; the school had to be closed down in 1868.[135] South in the Deccan, whatever little access the lower castes had to the new education generated considerable jealousy among the brahmins, who grumbled, "What have they to do with letters? Let them learn their own work, literature is our department."[136]

Thus caste was getting blended with colonial Western education; it was a case of "modernity of tradition", to use the phrase of political sociologists S. Rudolph and L. Rudolph. The preceptor of nationalist historiography, R.C. Majumdar, notes that "the mutual relations between the different castes in ancient Bengal cannot be precisely defined, but they had not developed into the rigid system such as prevailed in the nineteenth century A.D."[137] The implication for education in nineteenth-century Bengal was explained by an educationist to the Education Commission as follows:

> I am strongly inclined to the opinion that all or most of the subordinate inspecting officers recruited from the higher classes of the native community are not quite friendly to the education of the masses. These inspecting officers are unable to shake off completely the prejudices of their class, and many of them look on primary education, though not with utter distrust, at least with some apprehension.[138]

As required by the resolution of 1835, there were some efforts by the English-educated middle class to give a new orientation to popular languages as part of the downward filtration of knowledge. Thus we see the establishment of the Tattvabodhini Pathshala by Akshay Kumar Dutta at Calcutta in 1840, and the vernacularization of Sanskrit by Vidyasagar in the 1850s. But these efforts were ephemeral and remained isolated for some time. Also, they created a new, second linguistic barrier between the middle class and the masses.

The greater part of the nineteenth century witnessed the increasing companionship of two strange bedfellows, English and Bengali. The latter became "a doubly artificial language [with] forms belonging to the Middle Ages and a vocabulary [that was] highly Sanskritized."[139] This sprucing up was done in the interest of the Western educated, who needed a new Bengali language for day-to-day communications. It added yet another attribute to their bhadralok status.[140] Typically, the middle class in Bengal took pride in the "philological purity" of Bengali as a "daughter of Sanskrit".[141] Elsewhere, there were proposals to adopt vernaculars as the medium of higher education, and a vernacular university was being discussed in Punjab. But the Calcutta-based Indian Association, dominated by the Bengali middle class, was one of the first to oppose the idea, saying it would be "a thoroughly hopeless task."[142] From the people's point of view, this meant, to borrow the phrase of a linguist, rationing the flow of communication.[143]

This trend was seen also in the Hindi regions. Much to the chagrin of Grierson in Bihar, a Sanskritized "Banaras Hindi" was officially adopted as the medium of instruction, in preference to the popular tongue, after a long controversy over the question in the last quarter of the nineteenth century.[144] The story was not different in the North-Western Provinces, where a powerful Hindi literate class contributed to the decline of popular Hindustani.[145] Around the same time in Punjab, there was controversy over choosing Hindi or Urdu as the medium of instruction, and it was noted, "As a rule, where Hindus in the Punjab ask for Hindi, they mean Sanskrit."[146] As a counterpoint in Punjab, the government's attempt to Persianize Urdu in 1857 was favoured by the protagonists of the latter language.[147] In pre-colonial times, the suppression of channels of communication to the masses yielded intermittently to the rise of popular languages or the process of Prakritisation, as the linguists call it.[148] But the popular languages of the second half of the nineteenth-century were so contorted that they could no longer be so described.

The reactivation of high-caste interests in Indian education was perceived by a section of nineteenth-century intelligentsia, such as Mahendralal Sarkar, Bankimchandra Chatterjee and Jotirao Phule, as the chief hurdle before popular education.[149] As an exercise in soul-searching, this was certainly the right conclusion. But they failed to situate it in the context of the collusion of Indian middle-class interests in education with those of the colonial power, which were aimed at enhancing their influence in India.

In the late nineteenth century, the nationalist intelligentsia did start to perceive colonial policies as the source of the educational ills facing India. But the early phase of nationalism was preoccupied with the expansion of higher education, adding an Indian component to educational management, and increasing the science and technology content in higher education. Popular education did not hold their interest as much. At a broader level, the masses on the whole were not, at this time, the immediate concern of the nationalists. It was only gradually that the middle-class intelligentsia looked beyond sectional interests to broad-based national issues at political fora like the Indian National Congress. But this did not happen to popular education till the early decades of the twentieth century, despite the basic malady of Indian education.

Bengal had the largest middle class and, typically, it presented a peculiar case with two parallel systems of primary education: one coordinated with higher English education, and the other "designed to meet the simple requirements of the masses of the people and therefore complete in itself so far as it goes."[150] This did not seem to bother the intelligentsia; the leaders of the swadeshi movement in Bengal chose higher education over popular education while debating what the thrust of a national education should be.[151] Even the 1911 elementary education bill of Gokhale was impelled primarily by the political exigency of raising an intelligent electorate out of the illiterate masses, although comprehensive social reconstruction at the grassroots was the need of the hour.

Any primary education the country had became a weaning device, uprooting the masses culturally, and alienating them from their natural mode of life. This caught the attention of the Royal Commission on Agriculture of 1928, which said:

> In a population where only one man in six is even literate and where, until recently, little more than the minimum of secondary education sufficed to make employment under government or in some business house practically certain of attainment, it is obvious that the boy from the village who had acquired that education found himself in a very special position ... Scarcity of a desirable thing always gives it a high, even it be a fictitious value. That

value, in the case of secondary education for the boy from a rural area, has hitherto lain in the road it has opened out to him for work in the towns. This has contributed to the drift of educated boys from the village to the town, which still continues.[152]

By the time of the Wardha scheme, the colonial system had irreparably distorted the popular mind. Education and manual labour came to be considered opposites, and any new experiment was judged in terms of its expediency in leading to a white-collar job in town. This kind of prejudice, according to Gunnar Myrdal, tends to be strongest in a situation where popular education is least advanced.[153] Not surprisingly, the common people themselves opposed the Wardha scheme, which was anyway being shouted down by the middle class. The people's preference for the existing primary education has inspired scholarly criticism of the Wardha scheme, but this ignores its anti-colonial spirit and assumes the existence of a nationalistic, visionary middle class.[154] The scheme, with all its flaws, aimed at "a silent social revolution, fraught with the most far-reaching consequences," to use the words of Gandhi.[155]

Unprecedentedly, the Wardha scheme made the technical crafts, hitherto the exclusive domain of the bread-winning professions, the core of its school curriculum.[156] From the middle class it sought to exact a heavy compromise. The nationalist educationist J.P. Naik closely monitored the scheme for a long time as a government functionary. He was impatient to educate the masses, and clearly saw this as the central reason for opposition, even though he was not necessarily a supporter of basic education.[157] Naik's vehemence against middle-class hegemony can be seen in his book, *The Education Commission and After* (New Delhi, 1982), which is corroborated by contemporary developments.

Conclusion: the Past and the Present

In order to mollify Indian sentiments on the issue of mounting illiteracy, the colonial government initiated a crash programme called "adult education", or, as the Agriculgtural Commission called it, a "short-cut to primary education". In the 1930s, it invited the expertise of Christian missionaries, particularly Frank Laubach, who openly hobnobbed with American imperialism to protect missionary interests in India. The government had the concurrence of leading nationalist leaders, who naively joined hands with the missionaries when they took over the interim government in several states. The programme sought to equip the masses with basic literacy, but it was too limited to do so.

By the beginning of the Second World War, the whole issue of popular education was trapped in a vicious circle, with adult education and primary education needing the support of each other to wriggle out of the quagmire.[158] Strong political will was badly needed, but amidst larger political issues, the will of the nationalists was eroded by myopic middle-class interests, which had become deeply intertwined with those of the ruling power over the years. A hegemonic middle class had entrenched itself in the bureaucracy and social system; it would not accept any educational measure that could destabilize it. In the politically fluid, pre-independence years, it was this class that had a field day in Indian education, adding to the backlog of unfulfilled promises in respect of popular education.

The debate generated by Gokhale's elementary education bill had led to a series of acts on primary education for the masses, often prefixed with the word "compulsory". These acts, however, remained paper tigers, considering the lackadiasical attitude of the government. Underneath the causes espoused by the top echelon of the nationalists, the rank and file were more interested in maintaining the educational *status quo*.

In the early 1930s, R.V. Parulekar, Secretary to the Municipal Schools Committee of Bombay, expressed deep concern over the slow pace of progress in popular education. In a booklet entitled *Mass Education in India* (1934), he suggested a set of concrete steps within the official model. His points awoke a section of the intelligentsia, and a number of reports and reviews followed in the English and vernacular press of Bombay. But another section of the middle class said that Parulekar's suggestions emphasized quantity at the cost of quality. The denial of mass education was the basis of their social position, so their reaction was marked with extreme hostility. Ironically, the officers of the education department betrayed Parulekar by becoming front-line campaigners against him. Amidst acrimony, it was said that "Shri R.V. Parulekar should be drowned in the Arabian Sea with his book."[159] One section of the Maratha press even attempted to brand Parulekar's proposals casteist, arguing that they were tantamount to denying quality higher education to the lower classes.

Middle-class meddling with education, a legacy of colonialism, continues to this day. Of late it has become intense because of the policy of positive discrimination for government and university positions in favour of the OBCs (other backward classes), scheduled castes and scheduled tribes. The problem, it should be remembered, is a byproduct of uneven educational growth and suppressed universal primary education under colonialism. It is here that one may usefully look back to the traditions of the pre-colonial, proto-democratic system of popular education when attempting national educational reconstruction.

Indigenous popular education had an infrastructure rooted in Indian culture. Its door was open to most of the common people for elementary instruction within the framework of the caste system. By contrast, primary education in the colonial Western system lacked a sound structure, uprooted the people culturally, and widened the gulf between high and low in the social hierarchy. Pre-colonial elementary education was socially purposive and tended to be free of cost in a natural setting. But the colonial system's "general" elementary education used public resources for the benefit of those classes who were already educationally privileged, according to a candid official of the Indian Education Service.[160]

It is the educational requirements of these privileged few that has been dictating primary education in the country. They only expected it to provide a working link with higher education. Thus, it did not keep pace with "modern" developments elsewhere, especially the metropolitan West, during the colonial period. It is against this background that one must compare the abysmally low standards of schools catering to the masses, with the high standards of selected urban primary schools. The innovative "neighbourhood school" concept of the Kothari commission was conveniently covered up after much discussion. They were renamed "common schools" in the 1968 education policy, and in this form have been ritualistically resurrected in the new policy of 1986.

Notes

1. C.E. Trevelyan, *On the Education of the People of India*, London, 1838, pp. 135–36.
2. *Report of the Indian Statutory Commission*, Vol. I, Calcutta, 1930, p. 379.
3. R.V. Parulekar and R.P. Paranjape, "Literacy in India in pre-British days", 1940, in J.P. Naik (ed.), *Educational Writings of Shri R.V. Parulekar*, Bombay, 1956; R.V. Parulakar (ed)., *Survey of Indigenous Education in the Province of Bombay 1820–30*, Bombay, 1945; A.N. Basu, "Indigenous education", *Modern Review*, August, 1939; A.N. Basu, *Report on the State of Education in Bengal*, Calcutta, 1941; S. Nurullah and J.P. Naik, *History of Education in Modern India*, Bombay, 1945.
4. J.P. Naik, *Educational Reform in India: A Historical Review*, Kale Memorial Lecture, Pune, 1978.
5. Parulekar and Paranjape, *op. cit.*, p. 234.
6. G.P. Kelly and P.G. Altbach, *Education and Colonialism*, New York, 1978, p. 43.
7. J.P. Naik (ed.), *Educational Writings of Shri E.V. Parulekar*, *op. cit.*, p. xxiv.
8. Nurullah and Naik, *op. cit.*, chapter I.
9. H.R. James, *Education and Statesmanship in India 1797–1910*, London, 1911.
10. R.K. Mookerji, for instance, after keeping his research on ancient Indian education in cold storage for quite some time,

chose to publish his monumental work, *Ancient Indian Education: Brahmanical and Buddhist*, in 1939.

11. Edgar Faure *et al.*, *Learning To Be: The World of Education Today and Tomorrow*, Delhi, 1972 (reprint), p. 6.
12. S.C. Shukla, *Elementary Education in British India during Later Nineteenth Century*, Delhi, 1959; Kazi Shahidullah, *Pathsalas into Schools: Development of Elementary Education in Bengal 1854–1905*, Calcutta, 1987.
13. Dharampal, *The Beautiful Tree: The Indigenous Indian Education in the Eighteenth Century*, New Delhi, 1983; Joseph Di Bona, *One Teacher, One School*, Delhi, 1983.
14. P. Radhakrishnan, "Indigenous education in pre-British India: A profile", *Contributions to Indian Sociology*, No. 24, 1990.
15. Krishna Kumar, *Political Agenda of Education: A Study of Colonialist and Nationalist Ideas*, New Delhi, 1991, pp. 124–36.
16. David Leliveld, "Colonial knowledge and the fate of Hindustani", *Comparative Studies in Society and History*, Vol. 35, No. 4, October, 1993; C.R. King, *One Language, Two Scripts: The Hindi Movement in the Nineteenth Century*, Bombay, 1994.
17. National Council of Educational Research and Training (NCERT), *Education and National Development: Report of the Education Commission 1964–66*, Vol. II, New Delhi, 1970, pp. 5, 10.
18. Abbé J.A. Dubois, *Hindu Manners, Customs and Ceremonies*, 1906 (third edition), p. 376.
19. Debiprasad Chattopadhyaya, *Science and Society in Ancient India*, Calcutta, 1979 (reprint), p. 4.
20. Quoted in S.N. Chaturvedi, *History of Rural Education in the United Provinces of Agra & Oudh 1840–1926*, Allahabad, 1930, p. 49.
21. T.W. Rhys-Davis, *Buddhist India*, Calcutta, 1955 (sixth edition), pp. 71–72.
22. *Kautilya's Arthasastra*, translated by R. Shamasastry, Mysore, 1929, pp. 71–72.
23. S.D. Sankalia, *The University of Nalanda*, Delhi, 1952.
24. Quoted in P.N. Bose, *A History of Hindu Civilisation During the British Rule*, Vol. III: *Intellectual Condition*, New Delhi, 1975 (reprint).

25. D.D. Kosambi, *An Introduction to Indian History*, Bombay, 1975 (revised second edition), p. 284.
26. B.D. Metcalfe, *Islamic Revival in British India*, Princeton, 1992, p. 9.
27. N.N. Law, *Promotion of Learning in India*, Delhi, 1973 (reprint), p. xlvi.
28. K.K. Dutta, *Studies in the History of the Bengal Subah 1740–70*, Volume: *Social and Economic*, Calcutta, 1936, p. 1.
29. S.M. Jaffer, *Education in Muslim India*, 1936, pp. 231–33. S. Khuda Baksh, *Essays: Indian and Islamic*, Delhi, 1977 (reprint), narrates an interesting story of the origin and growth of the famous Khuda Baksh library at Patna out of that culture.
30. B.S. Goel and J.D. Sharma, *A Study of the Evolution of the Textbooks*, New Delhi, 1987, p. 38.
31. *Ibid.*, p. 37.
32. Yusuf Husain, *Glimpses of Medieval Indian Culture*, Bombay, 1962 (second edition, reprint), p. 77.
33. *The Nabobs: A Study of the Social Life of the English in Eighteenth Century India*, London, 1980 (second edition), p. 3; see also Parulekar, *Survey of Indigenous Education in the Province of Bombay 1820–30*, p. 5.
34. Arthur Mayhew, *Pre-Independence Educational Policy of India*, New Delhi, 1988 (reprint), p. 47.
35. Di Bona, *op. cit.*, "Adam's third report", p. 256.
36. G.M.D. Sufi, *Al-Minhaj Being the Evolution of Curriculum in the Muslim Educational Institutions of India*, Lahore, 1941, p. 65.
37. Satpal Sangwan, *Science, Technology and Colonisation: An Indian Experience*, Delhi, 1991, pp. 5–6.
38. Observation recorded by Dutch traveller Francisco Pelsaert (1620–27) in M.A. Ansari, *European Travellers under the Moghuls 1550–1627*, Delhi, 1975, p. 113; M.A. Laird, *Bishop Heber in Northern India: Selection from Heber's Journal*, Cambridge, 1971, pp. 46, 57.
39. S.M. Jaffer, *op. cit.*, p. 90.
40. S.A.A. Rizvi, *Muslim Revivalist Movements in North India in the Sixteenth and Seventeenth Centuries*, Agra, 1965, p. 399.
41. Macaulay's Educational Minutes, *The Proceedings of the Transactions of the Bethune Society*, Calcutta, 1870, p. 216.
42. S.N. Chaturvedi, *op. cit.*

43. Dharampal, *op. cit.*, p. 3.
44. In medieval Europe, trade, notary culture, warfare and, above all, Christianity's emphasis on reading the Bible made the three Rs all-important. See Peter Burke, *Popular Culture in Early Modern Europe*, London, 1978; Carlo M. Cipola, *Literacy and Development in the West*, Penguin, 1969; P. Vincent, *Literacy and Popular Culture in England*, Cambridge, 1990.
45. P. Vincent, *ibid.*, p. 1; E.P. Thompson, *The Making of the English Working Class*, Penguin, 1980 (reprint), p. 783.
46. E.P. Thompson, *ibid.*, pp. 782–83.
47. Harold Silver, *The Concept of Popular Literacy*, London, 1965, p. 20.
48. *Ibid.*
49. H.G. Good and J.D. Teller, *A History of Western Education*, London, 1959 (third edition), p. 295.
50. E.P. Thompson, *op. cit.*, p. 782.
51. K.K. Dutta, *op. cit.*, pp. 17–18.
52. Percival Spear, *op. cit.*, p. xiv.
53. David Kopf, *British Orientalism and the Bengal Renaissance*, Calcutta, 1969, p. 59.
54. Joseph Di Bona, *op. cit.*, "Adam's third report", p. 256.
55. Macaulay's Education Minutes, *op. cit.*, p. 255.
56. R.V. Parulekar, *Selections from the Records of the Government of Bombay*, Part I: *Education 1819–1852*, Bombay, 1953.
57. Joseph Di Bona, *op. cit.*, "Adam's second report", pp. 63–64.
58. S.K. Chatterji, *The Origin and Development of the Bengali Language*, London, 1970, p. 133.
59. Evidence of G.W. Leitner in *Education Commission: Report by Provincial Committee with Evidence taken before the Commission and Memorials addressed to the Education Commission*, Calcutta, 1884 (Hereafter Punjab Provincial Committee Report).
60. J. Thornton, *Memoir on the Statistics of Indigenous Education in the North-Western Provinces*, Agra, 1851?; H.S. Reid, *Report on Indigenous Vernacular Schools in Agra, Aligarh, Bareilly, Etawah, Farrukhabad, Mynpoory, Muthra, Shahjahanpur for 1853–54*, Appendix A, Table II, Agra, 1854, p. 70.
61. H.S. Reid, *ibid.*, Appendix K, pp. 149–65.
62. R.V. Parulekar, *Survey of Indigenous Education in the Province of Bombay 1820–30*, p. iii; Dharampal, *op. cit.*, p. 32.

63. Evidence of G.A. Grierson in *Education Commission: Bengal Provincial Committee Report.*
64. Radhika Prosunno Mookerjee, "A few notes on Hindi" in *Education Commission: Bengal Provincial Committee Report,* p. 403; S.K. Chatterji, *op. cit.*, p. 134.
65. K.K. Dutta, *op. cit.*, p. 12.
66. R.V. Parulekar, *Survey of Indigenous Education in the Province of Bombay 1820–30,* p. 12.
67. Letter dated 22 March 1882 from Siv Nandan Lal Ray, deputy magistrate, Bankipore, Bihar to G.A. Grierson, appended to the evidence of G.A. Grierson in *Education Commission: Bengal Provincial Committee Report.*
68. Robert E. Frykenberg, "Modern education in south India, 1784–1854: its roots and its role as a vehicle of integration under the company raj", *American Historical Journal,* **91**, 1, 1986, p. 45.
69. Joseph Di Bona, *op. cit.*, "Adam's third report", p. 240.
70. Dharampal, *op. cit.*, p. 27.
71. Joseph Di Bona, *op. cit.*, "Adam's third report", p. 223.
72. S.N. Chaturvedi, *op. cit.*, p. 27.
73. Joseph Di Bona, *op. cit.*, "Adam's third report", p. 223. The list includes Amara Kosha, Ashta Sabdi, Ashta Dhatu, Sabda Subanta, and the verses of Chanakya.
74. S.N. Chaturvedi, *op. cit.*, p. 22.
75. The only oft-repeated scientific work in Bengal was *Subhankar*, an arithmetical work.
76. Letter dated 17 August 1823 from A.D. Campbell, Collector of Bellary to the Board of Revenue, Madras in H. Sharp, *Selections from Educational Records,* Part I: *1781–89,* New Delhi, 1965 (reprint), pp. 67–68.
77. *Education Commission: Bengal Provincial Committee Report,* p. 73.
78. Joseph Di Bona, *op. cit.*, "Adam's second report", p. 61.
79. K.K. Dutta, *op. cit.*, p. 7.
80. R.V. Parulekar, *Survey of Indigenous Education in the Province of Bombay, 1820–30*, p. 12.
81. Joseph Di Bona, *op. cit.*, "Adam's third report", p. 255.
82. H.S. Reid, *op. cit.*, p. 6.
83. *Education Commission: Bengal Provincial Committee Report,* p. 69.
84. William Adam, *Third Report on the State of Education in*

Bengal Including some Account of the State of Education in Bihar and a Consideration of the Means Adopted to the Improvement and Extension of Public Instruction in Both Provinces, Calcutta, 1838, p. 135.

85. Evidence of G.A. Grierson in *Education Commission: Bengal Provincial Committee Report*.
86. Radhika Prosunno Mookerjee, *op. cit.*, p. 399.
87. Arnold's second report dated 25 June 1858 in J.A. Richey, *Selections from Educational Records,* Part II: *1840–59*, New Delhi, 1965 (reprint), pp. 301–2.
88. "A few notes on Hindi", *op. cit.*, p. 398.
89. S.N. Chaturvedi, *op. cit.*, p. 26.
90. Evidence of Rajendralala Mitra in *Education Commission: Bengal Provincial Committee Report*, p. 331.
91. Letter of Rajendralala Mitra dated 29 April 1868 to the magistrate of the 24 parganas in *Correspondence Relative to the Expediency of Raising an Educational Cess in Bengal*, Simla, 1870, p. 55.
92. Joseph Di Bona, *op. cit.*, "Adam's third report", p. 221.
93. *Education Commission: Punjab Provincial Committee Report*, pp. 35–36.
94. A.M. Monteith, "Note on the state of education in India, 1865–66" in *Selections from Educational Records of the Government of India*, Vol. I, *Educational Reports 1859–71*, Delhi, 1869, pp. 194–95.
95. Joseph Di Bona, *op. cit.*, "Adam's third report", p. 208.
96. His letter dated 29 April 1868 to the magistrate of the 24-Parganas, *op. cit.*, p. 55.
97. Evidence of K.S. Macdonald in *Education Commission: Bengal Provincial Committee Report*.
98. R.V. Parulekar, *Survey of Indigenous Education in the Province of Bombay 1820–30*, p. xlix.
99. *Ibid.*, p. xxviii, V.P. Khanolkar, *Indigenous Elementary Education in the Bombay Presidency in 1855 and Thereabout*, Bombay, 1965, pp. 20, 28.
100. V.P. Khanolkar, *ibid.*, p. xv.
101. Evidence of G.A. Grierson, *op. cit.*
102. *General Report on Public Instruction in the Lower Provinces of the Bengal Presidency of 1862–63*, Appendix A, p. 227.
103. *Education Commission: Evidence taken before the Bombay Provincial Committee and the Memorial addressed to the*

Committee, Calcutta, 1884, p. 452. (Hereafter Bombay Provincial Committee Report.)

104. Joseph Di Bona, *op. cit.*, "Adam's third report", pp. 205–6.
105. Hitesranjan Sanyal, *Social Mobility in Bengal*, Calcutta, 1981, p. 50.
106. *Ibid.*, pp. 54–55.
107. A.N. Basu (ed.), *Indian Education in Parliamentary Papers*, Part I: *1832*, Bombay, 1952, pp. 297–98.
108. *Ibid.*
109. Quoted in S.N. Chaturvedi, *op. cit.*, pp. 33–34.
110. Letter dated 18 August 1824 from General Committee of Public Instruction to the Governor-General of Bengal in H. Sharp, *op. cit.*, p. 97; and the Report of the Director of Public Instruction, Bengal, for 1881–82, quoted in the Evidence of Kristodas Pal, *Education Commission: Bengal Provincial Committee Report.*
111. Munro's Minute dated 10 March 1826 in H. Sharp, *op. cit.*, pp. 73–74.
112. William Adam, *op. cit.*, p. 201; Tapan Raychaudhuri, *Europe Reconsidered: Perception of the West in the Nineteenth Century Bengal*, New Delhi, 1988, p. 62.
113. Evidence of K.S. Macdonald and Mahendralal Sarkar in *Education Commission: Bengal Provincial Committee Report*; Bhudev Mookerjee in *General Report on Public Instruction in the Lower Provinces of the Bengal Presidency for 1862–63*, Appendix A, p. 229; Lal Behari Dey, "Primary education in Bengal", *Proceedings of the Transactions of the Bethune Society*, Calcutta, 1870, p. 111.
114. F.E. Keay, *A History of Education in India and Pakistan*, Calcutta, 1859 (fourth edition), p. 175.
115. E.P. Thompson, *op. cit.*, p. 782.
116. Quoted in William Adam, *op. cit.*, pp. 150–51.
117. For an example of how popular school textbooks were recast, see H.S. Reid, *op. cit.*, pp. 54–60.
118. C.E. Trevelyan, *op. cit.*, p. 195.
119. J.A. Richey, *op. cit.*, p. 365.
120. C.E. Trevelyan, *op. cit.*, pp. 166–67.
121. Henry Woodrow's introduction to Macaulay's educational minutes, *op. cit.*, p. 211.
122. Peary Chand Mitra, *Biographical Sketch of David Hare*, Calcutta, 1874, p. 61.

123. *Report of the General Committee of the Presidency of Fort William in Bengal for the Year 1830–40*, Calcutta, 1841, Appendix 1, pp. xiii–viii.
124. J.A. Richey, *op. cit.*, p. 376.
125. C.E. Buckland, *Bengal under the Lieutenant-Governors, Being a Narrative of the Principal Events and Public Measures during the Periods of Office from 1854 to 1898*, Vol. I, Delhi, 1976 (second edition), p. 9.
126. Report of the Inspector of Schools, Bihar, for the quarter ending July 1855 in *Report on Public Instruction in the Lower Provinces of the Bengal Presidency for 1855–56*, Calcutta, 1856, Appendix A, p. 9.
127. *Ibid.*, pp. 10–11.
128. C.E. Buckland, *op. cit.*
129. "There will be no distinction made except that of superior merit," C.E. Trevelyan, *op. cit.*, p. 183.
130. See for details, B.T. McCully, *English Education and the Origins of Indian Nationalism*, New York, 1940; Anil Seal, *The Emergence of Indian Nationalism: Competition and Collaboration in the Later Nineteenth Century*, Cambridge, 1968; Aparna Basu, *Growth of Education and Political Development in India 1898–1920*, Delhi, 1974.
131. J.H. Broomfield, *Elite Conflict in a Plural Society: Twentieth Century Bengal*, Bombay, 1963, p. 8.
132. *Report of the Sedition Commission*, Calcutta, 1919, p. 15.
133. J.A. Richey, *op. cit.*, p. 389.
134. See *Correspondence Relative to the Expediency of Raising an Educational Cess in Bengal*, Simla, 1870; Archana Mandal, "The ideology and the interests of the Bengali intelligentsia: Sir George Campbell's education policy (1871–74)," *Indian Economic and Social History Review*, January-March, 1975, pp. 81–98.
135. A.P. Howell "Education in British India," *Selections from Educational Records of the Government of India,* Vol. I: *Educational Reports, 1859–71*, New Delhi, 1960, p. 423.
136. Candy's report on the Deccan schools in 1840 in J.A. Richey, *op. cit.*, p. 154.
137. *The History of Bengal*, Vol. I, Dacca, 1963 (reprint), p. 575.
138. Evidence of Dwarka Nath Ganguli in *Education Commission: Bengal Provincial Committee Report*, p. 269.
139. S.K. Chatterji, *op. cit.*, p. 134.

140. J.H. Broomfield, *op. cit.*, p. 10.
141. K.M. Banerjee, "The proper place of oriental literature in Indian college education", lecture delivered on 1 February 1868, *Proceedings of the Transactions of the Bethune Society, op. cit.*, p. 161.
142. Memorandum from the Indian Association to the Secretary of State for India dated Calcutta, 27 July 1881 in J.P. Naik (ed.), *Selections from Educational Records of the Government of India,* Vol. II: *Development of University Education 1860–87*, Delhi, 1963, pp. 309–11.
143. D.P. Pattanayak, *Multilinguism and Mother Tongue Education*, Delhi, 1981, p. 112.
144. Evidence of G.A. Grierson, *op. cit.*
145. Krishna Kumar, *op. cit.*, pp. 124–36.
146. Evidence of G.W. Leitner, *op. cit.*, p. 358.
147. The Punjab government's resolve was "to make the Urdu language and the Persian alphabet the one language and the one alphabet in government schools": W.D. Arnold's first report dated 6 July 1857 in J.A. Richey, *op. cit.*, pp. 293–94.
148. D.P. Pattanayak, *op. cit.*, p. 112.
149. Evidence of Mahendralal Sarkar in *Education Commission: Bengal Provincial Committee Report*, p. 363; Bankimchandra Chatterjee, "Samya" in M.K. Haldar (ed.), *Renaissance and Reaction in Nineteenth Century Bengal*, Calcutta, 1977, p. 153; Jotirao Phule, "A statement for the information of the Education Commission" in *Education Commission: Bombay Provincial Committee Report*, pp. 141–42.
150. Alfred Croft, *Review of Education in India*, Calcutta, 1886, p. 196.
151. Sumit Sarkar, *The Swadeshi Movement in Bengal 1903–8*, New Delhi, 1973, p. 539.
152. *Report of the Royal Commission on Agriculture*, Bombay, 1928, p. 539.
153. Gunnar Myrdal, *Asian Drama: An Enquiry into the Poverty of Nations*, Penguin, 1972 (abridged edition), p. 320.
154. John Kurrien, *Elementary Education in India: Myth, Reality and Alternative*, New Delhi, 1983, p. 70.
155. M.K. Gandhi, *Educational Reconstruction*, Bombay, 1937, p. 34.
156. Krishna Kumar, *op. cit.*, p. 171.
157. J.P. Naik, *Elementary Education in India: A Promise to Keep*, New Delhi, 1975, p. 32.

158. Report of the Adult Education Committee of the Central Advisory Board of Education, 1939 in S.Y. Shah (ed.), *A Source-book on Adult Education*, New Delhi, 1989, p. 3.
159. Quoted by J.P. Naik in *Educational Writings of Shri R.V. Parulekar, op. cit.*, p. xix.
160. Arthur Mayhew, *op. cit.*, p. 229.

Educating the Labouring Poor in 19th Century Bengal: Two Experiments

SUMANTA BANERJEE

Bengali social reformers of the 19th century are known for efforts to develop and transform their society by agitating against practices like sati, child marriage and polygamy, and in support of widow-remarriage and female education. Almost all these attempted reforms, interestingly enough, revolved around the position of women in contemporary Hindu society, and were confined primarily to the upper and middle classes of that society.

What is perhaps less well known is their work in the neglected areas of rural peasant societies and the urban slums housing industrial workers. Attempts at mediating in agriculture through educational experiments began in the 1850s. Later, in the last quarter of the century, some middle-class reformers initiated exercises in educating and training particular sections of the labouring poor: the raiyats or peasant-tenants in the countryside, the artisans and craftsmen in Calcutta and other towns, and the mill-hands in the industries that developed on the outskirts of Calcutta in the 1870s.[1] These experiments were essentially an extension of the earlier social reform attempts. They were aimed at the

---

This article is based on the author's research in the field of communication at the National Institute of Adult Education.

labouring classes this time, and used structured pedagogic curricula. The initiators were the same Bengali intellectuals who had been a part of the social reform movement of the past and inherited its values.

There is a vast and growing literature of critical re-examination of the role of 19th century Bengali intellectuals in contemporary social and political developments.[2] Their views on education at the primary and higher levels are also being re-assessed in the context of the educational policies presently being implemented in West Bengal.[3] An analysis of some of their experiments in educating the rural and urban poor of the 19th century is relevant today, particularly when the government has undertaken its ambitious National Literacy Mission to make all adults functionally literate by the turn of the century. The pedagogues of the late 19th century professed a similar objective of providing the poor with the functional capabilities that would help them participate in development and improve their economic condition.

The present paper examines two 19th century educational experiments. The first was a school for peasant boys set up in 1863 in a village called Makla in the Hooghly district by the Uttarpara Hitakari Sabha, an organization of "bhadralok" reformers. The second was a broadsheet called *Bharat Sramajeebee*, brought out in 1874 by another bhadralok reformer and philanthropist, Shashipada Bandyopadhyay, with the aim of teaching industrial workers.

The paper is divided into two main sections, one devoted to the rural school, and the second to the broadsheet and a number of working-class activities which were organized around it. To explain the historical context in which these experiments took place, each section begins with a brief survey of the changes in the respective economic fields (i.e., agriculture and industry) during that period. The concepts used by the proponents of these experiments to educate the poor is also examined, as is their interaction with both the colonial rulers and the learners. The main empirical data on which the paper is based, quoted extensively in the two sections, are the curriculum of the rural school, questions and answers during tests there, the contents of the urban broadsheet, and reports of workers' responses to its editor's educational programme. A concluding section highlights the common features of both the experiments. It is suggested that educational programmes, whether carried out in schools and universities, or undertaken for the masses outside these formal structures, are not value-free. The curricula are shaped by the political beliefs, economic needs and social norms of those who formulate and implement them. It is further noted that educational activities do not take place in a vacuum; they emerge at certain historical junctures, from a variety of contemporary economic, social and political compulsions, and from individual motivations.

Both the Makla school and Shashipada Bandyopadhyay's broadsheet were founded at a time marked by the development of a new political mood among the Bengali bhadralok. The members of this group ranged from feudal landlords like the zamindars of Uttarpara who set up the Makla school, to urban middle-class professionals like Shashipada. They had been brought together by the system of English education introduced in the early years of the 19th century. Besides helping to cohere them as a social class, it encouraged their ambition to use English political and civil institutions to improve their status and prospects and assert their voices in decision-making.

Building institutions with reformist objectives like women's education, temperance, etc., endeared them to the British, and also helped the bhadralok claim a constituency (of "reformed natives") so as to bargain with the colonial administration for both personal benefits (like the title of rai-bahadur) and political concessions for their class in general. For instance, the zamindar of Uttarpara, Joykrishna Mukherjee (in whose domain the Makla school was established), was one of the founders of the British Indian Association, the main platform for dialogue and manipulation between the big Indian landlords and the colonial administration. His son Pearymohan was made a CSI (Companion of the Order of the Star of India) and given the title of Raja by the British government. Shashipada Bandyopadhyay also displayed the same instincts, mediating between the colonial administration and the British mill owners on the one hand, and the workers on the other.

It should be added that, in conceiving the idea of educating the poor and carrying it out in practice, these pioneers anticipated many present-day concepts of post-literacy and continuing education and the activities following from them. Also, the problems and failures they experienced quite often look similar to those faced by policy makers and practitioners today. We will look at some of these aspects in the concluding part of the present paper.

The Makla School for Peasant Boys

This school was established in 1863 in the village of Makla, Hooghly district, in 1863. It came in the wake of a number of developments in the agricultural scenario of Bengal: among other things, crop diversification and changes in land relations.

The cash crop indigo, an important item during the first half of the 19th century, fell into decline from the 1860s onwards. First, there were rising costs of production. Second, the peasants increasingly resented being forced to cultivate it by the planters. (This led to the famous "blue mutiny" in Bengal in 1859-60.) Better prices were available in the world market for alternative cash crops. This prompted the colonial state to promote the planting and export of these crops. The money-lending landlords, too, developed a stake in cultivating new crops. For instance, there was demand in the world market for jute to make bags. Besides, Hooghly district had experienced a sharp increase in population, which reached a density of more than 700 per square mile by the mid-nineteenth century. Such a population could be sustained by adopting intensive techniques of agricultural production, including a limited switch-over to cash crops like sugarcane, cotton and mulberry. These were high-value, labour-intensive crops. Quite understandably, enterprising landlords were keen to train their cultivators in the use of suitable technical inputs for their growth.

The same period, the 1860s, also witnessed changing land relations. The rent act introduced in 1859 by the British government in Bengal granted the right of occupancy to raiyats (tenants) in continued possession of their holdings for twelve years. The new act also allowed landlords to increase rents if the area under cultivation expanded, the value of the produce rose, or higher rates prevailed in the locality. These provisions were incentives to the landlords to cultivate high-value crops. But they made the tenants legally subject to high rental demands, since the landlords were anyway keen to expand cultivable area and produce high-value crops.[4] Furthermore, the landlords, particularly in places like Hooghly in West Bengal, were also the local moneylenders and grain dealers; they wielded tremendous power over their tenants and the peasantry. These agrarian land relations had a major influence on the attitudes of the latter, causing them to suspect and, when possible, resist any innovations sought to be introduced by the landlords.[5]

An understanding of the above historical context is necessary when seeking answers to why the reformers of 19th century Bengal undertook to educate the rural poor, and why their efforts evoked either lukewarm response or total rejection from the agricultural classes. Without trying to belittle the good intentions of the social reformers and educationists of that period, the author seeks to draw the attention of the historian of today to a conflict of interests between the landed classes (from among whom the reformers primarily came) and the raiyats or tenants who were the main target for education. This conflict could have thwarted all the pedagogic programmes for the rural poor in 19th century Bengal.

To come back to the Makla school, available evidence suggests that this was the first attempt in Bengal to train the sons of peasants in scientific agriculture. The school was set up by the Uttarpara Hitakari Sabha on April 14, 1863, just nine days after the Sabha itself came into existence (indicating the earnestness of the reformers). Among the founder-members of the Sabha were Rajkrishna Mukherjee and Bejoykrishna Mukherjee, brother and step-brother, respectively, of Joykrishna Mukherjee, the famous zamindar of Uttarpara.[6] The Sabha tried to link educational activities with developmental work and social reforms. For example, it provided free medical treatment to the rural poor and campaigned against alcoholism. It played an important role in educating the women of Uttarpara and neighbouring villages. This endeavour lasted into the first few decades of the 20th century.[7]

Contemporary records show that the Makla school had three classes with monthly fees ranging from two annas to six annas. (One anna used to be the sixteenth part of a rupee.) The subjects taught were agriculture, geology and botany. The one teacher, Rajkumar Bhattacharya, was designated "head pandit". He got a monthly salary of six and a half rupees.[8]

The village Makla, only a couple of kilometres from the headquarters of the Hitakari Sabha at Uttarpara, was in a fertile area. To the south of the village ran a canal that gave enough water for irrigation. The inhabitants were mainly agriculturists, from tenants to landless labourers. The Sabha had therefore chosen well in selecting this village for its objective of education in advanced techniques of cultivation.[9]

When it started in April, 1863, the Makla school drew only 12 students from among the local agriculturists. By and by, the number went up to 40, but before the year was up, 5 students left and 5 more died during an epidemic in November. The next year, very few sought admission and, after a few months, the organizers closed down the school; it had run for a little over a year. According to a latter-day observer, it had to be closed because "its teaching activities did not meet the approval of the peasantry."[10]

The school's curriculum included instructions in the use of fertilizers and other agricultural inputs, and lessons in physics and botany. The following questions from an 1863 examination, give us an idea.

- What is atom? How can you test atom? Is there atom in air?

- What is termed as "attraction" and how many types of it can you name? Leaves fall from trees, and water rises up to the trees. Which are the rules of attraction that govern them?
- What is a fertilizer? How many types of fertilizers are available? How are they made? Which fertilizers are needed to improve the production of particular crops?[11]

A modern researcher has unearthed the answers written down by one of the examinees that year. He was Pearymohan Malik, judged by the examiners as the best student.[12] To the first two questions, Pearymohan gave the following answers.

- Molecules make up matter; the minutest parts of matter which cannot be separated by any technique or machines, are called atoms. Whether conscious or unconscious, or vegetables—every matter is an aggregate of atoms. One can feel air by touch. There is atom in air.
- The term "attraction" is used for that tie that draws the atoms towards each other. Attraction is of three types—molecular, gravitational and chemical. When leaves fall from trees, it is gravitational. When a juice climbs up a tree, it is capillary attraction.

His answer to the third question depicts a more down-to-earth peasant boy.

> The blood (of animals) is extremely beneficial for saplings. If you grind bones into powder and spread them evenly across the fields, they will make good manure, and keep the soil loose. These are good for sugarcane and tuberous vegetables. Carcasses of animals, their flesh and nails among other remains, turn into good manure after they rot. It is because of this that trees grow easily in burial grounds. If you want to decompose animal bodies, bury them under the earth and spread lime over them. Different types of manure can be made from plants ... Rotting leaves and branches make good manure. Among mineral fertilizers ... lime is in use in cold climates. Mixed fertilizers are made from animal, plant and

mineral manures. Cow-dung and cow-urine are the most important among mixed fertilizers.[13]

Many among us today may be inclined to dismiss Pearymohan's answers as the outcome of the usual method of learning by rote practised in Indian schools. Some may even suspect that the answers were fabricated by his teacher Rajkumar Bhattacharya to impress his employers, the Hitakari Sabha. Such suspicions cannot be ruled out by present-day historians. The expert group set up to monitor the government's total literacy programmes has itself suspected "fudging/overestimation of achievement figures."[14]

However, while making allowance for the possibility of Pearymohan's answers being learnt by rote or fabricated by his teacher or someone else from the educated upper class, we should note the different ways the peasant boy answered the three questions. Equally important, we need to analyze the nature and style of the questions. They were set by the middle-class members of the Hitakari Sabha, in terms of the framework learnt by them in the Calcutta colleges. They used terms like "atom" and "attraction" which sounded totally alien to the peasant boys of Makla. It is necessary to keep this alienation in mind when we try today to understand why the Makla school attracted agricultural students at its peak, but then lost its appeal within a year, and finally closed down before it could complete two years.

There is only fragmentary evidence on the Makla school, but more cohesive data is available about similar, simultaneous experiments undertaken by the Uttarpara Hitakari Sabha in other fields. Based on these, we can at best hazard a few speculations about the reasons for both the brief success and the quick demise of what can be claimed a pioneering effort to train the sons of agriculturist families along vocational lines.

First, the questions quoted above, and therefore the curriculum, indicate a heavy bias towards abstract theories. There were five questions in all, three related to theories about matter, atoms, gravity, etc., and two on the daily experiences of the boys. One asked them how flowers blossom, and another asked about agricultural manure. The theories introduced to the students, although important, do not appear to be couched in the framework of their daily life. Was it this that alienated the students?

A modern historian says this on the collapse of the Makla school: "It was not possible to implant new ideas among the sons of peasants who had been used to cultivating fields by traditional means handed down to them from past generations. The peasants could not be convinced of the need for taking lessons in agricultural science to improve cultivation."[15] Similar views about the conservative nature of Bengali peasants were expressed frequently by bhadralok writers in the columns of 19th century newspapers. They looked down on the peasants as rustic yokels, and urged the state and landlords to "civilize" them and teach them modern techniques of cultivation.[16] But the reluctance of the peasants to adopt innovative techniques need not have been due to conservatism. In a situation where any surplus they produced went to swell the coffers of the landlords, why should they be enthusiastic about increased production and improved cultivation? It may be pointed out in this connection that the Makla students were recruited by the same landlord clan that had exploited their families through rack-rent and usury.

The main organizers of the school, the two brothers, Rajkrishna and Bejoykrishna Mukherjee, were scions of a powerful family of Uttarpara. Their elder brother, Joykrishna Mukherjee, paid Rs 90,000 to the government annually in land revenue, and earned 12% to 24% in interest on Rs 100,000 of "floating" rural credit. Half the tenants were in debt.[17] There had been a stormy dispute within the Mukherjee family centered around the village of Makla just before the establishment of the school there. The two founding brothers were also powerful zamindars who owned large estates in Hooghly. Both Joykrishna and his brothers had for long wanted to buy Makla from its landlord, a certain Dhar. In June, 1860, both Joykrishna and Rajkrishna produced deeds of sale, but on March 31, 1862, Joykrishna was convicted of forgery, and sentenced by the Sader Nizamat Court to five years with hard labour (the latter commutable to a fine of Rs 10,000). Joykrishna then used his official contacts to persuade the lieutenant-governor of Bengal, Sir Cecil Beadon, to get his sentence reduced to nine months. During his brief imprisonment, his tenants—the "ryots" employed on his lands and the victims of his rack-rent—breathed a sigh of relief. One ryot dared to write a letter to the *Bengal Hurkuru*. Published on April 21, 1862, it said the tenants felt "as if a dreadful tiger had been caught in a snare."[18] But once he got out of prison, Joykrishna is reported to have retaliated against those tenants who gave evidence against him.[19] Joykrishna's tenants were mortally afraid of him, knowing from past experience that he could be ruthless in revenge. Earlier, in December 1858, he had kidnapped a recalcitrant tenant, Madan Dey, and got away with it by serving four months of simple imprisonment.[20]

Thus, Makla school was opened in a village whose ownership was disputed between two powerful sections of an oppressive zamindar family. The two brothers who started the school were rivals of another brother. The latter, just released from jail and smarting because his brothers had put him there, was quite possibly bent on subverting whatever reformist measures they might have undertaken by terrorizing the peasant-tenants of Makla. These villagers would then have been caught in the crossfire between two factions of a despotic landlord family. This could partly explain the disinclination of the peasant families to send their children to the school. Knowing Joykrishna's vengeful nature and his ability to get away with anything, they may not have wanted to antagonize him by patronizing a school run by his rival brothers. Given this background, one can hardly blame them for their lukewarm response to the school.

In any case, the peasants surely did not deserve the patronizing behaviour of the bhadralok reformers who assumed that they were ignorant and idle and needed to be trained in better agricultural practice. Without access to more modern but expensive inputs and facilities, they had toiled for generations and produced a variety of crops from their fields.

They could claim better knowledge of their soil than their educators. The superior, authoritarian posture of the latter could well have put off the peasant families. A few years after the school closed, the contemporary poet Michael Madhusudan Dutta (1824–73) was invited to a lecture on agricultural education at the Uttarpara Hitakari Sabha. His comment on their endeavour was brusque and sarcastic: "It is all humbug! What's so great in giving a lecture on agriculture? Don't the peasants know how to sow paddy? (Otherwise) how are you folks feeding yourselves? What sort of agricultural wisdom do you pretend to impart to them?"[21] He was not denying the need for technological inputs and training to increase agricultural production; rather, he was warning his friends not to take the peasants for granted.[22]

Returning to the history of the Uttarpara venture, the winding up of the Makla school set its patrons rethinking. They did not give up the idea of agricultural education, although their efforts in that direction had been rebuffed by the peasants they had initially chosen as their constituency. Instead, they shifted their attention to the educated middle class, and sought to recruit them directly for agricultural production. Thereby they hoped to conduct it along the lines the peasants were intended to follow. Joykrishna Mukherjee submitted a plan to the government on March 15, 1864, suggesting agricultural education on a collegiate level. Presumably, he hoped middle-class graduates could be induced to take up farming activities and would eventually become "gentlemen farmers". He wanted them to replace his peasants, who were proving stubborn in the face of all educational and reformist endeavours.[23]

A few years later, Joykrishna's son, Pearymohan Mukherjee expressed more forthrightly his objections to peasant education. Addressing a meeting of the Bengal Social Science Association on February 11, 1870, he recalled the "evil consequences which have resulted to society by the smattering of instruction given to the sons of carpenters, potters and others of the artisan class, and the disinclination which they feel to practice the trades and occupations of their fathers." He added that there was "little reasonable ground to anticipate that the mental training and increased stock of knowledge imparted by education" would lead to any improvement. Instead, "the education of the general body of the zamindars and the middlemen could effect a more beneficial change in the condition of the ryots than could ever result from ... the sort of education which it is possible to give to the masses."[24]

By the end of the 19th century, the upper- and middle-class bhadralok reformers appear to have become convinced that agricultural education should be imparted to the middle classes rather than the rural poor. The Bargabashi School set up in Calcutta in 1886 had a special section devoted to teaching agricultural practices to its middle-class students. In 1899, an undergraduate agricultural course was started at Shibpur College near Calcutta. The new policy on agricultural education was neatly summed up in a typical editorial of the Bengali journal *Sangbad Prabhakar*: "In our opinion, when sons of respectable families, educated in scientific agricultural practices, employ the present peasant classes and take to agriculture as a subsidiary occupation, and cultivate paddy, pulses, jute, tobacco and other crops, at one go many learned boys will be able to earn money."[25] But fluctuations in demand in the world market frustrated such hopes. The jute economy in Bengal, which saw a brief era of high income for cultivators, ended in dramatic losses in the downturn of 1882-83 that followed shrinking demand in Western markets. Likewise, expansion in the mid-1880s was followed by a crisis in 1890-91 because of a depressed export market.

Bharat Sramajeebee

Around the time the Uttarpara Hitakari Sabha was initiating educational activities for rural peasants, another Bengali bhadralok social activist, from an industrial suburb of Calcutta, was planning similar work the among mill-hands. Shashipada Bandyopadhyay, a young Brahmo intellectual, started life as a reformer by organizing classes for middle-class women in his hometown, Baranagore, in the 1860s. He soon extended his activities to the jute workers of the area. He brought them together at a meeting in Baranagore on November 1, 1866; this led to the establishment of a night school for them. They were employed in jute factories of the Borneo Company in Kamarpara, Ariadaha and Kuthighata in the Baranagore area. Shashipada approached the company bosses at their headquarters in Calcutta, and managed to convince them of the need to educate their workers. They agreed to provide space for the night school in the premises of one of their factories. Shashipada and his brother Kedarnath taught the workers there, accompanying the lessons with magic-lantern shows to attract the workers.[26]

In August, 1870, Shashipada went a step further by organizing these workers in the Sramajeebee Samity, workingmen's club. It was a meeting place for the workers, and its sessions were held by rotation in the homes of members. He invited speakers from Calcutta to address the workers on topics like moral conduct, discipline in the workplace and temperance. At a "temperance association" he formed, workers pledged to abstain from drinking and gambling. He also established "anna banks" (piggy banks) to collect savings from the workers' earnings to see them through lean days. Subsequently, on his initiative the government opened a "savings bank" in Baranagore on November 4, 1871, with a deposit of Rs 300 contributed by the workers.[27]

The apex of Shashipada's work among the Baranagore jute workers was the publication in May, 1874, of the journal *Bharat Sramajeebee*. It was addressed to all industrial workers, and was the first of its kind in Bengal. A public notice issued under Shashipada's name at the launch stated that the journal aimed to educate workers in developing the right attitude towards their employers and colleagues, as well as towards society in general.[28]

Let us first locate Shashipada's pedagogical experiments for the working class in the context of industrial development in the last quarter of the 19th century. By this time, metropolitan capital had already entered the economy, and enterprises like jute and cotton mills, engineering concerns, coal mines, and tea plantations had been established. Jute- and cotton-mill workers formed the core of the growing working class, the first generation of industrial labour in Bengal. The bulk of these workers came from agricultural and fishing communities, and from the large groups of artisans and weavers who had been displaced from their traditional homes and workplaces in the villages surrounding Calcutta and its new industrial suburbs. As one perceptive modern historian has observed, these first-generation industrial labourers were "in the midst of a process of transformation, though of a slow and halting nature, into a working class."[29]

From contemporary records, we can recapture in some measure the mental attitudes and working behaviour of the raw recruits in the newly established mills. What affected them most was the switch from the seasonal rhythms of agriculture to the fixed hours and daily rhythms of factory work. Official reports repeatedly complain about their dilatory work habits: taking time off during working hours (for a smoke or a wash), high rates of absenteeism, etc.[30] They used such strategies because they were repelled by the long hours of work, often 15 hours from dawn to dusk. (This practice continued till 1911, when the Factory Act mandated that no worker could be employed for more than 12 hours, with a half-hour break after six hours of work.[31]) These first-generation immigrants from pre-industrial societies were also totally alienated from the production process and the end product.

Apart from the uncongenial and monotonous nature of the work, the workers were often antagonized by the ill-treatment of the European factory manager and his Indian subordinates. The latter included labour contractors known as sirdars or jamadars, who controlled recruitment, promotion and the granting of leave. The workers' alienation even led to the outbreak of violence. In 1875, for instance, at a factory in Serampore near Calcutta, the workers demanded the punishment of a jamadar, and stopped the spinner boys from entering the premises. Cases of assaults on European employers were also not unknown.[32]

It is against this backdrop that Shashpada's educational

endeavours assume importance. He addressed the psychological needs of a generation of labouring poor that had been uprooted from their natural socio-cultural environs to enter a world of strange working conditions and lifestyles. Simultaneously, he sought to cultivate in them the norms and values that he felt were necessary to make them suitable workers in the new industrial climate. His concepts were shaped by contemporary Bengali bhadralok attitudes towards the unlettered labouring poor, mixed with reformist zeal to transform them into a new working force attuned to the requirements of capitalist development. Just as the bhadralok felt that the peasants were too backward and conservative to respond to innovative techniques and therefore needed to be educated and motivated, Shashipada and his colleagues were patronizing towards the mill-hands. They attributed their uncooperative behaviour and dereliction of duty to inherent feeble-mindedness. (Today this is called low IQ, a fallacious label without scientific basis, but one that is cavalierly used by most Indian educationists and policy-makers.)

An idea of Shashipada's perception of working-class behaviour and his model of an alternative set of rules to guide the mill-hands can be gained from his lectures and statements, apart from his writings in *Bharat Sramajeebee.* Some of these lectures were in England, which he visited in 1871 at the invitation of an English educationist and social reformer, Mary Carpenter.[33] At a speech on September 23, 1871, Shashipada referred to the Indian workers and said, "The greatest drawback I have is that the working classes do not think labour is honourable. This makes a miserable state of society, little better than the brutes of creation." In his night school, he added, "I have been trying to teach them that labour is honourable, not to bring disorder and confusion amongst them but to bring class with class in sympathy with each other."[34]

The assumption that the working classes "do not think labour is honourable" was based on the irregular attendance and dilatory working habits that plagued industry. Shashipada apparently did not go into the deeper causes of such habits. It did not occur to him to find out why these first-generation immigrants who, a few years previously had worked well at their rural vocations, whether cultivation, weaving or other crafts, treated their labour in the jute and cotton mills disdainfully. It was not as if he was unaware of the bad working conditions in these mills. To be fair, he was one of the first to demand legislation to limit daily working hours and provide for breaks. He had acquainted himself with factory legislation in England, and in his speeches there he stressed the need to implement similar laws for Indian workers.[35]

When he addressed Indian workers in his journal *Bharat Sramajeebee*, however, Shashipada preferred to preach the value of labour discipline rather than how to organize themselves to bring about better working conditions. His stress was on developing a deferential working class rather than a self-reliant one. He tried to alleviate their working conditions through appeals to British social reformers or negotiations with the mill authorities in his home town, Baranagore. As a later observer noted, "If they (the mill-hands) faced any difficulties, they used to come to Shashipada Babu. He advised them to be peaceful, restrained and dutiful. He then went to the managers of the mills and discussed with them the grievances of the workers. The mill management had a lot of faith in Shashipada Babu. As a result, by mediation, he could easily bring about a just solution of the workers' problems."[36]

The moral lessons in his journal are couched in terms which combine the Protestant work ethic (introduced to Bengali middle-class students at the beginning of the 19th century) and deference to superiors in accordance with indigenous feudal traditions. Shashipada sought to encourage the work ethic among his readers by publishing stories about Europeans who had succeeded by individual endeavour and perseverance. The moral for Indian workers was that they, too, could become rich by improving their personal habits and emulating the industriousness of Western man.

Typical was the rags-to-riches story that appeared in one of the issues about the 18th century English inventor Richard

Arkwright, whose spinning machine and other innovations started the industrial revolution in Europe. After describing Arkwright's arduous efforts to rise from his poor background and finally reach the pinnacle of success as a rich industrialist, the article concluded:

> At the age of fifty, he started learning English grammar. At an age when people in our country choose to rest and sleep in comfort, he refused to shun labour. It was Richard Arkwright who pioneered the textile industry, through which the English nation has amassed such riches ... Bengali workers! With such a bright example before you, you do not have any reason for despair. Read the lives of these great characters, and follow their examples. You also will be happy in your lives.[37]

Another article was entitled "Many sons from poor families have become rich." It narrated the life-histories of several European intellectuals from the labouring classes who became successful through their personal industriousness. It ended with a typical appeal to its working-class readers:

> Those among you who are spending your lives in extreme distress can also become rich if you are diligent. Those who are idle—even if born in rich families—will eventually land up in misery. And those who are industrious, in spite of all the miseries that they might be suffering now, will eventually see happier days. Oh poor, don't despair then. Pull yourselves up, and you'll see the face of happiness.[38]

Along with this attempt to inculcate the European work ethic, Shashipada also appealed in the pages of his journal to the traditional religious values inherited from the past by the immigrant mill-hands. In an article entitled "Charitrayi manushyatva" (meaning "character alone defines human nature"), the writer narrates the stories of Rama from the myths and Chaitanya, the 16th century Bengali vaishnavite reformer, from history. He tried to convey the message that following these icons could help the workers become industrious and achieve salvation. The article ended with the appeal:

> A chandala became a friend of Ramachandra. Even though coming from a low caste, how could he have gained respect from Maharaja Ramachandra? It was due only to his good moral character. Follow the examples of these people. Your names also will be remembered by the world in future.[39]

Almost every issue of *Bharat Sramajeebee* carried lessons on morals in the form of easy-to-remember couplets and brief articles on issues like health, cleanliness, temperance, etc. Two of these couplets are given below.

> Aloshey deher peera, parisramey noy,
> Bina byaboharey chhuri morchay porey roy.[40]
> (The body falls sick out of idleness, not labour.
> Without regular use, a knife rusts away.)

> Nahik paitrik dhan, kiba khoti taye?
> Jano na soubhagya phaley srama saheelataye?[41]
> (What if you did not inherit wealth?
> Don't you know good fortune comes from work?)

The magazine also offered practical advice. For instance, one brief article entitled "Easy way to become rich" told the workers to save one paisa every day and, at the end of the year, lend the accumulated money to a "good person" at a monthly interest of two paise on each rupee.[42]

Shashipada's pedagogy was based on the conviction that the labourers should stay with their respective occupations and seek to improve their condition from within them. In one article on the peasantry of Bengal, the journal commented:

> A few from among this class have indeed started to pick up a little learning. But instead of good results from this, we fear that it would create more harm. It is desirable that, after becoming literate, people should improve the quality of the respective trades and occupations in which they are engaged. Once the son of a peasant learns the

> alphabets, he refuses to take up the plough; the son of an artisan wants to leave his profession and take up a job ... We are therefore appealing for the sake of the welfare of both our country and the labourers: be literate, and with close application of your minds invent new techniques in your respective occupations ... Otherwise, if you become "babus" with a little learning, the country will go to dogs, and there will be no end to your miseries.[43]

Evidently, Shashipada and his collaborators were keen on building up a generation of industrious, ambitious workers who, they hoped, would promote the development of Bengal. This streak of patriotism often came out in brief comments in *Bharat Sramajeebee*. Take the following couplet:

> Phalode Bharat khetra, jaloda gagan;
> Tabey kano paradheen anner karon?[44]
> (Indian soil is fertile, its skies pour water.
> Why then do we need foreign rice?)

Similarly, in an otherwise quite objective report on the British-Afghan war of 1879, the journal explained as follows the resentment felt by the king of independent Afghanistan at British interference:

> [The Afghan king] feared that, as in India where the English entered as traders initially and have now gradually conquered the entire country, in his country also they might enter and gradually bring it under their control.[45]

In a monthly summary of news from India and abroad, we find a snide comment. After reporting that the pulse "masoor ka dal" had been recognized internationally as nutritious, and that its gravy had become popular in England, the paper added:

> The Empress (Queen Victoria) has tested it and praised it a lot ... We fear, from now, masoor ka dal will become costly![46]

Shashipada thus tried to make his worker-readers aware of the colonial occupation of their country and their dependence on the ruling powers. At the same time, he tried to strike a compromise in his educational experiments between an ambivalent attitude to the colonial order and the workers' betterment. It was a difficult task, and like many of his liberal contemporaries in Bengal, he fell back on the theory of the work ethic. This conveniently avoided the embarrassing question of the inequality of opportunities between the privileged, educated middle classes and the dispossessed rural poor and industrial immigrants. It also overlooked the discriminations suffered by the educated Indian middle classes in relation to the members of the colonial race. In other words, the economic and social obstructions embedded in the structure were totally ignored in stressing that individual endeavour and enterprise alone could bring about a transformation in the workers' lives. A typical example from an article in *Bharat Sramjeebee* is entitled "Labour and perseverance". It starts by saying, "In this world, everyone is equal," but then continues,

> Both the king and his subject are equal. The rich and the poor are equal. The fool and the intelligent are equal. All of them are sons of the same God. God has granted all of them the same powers. Whoever makes good of those powers earns fame. And whoever misuses these powers granted by God, will be doomed to misery.

It then asks the "destitute peasants of Bengal" to

> labour and persevere ... You will also become famous and celebrated ... The members of the lower orders also become rich. We can find lots of such examples in history.[47]

The publication of *Bharat Sramjeebee* was closely linked with Shashipada's other activities among the factor workers of Baranagore: running the night school and working men's club, and periodic outings on holidays.[48] Initiatives like the setting up of "anna banks" and the campaign against alcoholism endeared him to the families of the workers. At a farewell address on the eve of his departure for England in 1871, the workers expressed their gratitude to him for looking after them like a father and reforming their lifestyle by weaning them away from drink and gambling. They also recalled how he nursed them when they fell ill, and arranged for free treatment and medicines for the poorest among them.[49]

It must be acknowledged that Shashipada Bandyopadhyay earned a larger measure of success with the industrial workers of Baranagore than the Uttarpara Hitakari Sabha among the peasants of Makla. One of the main reasons was his ability to integrate his reform efforts with active intervention in the daily problems and social life of the workers, including mediation in disputes with mill management, helping the workers to save money from their earnings, and looking after their medical needs. Furthermore, Shashipada came from a middle-class family, while the Uttarpara educationists belonging to the zamindar class, and were probably perceived as exploiters by the peasants. Another advantage was that industrial labour was just emerging and yet to get its bearings. Put to work in alien urban surroundings and unfamiliar with the production process, Shashipada's mill-hands were more inclined to depend on guidance from above, whether in technical or social matters. Shashipada offered them the emotional solace they needed. In return, they heeded his advice to become a deferential and disciplined work force.

But while the workers were willing to be compliant, did the mill management respond to their needs and ameliorate working conditions as expected by Shashipada and his pupils? Evidence given by industrial workers before the 1890 Commission on Indian Factories reveals that, even in Shashipada's Baranagore industrial belt, conditions had worsened since the 1870s when he started his reforms. For example, during the five years from 1880 to 1891, the export market for jute was depressed, so the mills reduced the work-week to four days. This meant a sharp decline in earnings, for the workers were paid on a daily basis. The situation was ironic because the mill management used to complain in the 1870s about poor attendance, and now, when the workes were willing, it could not afford to employ them full time.

Before the 1890 commission, almost every worker said he preferred working six days instead of four.[50] A 40-year-old worker, Noderchand, had been employed in the Baranagore jute mills for more than 20 years, which suggests that he might have witnessed Shashipada's experiments. He told the commission that he worked from 5 a.m. to 6 p.m. and earned a little over Rs 3 in a four-day week. More disconcertingly, he said that the mill management used to pay injured workmen their full wages, but they had now stopped doing so. Women and children (aged seven to nine years) worked the same hours as the men but earned less—14 annas for four days (according to Taroni, a woman worker employed in the same mill). There was a school in the area, said Noderchand, but it discontinued because the "children find themselves too fatigued to go to school after their work."[51]

Evidence before the commission also shows that the Baranagore mill workers had "graduated" during the 1870–90 period from their initial, rural working rhythms to the stage of an industrial proletariat, gradually modifying their habits to meet the compulsions of daily life in the working-class slums. Women workers in the Baranagore mills had begun to save and pay off their debts; some of them were even paying a few annas to other women to "baby-sit" their children while they were away in the factories. These were the Bagdi woman, Taroni, cited above, and a woman called Sookwaria from Chaprah.[52] We can only speculate whether the changing habits of the Baranagore workers were due to Shashipada's endeavours or their own down-to-earth experiences in the factories and slums. However, evidence before the factory commission from other industrial areas of Bengal do not show any basic differences.

In the end, we are left with questions but no certain answers. Did pedagogical efforts by well-meaning bhadralok reformers lead to any transformation in the socio-economic conditions of poor workers? Did the work ethic taught by these reformers and partly absorbed by the workers help them improve their living and working conditions? Some sections of the fledgeling working class of Baranagore did respond positively to Shashipada's reformist endeavours. By and large, however, it was organized trade unionism by the industrial workers of Bengal, beginning in the 1890s, that helped them improve their lot. By this time, the workers had changed from being first-generation migrants to a more self-confident, assertive working class. Organized forms of protest, like strikes against increased working hours, low wages, ill-treatment by jobbers, etc., were on the increase. The first trade unions were established at the beginning of the 20th century by middle-class nationalists. Moderate reformers like Shashipada Bandyopadhyay, who preached discipline in work and loyalty to the crown, were replaced by radical union leaders. The latter channelized the workers' growing militancy, and trained them to plan strikes and force the European management to concede their just demands. Thereby, they initiated them into the anti-imperialist nationalist movement of the period.[53]

Conclusion

Although the immediate impact on their subjects differed to a considerable extent, both the Makla peasant boy's school and *Bharat Sramajeebee* and associated activities had certain common features that are of relevance to today's pedagogical experiments among the labouring poor of India. Both the Uttarpara Hitakari Sabha and Shashipada Bandyopadhyay pioneered a teaching system to promote what is today called "functional literacy". This term is defined as the mechanism of reading, writing, counting and other basic knowledge that enables people to run their lives more efficiently, and improves productive capacity and occupational skills. The Makla school and Shahipada's night school sought to combine the three Rs with knowledge of better production techniques in agriculture, and disciplined behaviour for the new industrial production system.

In particular, Shashipada's broadsheet *Bharat Sramajeebee*

approached in large measure another educational activity that is being promoted among adult learners today, namely, "post-literacy". Broadly defined, this is the provision of appropriate activities and materials to persons with limited reading and writing abilities or experience.[54] Post-literacy programmes are carried out today through a range of activities, including newsletters or broadsheets written in a simple language and conveying information as well as instruction to their neo-literate readers. They are primarily directed at adult labourers who possess a limited range of basic skills, but who are outside formal and non-formal systems of education. When Shashipada started publishing his paper in 1874, he had already taught his workers the three Rs in the night school he set up in 1866-67. His broadsheet can therefore be described as a pioneering effort in "post-literacy" for industrial workers. Furthermore, a number of post-literacy programmes today are being linked with developmental activities and social reforms. Shashipada's attempts to encourage workers to open accounts in savings banks and his campaign against alchoholism thus anticipated modern linkages between literacy and development.

Both the Uttarpara and Baranagore experiments faced a problem that also plagues today's literacy programmes: sustainability. The Makla school lasted a little over one year, and though Shashipada's night school and broadsheet continued for more than a decade, they did not survive his death, losing their importance in the new political environment of the first decade of the 20th century. It was student alienation from the curriculum and teachers that halted the Makla school. In Baranagore, on the other hand, the learners were too dependent on Shashipada; when he made his exit, they failed to sustain the school and associated activities.

Incidentally, prior attempts had been made to educate the rural and urban poor, but they, too, failed to persist. We hear of a number of "free schools" in Calcutta in the 1830s, but they all folded up within a few years. In 1839, a mechanic's institute was set up in Calcutta to improve the skills of artisans. This effort also failed, since the goods made by the artisans could not complete in the market against manufactures imported from England. Contemporary observers blamed lack of resources and poor learner interest for the failure of these early attempts.

The Makla and Baranagore experiments were undertaken when the ruling powers were aiming to incorporate peasants and urban workers into new production systems. Developments in agriculture and industry in Bengal in the mid-19th century required a labour force that possessed suitable skills and was willing to work. This called for an educational process that went beyond literacy and taught socializing mechanisms that prepared the labourers mentally for the type of work they were expected to do. The socialization could be achieved by reinforcing traditional values on the one hand, and instilling the values of the capitalist economy on the other. The educational messages therefore emphasized collective deference and loyalty to superiors, and individual enterprise and perseverance for self-advancement and financial success.

In this strategy for building a work force that could contribute to increased production, pedagogues like Shashipada Bandyopadhyay and the members of the Uttarpara Hitakari Sabha played important roles. Shashipada was, indeed, moved by deep feelings of sympathy for the mill-hands, but he believed that their poverty could be overcome by changing the workers' lifestyles and helping them develop better habits and skills. The hope was to provide the workers selective access to upward mobility, while preserving the existing power structures. Similarly, the Uttarpara Hitakari Sabha wanted to bring about a peasant class well-trained in scientific methods of cultivation. These methods were becoming necessary for higher agricultural yields. In the process, the Sabha hoped to provide some economic benefits to the peasantry as well.

Both experiments turned out to be instruments to facilitate the integration of the labourers into the logic of the prevalent economic system and bring about conformity to it, instead of helping them deal critically with reality and alter existing circumstances. That neither of the ventures had a lasting impact on the learners was due to a variety of factors. In Makla, it was the alienation of the landlord pedagogues from a resistant peasantry caught in an unsure situation. In Baranagore, moral education gradually lost its appeal among the industrial workers, to be superseded by their overriding need to unionize and struggle for their demands. As suggested earlier, the initiation of educational programmes and the choice of curricula are determined in large measure by the historical convergence of socio-economic and political requirements, and individual or group ambitions. The success or failure of these programmes also depends on the confluence of the objectives of those who teach and the needs of those who are taught.

Notes

1. A project was undertaken in the 1870s by the social reformer Keshub Chandra Sen through a broadsheet called *Sulabh Samachar*, meant primarily for the artisans and small traders of Calcutta. It has been analyzed by the present author in a paper, "Popular education in colonial Bengal and its legacy: an examination of a 19th century Bengali broadsheet", presented at the national seminar on "education, development and underdevelopment" organized by the Developing Countries Research Centre and the Centre for Professional Development in Higher Education, University of Delhi, August 7, 1994.
2. Reference can be made to the writings of Susobhan Sarkar, Benoy Ghosh, Suprakash Ray and Ranajit Guha, among others.
3. See Poromesh Acharya, "Bengali bhadralok and educational development in nineteenth-century Bengal", Occasional Paper 2, Shiksha Bhavan, Calcutta, January, 1995.
4. An idea of the way the landlords of Hooghly district (site of the Makla school) increased land rents and promoted the cultivation of cash crops in the last quarter of the 19th century is available from a contemporary account by a British official: "Rates of rent are high in Hugli district, and have considerably increased of late years. First-class paddy land, which formerly

ranted for 15s an acre, now pays from £1 1s to as much as £1 16s ... Mulberry and tobacco lands are rented at £1 4s to £3 an acre, and sugarcane lands at from £1 4s to £2 8s." see the chapter on "Hugli" in W.W. Hunter (ed.), *Imperial Gazeteer of India*, Vol. IV, London, 1881.

5. For this brief historical summary of land relations and crop diversification in Bengal in the 1860s, I have depended heavily on the excellent analysis of agrarian developments in colonial Bengal by Sugata Bose in his book *Peasant Labour and Colonial Capital: Rural Bengal since 1770*, Cambridge University Press, 1993.
6. Joykrishna Mukherjee (1808–1888) was the founder of the famous Uttarpara zamindar family. His father was banian to the Britain regiment that laid siege to the Bharatpur fortress in 1824. After its capture, he and other members of the regiment received a share of the prize money given by the East India Company. The young Joykrishna accompanied his father on the Bharatpur expedition, and later became a record-keeper in the collector's office in Hooghly. He invested the prize money in land, acquiring large, valuable properties spread over six districts. He was ranked among the largest landowners of Bengal. He set up several schools, a college and a public library in Uttarpara.
7. See Basanta Kumar Samanta, *Hitakari Sabha: Stree Shiksha O Tetkaleen Bangasaraj*, Sahityaloke, Calcutta, 1987.
8. *Ibid.*, pp. 75–76, reproduces from the *Indian Agriculturist* of July 2, 1883, the objectives of the school as explained some years later by the members of the Sabha: "In a purely agricultural colony such as this is, we want the children to grow up to be useful members of the community, and this is the end that should be aimed at in their early training."
9. *Ibid.*, p. 76–77 The peasant children who attended the school were too young to handle the plough or help their fathers in other agricultural operations, and were therefore spared for the lessons.
10. *Ibid.*, p. 75.
11. *Ibid.*, p.77.
12. *Ibid.*, pp. 77–78.
13. *Ibid.*, p. 76.
14. "Evaluation of literacy campaigns in India", report of the expert group, National Literacy Mission, Ministry Of Human

Resources Development, Government of India, New Delhi, 1994, p. 38.

15. Basanta Kumar Samanta, *op. cit.*, p. 76.
16. See *Sangbad Prabhakar*, 27 Agrahayan 1270 (Bengali era, approximately 1863), quoted in Benoy Ghosh (ed.), *Samayik Patrey Banglar Samajchitra*, Vol. I, Calcutta, 1978. p. 109. See also *Sangbad Prabhakar*, 24 Agrahayan 1299 (approximately 1892), quoted *ibid.*, Vol. II, pp. 118–19. Also *Education Gazette*, 9 Baisakh 1278 (approximately 1871), quoted *ibid.*, Vol. III, p. 181.
17. Report of the Indigo commission, answers 3807, 3821 and 3825, quoted in Ranajit Guha, "Neel darpan; the image of a peasant revolt in a liberal mirror", *Journal of Peasant Studies*, **2**, 1, 1974, pp. 36–37.
18. Nilmani Mukherjee, *A Bengal Zemindar*, Firma K.L. Mukhopadhyay, Calcutta, 1975, p. 173.
19. *Somprakash*, February 2, 1863.
20. *Ibid.*
21. Nagendranath Shome, "Madhu smriti", in *Bharatvarsha*, Vol. II, No. 5, Baisakh 1324 (Bengali era), quoted in Basanta Kumar Samanta, *op. cit.*, p. 87.
22. Madhusudan's views were confirmed some years later by an agricultural expert who exploded the erroneous belief, current among Bengali bhadralok, that the peasants were an idle lot, lacking innovative ideas. In 1889, the government deputed Dr. J.A. Voelcker, consulting chemist to the Royal Agricultural Society, to conduct an investigation into Indian agricultural techniques and suggest improvements. After travelling through the agricultural areas of India, Voelcker observed: "The ideas generally entertained in England, and often given expression to even in India, that Indian agriculture is, as a whole, primitive and backward, and that little has been done to try and remedy it, are altogether erroneous ... To take the ordinary acts of husbandry, nowhere would one find better instances of keeping land scrupulously clean from weeds, of ingenuity in the device of water-raising appliances, of knowledge of soils and their capabilities, as well as the exact time to sow and to reap, as one would in Indian agriculture." Quoted in R. Palme Dutt, *India Today*, People's Publishing House. Bombay, 1947, p. 182.
23. Basanta Kumar Samanta, *op. cit.*, p. 71.

24. Transactions of the Bengal Social Science Association, Vol. IV, 1870.
25. *Sangbad Prabhakar*, 1299 (Bengali era), quoted in Benoy Ghosh, Vol. II, *op. cit.*
26. Kanailal Chattopadhyaya (ed.), *Bharat Sramajeebee*, Devalaya Trust, Calcutta, 1975, p. 10.
27. *Ibid.*, pp. 10–14.
28. *Ibid.*, p. 17. Only one file containing the 1879 issues of *Bharat Sramajeebee* has been unearthed till now. This suggests that the broadsheet continued for at least five years after its inception. We hear of the journal reappearing in a "new sequence" under a different editor in 1885, indicating the end of Shashipada's direct editorship before that year. Although it might seem unfair to analyze Shashipada on the basis of just one annual file, we have tried to link his views with those expressed in lectures, night-school experiments, etc.
29. Ranajit Das Gupta, "Material conditions and behavioural aspects of Calcutta working class, 1875–1899," Occasional Paper 22, January, 1979, Centre for Studies in Social Sciences, Calcutta, p. 8.
30. *Ibid.*, pp. 12–23.
31. Sunil K. Sen, *Working Class Movements in India: 1885–1975*, Oxford University Press, New Delhi, 1994, p. 13.
32. Ranajit Das Gupta, *op. cit.*, pp. 30–31.
33. Mary Carpenter, who was instrumental in inspiring Keshub Chandra Sen to turn his reformist zeal to the artisans of Calcutta, visited Baranagore in 1867 and met Shashipada Bandyopadhyay. She evinced interest in his work among the workers.
34. Albion Rajkumar Banerji, *An Indian Pathfinder: Being the Memoirs of Sevabrata Sasipada Banerji by his son Albion Rajkumar Banerji*, Devalaya Trust, Calcutta, 1971 (reprint), pp. 36–37.
35. Kanailal Chattopadhyaya, *op. cit.*, p. 10.
36. Kuladaprasad Mullick, *Nabayuger Sadhana*, Calcutta, 1913, pp. 175–76, quoted in Kanailal Chattopadhyaya, *op. cit.*, p. 21.
37. *Bharat Sramajeebee*, Baisakh 1286 (Bengali era).
38. *Ibid.*, Magh 1286.
39. *Ibid.*, Falgun 1286.
40. *Ibid.*, Sraban 1286.
41. *Ibid.*, Kartik 1286.

42. *Ibid.*, Magh 1285.
43. *Ibid.*, Agrahayan 1286.
44. *Ibid.*, Kartik 1286.
45. *Ibid.*, Paush 1286.
46. *Ibid.*, Sraban 1286.
47. *Ibid.*, Paush 1286.
48. One such outing was described in a report published in the *Indian Daily News* of December 11, 1873, quoted in Kanailal Chattopodhyaya, *op. cit.*, pp. 19–20.
49. Kanailal Chattopadhyaya, *op. cit.*, p. 15.
50. See copy of "A Report of the Recent Commission on Indian Factories", India Office, February 1891, London.
51. Evidence given before the twenty-fifth meeting of the Factory Commission on October 30, 1890. Quoted *ibid.*
52. *Ibid.*
53. Strikes crippled the Ghoosery cotton mill in Bengal for days together in 1881, and again in 1890. In October 1895, there was a strike in the Budge jute mills, accompanied by violent clashes with the police and European managers. See Ranajit Das Gupta, *op. cit.*, p. 34, and Sunil K. Sen, *op. cit.*, pp. 24–25.
54. Alan Rogers, "Education research using literacy: A new approach to post-literacy materials", November, 1994, No. 10, Overseas Development Administration, London, p. 2.

Marginalization of Popular Languages and Growth of Sectarian Education in Colonial India

NARESH PRASAD BHOKTA

Colonial rule made a deep impact on the socio-economic structure of Indian society, leaving hardly any aspect of it unaffected. A process of centralization was started in the political and administrative spheres. Its counterpart in socio-cultural life was the standardization of Indian languages and scripts. For sheer administrative convenience, the colonial government took many decisions that affected the linguistic landscape of the country and sealed the fate of many popular languages during the nineteenth century.

Indians who spoke English also played a role in accelerating the speed of marginalization of popular Indian languages. Colonial rule produced congenial conditions for the development of a new middle class that looked down upon prevalent socio-cultural institutions and popular languages. In Bihar and the North-Western Provinces, this growing middle class tried to emphasize its separate cultural identity by developing a highly Sanskritized Hindi called shisht bhasha or sophisticated language. Urdu protagonists, too, began to borrow a large number of words from Persian and Arabic sources. Both groups completely ignored the lok bhashas, the languages of the common people, like Magahi, Maithili, Bhojpuri, Awadhi and Braj Bhasha. The new languages, i.e.,

Sanskritised Hindi and Persianized Urdu, satisfied the cultural needs of the emerging middle class but failed to meet the cultural and occupational needs of the masses. Thus a rift was created that has not yet been bridged. In fact, most of the leaders of the national movement belonged to the new middle class. They were the most vocal supporters of the khari boli form of Hindi and tried their best to popularize it at the cost of the lok bhashas.

Let us now make a brief survey of the linguistic position in nineteenth-century Bihar and the North-Western Provinces. At the very outset, it should be clear that the writing of modern Hindi prose started only at the beginning of the nineteenth century. Almost all the leading linguists accept the comparatively recent origin of this kind of Sanskritized Hindi. Suniti Kumar Chatterjee, the doyen of linguistic studies in India, writes:

> The khari boli form of Hindi ... is one of the youngest of the Indian languages. As a matter of fact, it did not come into literary use in any appreciable scale before 1800, and its effective literary use started only after 1850.[1]

Hazari Prasad Dwivedi, the distinguished historian of Hindi literature, also says that the writing of modern Hindi prose started only in the nineteenth century.[2] According to him, this development was highly influenced by the British impact on Indian culture and society. Jotirindra Das Gupta, too, concedes that standard literary Hindi "is a relatively recent speech, barely a century and a half old."[3]

G.A. Grierson,[4] who made the most systematic, sophisticated analysis of the language situation in India, separated the dialects and/or languages in the large Hindi family into three distinct groups on the basis of their grammatical structure. Each group was recognized as a distinct language, giving Bihari, eastern Hindi and western Hindi. In the Bihari group, Grierson gathered a number of related dialects with similar phonology, grammatical structure and vocabulary.[5] The three important ones were Maithili, Magahi and Bhojpuri. Deposing before the Indian

Education Commission of 1882–83, Grierson thus described the separate existence of a Bihari language:

> The mistaken idea about Hindi being the language of Bihar is due, I think, to the idea which has been prevalent since the time of Colebrooke that the language of the "gentoos" was the same all over India. It took a long time to discover the existence of Bengali. Then, later still, the Assamese, Uriya and Punjabi were discovered, and last of all Bihari has remained uncared for and unloved except by its own speakers. Hence has arisen, too, the idea that Bihari has no literature. It really has one as large as Hindi before Hindi was brought to the front by the English. Curiously enough, the best part of the Bihari literature has been adopted by Bengalis as their own, while its very existence is denied by those who pretend that Hindi is the language of the country.

In the North-Western Provinces and Oudh, different languages and dialects related to eastern and western Hindi were being used. Eastern Hindi included three dialects: Awadhi, Bagheli and Chattisgarhi. Most important was Awadhi, which was used in the whole of Oudh province. Western Hindi also had several recognised dialects; most important were Hindustani, Braj Bhasha, Kanauji and Bundeli. Hindustani, which was based on khari boli, gradually became a recognized literary form of western Hindi. The home of Braj Bhasha was the central Doab and the region immediately to its south from near Delhi to Etawah. Surdas and Bihari Lal were celebrated poets of Braj Bhasha.

The development of these popular languages was directly related to the bhakti movement between the fourteenth and seventeenth centuries. The movement's teachers came from different social backgrounds. Many of them were artisans or belonged to the peasantry. A few brahmins joined the movement but its adherents were mainly from the lower castes.[6] The teachers made a strong plea for social equality by discarding the caste system, brahminical form of worship and institutionalized religion. One of the most important features of these teachers was that they spoke entirely in the local languages of the people; they even composed their verses in these languages. Declared Kabir, a revolutionary social reformer and leading preacher of the time, "Sanskrit is the water in a well, the language of the people is the flowing stream."[7] The great bhakti poet Vidyapati declared in no uncertain terms, "Sanskrit is incapable of pleasing many, Prakrit is dry only. Desila bayana (local language) is sweet to all."[8] These preacher-poets believed in mass contact, and for this they found the popular languages quite necessary. A high quality of literature resulted from their efforts, proving that the popular languages were not only well suited for the socio-cultural needs of the people but were also capable of expressing such subtle religious ideas as atma, brahma and mukti.

To get a better insight into the language situation of nineteenth-century India and its specific role in the field of education, let us look at Brann's three-language formula.[9] Though this conceptual framework was developed for sub-Saharan Africa, it is equally relevant to the Indian context. Brann suggests that the language situation in a multilingual country is best described as trilingual acquisition of the local language (L1), the regional language (L2), and the received or link language (L3). His formula is based on the functions of a language, including domains and registers of use, and the specific objective or motivation of the speaker. It is also based on standard geographical and demographic distinctions such as areal spread and the size of the group using the language. These factors are summarized in Table 1.

TABLE 1 Brann's three-language formula for education

Factor	*L1*	*L2*	*L3*
areal spread	local regional	regional national	national international
demography	minor 1000m–1m	major 1m–10m	maxi 100m

TABLE 1 Brann's three-language formula for education

Factor	*L1*	*L2*	*L3*
domain	home community	community school	school nation-world
motivation	affective conative	conative cognitive	cognitive ideational
language register	familiar communal	communal official	official specialized
language terminology	vernacular dialect chthonolect	lingua franca national language demolect	national language world language metalect

TABLE 2 Popular languages in Bihar and NWP in the 19th century

Language	*No. of speakers*	*Areal spread (sq. miles)*
Maithili	10,000,000	
Magahi	6,239,967	
Bhojpuri	20,000,000	
Bihari[10]	36,239,267	90,000
Awadhi	16,143,548	
Bagheli	4,612,756	
Chattisgarhi	3,755,343	
Eastern Hindi[11]	24,511,647	1,87,500
Hindostani	16,633,163	
Bagheli	2,165,784	
Braj Bhasha	7,864,274	27,000
Kanauji	4,481,500	
Bundeli	6,869,201	
Western Hindi[12]	38,013,928	

Brann says that all these types of languages may be used in the education system but, most commonly, it is L2 and L3 that are utilized. When an L1 language is used for educational purposes, it is frequently as a bridging language in the first grades of primary education or in adult education programmes. For further participation in formal education, learning an L2 or L3 is necessary. Here, our argument is that all the popular languages of Bihar and NWP had all the essential features to qualify for Brann's group, L2. Table 2 substantiates our point.

These popular languages were used as the medium of instruction in a large number of indigenous schools. In the vernacular schools of Bihar, instruction was through the language of the locality, i.e., Bihari or its dialects, even though the colonial government, missionaries and English-educated Indians tried their best to introduce the shisht bhasha or sophisticated Hindi. In his evidence before the Indian Education Commission in 1882, Grierson remarked:

> Hindi, which is the vernacular taught in the (government) schools of Bihar, is not the dialect of the people ... By school I mean aided primary schools. In unaided (indigenous) schools as a rule, Hindi is not taught but Bihari. In these unaided schools, teaching is not by the book but by dictation, and so the art of reading is not forced into the Hindi channel as it is in the primary aided schools, where books in the Hindi language are also distributed.

Grierson makes clear the differing social bases of those two systems by pointing out:

> There were two classes of people who normally went to primary schools: one was the villager's son who preferred his unaided village school (pathshala), where instruction was given in his own language. The other class was the comparatively educated classes, who sought a kind of middle-class education so that they might be able to appear in public and take a public share in bazar.[13]

The *Bihar Bandhu* of 18 August 1881 describes similarly the social bases of the people who used these two kinds of languages. It informs us that a good number of sarswar, gaud, sandhya, and some shakadwipi and kanujya brahmins used Sanskritized Hindi, but those brahmins who were engaged in any kind of manual labour spoke the language of the common people. Among the kshatriyas and kayasthas, village dwellers spoke in the Bihari languages, and town dwellers in the khari boli. The lower stratum of the banias, including sub-castes like kalwar, banwar, etc., and most lower-caste people, e.g., kahar, kurmi, dhanik, teli, tamboli, halwai, etc., used popular languages like Bhojpuri, Maithili, Magahi, etc.[14] In brief, those higher classes that did not do any manual work preferred Hindi, while peasants, artisans and petty shopkeepers used regional languages for all their cultural and economic functions. By adopting Hindi as the medium of instruction in the schools of Bihar, the government therefore denied educational opportunity to the large mass of the rural population.

Like Bihar, local languages were used for elementary education in the indigenous vernacular schools of the North-Western Provinces, too, though here, the khari boli form of Hindi or Hindustani was more popular, at least with town dwellers. Of the indigenous vernacular schools of this area, Muir says, "The object of tuition [was] merely to give the power of communicating and interpreting the commonest ideas in the usual colloquial languages."[15] The epithet "colloquial" undoubtedly implies the vernaculars of the people, namely Awadhi, Braj Bhasha and Hindustani. The order of the alphabets was taught in these schools by means of poems known as barakharis or dwadaksharis. These poems were in Awadhi or Braj Bhasha.[16] Buchanan informs us that in the "Hindi" schools of Gorakhpur in the North-Western Provinces, very young students could recite from the works of Tulsidas, Kesavadas, Bihari, etc.[17] It is well known that these poets composed in Awadhi or Braj Bhasha. The books taught in these schools, e.g. *Sudama Charita, Sunder Khad* and *Sunder Sudama,* were also in lok bhashas like Awadhi, Braj Bhasha and Maithili, not in Hindustani or khari boli.

The lok bhashas had met the needs of the masses in the North-Western Provinces and Bihar for centuries. These languages were now being used as the medium of instruction in a large number of indigenous vernacular schools. But the colonial government and its "illegimate progeny", the English-educated Indian middle class, found them coarse, incapable of portraying the new world.

The new Indian middle class consisted mainly of landlords created by various land settlements and revenue rules.[18] It included Indians educated in English who either worked or aspired to work in the ever-growing administrative and judicial offices. Uprooted from its traditions, the new class tried to acquire an identity by developing a new language based on the khari boli of the Delhi region. To make it more sophisticated, there was profuse borrowing of words from classical languages.

Nor can we ignore the role played by the colonial government, British officials, and Christian missionaries and the leaders of the national movement in the development of Sanskritized Hindi and the marginalization of popular languages. Sir Erskine Perry, the principal of Delhi College, classed Maithili as a dialect of Bengali.[19] B.H. Hodgson, the company's Resident in Nepal,[20] while arguing in favour of vernacularization, forgot the existence of Maithili, Magahi, Bhojpuri and even of Oriya and Assamese, arguing that only three languages, Bengali, Hindi and Hindustani existed in the whole of the Bengal presidency.

Hazari Prasad Dwivedi maintains unequivocally that modern Hindi writing started under the fostering care of the Fort William College, which was established in 1800 to train recruits to the Indian Civil Service.[21] Here, Guilchrist guided the Oriental language experts Lallu Lal and Sadal Mishra in developing a new form of written Hindi. According to Dwivedi, the new language became stronger day by day, and the shisht jan (higher classes) increasingly adopted this "Sanskrit mishrit bhasha". The process of Sanskritization ended up becoming so vigorous that a professor of Banaras remarked, "When a Hindi writer takes his pen in his hand, he ceases to be sober, and becomes Sanskrit-drunk."[22]

Like the Indian middle class, the colonial government, too, found the lok bhashas "uncultivated", "barbarous" and "rude", unsuited to be the medium of instruction in government and aided schools. The British government always believed that the Indian who knew English and also had a good command of Sanskrit was best suited to write textbooks and create a better kind of literature in Hindi. We come across several references like this in the official records: "Individuals who are proficient both in Sanskrit and English will be the persons qualified to compose elegantly or teach efficiently in Hindi."[23]

Another factor that accelerated the Sanskritization of Hindi was Bengal and the development of the Bengali language. The emerging Bihari middle class wished to follow the example of the Bengali bhadralok, who had developed a Sanskritized Bengali they called sadhu bhasha, as opposed to the common or laukik bhasha, some three or four decades earlier. As we mentioned, the writing of modern Hindi prose was started by Lallu Lal and Sadal Mishra at Fort William College in Calcutta. The leading Bengali intellectual of the day, Raja Ram Mohan Roy, also wrote a couple of books in Hindi. According to Dwivedi, these three men were the "pioneers of Hindi prose."[24] Our argument is that all of them were writing in Calcutta and were certainly influenced by the style of Sanskritized Bengali.

The Calcutta School Book Society, established in 1817, also played an important role in popularising the khari boli form of Sanskritized Hindi. It published schoolbooks in all the major languages of the Bengal presidency. During the period 1817–35, a total of 23,750 Hindi books were printed, of which 19,087 were distributed. Between 1835 and 1854, the society published 65,100 Hindi books and distributed more than 47,000.[25] Thus, it was a Calcutta society that set the pattern of Hindi textbook writing.

The first two Hindi newspapers, *Udant Martand* (1824) and *Banqdoot* (1826), were also published from Calcutta. They were followed by many other leading Hindi journals and newspapers, e.g., *Praja Mitra, Sudha Varshan, Bharat Mitra, Sarsudha, Nidhi* and *Uchit Vakta*. Almost all the editors were brahmins, and the newspapers played an important role in popularizing Sanskritized Hindi and the Nagari script.

The expansion of the colonial administration into north India during the nineteenth century resulted in the migration from Bengal of a series of Bengali communities. They were very vocal in advocating Hindi as a link language in north India, and constantly campaigned for the adoption of Hindi in schools and courts. It was the Bengali intellectual and Inspector of schools for the Bihar circle, Bhudev Mukherjee, who was largely responsible for the introduction of Hindi in the law courts and schools of Bihar.

Thus, we find an explicit and close relationship between nineteenth-century colonial policies, the socio-cultural identity of the emerging middle class, and Sanskritized Hindi, with all these factors reinforcing each other. In reaction to this, the Muslim intelligentsia began to identify Urdu more closely with their social, cultural and economic interests. To distinguish Urdu as a separate language, they began to make it more and more Persianized. About the negative results of these trends, Paul R. Brass says, "In this process, the Hindi-Urdu controversy of the late nineteenth century widened the divergence between the languages of the educated urban elites and the rural masses who, Hindus and Muslims alike, spoke a variety of dialects."[26]

In the second half of the nineteenth century, the emerging Hindu middle class started agitating to introduce Sanskritized Hindi in the government's courts and schools. Their first major victory was the acceptance of Hindi as the medium of instruction in government and aided schools of Bihar. The Lieutenant-Governor of Bengal, George Campbell, declared in 1871 that neither Urdu nor Bihari would be used any longer in the vernacular schools of Bihar. He made it obligatory for the teachers of government and aided schools to use Hindi as the medium of instruction. Earlier, the use of local languages and the practical knowledge that was imparted in these pathshalas had encouraged boys from the deprived sections of society and lower castes such as kahar, kurmi, kairi, napit, teli, mahuri and gandhabanik to attend them in large numbers. But the new language had no connection with their socio-cultural life, and undoubtedly discouraged them from further participation in the education system.

There used to be hardly any textbooks in the vernacular pathshalas. This is particularly true of Bihar and the North-Western Provinces.[27] In his third report of 1838, William Adam says that out of 365 indigenous vernacular schools in Tirhoot and South Bihar, only 13 had any kind of written books.[28] Most of the instruction was in oral form. When the British system of education was introduced in Bihar, the use of some textbooks became compulsory. However, they got written not in the language of the common people, but in the khari boli form of Hindi, which was beyond their comprehension. One of those who initiated a large-scale school textbook programme was Bhoodeb Mookherjee, Inspector of schools for the Bihar circle.[29] Another was the Maharaja of Darbhanga, who awarded annual prizes to encourage the writing of textbooks in Hindi for different subjects.[30]

The introduction and encouragement of Hindi in the schools of Bihar discouraged the sons of cultivators and artisans, who used only the vernacular of their locality, from joining government-aided schools. These poor sections of society did not find their textbooks relevant to their cultural and economic needs. Even the spoken language was alien to these village folk. Many persons, including Grierson, voiced their resentment at the introduction of "high Hindi" and books written in it in the schools of Bihar. The Indian Education Commission of 1882–83 says about this:

> A larger objection was brought against the language, Hindi, as the medium of instruction in the primary schools of Bihar. This was said to be a language not understood at all by the boys in many parts of the province, and little even by the teachers. The essence of the objection is that the Hindi of the textbooks is what is known as "high Hindi", and that while this form is closely allied with the dialects of northern India from Allahabad to Delhi, it is too far removed from those of

> the eastern group, that is, chiefly, the dialects of Bihar, to be safely used in schools as the standard or literary form of the language.[31]

National unity was being seriously threatened by the Hindi-Urdu controversy of the late nineteenth century. The Arya Samaj emerged as the most important champion of Hindi. Its founder, Dayanand Saraswati, made it obligatory for every member to learn what he called the Arya bhasha. The Samaj's efforts to popularize Hindi was most successful in the Punjab,[32] and the Hindi-Punjabi-Urdu controversy there was the direct result. In opposition, Sir Sayyid Ahmad Khan, a vocal champion of vernacular education, proposed establishing vernacular schools, colleges and even a university in Urdu, which he viewed as the only language of north India.[33] The leaders of both communities tried to mobilize support for their respective languages, ignoring the basic fact that language had connection with locality, not with the different religious communities resident there.

Meanwhile, the leaders of the national movement tried to use Hindi or Hindustani as a symbol of the cultural unity of "the nation in the making", and as a tool in their struggle against colonial rule and the English language. Gandhi wanted to adopt the mother tongue as the medium of instruction at all levels at once,[34] but failed to do justice to the lok bhashas of northern India. In his basic education scheme, Hindustani became a compulsory subject, while the medium of instruction was the language of the province. The exception was the whole of the United Provinces and Bihar, where he failed to see the existence of any language other than Hindi or Hindustani. He declared in no uncertain terms, "Hindi must rule supreme."[35]

Lala Lajpat Rai thoroughly discussed the question of national education in his celebrated work, *The Problem of National Education in India.* There, he gives a fairly representative idea of the language policy of the nationalists:

> The vernaculars, to be adopted as medium of instruction, should be as few as may be compatible with the educational

> interests of the children. A certain amount of efficiency will have to be sacrificed at the altars of provincial integrity and national unity. For example, it will be absurd to insist that for primary education of the Bengalees, the different dialectic variations of the spoken language be recognized, or that Ooriya be raised to the status of a language, or that in the Agra division of the Upper Provinces, education be imparted in Braj Bhasha ... and so on.

In other words, the leaders of the national movement were no more ready than the colonial rulers to give lok bhashas like Oriya, Maithili and Braj Bhasha their rightful place.

The controversy in Bihar over the question of education in one's mother tongue remained unresolved even in 1939, when the administration was in the hands of Congress leaders. An educational reorganization committee was formed to decide the question. One of its members, Amarnath Jha, strongly pleaded the case of Maithili as the medium of instruction in the schools of Mithila, but two other members, Rajendra Prasad and Sachchidanand Sinha, put forward equivalent claims for Bhojpuri and Magahi. Meanwhile Bengali, the mother tongue of only a few lakh people in Bihar, was recognized as one of the province's vernaculars and accepted as a medium of instruction. In contrast, Maithili and Bhojpuri, the mother tongues of millions, were denied the same status.[37]

The aboriginal tribes of Chota Nagpur and Santhal Parganas had their own distinct culture and languages, but they, too, were forced by the government to study through Hindi or Urdu.[38] In fact, the colonial government did not have a coherent policy regarding the language to be used in tribal schools. An English official called J.N. Crownford visited the Chota Nagpur government school on 30 September 1850, after which he agreed that "Nagari was as foreign a language for the Kols as English." Nevertheless, he suggested that the Kols should be taught in Bengali![39] H.L. Harrison, Inspector of schools for the south-west division, argued:

> Considerable difficulty is experienced in Chota Nagpur, as elsewhere, by the different languages current in the district. The two municipal tribes are the Uraons and Mundaries ... Each of these tribes has a language of its own ... It was therefore resolved to adopt Hindi as the medium of instruction of every kind.[40]

Nobody realized that, once a child was in school, the greatest handicap he could suffer was unfamiliarity with the language of instruction.[41] Even Harrison later wrote, "The village schools are open to all but ... the Coles exhibit the extreme of indifference or, rather, aversion to education."[42]

In the North-Western Provinces, the new high Hindi became fairly popular because of proximity to the Delhi region, whose khari boli formed its basis.[43] Furthermore, Banaras, the seat of Sanskrit learning and brahminical culture, emerged as the centre for the cultivation and diffusion of the new Sanskritized Hindi. Another impetus was the adoption of the four-volume series by Ram Suran Das as textbooks in the government vernacular schools of the area. This series was popular because it was written in simple Hindi, and because two of its four volumes dealt with commercial and agricultural accounts, subjects of local interest. It provided a sound model for subsequent schoolbooks; only, the later writers borrowed Sanskrit words in large numbers. About the futility of such an exercise, G.A. Grierson remarks, "Nine-tenths of the Sanskrit words which one meets in modern Hindi books are useless and unintelligible."[44]

To summarize our discussion, the social and economic policies of the colonial government created conditions favourable to the growth of a middle class. This class found the prevalent cultural institutions and popular languages unable to fulfil their aspirations. In collusion with the colonial government it developed a highly Sanskritized Hindi called shisht bhasha or high Hindi, and got it adopted as the official language in government schools and offices. This language was different from the popular languages spoken by the masses, so their children could not adapt to the education imparted in it. Particularly in Bihar, the popular languages had met the cultural and occupational needs of an overwhelming majority of the people for centuries. These languages have now become marginalized.

Notes

1. S.K. Chatterjee, "Language and literature", in R.C. Majumdar (ed.), *The History and Culture of Indian People*, Vol. VI, Bharatiya Vidya Bhavan, 1960, p. 499.
2. Hazari Prasad Dwivedi, *Hindi Sahitya*, 1955, p. 369.
3. Jotirindra Das Gupta, *Language Conflict and National Development*, University of California Press, 1970, p. 50.
4. G.A. Grierson, *Linguistic Survey of India*. This is a monumental work published in 19 volumes from 1903 to 1928. It has had an impact on almost all subsequent studies on the language situation in India, including the first detailed tabulation of language data of the 1961 census.
5. L.P. Vidyarthi, "Cultural and linguistic regions in India: Bihar, a case study", in Arbinda Poddar (ed.), *Language and Society in India*, p. 126.
6. Romila Thapar, *A History of India*, p. 308.
7. S.K. Chatterjee, *op. cit.*, p. 563.
8. Amresh Pathak, "Maithili literature in Bihar", in K.K. Datta (ed.), *Comprehensive History of Bihar*, Vol. III, Part II, K.P. Jayaswal Research Institute, Patna, 1976, p. 538.
9. C.M.B. Brann, *Trilingualism in Language Planning for Education in Sub-Saharan Africa*, UNESCO, 1981, p. 7.
10. G.A. Grierson, *op. cit.*, Vol. V, Part II, p. 5.
11. *Ibid.*, Vol. I, Part I, p. 158.
12. *Ibid.*, Vol. IX, Part I, pp. 1–2.
13. G.A. Grierson, evidence before the Indian Education Commission (1882–83), Bengal province report.
14. *Bihar Bandhu*, 18 August 1881.
15. Quoted by H.S. Reid in *Report on Indigenous Education and Vernacular Schools*, 1851, p. 73.
16. S.N. Chaturvedi, *The History of Rural Education in United Provinces of Agra and Oudh*, Indian Press, Allahabad, 1930, p. 20.

17. R.M. Martin, *History, Antiquities, Topography and Statistics of Eastern India*, Vol. II, 1838, pp. 429–30.
18. Bipan Chandra says that by the second decade of the nineteenth century, nearly half the landed property had been transferred from the old zamindars to merchants and moneyed classes living in towns. See *Modern India*, NCERT, 1971, p. 188.
19. G.A. Grierson, *Linguistic Survey of India*, Vol. I, Part I, p. 15.
20. B.H. Hodgson, *Pre-eminence of the Vernaculars, or The Anglicists Answered*, Serampore Press, Calcutta, 1837, p. 18.
21. Hazari Prasad Dwivedi, *op. cit.*, pp. 370–374.
22. G.A. Grierson, *op. cit.*, Vol. I, Part I, p. 130.
23. J. Richey, *Selections from Educational Records*, Calcutta, 1922, p. 255.
24. Quoted in Reena Chatterjee, *Impact of Raja Ram Mohan Roy on Education in India*, S. Chand, New Delhi, 1983, p. 108.
25. N.L. Basak, *Vernacular Education in Bengal*, Bharat Book Stall, Calcutta, 1974, pp. 309–310.
26. Paul R. Brass, *Language, Religion and Politics in North India*, Cambridge University Press, London, 1974.
27. H.S. Reid says, "In the Hindi schools, no textbook is used; all knowledge is orally communicated." *Op. cit.*, p. 73.
28. William Adam, *Reports on the State of Education in Bengal*, edited by A.N. Basu, Calcutta, 1941, p. 253.
29. *Bihar Bandhu*, 16 Dec. 1879, pp. 3–4.
30. *Bihar Herald*, August, 1880.
31. *Report of the Indian Education Commission (1882–1883)*, p. 343.
32. Ramchandra Shukla, *Hindi Sahitya Ka Itihas*, Nagari Praharini Sabha, Kashi, p. 305.
33. *Report of the members of the select committee for the better diffusion and advancement of learning among Muhammadans of India*, Banares, 1872.
34. *Harijan*, 30 July 1938.
35. *Ibid.*
36. Lajpat Rai, *The Problem of National Education in India*, Publication Division, 1966, p. 77.
37. Assembly Interpretation File No. 50, Sinha Library, Patna.
38. Home, Education, No. 424, 28 July 1863.
39. Jata Shankar Jha, *Education in Bihar*, KPJRI, Patna, 1979, p. 255.
40. Home, Education, No. 1068, 7 November 1864.

41. Brimer and Pauli, *Wastage in Education: A World Problem*, UNESCO, 1971, p. 24.
42. Home, Education, No. 1068, 9 November 1864, para 15.
43. Shakespear, *Memoir on the Statistics of the Northern Provinces of the Bengal Presidency*, Baptist Mission Press, Calcutta, 1948, pp. 11–12.
44. G.A. Grierson, *op. cit.*, Vol. I, Part I, p. 130.

Decline of Vernacular Education in Bihar in the Nineteenth Century

HETUKAR JHA

There was a well established network of village schools in the rural areas of Bihar during the early decades of the nineteenth century. William Adam inspected 285 such schools in the district of South Bihar and 80 in the district of Tirhut in the painstaking survey of indigenous mass education which he conducted between 1835 and 1838 in Bihar and Bengal.[1] In the schools of South Bihar, only 37.5% of the total number of students belonged to upper-caste groups; the rest, including 1.61% scheduled-caste students, belonged to 44 lower castes such as gandhabanik, koiri, goala, napit, barhai, kalwar, mali, kandu, churihar, beldar, dosadh, dhobi and musahar. Similarly, in Tirhut, only 31.07% of the total number of students belonged to the upper castes.[2] Details are given in Tables 1 and 2. A little before Adam's survey, Buchanan had estimated the number of schools in 1811 at 765 in the district of Patna-Gaya.[3]

The teachers in these schools were a mixed lot caste-wise; Adam did not notice a monopoly by any particular community.[4] The syllabi were more or less uniform in both districts: agricultural accounts, commercial accounts, and some books in the vernacular. In the north-eastern part of north Bihar, the medium of instruction was Maithili.[5]

The uniformity of syllabi and the spread of the school network over a vast tract indicate that education had become institutionalized as part of rural life. This must have taken a

TABLE 1 Village schools in South Bihar in 1835–38

	No. of students		No. of students
Upper castes		Scheduled castes	
1. Magadha*	468	1. Dosad	23
2. Brahmin	256	2. Pashi	22
3. Kayastha	220	3. Dhobi	1
4. Rajput	150	4. Musahar	1
Total	1094 (37.5%)	Total	47 (1.61%)
Lower castes		Lower castes	
1. Gandhabanik	540	21. Bhatta	15
2. Teli	271	22. Sanyasi	14
3. Koiri	200	23. Banawar	14
4. Kahar	102	24. Lohar	13
5. Halwakar	66	25. Lahari	13
6. Sunri	56	26. Kumar	10
7. Kurmi	55	27. Kandu	9
8. Swarnkar	51	28. Yugi	8
9. Mahuri	42	29. Beljar	8
10. Napit	39	30. Bundela	4
11. Goala	38	31. Patowar	4
12. Barhai	35	32. Vaishnava	2
13. Suvarnabanik	31	33. Khatki	2
14. Aguri	21	34. Tanti	1
15. Luniar	20	35. Mahla	1
16. Kansyabanik	20	36. Baiti	1
17. Kshtriya	18	37. Chhatri	1
18. Kalwar	18	38. Barayi	1
19. Mali	16	39. Churihara	1
20. Tamil	16	40. Kayali	1
		Total	1778 (61%)

*Bhumihar brahmin.

TABLE 2 Village schools in Tirhut in 1835–38

	No. of students		*No. of students*
Upper castes		Scheduled castes	
1. Rajput	62	1. Pashi	5
2. Kayastha	51		
3. Brahmin	25		
4. Magadha	18		
Total	156 (31.07%)		(0.99%)
Lower castes		Lower castes	
1. Sunri	72	14. Koiri	5
2. Kalal	40	15. Dhanuk	5
3. Gandhabanik	32	16. Tamil	4
4. Teli	29	17. Kamar	4
5. Mayra	28	18. Kansari	4
6. Swarnakar	25	19. Napit	4
7. Kandu	18	20. Kaivarta	2
8. Aguri	17	21. Chhaipikar	2
9. Karmi	11	22. Parsua	2
10. Luniar	9	23. Lahari	2
11. Goala	8	24. Sutar	2
12. Kshatriya	7	25. Kahar	2
13. Mahla	6	26. Khatti	1
		Total	341 (67.92%)

long time, so the system might well have existed in the rural areas since at least the pre-modern era. The schools managed to equip peasant children from different castes and communities with enough competence to carry out their future professional obligations.

It was this education that Fraser favoured, and in 1823 he asked the General Committee of Public Instruction to support it.[6] William Adam, of course, canvassed for it seriously. But in 1835, William Bentinck accepted Macaulay's pleas in favour of English education. The latter believed in the filtration theory of education and therefore ignored mass education. Following the 1835 decision, the vast network of vernacular village schools gradually collapsed. They owed their existence to the village lands granted to them for maintenance, and the weekly fees (in both cash and kind) given to the teachers by the villagers. The villages themselves lost the lands, since the British authorities were not prepared to leave any land revenue-free.[7] Having thus lost their base and the patronage of the authorities, these schools, where students of all castes and communities had been given cost-free instruction in vernacular languages, were eventually forced to become extinct.

There were some in Bihar who valued the old educational system and later tried their best to revive it. S. MacIntosh, the headmaster of Patna High School during the 1840s, was one such person. On his own he established 11 vernacular schools in the neighbourhood of Patna, and both the Hindu and Muslim communities sent their children to them enthusiastically. According to the records of the Council of Education for the year 1844, there were 647 students comprising 57 brahmins, 5 babhans (bhumihar brahmins), 34 kshatriyas (rajputs), 128 vaishyas, 366 shudras and 57 Muslims.[8] MacIntosh's efforts were quite successful, but eventually, he ran out of funds and had to close the schools.[9] The colonial education policy was elitist and biased towards urban areas. Vernacular education for the masses meant centres spread all over the rural hinterland. How could the authorities spare money for a system that did not conform to their policy?

However, efforts to revive vernacular education in Bihar were made again a few decades later, this time under the leadership of the Darbhanga Raj. This estate was under the court of wards since 1860. Its General Manager, J. Furlong, wanted to spread elementary education among the tenantry and, in 1866, devised a scheme to do this. He corresponded with the government to get its approval, and also wrote letters to the proprietors of the indigo factories located in the jurisdiction of Darbhanga Raj to contribute. The government's sanction came in due course, and indigo factory owners like M.H.L. Gale of Pandaul, George Falkner of Muzaffarpur, Saunders and J.F.K. Misselback of Purnea, and J. Macrae of Huttawry agreed to contribute 0.5% of their total rental.[10] Accordingly, 26 vernacular schools were opened in the following villages within the jurisdiction of the Raj: (1) Serai Bakerganj, (2) Sripur Gahar, (3) Jhanjharpur, (4) Dahibhat Madhopur, (5) Behta, (6) Bhija, (7) Rusiari, (8) Bhowarah, (9) Harinagar, (10) Bilaspur, (11) Jale, (12) Dhurwarrah, (13) Bajitpur Thukra, (14) Koili, (15) Nagarbasti, (16) Bahera, (17) Kamrauli, (18) Simri, (19) Sariso-Pahi, (20) Kusma, (21) Mokarampur, (22) Narar, (23) Narahiapatti, (24) Kanhauli, (25) Bhagwatipur, (26) Arair. The selected villages were probably considered important in their respective localities.

Unlike MacIntosh, Furlong paid attention to the funds required to run the schools. The schoolhouses were built by the Raj, and an amount of Rs 38 per school was earmarked for monthly expenditure.[11] The Commissioner of Patna division considered this amount too much. In a letter to the Collector of Tirhut on June 8, 1869, he wrote:

> It appears that the average monthly cost of each school is about Rs 38. This, I think, is far more than was originally intended. It is my impression that cheap village schools should be maintained by the Raj. All we attempt is to bring about a taste for education by introducing a few schools where children can learn the rudiments of the languages they are to speak and write.[12]

The Raj, however, continued to spend the amount and, by 1871, many of the schools had become fully established. Although 5 schools soon closed due to management problems, the remaining 21 had more than 700 students, most of them from the lower castes.[13] The Raj authorities were happy to note the success of their scheme. Subsequently, they appointed a deputy inspector of schools to supervise their working. In 1873, five more schools were established in the district of

Munger. The entire Raj network of vernacular schools served rural Bihar society by imparting primary education to the children of tenants, particularly those from the lower castes.

Unfortunately, most of these vernacular schools were closed by the end of the nineteenth century upon the death of the enlightened head of the Darbhanga estate, Maharaja Lakshmishwar Singh. The reasons were many. According to Raj records:

> In some localities, the ryots for whose benefit these schools had been established were averse to education, and preferred their children helping them in the field to receiving instruction in the school. In some localities, the ryots of some villages behaved very badly and stopped paying rents to the Raj, and consequently, the Raj either shifted the school to some other village or abolished it. Yet another cause for the unpopularity of these schools was the growing tendency among the people to give their children English education.[14]

It is probable that the first two reasons for withdrawing support—the lack of interest and conflict over payments—were highlighted by the Raj. To see why, we should take a closer look at this estate.

Of all the zamindaris of Bihar, only Darbhanga Raj considered it important enough to educate the peasantry to launch a full-fledged scheme for it.[15] This occurred when the Raj was under the administration of the court of wards. Then, in 1879, the management went into the hands of the proprietor, Lakshmishwar Singh. When he died, his younger brother, Rameshwar Singh, took over the estate in 1898–99. Rameshwar was more orthodox and promoted Sanskrit education, so vernacular education fell from favour. The first two reasons cited by the Raj for closure could not have been completely absent at the time of Furlong. Yet his scheme had been successful. Lakshmishwar Singh, too, realized the importance of the scheme and continued to support it. But when Rameshwar Singh took over, he could conveniently use the above-mentioned factors to stop further support to vernacular education.

The third factor noted in the Raj records is the increasing popularity of English education. In this connection, O'Malley writes:

> The number of middle vernacular schools, i.e., schools which read up to the middle scholarship, but in which the vernacular is the only recognized medium of instruction and forms the only course of studies, was 22 in 1880, and has declined steadily ever since ... All these schools are situated in the interior of the district, and are maintained entirely by the Darbhanga Raj ... The constant decrease in the number of schools, as well as in that of the pupils attending them, accompanied, as it has been, by a corresponding rise in the number and attendance of the high and middle English schools, conclusively proves a growing preference for English education among the people.[16]

Thus, what O'Malley says accords with the Raj records. However, while English education had earned social value at the end of the nineteenth century, only the upper castes preferred it. Even among them, only the kayasthas and bhumihar brahmins had taken steps to promote English education. The rest of the Bihar upper castes, rajputs and maithili brahmins, were not so serious about it.

The kayasthas were the first to establish a caste association in Bihar: the *All-India Kayastha Sabha*, established 1887.[17] The bhumihar brahmins followed suit in 1889 with their *Pradhan Bhumihar Brahman Sabha*.[18] These associations were mainly aimed at getting more and more of their (male) members educated in English, for this secured jobs in administration. These jobs carried authority and were valued in their society. The rajputs were attached to their zamindaris and did not wish to work under anyone; they had enough of their own to manage. They were reported to be very arrogant and superstitious, fearing religious conversion through English education.[19]

The brahmins of Mithila were too orthodox to allow their children to learn English, so the progress of English education in this community was very slow. In the 1860s, Lakshmishwar Singh and Rameshwar Singh were the first maithil brahmins to get English education. The first graduate from this group was Vindhyanatha Jha, who passed his B.A. examinations in 1888. A maithil brahmin directory prepared in 1917 records 6 M.A.s, 39 B.A.s, 41 I.A.s and 155 matriculates.[20] It is obvious from these figures that English education was not at all valued by many brahmins of the nineteenth century. The lower castes formed their own sabhas later, in the first two decades of the twentieth century,[21] presumably in imitation of the kayasthas and bhumihar brahmins. They had not yet organized themselves in the nineteenth century.

Therefore, since English education was preferred by only two caste groups, one cannot ascribe the decline of vernacular education to the people of Bihar in general. The other castes either considered it defiling or thought it was beyond their reach. For them, the system of vernacular education could have proved useful. Also, the vernacular schools were located in the villages, while the English schools were in urban areas only. Worse, the government made efforts to convert vernacular pathshalas and maktabs into government primary schools. In his study of Patna district, Hagen writes in this context:

> In one year, 1872 to 1873, primary schools on the government rolls went from zero to 264. These were not created like the higher schools had been, but rather, it was a matter of negotiating with the teachers of indigenous primary schools, only pathshalas at first, and then the maktabs after 1877, regarding whether they would accept a monthly stipend and materials in exchange for inspection and government recognition. This then did not constitute the creation of primary schools in the district, but rather the annexation of the indigenous system, and the beginning of their cultural transformation.[22]

Vernacular education also lost the support of the elites, so it virtually ceased to be part of any recognized educational system by the end of the last century. However, it seems that some people tried their best to continue it where they could afford to do so. The notes appended to the first cadastral survey of Bihar in 1900–1901 mention the existence of vernacular schools in the following villages: Baghant (Gopalpur pargana), Kathra (Lvam pargana), Haraitha (Dharaur pargana), Punahad (Dharaur pargana), Korthu (Dharaur pargana), Bangrahta (Ahis pargana), Dumri (Ahilwar pargana), Afzala (Ahilwar pargana), and Akharpur (Ahilwar pargana).[23] All these villages were in Bahera thana of Darbhanga district. The villagers found this education useful, and somehow managed to secure local support for it.

In general, though, the present century has seen continued suppression of vernacular education. The report of the census of 1911 records the declining popularity of vernacular schools in Bengal and Bihar.[24] It was prepared by O'Malley, who had earlier noted the same decline in the *Darbhanga District Gazetteer* of 1907. He had then ascribed it to the rising popularity of English education. As has already been pointed out, this assertion is valid only for two caste groups, not all the people. Later, in the *Report on the Progress of Education in Bihar for the Year 1937–38*, one finds the following: "The Patna district board has recently decided to convert all their middle vernacular schools into middle English schools."[25] Clearly, the process of annexing the vernacular system to the government primary system, begun in 1872-73, continued unabated.

In 1937-38, the senate of Patna University asked the government to appoint a committee to plan the reorganization of primary, secondary, university and technical education in Bihar.[26] The committee that was subsequently formed had T.K. Shah as chairman, with Sachchidanand Sinha (vice-chancellor of Patna University), Rajendra Prasad, H.R. Batheja, Zakir Hussain, Amaranatha Jha and others as members. At its first meeting in 1939, the committee decided that the mother tongue would be the medium of education at the primary stage in order to enhance literacy in Bihar. They had returned to the essence of vernacular education. But the mood changed in

1940; the members reversed themselves and opted for Hindi as the common medium for all the different zones of Bihar. Amaranatha Jha was the only dissenter, but his efforts were in vain; the elite of Bihar represented in the committee sealed the fate of vernacular education in this state.[27]

To recapitulate, vernacular education was ignored by the colonial government because it favoured English education. The Darbhanga Raj had boldly launched a scheme for its revival in the second half of the nineteenth century, but eventually withdrew its support. In the present century, even before independence, the political and intellectual elite of the state were divided into conflicting camps that favoured Hindi, Hindustani or Urdu.[28] They ended up suppressing the local vernaculars and introducing Hindi. This language was never the mother tongue of any section of the vast rural population of Bihar.

Notes

1. A.N. Basu (ed.), *Reports on the State of Education in Bengal (1835–1838) by William Adam*, University of Calcutta, 1941, pp. 243–245.
2. *Ibid.*, pp. 245–247.
3. James Ray Hagen, *Indigenous Society: The Political Economy and Colonial Education in Patna District—A History of Social Change from 1811 to 1951 in Gangetic North India*, Ph.D. thesis, University of Virginia, University Microfilms International, 1981, pp. 256–257.
4. A.N. Basu, *op. cit.*, pp. 243.
5. *Ibid.*, pp. 247.
6. Henry Sharp (ed.), *Selections from Educational Records*, Part I, Government Printing Press, Calcutta, 1920, pp. 13–14.
7. C.J. Stevenson-Moore, *Final Report on the Survey and Settlement Operation in the Muzaffarpur District, 1892–1899*, Government Printing Press, Patna, p. 85.
8. J.S. Jha, "Education in Bihar", in K.K. Dutta (ed.), *History of Modern Bihar*, pp. 396–400.
9. *Ibid.*
10. J.S. Jha, *Beginnings of Modern Education in Mithila: Selections*

from the Educational Records of the Darbhanga Raj, K.P. Jayaswal Research Institute, Patna, 1972, pp. xii–xiii and pp. 9–11.

11. *Ibid*., pp. xiii.
12. Quoted by J.S. Jha, *op. cit*., p. 18.
13. *Ibid*., pp. xiv–xv.
14. *Ibid*., pp. xiv–xv.
15. *Ibid*., pp. x.
16. L.S.S. O'Malley, "Darbhanga", *Bengal District Gazetteers*, Bengal Secretariat Book Depot, Calcutta, 1907, p. 137.
17. J.S. Jha, *Early Revolutionary Movement in Bihar*, K.P. Jayaswal Research Institute, Patna, 1977, pp. 14–15.
18. *Ibid*., p. 17.
19. See Lantour's report quoted by J.S. Jha, *Beginnings of Modern Education in Mithila, op. cit*., p. xvi.
20. Yoganand Kumar, *Maithil Brahman Directory* (in Maithili), Darbhanga, 1917, pp. 9–29.
21. J.S. Jha, *Early Revolutionary Movement in Bihar, op cit*., p. 17.
22. James Ray Hagen, *op. cit*., p. 379.
23. Notes on about 7,000 villages located on both sides of the river Ganga were collected by the author in the 1970s. The village notes referred to here form part of this collection.
24. L.S.S. O'Malley, *Census of India*, 1911, Vol. V, Part I, Bengal Secretariat Book Depot, Calcutta, 1913, p. 366.
25. *Reports on the Progress of Education in Bihar for the Year 1937–38*. Government Printing Press, Bihar, Patna, 1939, p. 26.
26. *Ibid*., p. 15.
27. Detailed proceeding of this committee have been cited by the author in this context in *Amaranatha Jha* (series on the makers of Indian literature, in press), Sahitya Akademi, New Delhi, pp. 95–102.
28. For details see Z.A. Ahmad (ed.), *National Language for India*, Kitabistan, Allahabad, 1941.

Law and Politics of Primary Education in Bengal

POROMESH ACHARYA

In Bengal, a close relationship can easily be traced between the spread of school education and the rise of communal politics. It is true that communal strife between Hindu and Muslim bhadralok had sharpened at the turn of the 20th century due to the partition of Bengal. However, communal conflict also surfaced every time the government mooted an act on either primary or secondary education. It occurred, for example, in the 1920s when a primary education bill was introduced in the Legislative Council, and in the 1930s when a secondary education bill came up in the Legislative Assembly. Thus, there seems to be an interesting link between educational development and the rise of communal politics. This paper will attempt a descriptive discourse on the law and politics of primary education in Bengal. It will describe successive primary education acts in terms of decentralization of management and functional modality.

The demand for free and compulsory primary education in Bengal was first raised in 1869 at a meeting of the Bethune Society of Calcutta by Lal Behari Dey, the famous author of *Bengal Peasant Life* and *Folk Tales of Bengal* (Bagal, 1367, p. 109). But it was not until 1904 that the government of India, through a resolution on its Indian Education Policy, accepted that the extension of primary education was a state responsibility. It declared that the rapid spread of elementary education was "one of the foremost duties of the state" (Sen,

1941, p. 177–178). It is interesting to note that it was Governor-General Curzon who was responsible for this change in policy. Throughout the previous century, the policy was one of "downward filtration", despite attempts by Mayo and Campbell to tilt it towards primary education. It was the Hindu bhadralok who had successfully stalled these attempts (Acharya, 1995, pp. 670–673). They wished to confine education to the higher classes. A few exceptions were Lal Behari Dey, Keshab Chandra Sen and Bankim Chandra Chattopadhyay.

Until 1904, even the Indian National Congress never demanded free, compulsory primary education, although it had passed resolutions every year since its inception for higher and secondary education. In that year, finally, it thanked the government for its increased outlay on primary education, and asked for a larger allotment "to spread primary education more widely among the mass of the people, and to make a beginning in the direction of free and compulsory education." It was only in 1906 that this request became a demand (Chakrabarty and Bhattacharyya, 1935, pp. 132–133). In fact, the Indian National Congress moved only after Curzon took the initiative (Basu, Aparna).

All this proves the apathy of the Indian elite towards education for the common people. In Bengal, it went a bit beyond apathy. School education there had been developed at the private initiative of the Hindu bhadralok. Government policy was to encourage such initiatives through aid and inspection. The small grants-in-aid they got helped the landed gentry run their schools. However, higher education was far more expensive and needed substantial state support, even for the landed gentry. These people, mostly Hindus in Bengal, followed the British in viewing higher education as the apex of a ladder they had to climb. Funds for education were limited, and primary education could only grow at the cost of higher education, at least, so the bhadralok perceived. The alternative of an education cess was considered an infringement. It might lead to permanent settlements in violation of their land rights. Although not really hostile to primary education, the bhadralok would not allow it to spread at the cost of their own educational interests.

Gradually, however, a perceptible change took place in the attitudes of many Indian political leaders. The concept of primary education as a state responsibility was, by and large, accepted in principle. Gopal Krishna Gokhale demanded it in the Imperial Legislative Council on 19 March 1910:

> It is this, that without a resort to compulsion, no state can ensure a general diffusion of education among its people. England, with her strong love of individualism, stood out against the principle of compulsion for as long as she could, but she had to give way in the end all the same.

Gokhale wanted an Indian equivalent of the English Education Act of 1870, empowering local bodies to make elementary education compulsory and free in their areas.

District education boards, introduced in the 1880s, had been active in elementary education (Roy, 1936, p. 89). However, for want of adequate funds, they could not extend it. They relied more on aiding "privately" managed institutions rather than maintaining their own schools. Most district boards were anyway under the control of Hindu bhadralok. Any shift of responsibility for primary education from district boards to other bodies would appear to them as a threat.

Gokhale failed to carry his bill in the Imperial Legislative Council, but his moves had an impact on government education policy. His proposals in the Council over three successive years set the future direction of free, compulsory primary education. The government framed an education policy in 1913, but it was only in 1919 that, for the first time, an act was passed to expand and regulate primary education in Bengal. By the 1920s, universal, compulsory, free primary education had moved onto the agenda of educational discourse in Bengal. While accepting this goal, the various communities of Bengal could not agree on how to get there. The main differences concerned the management and administrative structure needed to regulate the primary schools at the district level.

L.S.S. O'Malley, the Director of Public Instruction in Bengal, appointed E.E. Biss in 1920 to draw up a programme for the expansion and improvement of primary education. In 1921, the district boards met at a conference and resolved that "the intention of making primary education free and compulsory as soon as possible be accepted as a directive idea" (Biss, 1921, p. 20). Biss also submitted his report in 1921, and in that year, the 1919 act was amended to cover first, all the municipalities, and later, the union boards under the Bengal Local Self-Government Act of 1885. For long, however, the act remained a dead letter, except in the Calcutta corporation and Chittagong municipal areas. A bill was mooted in 1927, but the comprehensive Bengal (Rural) Primary Education Act was passed only in 1930 to enable a partial decentralization of the system.

The 1930 act constituted district school boards separate from the existing district boards. Their job was to establish new schools where required, give recognition and aid to privately initiated schools, maintain the schools, and manage the provident funds and other annuities of the teachers. They were also to conduct surveys to ascertain the requirements for primary education facilities in each district, and to appoint teachers according to these requirements. They were further authorized to levy an education cess and make primary education compulsory where possible. However, the union boards were made responsible for enforcing the compulsion in their jurisdictions. It was expected that compulsion could be introduced within ten years.

To monitor the system, a Sub-Inspector of schools supervised every 100 schools under a district inspectorate which, in turn, was under the direct control of the Director of public instruction. The sub-inspectors had to visit the schools at regular intervals and then report to the district Inspector of schools. The district school boards would give recognition and aid only on the basis of these inspection reports. Thus, the school Inspectors played the role of intermediaries between the school and the district- and state-level authorities. The inspectorate was also a monitoring agency.

Through a resolution passed in March, 1937, the Bengal government constituted a central primary education committee to prepare the curricula, arrange approvals for textbooks, and formulate policies for efficient functioning of the system. This committee was of the opinion that English should not be taught in primary schools and the primary departments of secondary schools (Sen, J.M., 1941, pp. 205–243). Even earlier, E.E. Biss had opined that English should be taught as a special subject from Class III, and only in those schools where competent teachers were available (Biss, 1920, pp. 19, 20).

Noteworthy is the hierarchical system of management, with different layers and parallel structures, that had been created. Policies were determined by the state-level authority, they were carried out by the district school board, and supervision was done by the inspectorate. Finally, the school committees and teachers were responsible for translating policy into practice. For some aspects, like enforcing universal enrolment, yet another agency, the union board, entered the scene. By a 1946 order of the state government, an attendance committee for each rural school had to be appointed by the union board or panchayat. This committee had to secure proper attendance in its school, else the appointing authority could suspend it. In Calcutta, however, managing committees were retained. The entire process was supervised and monitored by the inspectorate, which was accountable to the directorate of education. The whole system worked only so long as primary education grew slowly, but when, after independence, it acquired momentum, the system's weaknesses became apparent.

In 1950, major amendments were made to the 1930 act to get closer to the goal of universal, compulsory primary education in West Bengal. The new act said that compulsion could be introduced "in any area lying within the jurisdiction of a union board, union committee or panchayat," and that "once a pupil in the rural areas is admitted to Class I of a primary or junior basic school, he or she must continue till the course is completed." A quinquennial review on the progress of education in West Bengal from 1947-48 to 1951-52 claimed: "A ten-year scheme for the introduction of compulsory primary education in the rural areas made considerable progress during the period under review. Compulsion was introduced in 94 unions and 3,664 villages." About the difficulty in making education compulsory, the review says, "Parents and guardians often required the assistance of boys of school-going age in their work, and this was made an excuse for non-attendance at school. There were indeed attendance committees and provisions for penalty, but these local committees were seldom inclined to take strict measures against delinquents" (Quinquennial Review, 1959, pp. 4, 5).

To extend free, compulsory primary education to the municipal areas, the West Bengal government passed another act in 1963. However, progress in these areas was anything but satisfactory. In 1964, only the municipalities of Khardah (24-Parganas district) and Jangipur (Murshidabad district) introduced free, compulsory primary education, while it had been in force before 1963 in five wards of Calcutta Corporation. A septennial review on the progress of education in West Bengal from 1957-1958 to 1963-1964 reported that only 81% of the children aged 6–11 were attending school in the compulsory areas in 1963-64, against 79.6% percent in 1960-1961. This was despite the fact that there was provision for supplying all the approved textbooks and writing materials (slates and pencils) free of cost to needy children (25% of the enrolment). Another statistic showed that, in 1963-1964, 78.6% of the total child population in the age-group 6–11 had enrolled, compared to 76.4% in 1962-1963, 68.3% in 1960-1961 and 65.3% in 1955-1956 (Septennial Review, pp. 11, 12, 13). Unfortunately, a 68% drop-out rate renders these enrolment figures meaningless, even if we take them at face value.

The 1930 act had provision for school attendance committees to ensure universal enrolment and retention of children in compulsory areas. The union boards were entrusted with the task of constituting these committees. They were responsible for compulsory attendance, but had no role to play in policy-making or even preparing the curricula of their choice. They merely had to follow the course determined for them by higher authority. It was no wonder that the union boards were not too enthusiastic about trying to make school attendance compulsory within their jurisdictions.

According to the quinquennial review, "the local bodies to whom the task of organizing and administering primary education was entrusted could not discharge their duty satisfactorily mainly because of party politics and communal dissension" (Quinquennial Review, 1959, p. 19). Ananthanath Basu, a renowned educationalist of the time, wrote (*Primary Education in India: Its Future*, pp. 12, 13):

> The cause of the failure of the local authorities to implement the provisions of the primary education acts and to build up a well-organized system of compulsory primary education are not far to seek. Firstly, we may note that, under the provision of the ... acts, the option of introducing compulsion rested with the local authorities. There was no provision in them for a central directive authority. Secondly, the imposition of the education cess was also left to the option of the local authorities. One who knows anything about these boards can easily imagine what may have been the result of such option. No elective body, specially of the type of these district and municipal boards, would care to introduce a new cess and face unpopularity and risk defeat in elections ... The fate of compulsion under such circumstances was naturally sealed, and a universal system of compulsory primary education still remains an unfulfilled dream of educationists and politicians.

The passage of the 1930 Bengal (Rural) Primary Education Act did not follow a smooth course. First, a comprehensive bill was drawn in 1927 by the Secretary of the education department of the government of Bengal. Then the permission of the government of India had to be obtained. Meanwhile, the Bengal education minister, B. Chakravarty resigned, and a new minister Nawab Musharruf Hossain introduced the bill to the Bengal legislative council in August, 1928. Justifying provisions in the bill for a new cess and a separate administrative body called a district school board, he said:

> It is not difficult to show that the present system can only be reorganized by the expenditure of a large sum of money. This the present bill aims at providing in part, if not entirely. I should like to say that the bill aims at taxing those who are owners of land, either as zamindar or tenancy holder or as an occupancy raiyat, and those people who carry on trade as a profession but are not owners of land. It may be said here that the bargadars, adhairs and other labourers will not have to contribute anything towards the fund ... After careful consideration, 4 pice on the raiyats and 1 pice on the landlords has been proposed in the bill, and it is not difficult to see that these proportions are equitable.

He calculated that the landlords would have to pay 1/56 of their net income, while the raiyats would pay 1/288 theirs. Regarding the setting up of district school boards, he said (Council Proceedings, pp. 519–520):

> Important provisions of the bill deal with the establishment of district school boards for the purpose of administering the act. I cannot too strongly emphasize the necessity of utilizing, in the initial stage, the most expert administrative machinery available. The problems which will confront the boards will be novel and far from easy to solve. In order to ensure that the scheme will have the best possible start, it is proposed to have a strong official element on the boards during the first few terms of their operation and, later, to increase the non-official element.

The entire debate on the bill centred on the new education cess and the constitution of district school boards separate from the existing district boards. Initially, the main opposition to the bill was nationalistic. J.L. Banerjee, a nationalist leader with strong secular views, said that the constitution of a separate district school board amounted to transferring administrative control from an elected non-official body to an *ad hoc* official body headed by an English district magistrate no way superior to Indians. Banerjee rejected the argument of efficiency and, noting that the district boards had come under non-official control only six years before, he saw a plot to transfer power back away from them. He argued (Council Proceedings, 1928, pp. 521–526):

> If the government had been *bona fide* in their desire of promoting self-government and of promoting the spread of education, they would have entrusted the work of administering the proceeds of the new education cess to the district boards, and would not have gone out of their way for the purpose of creating a new machinery altogether ... Apart from these very vital and fundamental considerations, there is another glaring defect in the bill. Throughout the bill, from the first to last, there is not one word about education—how instruction is to be imparted, how the curriculum is to be drawn up, and who are to be the final authorities for settling these points. Here is an education bill introduced by the honourable minister for education which is directly silent on the vital question of education itself. It is a bill not for the purpose of spreading education but for raising funds and administering the same by the agency of government officials.

Banerjee was joined by J.M. Sengupta, a leader of the National Congress, in questioning the *bona fide* intentions of the government. Another opponent was Maulvi Abdul Karim, who said (Council Proceedings, 1928, pp. 529, 535, 536):

> The ... bill, as it stands at present, is open to much justifiable criticism ... I think it would be unwise to make primary education compulsory until the system is so

> revised as to make it really useful to the masses. The prevailing system, which has been in operation for about half a century, has not improved either the knowledge or the condition, specially of the rural population; it has not made the cultivators better cultivators, nor the artisans more efficient artisans. On the contrary, it has proved detrimental to their interest, in as much as it has created in them a distaste for manual labour and for their hereditary callings and modes of living. They ... know nothing else by which they can make an honest living. They are thus not only unemployed but also unemployable, and they accelerate rather than retard the decadence of indigenous arts and help to aggravate the economic difficulty prevailing in the country.

He felt the only way to educate Muslim boys was to combine the secular education of the pathshalas with the religious education of the maktabs. Without such a combination, compulsory primary education would be resented by the Muslim community, he said. Abdul Karim was silent about separate district school boards and the proposed education cess. Indirectly, he was unhappy with the present, expensive primary education, and was all praise for the inexpensive, indigenous pathshalas.

Banerjee and Sengupta were not against the education cess, but would not allow full official control over the fund, fearing the people would not get their money's worth. They also considered it iniquitous to levy 4 pice from the poor tenants and 1 pice from the zamindars. On the other hand, Surendra Nath Roy and Raja Bhupendra Narayan Sinha Bahadur of Nashipur opposed the new tax altogether. According to them, the peasants were already overtaxed, and the zamindars would not benefit by the measure either directly or indirectly (Council Proceedings, 1928, pp. 541, 544–45).

Maulvi Tamizuddin Khan also spoke on the education cess: "It is no doubt regrettable that government has not been able to find money without fresh taxation for the discharge of one of its primary functions. It is also true that the people are already overtaxed. The objection raised against the bill on the score of overtaxation is therefore a legitimate one." However, he said the cess would bring good, and since "the government cannot and will not spend the requisite money out of its existing resources, [the raiyats would] gladly submit to the assessment." He made an interesting observation in this regard: "The brahmins and the baidyas, cent per cent of whom are literate, will not be benefited by the act. Mussalmans, namasudras and other low-class denominations of the Hindu community are the people who will reap the greatest benefit, and surely they have reasons to be enthusiastic over the measure." Tamizuddin Khan opposed separate district school boards, saying the district boards were competent enough to carry the responsibility of primary education, even at a lower cost. He said, "It is regrettable that government [proposes] to deprive the district boards of what is almost universally believed to be their legitimate right" (Council Proceedings, 1928, pp. 543–550).

Maulvi Abul Kasem supported both separate district school boards and a fresh tax, but said the tax was not equitable. He thought that "there should be statutory provision [in the Bill] for a substantial contribution by government towards the expansion of primary education. They may, if they like, and if their finances do not allow, curtail the expenditure on higher education, but they must make a substantial contribution out of the provincial resources." (Council Proceedings, 1928, pp. 559–560).

Ultimately, the bill was referred to a select committee of 32 members. But the Bengal Legislative Council was itself dissolved in 1929, so the committee's amended bill was automatically dropped.

Even before the 1927 introduction of the bill, opinions had been collected from district boards, government officials at district level, teacher's organizations, and a few religious and community organizations. They all opposed the bill on the two grounds mentioned above. (Collection of Opinions on the Bengal (Rural) Primary Education Bill, 1927, B.G. Press, 1928). Everyone felt that separate district school boards were not at all necessary, as the district boards were quite competent to look after primary education in their respective districts. If necessary, an education committee comprising a few members of the district board, persons interested in education, and concerned government officials could be formed for the task of expanding the facilities for primary education. The committee would work under the direct control of the district board. By contrast, the bill would create multiple authorities and cause confusion. Also found objectionable was the fact that the district school board would be an official body with nominated members and headed by a district magistrate. Such a body would probably fail to encourage the popular initiatives essential for the successful implementation of any scheme of popular education.

An opinion from 1936 goes as follows (Roy N.C., 1936, pp. 92–94):

> I do not think that the policy underlying the introduction of the separate school boards is in any way justifiable. It has been proved in different countries that local bodies become efficient instruments of administration only when different functions are concentrated in the same authority. When a body is commissioned to perform only one particular duty, it is unlikely that a sufficient number of able and desirable candidates will come forward to contest its membership ... Its administration also becomes unnecessarily expensive ... The members of a board which is concerned with several duties develop that sense of proportion and that practical imagination which can hardly be expected of people who are entrusted with the performance of one special duty ... The application of the act of 1930 has weakened the district boards without strengthening the cause of elementary education in this province.

In this connection, the Khulna district board maintained that it accorded "full support to the proposal of taking the union boards into confidence and working through them where possible. But if the school board is a district body separate from the district board, the union boards will have another master added to their already too many masters, the inevitable result being ultimate inefficiency" (Collection of Opinions, *op. cit.*, p. 4).

Except Birbhum, all the other district boards, landholder's associations, the All-Bengal and other district-level teacher's associations, and community organizations like Anjuman-i-Islamia were united in opposing fresh taxation in the form of an education cess to expand primary education. The consensus was that it was government that should bear the cost of free, compulsory primary education. Some, like the district board of Burdwan and the landholder's associations of Mymensingh, felt that there were enough primary schools, and the problem was the quality of education. Quite a large section of the landed gentry held this view, as did E.E. Biss, who observed, "What is needed in Bengal is not an increase in the number of primary schools but their proper and systematic organization and distribution on a well-defined plan." Biss noted that Madras had fewer schools but more students than Bengal. He also did not think compulsion could be introduced in the near future; he advocated free schools instead (Biss, 1921, p. 16). A few other organizations also thought that it was premature to introduce compulsion before the people were prepared for the measure. Some organizations like Anjuman-i-Islamia wanted teachers to be paid partly by monthly salary and partly by reward on the basis of results. They also wanted to pay the teachers a government pension. Another suggestion was to allow needy agricultural families to utilize the labour of their children by adjusting school hours, preferably in two shifts. Hardly any of these opinions was reflected in successive primary education bills.

After a new Legislative Council was constituted, McAlpin, as member-in-charge of education, introduced a fresh bill on 5 August 1929. It was based on the recommendations of the 1928 select committee with a few modifications. It was referred to another select committee of 45, mainly swarajist members, which made some radical changes. A new minister of education, Khaja Nazimuddin presented the new committee's report in March, 1930, and then moved for the withdrawal of the bill. Due to strong opposition from Swarajist members of the Council, the motion was carried by the narrow margin of three votes. Mitra (1930, p. 207) says the bill was withdrawn because it had been too heavily modified. A new bill was published in the *Calcutta Gazette* of 10 April 1930. At this point, the entire process took a communal turn, but the ground had been prepared earlier by the former minister, Nawab Musharruf Hossain.

In April, 1928, Musharruf Hossain had asked the Director of Public Instruction to issue a circular urging inspecting staff to explain to the people the main features of the 1928 bill and gather their opinions. Thousands of copies of two leaflets were distributed. Both were on the subject of promoting primary education in Bengal, but one was directed at the Muslims alone. Sen (1941, p. 218) says that "as a result of these steps taken by the education department, hundreds of meetings were held all over the province and the response was remarkable." The steps may have been in the right direction, but the second leaflet set a trend. Nazimuddin had used this trend to counter the Swarajists and turn the primary education bill into a communal issue.

Before introducing the bill, the minister had toured the Muslim-majority districts of Chittagong, Noakhali, Faridpur, Jessore, Bakerganj, Dacca and Mymensingh to campaign for it. He managed to create a frenzy to ensure the support of Muslim members of the Council. Fazl-ul-Huq, a prominent member, described it as "fever heat." The minister Nazimuddin did it again in the 1940s in connection with secondary education, but that is a different story.

When he introduced the bill to the Council on 13 August 1930, he spoke as follows (Council Proceedings, 1930, p. 207):

> This bill is based, more or less largely, on the report of the first select committee which was presided over by Nawab Masharruf Hossain. The modifications are slight. The most important is the ratio of the cess ... In the bill, we are providing that the ratio should be 1½ pice for the

> landlords and 3½ pice for the tenants. This is what may be called a compromise. [Both the] select committees altered the ratio of the cess, and made it 2 pice for the zamindars and 3 pice for the tenants in the first instance, and in the second, 2 pice for the zamindars and 2 pice for the tenants.

Note that the second select committee, composed mainly of swarajists, had reduced the total amount of cess while dividing it equally between zamindars and tenants. This was not acceptable to the British government. In fact, Council proceedings show that the official and European members always pulled strings from behind and had the last word. It would not have been possible for Nazimuddin to carry the bill without the support of these persons, even if he had all the Muslim members on his side.

A speech by A.K. Fazl-ul-Huq in the Council in connection with the 1930 bill reveals how communal frenzy had been created to compel Muslim members to vote for the bill even if they opposed it (Council Proceedings, 1930, pp. 237–238):

> I am bitterly opposed to the bill, not because I am less anxious than even the hon'ble minister himself to see a bill introduced for primary education in Bengal, but because I feel very strongly that to tax the overtaxed people even on such a measure is an act of absolute cruelty to the teeming millions whose interests are in our sacred trust. But the tour of the hon'ble minister throughout the Mohammedan districts of Bengal has created such an unprecedented enthusiasm that the feelings of the people have been worked up to fever heat, and even the poor clients who come to me for professional service ask me not to betray the Mohammedan cause by opposing the bill ... I for one cannot understand how the cause of primary education can be the cause either of the Musalmans or of the Hindus. I feel that the cause of primary education is as sacred a cause of the Musalmans as of the Hindus. I therefore found that the position was becoming delicate

> and that, although I was personally opposed to the bill, I promised the members of my group and conveyed that promise to the hon'ble minister, that I would be prepared to go with him to the lobby.

Fazl-ul-Haq fervently appealed to the minister to concede the demand of the vast majority of Hindu members that the bill should be referred to a select committee. He cautioned Nazimuddin against playing the game of the official members. He says (Council Proceedings, 1930, p. 239):

> My feeling is that we should support this motion for select committee. There is no denying the fact that the vast majority of Hindu members ... are in favour of a reference to the select committee. The Mohammedan members seem to be as keen on opposing this motion, and having this bill discussed and passed here and now. Sir, anything that divides the Indian members of this House into two watertight compartments should be most strongly opposed by everyone who has the good of the country at heart ... I would ask the hon'ble minister, who is himself a Mohammedan, and the Mohammedan members of this House, whether it will really be a triumph to vote down the Hindu members of this House with the help of [British] officials.

In the 1940s, ironically, Fazl-ul-Haq faced opposition, this time from the Hindu members of the Bengal Legislative Assembly, when he introduced the secondary education bill. On that occasion, too, Nazimuddin clinched the issue with the help of European members (Acharya, 1993, pp. 168–204).

On the day education minister Nazimuddin introduced his bill, the minister for local self-government, Kumar Shib Shekhareswar Ray, resigned in protest. As noted, the Swarajists (mainly Hindus) objected to the setting up of a separate school board to act as a censor on the elected district board, which had become non-official only six years ago. They thought the whole process was designed to scuttle the movement towards self-rule. They believed the British were playing the game of divide and rule. By contrast, many of the Muslim members of the Council thought it gave them an opportunity in local politics. The district boards were generally controlled and dominated by Hindus, so a separate, district-level official body with nominated members might give them some voice in politics at the district level. Provincial autonomy had sharpened political differences between Hindu and Muslim gentry. Local self-government and education were two issues that generated much heat and communal tension. It is unfortunate that both the primary and secondary education bills became acts through a process that contributed a lot to turn Bengal politics communal.

The motion to refer the bill to a select committee was made on 25 August 1930 by Sarat Kumar Ray. The minister objected that the bill had already undergone two select committees. He did not want any more delay. As we saw, a few Muslim members like Fazl-ul-Haq appealed to him not to accentuate the antagonism between the two communities by being so rigid. But Nazimuddin did not yield and the motion was put to a vote. All the Muslim and official members voted against, and most of the Hindu members voted in favour. The motion was defeated and the Hindu members walked out in protest. Along with the motion, lost also was the amity between the two communities.

On 26 August, the primary education bill finally became an act in the absence of the Hindu members of the Council. A few Muslim members such as Fazl-ul-Haq, Abdul Karim and Tamizuddin Khan moved some minor amendmends, but all of them were opposed by the European member, A.J. Dash, and rejected. Abdul Karim's amendment read, "A central committee of educated experts, of whom one-third shall be official and two-thirds non-official, shall be constituted to prescribe the syllabus of studies for primary schools under this act, provided that the local government shall have power to dissolve or reconstitute this committee if necessary."

The minister Nazimuddhin was a pawn in a game planned by the official and European members. It is no wonder that a bill passed in this way could not yield the desired result.

Despite the force of an official act, primary education could only limp along in Bengal. A 1941 analysis viewed the situation thus (Sen, 1941, p. 236):

> The actual position is that, apart from a few primary schools controlled by local authorities, mission schools, and the primary classes of secondary schools, the primary school organization of today is of very doubtful value. Far from there being 64,000 useful primary schools in the province, it is safe to say that the number of schools which are effectively contributing towards the removal of illiteracy is not more than 5,000 at a generous estimate.

The number of primary schools, teachers and students has increased remarkably after independence, but conditions did not change in any qualitative way. By 1950, the primary education act of 1930 had been enforced in almost all the districts of West Bengal. It was extended in 1964 to the newly formed district of Purulia as well. As opposed to the rural emphasis of the 1930 legislation, an urban primary education act was passed in 1963 to provide for free and compulsory primary education in the municipal areas of West Bengal. It required the commissioners of every municipality to submit detailed proposals within a year. Although attendance committees had been set up as far back as 1946 for the rural areas, compulsion was not really given effect in any municipality or district school board. Low enrolment and high drop-out rates continued as before. With increase in the number of government schools and teachers came politics, and corruption in appointments and maintenance.

In 1969, the government replaced all district school boards by advisory committees. However, without any statutory provisions, these committees remained informal in character. Virtually all control over primary schools was in the hands of the local district inspector of schools, while school management came under the direct control of the directorate of public instruction. The advisory committees took on more members in 1970, and district magistrates became *ex officio* chairmen. The district inspectors of schools, however, remained the chief executives and member-secretaries of the committees. Successive office orders kept reconstituting the committees without any change in their real status. During the period from 1965 to 1975, school education seemed to go nowhere. The advisory committee's members were nominated, so they all belonged to the ruling political party. There was unprecedented politicization, which almost ruined the system.

In this context, the government of West Bengal passed another primary education act in 1973 in order to restructure state- and district-level authorities. Superseding all previous acts, new bodies such as the West Bengal board of primary education and district primary school councils were created at state and district levels. The membership of the board and the councils were both elected and nominated, and these organs were separated from the zila parishads. The elected members were from different categories of electorates, such as primary teacher members of the legislative assembly. Persons interested in education were nominated by the state government. There were also government officials as *ex officio* members. The process of constituting the board and councils was made very cumbrous. One wonders if this was done to maintain state control over these bodies.

Like the district school boards, the district primary school councils were separate bodies, without an organic link or relation to the local self-government (zila parishads). The former had been under the direct control of the state government, which could both direct them and supersede them by order. By contrast, the 1973 act created a state-level authority between state council and district council. In this centralized, hierarchical structure, the district councils were placed under the overall control and supervision of the state board. For all practical purposes, they would have no autonomy in matters of policy formulation, curriculum preparation, etc. While all meetings of the old district school boards were open to anyone who wished to attend as an observer without the right to speak or vote, the district primary school councils were closed bodies, as was the West Bengal board of primary education.

The state board of primary education was the real controlling body, answerable only to the state government. There was no ambiguity of roles between the policy-making state board and implementing district councils. However, the relation between the councils and the local zila parishads was overlooked altogether in the new act. If anything, the role of the zila parishad in the educational administration of the district had been undermined. One wonders what the Swarajists would have done under such circumstances.

Both the primary education and panchayat acts of West Bengal were passed in 1973, but up to the amendments of 1993, there are no clauses clearly distinguishing between panchayats and administrative bodies on primary education. This is surprising because there are provisions in the panchayat act for constituting shiksha sthayee, sanskriti sthayee and krira sthayee samitis at the panchayat and zila parishad levels to look after the development of elementary education in their areas. There is also provision for funds to maintain primary schools. But there is no statutory provision for the inclusion of any representative of the primary school councils in these sthayee samitis. As noted, even the relation between the bodies is not defined in the two acts.

Despite the hierarchical structure and centralized character of the management and administrative system described above, the state authority of education claims to have achieved decentralization of education. No elections have been held to date in accordance with the West Bengal education act to constitute either the state board of primary education or the district primary school councils. Instead, an amendment to the act passed in 1987 allowed the state government to instal *ad hoc* committees in 1990 at the state and district levels. These committees are still functioning as board and councils. Most of their nominated members belong to the ruling political party. Thus, what happened in 1969 has only been repeated, but with statutory power. In the process, the politicization of educational administration has become complete, flouting all democratic norms. It is like a return to the colonial system but minus the efficiency. The increasing availability of funds for elementary education has also fuelled corruption. Without adequate infrastructure to absorb the funds, the system can, in fact, be ruined. It is no wonder that court cases take away much of the time at the various levels of administration. Despite the tall claims of the state government, there is no doubt that primary education in West Bengal is in very bad shape. Recent studies show that learning outcomes after four years of schooling are anything but satisfactory (Acharya 1994 and 1996: Roy, Mitra and Roy, 1995).

In conclusion, it can be reasonably said that the Bengali bhadralok—whether Hindu, Muslim, nationalists or communists—made universal primary education an issue of power politics at the cost of the interests of the common people. While laws have been framed, the people for whom universal education was meant remained in the background as passive spectators. The present situation could not be worse; never before was there such a gap between claims of success and reality. In 1941, J.M. Sen found that only 5,000 primary schools out of 54,000 were contributing effectively towards the removal of illiteracy. The figure must be about the same today, despite all the money that has been pumped into the system. After innumerable commissions and committees on education, solutions are still out of sight.

Notes

1. All-Bengal Primary Teacher's Association, *Guide to Primary Education (Acts, Rules and Government Orders)*, Calcutta, 1978.
2. Acharya, Poromesh, "Education and Communal Politics in Bengal: A Case Study", in Krishna Kumar (ed.), *Democracy And Education in India*, Nehru Memorial Museum and Library, Radiant Publisher, Delhi, 1993, "Bengali bhadralok and educational development in 19th century Bengal", *Economic and Political Weekly*, Bombay, Vol. XXX, No. 13, April 1, 1995; "Problems of universal elementary education", *Economic and*

Political Weekly, Bombay, Vol. XXIX, No. 49, December 3, 1994; *Educating West Bengal: Problems of Participatory Management* (monograph), Siksha Bhavan, Calcutta, 1996.

3. Bagal, J.C., *Bethune Society*, Bangiya Sahitya Parishat, Calcutta, 1367.
4. Basu, Ananthnath, *Primary Education in India: Its Future*, Calcutta, 1946.
5. Basu, Aparna, *The Growth of Education and Political Development in India, 1890–1920.*
6. Biss, E.E., *Report on the Expansion and Improvement of Primary Education in Bengal*, Bengal Secretariat Book Depot, Calcutta, 1921.
7. Chakrabarty, D. and C. Bhattacharyya, *Congress in Evolution*, Book Company, Calcutta, 1935.
8. Government of Bengal, *Collection of Opinions on the Bengal (Rural) Primary Education Bill 1927*, B.G. Press, Calcutta, 1928; *Council Proceedings: Official Report, Bengal Legislative Council*, Calcutta, 1928; *Council Proceedings: Official Report*, Calcutta, 1930; *Report of Public Instruction in Bengal*, Calcutta, 1940.
9. Government of West Bengal, *Report on Public Instruction for the Year 1949–50*, Calcutta. 1953; *Quinquennial Review on the Progress of Education in West Bengal for the Years 1947–48 to 1951–52*, Calcutta, 1959; *Rules Framed Under the Bengal (Rural) Primary Education* Act, *1930*, Calcutta 1966; *The Bengal (Rural) Primary Education Act, 1930, as Modified up to the 1st January 1969*, Calcutta 1969; *Septennial Review on the Progress of Education for the Period 1957–58 to 1964–65*, Calcutta, 1970; *The West Bengal Panchayat Act, 1973, and the West Bengal Panchayat (Election) Rules*, Calcutta, 1974; *The West Bengal Panchayat Act, 1973, as Modified up to the 1st January 1988*, Calcutta, 1988; *The West Bengal Panchayat Act, 1973, as Corrected up to the 1st January 1993*, Calcutta, 1993; *The West Bengal Primary Education Act, 1973 as Corrected up to the 1st January 1993*, Calcutta, 1993.
10. Government of India, *Selected Educational Statistics*, New Delhi, 1993.
11. Mitra, N.N., *The Indian Annual Register*, July–Dec., Vol. II, Calcutta, 1930.
12. Mukhopadhyay, Gopal, *Mass Education in Bengal (1882–1914)*, Calcutta, 1984.

13. Roy, N.C., *Rural Self-Government in Bengal*, Calcutta University, 1936; *A Critical Study of Some Aspects of Public Administration in Bengal*, University of Calcutta, 1945.
14. Roy, Samir, Subir Mitra and Surja Sankar Roy, *Achievement Levels of Primary School Children at the End of Class IV* (monograph), ISI and SCERT, Calcutta, 1995.
15. Sen, J.M., *History of Elementary Education in India*, Calcutta, 1941.
16. West Bengal Board of Primary Education, *A Handbook on Primary Education (Extracts from Relevant Acts, Rules and Orders)*, Calcutta, undated.

13. Ray, N.C. *Rural Self-Government in Bengal*, Calcutta University, 1936. *A Critical Study of Some Aspects of Public Administration in Bengal*, University of Calcutta, 1945.
14. Roy, Samir, Subir Mitra and Sumi Sankar Roy. *Achievement Levels of Primary School Children at the End of Class IV* (monograph), IGI and SCERT, Calcutta, 1995.
15. Sen, J.M. *History of Elementary Education in India*, Calcutta, 1941.
16. West Bengal Board of Primary Education. *A Handbook on Primary Education (Extracts from Relevant Acts, Rules and Orders)*, Calcutta, undated.

SECTION III: SOME LEADING EDUCATIONAL THINKERS

Maulana Azad's Perception of Muslim Education

V.N. DATTA

In his biography of his father, S. Gopal writes that Maulana Azad was "a symbol and not an administrator, and his preference for the educational portfolio became a national disaster." Professor Gopal holds Azad and the "henchmen" in his ministry responsible for stifling substantial development in education for about eleven years. He concludes that, because of Azad's ineptitude, India "has still a long way to go in achieving even the minimum standards and objectives in education."[1]

Aijaz Ahmad has presented an intellectual portrait of Azad by tracing the evolution of his ideas through successive stages. He writes in the course of incidental observations, that Azad "left behind neither a personal influence on the actual system of education nor on any work on educational policy." Ahmad laments, "[Though] we know what Nehru's foreign or economic policies were, we know nothing of Azad's educational policy beyond some superbly written addresses which provide us with some general statements of decent desire."[2]

Like other contemporary political leaders who fought for India's independence and languished in jail for a number of years, Azad lacked administrative experience. The Secretary of State, Lord Pethic-Lawrence, noticed this when Azad met him during discussions on the Cabinet Mission proposals in 1946. He wrote that Azad was "ignorant of administrative necessities."[3]

Towards the close of his biography of Nehru, Gopal

concedes that his failure lay in the implementation of his policies, and that several candles remained unlit. He observes philosophically, "there is a limitation to the achievement of an individual or a generation." This measure should apply to Azad as well.

I will not try to assess Maulana Azad as education minister. A ministerial performance is collective, like that of an orchestra. It is difficult to know in matters of government who had the most skill or key role in laying down policy, unless the dominating ideas are as clear and loud as "non-alignment", the linchpin of Nehru's foreign policy. Azad's "henchmen" bristle at the accusations, and claim in a commemoration volume edited by Humayun Kabir that his performance as education minister was not bad. However, commemoration volumes published to mark the death of eminent persons are usually laudatory in tone and trite in judicious appraisal.[4]

Azad did bring into his ministry outstanding educationists like Tara Chand, K.G. Saiyidain, Humayun Kabir, Shanti Sarup Bhatnagar and Prem Kirpal to prepare comprehensive plans for education. He was convinced that education would do better in the hands of educationists rather than bureaucrats. Furthermore, it was during his tenure that the University Grants Commission (UGC), the Central Board of Secondary Education (CBSE), a central board of textbook research and various national laboratories were set up. Plans were prepared for a national museum and national library, and the activities of the National Archives and Department of Archaeology were expanded. Three academies were established for the arts, literature and music, and a project for the completion of a Sanskrit dictionary was taken up. The Indian Council of Cultural Relations also started working to promote cultural relations with foreign countries, particularly those in the Middle East. Also, the adult education scheme received special impetus. This list of institutions shows that much thought and planning went into laying the foundation for the future development of education in India. A decade is not long enough to enable one to see the fruits of these initiatives, for education was almost ignored in the first five-year plan.

Assessing Azad in his essay, Prem Kirpal concludes, "there was some success, some failure, [but] on balance the final picture is creditable."[5]

Azad was by no means a technical or theoretical expert trained in the discipline of education. He did not offer any educational formula or methodology. Neither can it be said that his interest in education was amateurish, for he did not express casual views on the subject like some of our worthy politicians. Education is often viewed as a field for all and sundry, and there are many who adopt the postures of experts and indulge in vague generalities.

Azad was deeply interested in education because he retained the memory of the oppressive, authoritarian mode of instruction to which he had been subjected. His ideas on education were thus derived from his own personal experience. He did not produce a treatise on education but, like Erasmus and Francis Bacon, his ideas were "dispersed meditations" scattered over his autobiographical writings. However, rather than mawkish personal criticism, his powerfully expressed thoughts reflected strong convictions and bitter experience. From this angle, what he thought and wrote on education is a consequential, important achievement.

Azad's self-education and development provides a sharp contrast between what his family intended for him and what he wanted for himself; it is a contrast between repressed, dutiful childhood and the liberated, adult existence of a free thinker. His father, Maulana Khairuddin, was a reputed Arabic scholar, religious divine and a sufi of the Qadriya school. Under his eagle eye, Azad learned the Koran by rote and completed the *Dars-e-Nizami* (made famous by Mullah Nizamuddin in Aurangzeb's time and prevalent since the eighteenth century) when he was only fifteen, taking one-third the normal time. Sir Sayyid Ahmad Khan has given details about the *Dars* in his *Tahzib-al-Akhlaq*. It was a rigorous course of studies that included metaphysics, arithmetic, physics, geometry, astronomy, scholastics, Muslim law, Muslim principles (*hadith*), lexicography, medicine and *tafsir*.[6] For relief from such an intensive course, Azad sought solace in Sayyid's literary works, which his father had banished from his education.

A parent is seldom a good teacher of his own children, and an authoritarian parent can smother a child's natural creativity. In his last literary work, *Ghubar-e-Khatir*, which Azad wrote while incarcerated in Ahmednagar fort, he gives a vivid account of the type of education he received and of the bold resistance he was compelled to offer against it. His father and teachers, he says, had a medieval cast of mind, clung to obsolete traditions, were hostile to new ideas, and believed they were infallible. He wrote, "The intellectual world in which my family lived was totally irrelevant to the needs of the times. I felt as though I were living in an India of a hundred years past."[7]

In *Ghubar-e-Khatir*, Azad assailed the pivotal position held by the *Dars-e-Nizami* in the scheme of Muslim education. Each of the various courses of study he followed he calls *nakis* (worthless).[8] Azad divided the *Dars-e-Nizami* into two parts: *ulum-e-deniya* (religious sciences) and *maqulat* (rational sciences). The former included revealed knowledge, Koranic *tafsir*, *hadith* and *figh*. *Maqulat* concentrated on grammar, logic, philosophy and mathematics.

According to Azad, studying the *ulum-e-deniya* involved reading selected texts which gave some information on the content and meaning of words and taught the art of writing, but it was learning by rote and neglected the larger aspects of subjects. It taught Islamic divinity pedantically, without the Koran's style of beauty and power. Although it produced some accomplished *maulvis* who possessed logical finesse and a type of scholasticism, Azad felt these men lacked breadth of outlook; they sought truth in words and quoted texts with unquestioning trust. He condemned this type of study as completely antiquated and superficial.

With the exception of astronomy, the *maqulat* (rational sciences) course dwelt on classical ideas and said very little about recent discoveries. There was also no scope for the study of comparative religion, and European languages and science. Too much reliance was placed on compliance to *taglid* (authority), while *ijtihad* (reason) was ignored. Quoting the poet Saadi, Azad said the type of knowledge imparted through such courses was like a body without a soul.

Like Ram Mohan Roy in the 19th century, Azad was a convinced, forward-looking reformer. Azad's opposition to traditional Muslim education was a counterpart to Roy's rejection of Sanskrit education.[9] Yet Maulana Azad was one of the finest products of Islamic culture, according to K.G. Saiyidain.[10] The whirlwind of Indian politics consumed most of his time from 1920 onward. If he had stayed out, I feel he would have attained the intellectual stature of a Bacon or Erasmus, distinguished for erudition and a wide sweep and profundity of thought. To Aijaz Ahmad, Azad's writings do not suggest any special erudition other than traditional knowledge.[11] But this notion should be dispelled by, for example, a reading of Azad's introduction to Radhakrishnan's *History of Philosophy*.

Maulana Azad chose the arduous path of finding things out by himself. Assailed by doubt, Sir Sayyid's writings opened a whole new world to him. He came to accept doubt as essential for intellectual advancement. Questioning all established knowledge, he began to doubt the existence of God and became an agnostic like Bertrand Russell. But unlike Russell, who remained agnostic all his life, Azad found comfort in Islam, becoming one of its greatest exponents and votaries.

Because of his intellectual background, cultivated literary tastes and flair for writing, nothing suited Azad's talents better than journalism. He recognized its force as a vehicle for the diffusion of ideas that could reform the Muslims, particularly the ulema. He came to journalism like a duck to water, and all his life, directly or otherwise, never parted from it. After four years of writing intermittently for some Urdu journals in both verse and prose, Azad launched his own journal, *Lisan-al-sidq* (voice of truth), at the age of sixteen.

This journal maintained quite a high literary standard. It was used by Azad to promote education among the Muslims. In his writings there, he made a distinction between good and bad books, promoting only those that contained modern knowledge, and were free from puerile fables and fancies. He protested the publication by the Anjuman-e-Taraqi-e-Urdu of books dealing with trite themes, noting that only one book out of five hundred published by this organization was worth studying.[12] He advocated Urdu as the language for India, but with the adoption of convenient English words like ticket, rail and engine. He also urged Muslim society to refine their literary tastes and cultivate a scientific temper for their social and educational advancement. His views appealed to a large section of the Muslim community.

Azad's association with the prestigious religious journal *al-Nadwa,* edited by Shibli Naumani, deepened his understanding of Islamic history and theology, and also widened his interest in European learning and science. He launched two more journals, *al-Hilal* on 12 July 1914 and *al-Balaq* on 12 November 1915, with the object of regenerating Muslim society, which he felt was socially, politically and economically backward. He was convinced that it was Islam that would strengthen the moral fibre of the Muslim community. Two passions dominated his life at this stage: preaching faith in the pure spirit of Islam, and diffusing Western learning and sciences among the Muslims.

Through these widely-circulated journals, he hoped to give the Muslims nationalistic fervour so they could free themselves from foreign rule. Thus, Azad tried to forge a link between religion and nationalism. Like Machiavelli, he had recognized the usefulness of religion for disciplining society and building nationalism by encouraging the virtues of suffering and humility. These two papers, *al-Hilal* and *al-Balaq*, were part of a crusade to make Sayyid's politics look obsolete. He declared, "No country can be a slave any longer in the twentieth century."[13] His journals were designed to shake Muslim politics out its supineness. Here is a typical trumpet call to the Muslims:

> Whence to obtain the bugle to awaken the nine crore of Muslims who are sleeping ... Where are the eyes which claim to shed tears for the Muslim brethren, where the

> hearts which are friends of the wounds of the fallen community ... The enemy is breaking open the doors of the town and the inmates are weeping over their lot ... Those who consider weeping a courageous act and despondency a vitality of life, listen. Your house is on fire ... The storm is raging and the fierce flames are leaping but there is none, none whatsoever among you to fetch water. If you are waiting for this time, then surely the time is come. If you are waiting for the boat to sink, then also there is not much time left.[14]

In *al-Hilal*, Azad wrote as a proponent of modern knowledge. He started a column called "Muzakira ilmiya" (scientific view), which had articles on radium, Scott's expedition to the south pole, Montessori's educational experiments, J.C. Bose's botanical investigations, and Darwin's theory.[15] For him, education was not just a means to get a job, but a tool to create a genuinely religious, humanistic, scientific outlook. He found no incompatibility between the true spirit of Islam and modern scientific knowledge. This was similar to Ram Mohan Roy, who had demanded not only Western learning and sciences, but the revival of ancient learning as well.

After his plunge into politics, Azad could not find the time for journalism, but the freedom struggle gained thereby. However, he continued to articulate the same convictions: reform of Muslim education, advocacy of scientific temper, and promotion of Urdu. After independence, Azad tried to overhaul Persian and Arabic teaching. In a speech at Lucknow on 22 February 1947, he said that Persian and Arabic studies neglected rhetoric and writing, and emphasized the interpretation of texts rather than original sources. He also pointed out that the non-religious parts of these courses relied on learning by rote and proofs through long-winded dialogues.[16]

Azad criticized the British government for having ignored the place of religious instruction in the scheme of education. He did not agree with the notion that religious education impeded intellectual advancement, arguing that eliminating it had led to the neglect of human values.[17] However, he wanted to bring religious education under government control, not leave it in the hands of local educational authorities, where it might be used to foster bigotry and fanaticism.[18]

The goal of education, according to Azad, was to make man realize his uniqueness and strive to attain the higher reaches of thought. Students should be taught the concepts of *fiqr* (reason), *zikar* (observation), *tadabur* (exploring the Koran), and *ijtehad* (forming independent opinions). He said:

> In both the East and West, the present systems of education have given rise to various paradoxes. In East we find a distinctive emphasis on individual salvation. The Eastern mode of thought, with its preoccupation with individual salvation, has at all times paid inadequate attention to the growth of society. In fact, considerations of social welfare have at times led to the growth of totalitarian society in which the individual has been suppressed. Today, when East and West have been brought nearer each other through the operation of science, it is necessary that bias, whether in favour of the individual or of society, should be rectified, and a system of education evolved which will give due regard to both individual and social values.[19]

Azad's ideal man was not an ascetic, but a *mard-e-momin*, one who has a will, creative intelligence and compassion. Without being too attached to things, such a person must be animated by social purpose. When he was assailed in the Lok Sabha on 20 May 1954 by Purshottamdas Tandon and others for discriminating against Hindi, Azad said:

> Forty years ago, when nobody had even heard of my friends sitting around here, I decided to dedicate my life to the service of the country. I am talking of 1907, when I was 18 or 19 years of age, and joined the Revolutionary Party of Bengal. Since then my life has been an open book. I have no desire left with me. A great part of my

> life is over and whatever is left will soon end. What is it that made me consecrate my life to the service of my nation? When a man expels personal interest from his life, he is free and detached. Do you know what it means to be free and detached? ... Not even the sharpest sword can touch [such a person] because it can pierce his body but not his soul.[20]

Maulana Azad had warned that the Muslim League should have no place in the country, but it continues to flourish. He had sought a complete change in Muslim education, but the kind of religious instruction he opposed continues to be imparted in thousands of madrasas, breeding religious intolerance. Our higher Muslim educational institutions once prided themselves on fostering a truly nationalist spirit; now narrow-mindedness and communal feelings have gained ascendancy there. It is these very trends that led to the two-nation theory of which Azad was an inveterate and consistent foe.

Notes

1. Sarvepalli Gopal, *Radhakrishnan, a Biography*, Delhi, 1989, pp. 287–288.
2. Aijaz Ahmed, "Azad's careers: routes taken and not taken", in Mushirul Hasan (ed.), *Islam and Indian Nationalism*, New Delhi, 1992, p. 159.
3. Nicholas Mansergh (ed.), *The Transfer of Power*, Vol. VII, London, 1987, p. 317.
4. Humanyun Kabir (ed.), *Maulana Azad: A Memorial Volume*, Bombay, 1959.
5. Prem Kirpal, "The Educationist", in Syeda Saiyidain Hameed (ed.), *India's Maulana*, New Delhi, 1990, Vol. I, pp. 185–97.
6. A.A. Fyzee, *A Modern Approach to Islam*, New Delhi, 1963, pp. 63–68.
7. Maulana Azad, *Ghubar-e-Khatir*, edited by Malik Ram, New Delhi, 1983, p. 95.
8. V.N. Datta, *Maulana Azad*, Delhi, 1990, p. 14.
9. J.C. Ghosh, *The English Works of Raja Rammohan Roy*, Calcutta, Vol. I, 1920, p. 473.

10. K.G. Saiyidain in *India's Maulana*, Vol. I, *op. cit.*, p. 64.
11. Aijaz Ahmed, *op. cit.*, p. 164.
12. Lisan-al-sidq, January, 1905.
13. *al-Halal*, 18 December 1912.
14. *Ibid.*, 16 June 1913.
15. V.N. Datta, *op. cit.*, p. 71.
16. *Khutbat-e-Azad*, edited by Malik Ram, New Delhi, 1981, pp. 310–329.
17. *Khutbat, op. cit.*, p. 179.
18. *Speeches of Maulana Azad (1947–55)*, New Delhi, 1959, p. 4; Salamat Ullah in *Muslim Education in Secular India*, Chandigarh, 1994, p. 102.
19. Syeda Saiyidain Hameed, *op. cit.*, Vol. I, p. 74.
20. *The Selected Works of Maulana Azad (1953–54)*, Vol. II, edited by Ravinder Kumar, New Delhi, 1992, p. 182.

Tagore's Educational Experiments at Santiniketan and Sriniketan, 1901–1941

UMA DAS GUPTA

Rabindranath Tagore established his first school in 1901 at Santiniketan in rural Bengal, 100 miles north-west of Calcutta. He claimed it was a "poet's school", not a nationalist institution, for he did not belong to the movement. If anything, for Rabindranath, the institutions at Santiniketan and Sriniketan were personal retreats. Earlier, he and others in his illustrious family had thrown themselves into the heart of the swadeshi movement. He gave it many soul-stirring songs. At his school, however, he dedicated himself to building an Indian self-respect away from the limelight of the political movement.

Both Rabindranath and Gandhi looked to India's own past for the revival of its cultural identity and self-respect. While Gandhi searched among folk traditions, Rabindranath drew from classical traditions while acknowledging the influence of the European renaissance on the modern Indian mind. All the same, few Indians have used the folk within the classical as creatively as Rabindranath. This can be seen abundantly in the way art, music and even just living were taught at Santiniketan and Sriniketan. It is noteworthy that, when he returned from South Africa with the boys from his Phoenix School, Gandhi took them first to Santiniketan in 1915, although he soon moved on from there with the boys.

It is difficult to put labels on Rabindranath; he was a little too unique for that. Still, one can say that he was committed to the cause of nationalism, only his emphasis was more on culture than any other elements. Thus, his school lay at the confluence of many historical and cultural ideas, and was called a "centre of Indian culture" quite early in its evolution. It finally took the name Visva Bharati, which can be translated to mean world learning or world culture. Both in the context of India as well as in his response to the world situation, Rabindranath's nationalism was humanitarian and cultural, hardly ever political, although his nationalist participation ranged from reciting poetry at the Hindu mela of 1876 to composing patriotic songs against the partition of Bengal.

At his Santiniketan and Sriniketan centres, however, he ensured there would be no politics, only nation building through the development of the Indian personality. Like Gandhi, he wanted to overcome India's weaknesses rather than blame the British for their strengths. This was a quest for self-respect. Gandhi sought it in moral and political ways; Rabindranath looked for it in India's humanitarian and cultural heritage. His poem, *Chito jetha bhay shunya* ("where the mind is without fear and the head is held high"), his song *Jana gana mono* (our national anthem), the novel *Gora*, essays such as *Nation ki* ("what is a nation"), the lectures on nationalism for which he was jeered at in post-war Japan, his debate with Gandhi over non-cooperation, all point to that effort.

In this paper, I argue that it is this cultural approach that was Rabindranath's contribution to Indian nationalism. It involved a rearrangement of Indian sensibilities and a reformulation of Indian emotions to claim a place for the country in the modern world. The canvases for this work were his schools at Santiniketan and Sriniketan. From the work he did there, he made it clear that he was not opposed to Western knowledge, only to imperial rule.

In his essay, *The Illegitimacy of Nationalism: Rabindranath Tagore and the Politics of Self*, Ashish Nandy asks an important question (p. 80): why did Rabindranath hold his position when "nationalism, patriotism and anti-imperialism were a single concept for most Indians"? Nandy says that it is in the answer to this that we can see what linked Rabindranath to Gandhi and what separated them. Nandy's answer is that both of them thought and felt morally in constructing a framework within which to work towards the goal of Indian unity. But while Gandhi chose politics as an essential means of testing his ethics in the conditions imposed by imperial rule, Rabindranath stayed away from politics even though he sometimes participated in it. Nandy rightly argues that Rabindranath's universalism arose out of his concern for the inherent openness of Indian civilization, its history of absorbing peoples from other traditions. He used this concern to try and construct a "national" ideology that would go beyond the boundaries set by nationalism. Partha Chatterjee's discussion on Gandhi (and also, in passing, on Tagore) in his book, *Nationalist Thought and the Colonial World: A Derivative Discourse*?, points out another set of similarities and differences between Rabindranath and Gandhi within the nationalist discourse. A glimpse there might help us understand Rabindranath's educational and cultural work in relation to Gandhi's work in the same sphere. I attempt to do this, albeit peripherally, because one of the themes of this seminar is nationalist educational philosophy.

Both Gandhi and Rabindranath were concerned about the divisions within Indian society: divisions that had their roots in the past but which colonialism had brought to the surface. Both focused on the peasantry as the largest class within Indian society. What especially troubled Rabindranath about the situation in the 19th and 20th centuries was that, while the peasant was still almost paralysed by his traditions, the Western-educated urban Indian had become gradually indifferent to him. However, perhaps as a fallout of colonial domination, both groups had taken to "begging" the alien rulers to cure the ills of their own society. This humiliation was Rabindranath's concrete target: not the ruler but rather the mentality of the ruled. His solution was an education that would bring the urban elite and the village folk closer. The town would bring modern science and technology, and the village its traditional knowledge and skills, which the urban dweller was beginning to neglect. The curriculum of the Santiniketan school reflects this approach.

Gandhi took a tougher line. He wanted no truck whatsoever with science and technology, civil society or "progress", whether for the elite or the peasantry. But as Partha Chatterjee points out (p. 100):

> Gandhism, like Russian populism, was not a direct expression of peasant ideology. It was an ideology conceived as an intervention in the elite-nationalist discourse of the time, and was formed and shaped by the experiences of a specifically nationalist movement ... In the Indian case, the largest popular element of the nation was the peasantry. And it was the Gandhian ideology which opened up the historical possibility for its appropriation into the evolving political structures of the Indian state.

From this significant standpoint, Rabindranath can also be legitimately regarded as an "interventionist". Only, his solution was more fluid and creative, and played out within cultural and emotional parameters.

The success of Rabindranath's ideology depended a lot on a change of heart within the classes. (Compare and contrast Tagore's "Hind swaraj" and Gandhi's "swadeshi samaj".) What Rabindranath was aiming for was a state of almost perfect cultural and aesthetic understanding: first, between two classes of people within the same society, and second, between Indian civilization (even Eastern culture) and Western scientific progress. The former he sought to bring about through his home-grown education, and the latter by sharing and learning from each other's contribution to civil society. Such an ideal state, he felt, would be free of cultural domination by one group over another and even generate political change. Furthermore, it would accomodate individualism and, at the same time, allow the individual to appreciate and assimilate the variety offered by the world at large. It is likely that the poet's school at Santiniketan and its rural extension at Sriniketan were developed along those very lines. We shall examine their workings as we go along.

Let me begin with the origins. The educational institution known today as Visva Bharati was founded by Rabindranath Tagore in 1901. It started as a school that allowed its students to creatively appropriate and enjoy the teaching given to them. Rabindranath believed intensely in freedom, and wanted the children being taught in his school to have as much joy and freedom as possible. Study was not separate from "life", as he felt was the case in the English-medium schools of the time. Teachers and pupils were told to work together as one family on a "religious" basis, in harmony with their natural surroundings like the hermit schools of the past.

In 1918, he enlarged the scope of the school, making it what he called a "centre of Indian culture." He wished to link Santiniketan with the world, or at least with other parts of Asia, so he added advanced studies in vedic and classical Sanskrit, as well as in Arabic and Persian. Along with these literary studies, a school of Indian art and music helped fulfil the poet's purpose. He widened his own and the school's horizon further after his tour of post-war Europe in 1920–21. To bring East and West together in common fellowship, he invited Europe's leading Indologists to study and teach at Santiniketan, "the guest house of India."

Visva Bharati became a formally registered institution in 1921 and, in 1922, its rural reconstruction work at Surul, a village two miles from Santiniketan, was also formalized. An agricultural centre had been functioning there for ten years as part of the curriculum of the Santiniketan school. The school, university and centre for rural reconstruction still make up today's Visva Bharati University at Santiniketan and Sriniketan. They are all based on their founder's conviction that an educational institution cannot be manufactured; it is like a limb on the body of society which grows along with the entire organism. Santiniketan was the antithesis of the current system of education, which he considered "machine-made", alien to Indian tradition, and "destructive of the spirit of

Man." He called it "an indigenous attempt in adapting modern methods of education in a truly Indian cultural environment." It was Rabindranath's effort at "constructive" swadeshi.

While Rabindranath's interest lasted, Santiniketan succeeded as a beautiful way of life for many. When, around twenty years ago, I travelled in many parts of India searching for the institution's students from the twenties and thirties, I met many who exuded that feeling. K.V. Muthuswamy (born 1919) was a student at Kala Bhawana, Santiniketan, from 1938 to 1944. When I met him at his Coimbatore residence on May 26, 1980, he told me:

> My father was a scientist and a widely travelled man. He wanted to put me in a school of Indian culture. Initially, he had put me in Madanapalli, Annie Besant's school. But the school was closed down when Annie Besant was interned. By then my father knew well of Santiniketan and sent me there. There was none other like Santiniketan.[1]

V. Balgangadhar Menon from Kerala (born 1916) attended the Santiniketan college from 1933 to 1937 because he was looking for a national school with a cultural environment. Interviewed on May 27, 1980, at his residence in Palghat, Kerala, he told me:

> I had already taken part in satyagraha. After that, I could only continue my education in a nationalist institution. Santiniketan and Sabarmati were the only two institutions which came to mind in this connection. I had heard of many brilliant students who had boycotted government colleges at Gandhi's call and gone to Santiniketan and Sabarmati and made good. I, too, had a recommendation for Sabarmati from Kellappan, the father of the nationalist movement in Kerala. But I hankered for a more cultural and philosophical education. So I wrote off myself for admission to Santiniketan supported by my eldest brother.[2]

V. Gopala Reddy (born 1907) was also from a background of

nationalist participation. He spent the years 1924–27 at the Santiniketan college. He told me at his Nellore, Andhra Pradesh residence on May 5, 1982:

> I was thirteen and a half when I boycotted government school at Gandhiji's call for non-cooperation. My brother and I were immediately sent off to the Andhra Jatiya Kalachala at Masulipatam, where I stayed for four years. By then I had read Tagore and felt greatly attracted towards him. By then also, my brother had visited the Indian National Congress in Calcutta, as well as Santiniketan. I was determined to leave Masulipatam for Santiniketan. My nationalist commitment was not at all hampered [there]. On the contrary, there were other things that equally attracted me. There was music, art; I loved that in Santiniketan. I began to learn other Indian languages in Santiniketan—Tamil from my Tamil friends, Gujarati from my Gujarati friends. I did not care about Chinese and Tibetan studies, which were then being pursued at Visva Bharati. Sten Konow from Norway and Vincent Lesny from Czechoslovakia were then teaching [there]. I did not feel particularly [strongly about] the idea of Visva Bharati. I said to myself, let me first learn about Bharat Bharati before I know Visva Bharati.[3]

Prime Minister Indira Gandhi (1917–1984) spent a year at the Santiniketan college in 1933–4. At her Parliament House office in New Delhi, she told me on April 12, 1982:

> Santiniketan revived in me certain traditions which I used to know in my childhood. These traditions, which were a very essential part of my grandfather's household at the time of my childhood, became a little inconsequential in our own household after my grandfather's death. But when I was at Santiniketan, these were revived in me—traditions like observing Vasant Sri Panchami. I have observed them in my own life ever since.[4]

I interviewed Mrinalini Sarabhai on January 2, 1980, at her

dance academy Darpana in Ahmedabad. She was at Santiniketan between 1939 and 1940, and was literally overcome even after all these years as she recalled her life there:

> What was wonderful was the very creative atmosphere I found there. For the first time in my life, I felt that there was nothing impossible creatively. That was perhaps because it was a world full of dance and music, and I loved that. But it was also because I felt my inner life was coming true for the first time. It was as though I was touched at Santiniketan. I was lucky. So many of us live through life without being touched. You see, there was a deep Indianness in me which my family never understood. My family thought I was a freak. I found my Indianness flowering in all its beauty when I was in Santiniketan.[5]

One can add to these examples from the testimony of people who were "touched" by the Santiniketan way of life. What is clear from their experience is that they had individually and together learned to appreciate and identify an Indian culture. Whether Rabindranath could do all he wanted with his educational experiments at Santiniketan and Sriniketan is doubtful. In his own lifetime, he had started to voice disappointment over Santiniketan. "I have no special love," he wrote, "for the school and college departments of Santiniketan, a borrowed cage that treats the students' minds as captive birds whose sole human value is judged according to the mechanical repetition of lessons by an educational dispensation foreign to the soil." Perhaps both Santiniketan and Sriniketan fell short of their founder's goal of creating an Indian who would become the social conscience and cultural leader of his society. That was his manifesto, as we have understood it, for a "swadeshi samaj".

Furthermore, although the institutions of Santiniketan contributed amply to the cultural enrichment of the elite, the village of Sriniketan hardly changed. Artisan cooperatives and a boy-scout movement for village self-help had been established there, as also laboratories for better agriculture and clinics for better health. But in the end, the most important addition to Sriniketan was the Silpa Sadana, which produced handicrafts. Here the villagers made aesthetically pleasing items based on designs which came from Santiniketan, mainly its art school. Mats, durries, fine woodwork and other items were made in an art style characteristic of Santiniketan. Many Calcutta homes in the thirties and forties, even those of the Sarabhais in Ahmedabad later on, used art work from Sriniketan.

Today, Santiniketan and Sriniketan are still not truly integrated. Rural Sriniketan considers itself dominated by Santiniketan. It is a fact that, although Visva Bharati is entirely a rural university, with Santiniketan and Sriniketan lying within two miles of each other, there is a different atmosphere at the two places. It is as if Santiniketan has become a "town", while Sriniketan remained a "village". All the same, these two places taken together and, of course, Gandhi's own educational and village programmes, have given to the government of independent India significant ideas about what can be done for village development. It is acknowledged that the work done at Santiniketan and Sriniketan were precursors of the country-wide village block development programmes and the cottage-industries movement. The knowledge that the government has taken over some of what the poet's school had begun for the cultural unity of the country could not have been disappointing to the founder.

Notes

1. Interview with K.V. Muthuswamy (b. 1919) on May 26, 1980, at his residence in Coimbatore. Muthuswamy was a student of Kala Bhavan, Santiniketan, during 1938–44.
2. Interview with V. Balgangadhar Menon (b. 1916) on May 27, 1980, at his residence in Palghat, Kerala. Balgangadhar was a student of the Santiniketan college department during 1933–37.
3. Interview with V. Gopala Reddy (b. 1907) on May 5, 1982, at

his residence in Nellore, Andhra Pradesh. He was a student of the Santiniketan college department during 1924–27.

4. Interview with Indira Gandhi (b. 1917) on April 12, 1982, at the Prime Minister's parliament House Office, New Delhi. Indira Gandhi was a student of the Santiniketan College department.
5. Interview with Mrinalini Sarabhai (b. 1923) on January 2, 1980, at her residence in Ahmedabad. Mrinalini Sarabhai was a student of dancing in Santiniketan during 1939–40.

The Contribution of Male Intelligentsia to Women's Education in Bombay Presidency during the Colonial Period

GAURI SRIVASTAVA

During the colonial period, the three important agencies that promoted women's education were the Christian missionaries, the male intelligentsia and the British government. The missionaries were pioneers in this field, but the thread of their activity was gradually taken up by educated Indian men. We will attempt in this paper to examine their contribution.

I use the term "male intelligentsia" to include Indian men who had been educated in the Western system.[1] This system laid emphasis on democratic, liberal, rational and humanitarian principles[2] as set out by Mill, Comte, Spencer and others. Mill's *Subjection of Women* (1869) became popular among the Indian educated, who often spoke in favour of female equality. Comte wrote about the absolute necessity of women's equality. His ideas had a major impact on the intelligentsia of both Bengal and Bombay.

Among the Bombay men who took up liberal ideas in their writings and speeches were Gopal Hari Deshmukh, G.G. Agarkar, Mahadev Govind Ranade, Kashinath Trimbak Telang and R.G. Bhandarkar. Agarkar wrote, "It is a shame that people like us, whose eyes are open, who know that there are other countries besides India, and who know that there exist great philosophies besides those found in Sanskrit books, should also become so narrow minded and act like blind people."[3] Western ideas helped these men examine their society to find out what retarded it. It became clear to them that, in addition to the caste system, social progress was blocked by old customs and traditions, particularly those that affected women: infanticide, child marriage, enforced widowhood and purdah.

There was also the realization that the knowledge imparted in traditional centres like tols and madrasas emphasized religion but failed to promote reason and logic. The old education was anyway confined to the upper castes. Raja Ram Mohan Roy, described as the father of modern India, was one who felt this way. To regenerate the Indian mind, he said, Western literature and sciences should be propagated. He petitioned the government to abandon its project for Oriental education and take up, instead, the teaching of Western science and literature.[4]

Institutional changes were needed, and one way to bring them about was outright, sudden change. The proponents of this method believed that conscience alone must be the guide of human conduct.[5] Another school of thought sought to reinterpret old Indian religious texts. They believed the present social, educational and political malaise did not exist in ancient India, particularly the period associated with the Rig Veda. For example, Raja Ram Mohan Roy[6] denounced the practice of sati, then widely prevalent in the Bengal presidency. Neither the *Vedas* nor the *Yajnavalkya* supported it, he said. He argued that even Harita and others did not support involuntary sati. Ishwar Chandra Vidyasagar stated that widow remarriage was sanctioned by the *Parasara Samhita.*[7] According to Ranade:

> A true reformer has to write upon a clean slate. His work is more often to complete the half-written sentence. We cannot break with the past altogether, for it is a rich inheritance, and we have no reason to be ashamed of it.

> But while respecting the past, we must ever seek to correct the practical growths that have encrushed it.[8]

A third group of reformers believed persons should take pledges irrespective of the opinions of society, the command of religions or personal convenience. Thus Karve pledged to marry a widow when his first wife expired. In his own words:

> The question of second marriage now confronted me. As soon as the marriage season arrived, friends and acquaintances began to approach me for marriage on behalf of guardians of marriageable girls. I told them that I was going to marry a widow.[9]

When he finally married the widow Anandibai, he had to face a lot of criticism and opposition, particularly from brahmins.[10] Similar views were expressed by Gopalrao Joshi:

> I wish to marry a widow, not necessarily a brahmin. Caste does not matter [nor whether she] belongs to a good family. A widow with a child will also do. What matters is that she should be a woman and a widow.[11]

Ranade, too, wished to marry a widow after his first wife died, but did not do so under parental pressure. In 1889, around 549 members of the Indian National Social Conference pledged to abstain from alcoholic drinks, cease the practice of dowry and child marriage, endorse widow remarriage, and educate their daughters. Ranade was among those who took the oath.[12]

There were also many who wanted reform, but perhaps due to moral cowardice, chose to compromise with tradition rather than act upon their honest beliefs. For example, despite the vigour of his attack against brahmin priests, Gopal Hari Deshmukh submitted to their demands and undertook penance (prayaschitta) for having attended the remarriage of a Hindu widow. He cited personal reasons for doing so: his daughter's in-laws threatened to get a new wife for their son.[13] Similarly, Justice Ranade pledged to marry a widow when his wife died, but ended up tying the knot with a virgin as tradition required. Justice Telang had vociferously opposed the tradition of child brides, but when the time came, he married off his own daughter at the age of ten.[14] A debate was organized in 1871 by the Shankaracharya of Poona on whether or not widow marriage was sanctioned by religion. Five shastris (priests) represented the orthodox camp, and five others the reformists. The outcome was against widow remarriage, but it was alleged that one of the nominees of the reformists, who was really in favour of widow marriage, voted against it under pressure.[15]

Finally, a fifth set of reformers wanted state compulsion, i.e., they sought to involve the legislature. Notable among them were Ishwar Chandra Vidyasagar and Malabari. Due to their efforts, the government passed the widow remarriage Act in 1856. An age-of-consent bill, passed in 1891, raised the legal age at which girls could marry from ten to twelve.[16] It should also be noted that some reformers, like Ranade, believed in adopting any method that suited the immediate purpose.[17]

The period also witnessed a controversy regarding whether or not social reform should be given precedence over political reform. Raja Ram Mohan Roy was one who thought so; he felt that religious and social reform were prerequisites to any enhancement of India's political stature.[18] "This interdependence is not accidental but is the law of our nature," he said.[19] Malabari and Ranade also stated that if Indians wanted to acquire the political institutions of the West, they would first have to assimilate at least some Western "moral and social usages".[20] Similar thoughts were expressed by R.G. Bhandarkar and Viresalingam Pantulu.

By contrast, an important activist who preferred political to social reform was Balgangadhar Tilak.[21] Although he was not against social reform, he objected to all kinds of social legislation, for then a foreign government would have to be entrusted with the power to make social changes. It was only when political conditions were bettered, he said, that society would slowly and spontaneously improve itself, aided by education and the consciousness of social evils.[22]

Despite the existence of all these methods and

controversies, both individual reformers and the societies (samaj) established by them focused on major issues. On the social front, they tackled the caste system and customs affecting the status of women, such as purdah, child marriage and enforced widowhood. In the field of education, they promoted primary, secondary and even, to some extent, vocational education, by setting up institutions, and writing educational journals and pamphlets.

Regarding the condition of women, there was a gradual realization that no amount of legislation would bring about a drastic change in social customs and traditions. The status of women would not improve significantly unless women were themselves made aware of the need for reform. Education could do this, and also help them perform the roles of mother and wife better. In the Bengal Presidency, the reformers hoped to make women gradually disassociate themselves from the activities of the zenana and andarmahal.[23] Thus, instead of imposing charge from above, a better course would be one where women themselves came forward and demanded reforms.

B.M. Malabari stated:

> The solution of India's problems is in the laps of the women of India. It is because [women] are ignorant and shut off from life that we have no real home life and, consequently, we are deprived of those silent but all-powerful influences which mould the child's character and fit men to be heroes. It is in the development of women's true nature that we must seek the future greatness of our people. In the moral and spiritual education of men, refinement of life, improvement of the home, upbringing of children, and implanting true faith in the hearts of men, the sphere of women is absolutely boundless. Who but women can inspire men with a high-minded resolve for noble deeds? Who but women can help the organization of charity, and provide comfort for the desolate, the ignorant and the friendless, and bring to the sick and the weary the love

> of a mother? … If we think education and freedom is good for women, we must not think of personal inconveniences.[24]

He added, "Unless women are educated and emancipated from the bounds of ignoble customs, there can be little hope for the future."[25] Vithaldas Thackersey felt that the index of a progressive nation lay in the education of women:

> Progressive womanhood is a sure symbol of a progressive nation; enslaved, illiterate and ignorant womanhood is no less a sure symbol of a degenerate, backward or dependent country.[26]

Similar views were expressed by V.R. Shinde. He felt that unless the condition of women was improved, there would be no social progress, indeed no progress at all.[27] A champion of the lower castes like Phule, he was convinced educating their girls would release them from the shackles of superstition and slavery, improve their families, and bring about a general elevation of their caste.[28]

This line of thinking was echoed by the Gujarati intelligentsia. Dalpatram, a well-known poet, wrote that there were many advantages in educating one's daughter, including, he said, the prevention of petty quarrels among women. He added, "If a father gives dowry to his daughter, the husband [will] usurp it; if education is given to her, no power on earth [can] deprive her of her wealth."[29] The poet Narmada urged girls to "study, study and study." He claimed that men would benefit if women were educated:

> An educated wife will help her husband; he will be able to talk to her and share his joys and sorrows … An educated man cannot share his life with an illiterate wife. Education will make a woman a better wife, a better daughter-in-law and a better mother.[30]

However, it was difficult making people break away from established traditions, particularly those legitimized by religion, and follow the reformers.[31] Thus, although a widow remarriage act was passed in 1856, it remained a dead letter. It was reported in 1890 that there had been only 500 widow remarriages. People were also cynical about the reformers. A story current at the time told of a young reformer who proclaimed he would marry a widow and none other. But the marriage never took place because of social ostracism, not just at the hands of the orthodox, which he was ready to face, but also from the group that had inspired his action.[32] On this issue, Karve and others felt that many widows who would never think of marrying again would come forward eagerly to avail the benefits of education. He said, "Why not then take up the work of providing educational facilities for the widow? After all, the object is to enable them to have a new and happy life."[33] He added that education would also make them self-supporting, and help them think for themselves.[34]

It was the Bengal Presidency which took the lead in tackling women's social and educational issues in the early 19th century. The prominent reformers were Raja Ram Mohan Roy and Ishwar Chandra Vidyasagar. The former was a crusader against sati, which, he said, was barbarous. It was not prevalent in the Vedic period; it was a modern encroachment directly connected with inheritance rights.[35] That is, the custom existed wherever widows had a right to inherit. It was because of articles in his journal *Sambad Kaumudi* and other efforts that sati was abolished in 1829.

Ishwar Chandra Vidyasagar fought to allow widow marriages, and got a widow remarriage act passed in 1856. Unlike Ram Mohan Roy, who only spoke in favour of women's education, Ishwar Chandra Vidyasagar established schools for girls and went on to become inspector of girl's schools in Bengal.

In their private capacities, some British officials, too, promoted women's education. In the Bengal Presidency, one of them was J.E.D. Bethune, the law member of the Governor-General's Exective Council and the President of the council of education from 1848 to 1851. He opened a school for girls in 1849; within a short-time it had attracted a large number of girls.[36] Its success lay in the fact that, gradually, it also started providing higher education for its women.

In the Bombay Presidency, one of the first to voice concern regarding women was Vishnu Shastri Pandit, who took up the cause of widows, founding the Vidhva Vivahottejak Mandal (society for the encouragement of widow remarriage).[37] As a result of his efforts, the remarriage of two brahmin widows took place at Belgaum in 1842.[38] Similar work was undertaken by Dadoba Pandurang, who founded the Paramahans Mandali (divine society) in 1840. It had the objectives of abolishing caste and idolatry, besides fostering widow remarriage.

The printed media of Bombay straddled both camps: orthodoxy and reform. Among the reform journalists was Gopal Hari Deshmukh, who wrote under the pen-name Lokahitwadi. In his column, "Shatapatre" (hundred letters), he made scathing attacks on the "monstrous, outdated customs and usages in Hindu society, and the inhuman treatment of women, particularly widows."[39] Jambhekar published a monthly journal, *Digdarshan* (show the way), and a weekly journal, *Bombay Durpan*. Both supported widow remarriage, the liberalization of caste formalities, and the readmission to Hindu society of persons who had been converted to Christianity.[40]

One of the early social reformers of Gujarat was Mehtaji Durgaram Mancharam. In 1844, he organized the Manav Dharma Sabha (universal religious society) to discuss social problems like the treatment meted to widows and the caste system.[41] The thread of his activity was picked up by the poet Narmada mentioned earlier. Most Gujarati reformers were associated with the Gujarat Vernacular Society of Ahmedabad, founded in 1848 under the inspiration of Alexander Forbes. The society's main work was in the field of women's education, and its journal *Buddhi Prakash* carried articles on the subject.[42]

Prominent in Bombay was the Student's Literary and Scientific Society. It was founded in 1848 at the Elphinstone Institution with the support of Elphinstone professors and under the leadership of four distinguished alumni: Dadabhai Naoroji, Naoroji Furdunji, Sorabji Shapurji Bengali and Bhau Daji. All the Society's members had in common the same background and schooling. To begin with, the Society acted merely as a sort of evening class for former students. They would come to hear papers read on scientific subjects like metallurgy, and social questions such as education, the status of women in society and women's education.[43] But there were linguistic and social divisions within the Society, and it soon split into three parts: the Gujarati Dhyan Prasarak Mandali (chiefly for the Parsis), the Marathi Dhyan Prasarak Sabha, and from April, 1851, the Gujarati Hindu Buddhi Vardhak Sabha. Each of these published its own journal, and attempted to produce cheap pamphlets on scientific and other subjects in its own language.

Although a project to build girl's schools under its auspices was originally mooted by the parent society, it was the Parsi branch that, in 1849, started morning classes for women. By 1854, there were nine schools for girls, and one member, Jagannath Shankarset, housed a Marathi school in his own compound and sent his daughter to it. In fact, it was the Parsis who were the first to realize the importance of female education and social reform in Bombay Presidency. The earliest girl's school in Bombay was founded by Cursetjee Nurserwanjee Cama and Sir Jamsetjee Jeejeebhoy.[44]

In their private capacities, the Maharashtrians also established schools for girls. Jyotiba Phule was a low-caste gardener, but he established a school for girls in 1851.[45] By 1852, he had built three more and one school for the "untouchables". Jyotiba's schools seem to have done a good job. According to the annual report of 1853, the performance of girls was better than that of the boys.[46]

Thus we find that, by 1854, the intelligentsia in the Presidencies of Bengal and Bombay had succeeded in getting social legislations passed and establishing educational institutions that promoted women's education. These two Presidencies led the way in the post-1857 period, too. In Bengal, the Brahmo Marriage Act passed in 1872 made child marriage illegal, sanctioned inter-caste widow marriage among the brahmins, and forbade polygamy. However, the impact of the act was confined to the reformed groups only, and could not acquire a wide base.[47] The brahmins themselves were split over the act, so it did not become popular. Regarding education, Sasipada Banerjee contributed by establishing schools for girls in 1865 and 1871.[48] More imortantly, he established an institution for women's higher education. In Bombay, the Parsis continued their efforts by establishing the Parsi Girls' School Association in 1865.[49] It looked into all aspects of school education for women. The Parsis were also successful in 1865, in getting passed a specifically Parsi marriage and divorce act. This act made bigamy a criminal offence and helped emancipate Parsi women by giving them a legal status in society.[50]

To go beyond the regions onto a national platform, Mahadev Govind Ranade initiated the Indian Social Conference in 1887. Just as the Indian National Congress took up political issues, the conference took up social questions that were of national dimensions.[51] Debates were held on social evils like child marriage and enforced widowhood. The period also witnessed the passing of the age-of-consent act in 1891; this showed that the government was not totally against social reform. The act increased the marriageable age of girls from 10 to 12. The man behind the new law was Malabari, who got it passed despite stiff opposition.[52]

Around the same time, Karve established various educational institutions for women. From the Anath Balikashram for widows founded in 1896, he went on to establish Bombay's first women's university in 1916. It is clear that his ideas had evolved over the period.

Some members of the Hindu upper castes also educated their daughters, wives and sisters at home. In the patriarchal society of Bombay, however, only a few saw the need for this. Ananta Shastri, a chitpavan brahmin, educated his daughter, Ramabai, in the sacred Sanskrit texts. She was later given the titles of Pandita and Saraswati by the learned brahmins of Calcutta.[53]

Among the Muslims, Badruddin Tyabji was the first in Bombay to send his daughters to a girl's school. This was the one at Mazagaon set up under the auspices of the Zenana Bible

Medical Mission in 1876. His daughters continued their schooling till they were fifteen or sixteen. They rode horses in the outskirts of the city, and had already started uncovering their faces outside busy localities. In fact, their family had the distinction of being the first to discard the purdah.[54] In 1904, Badruddin sent his daughters to boarding school at Haslemere in England to continue their education. The Parsi reformer Maneckji Cursetji also gave his daughter a thorough knowledge of English, and his example was followed by Framji Cowasjee Banajee and Jamsetjee Jeejeebhoy.[55]

When Ananta Shastri give his daughter an education, he taught his wife to read as well.[56] Social persecution did not discourage him, even though he had to take shelter in the forest of Gungamal in the Western Ghats. Ranade, too, educated his second wife, Ramabai. She says in her autobiography:

> He asked whether I could read and write. I could do neither. So that very night I was given a slate and a pencil and the first lesson of seven syllables, shriganeshyanamah, was taught. It was my first chance to handle a slate and pencil, and my first glimpse of the alphabet. It took nearly two hours for me to be able to read and write those seven letters ... I was taught the alphabet and the barakhadis (Devanagari alphabet) and, after about a fortnight, I read the first lesson of the first reader with some help.[57]

Anandibai Joshi was the first Indian woman to receive a degree in medicine from Philadelphia. She was taught initially by her husband, Gopalrao Joshi. As he had said:

> I have certain expectations from this marriage. I will educate my wife [and] I will also teach her English. She will be required to study the whole day.[58]

Gopalrao bought his wife school books on Marathi, arithmetic, grammar, Sanskrit and English, saying from now on she must no longer ask why this and why that. He says that, eventually, "a thirst for knowledge was kindled within her, and she felt like grasping all that was offered to her immediately."[59] Another woman educated by her husband was Kashibai Kanitkar, who went on to become active in women's issues. She says her husband did not approve of her ordinary looks but, as she once heard him tell somebody, if she educated herself, it might be possible to live with her.[60]

It was mostly upper-caste men who educated their wives. An exception was Savitribai Phule. Afterwards, she assisted her husband, Jyotiba Phule, as a teacher. Though she had to face severe social persecution, she was not discouraged, and carried on teaching with determination.[61]

Joshi, a friend of Karve, encouraged his sister Godhubai, later Anandibai Karve, to join the Sharda Sadan for her initial schooling. Another student of this place was Venubai Namjoshi, a cousin of its G.G. Agarkar.[62] Venubai went on to do her matriculation, and assisted Karve when he founded his Anath Balikashram.[63]

In conclusion, one can say that both the formal institutions established by the (male) intelligentsia and their private efforts succeeded in instilling among a tiny section of women the desire for education. Journals on social and educational issues were part of these efforts. The aim was to create an awareness among women and help them overcome irrational customs. In the Bengal presidency, Sasipada Banerjee founded the first women's journal in Bengali. It was run by his two daughters, and staffed exclusively by women. In the Bombay presidency, journals that carried similar messages were *Stri Bodh* and *Rast Goftar*. The former was started in 1857 by Cursetjee Nurserwanjee Cama; the latter was begun in 1851 by Dadabhai Naoroji.

Notes

1. The Bombay intelligentsia of the period may be defined as all those educated in English at the collegiate classes of Elphinstone Institution before the founding of Bombay University, as well as those who got degrees at this university afterwards. The term also includes those who attended

professional institutions such as Grant Medical College and government law classes, both before and after degree programmes were begun. See Christine Dobbin, *Urban Leadership in Western India—Politics and Communities in Bombay City 1840–1855*, p. 28.

2. Neera Desai, *Women in Modern India*, pp. 55–57.
3. Charles H. Heimsath, *Indian Nationalism and Hindu Social Reform*, pp. 16–17.
4. S. Nurulla and J.P. Naik, *A Student's History of Education in India: 1800–1916*, p. 194.
5. H.V. Derozio and his followers felt that rapid changes in the existing social institutions would not only reform society but also lead to all-round progress.
6. K.K. Datta, *Social History of Modern India*, pp. 260–265.
7. Ishwar Chand Vidyasagar, *Marriage of Hindu Widows*, pp. 15–16.
8. S. Natarajan, *A Century of Social Reform in India*, p. ix.
9. D.K. Karve, *Looking Back*, pp. 47; *Atamvrith va Charit*, pp. 7, 50–51.
10. *Ibid.*, pp. 50–51.
11. *Ibid.*, pp. 50–51.
12. N. Desai, *op. cit.*, pp. 82–83.
13. Charles H. Heimsath, *op. cit.*, pp. 23–24.
14. A.K. Bhagwat, *Maharashtra—A Profile*, p. 336.
15. D.K. *Karve, op. cit.*, pp. 43–44.
16. R.P. Karkaria, *India: Forty Years of Progress and Reform, Being a Sketch of the Life and Times of Behramji N. Malabari*, p. 129.
17. *Indian Worthies*, Vol. I, Bombay Manoranjak Grantha Prasarak Mandali, 1906, p. 57.
18. Raja Ram Mohan Roy told Bentinck, when he met him for the first time, that he opposed legislation on sati because the British, a foreign power, should not interfere with Hindu customs. He felt that reform should come from within Hindu society through education and persuasion. For details, see V.N. Datta, *Sati: A Historical, Social and Philosophical Enquiry into the Rite of Widow Burning*, pp. 119, 129–132, and Charles H. Heimsath, *op. cit.*, p. 11.
19. S. Natarajan, *op. cit.*, p. 66.
20. Charles H. Heimsath, *op. cit.*, p. 21.
21. In 1889, Tilak was one of the first to sign a pledge to educate

his daughters and not get them married below the age of 10. For details, see S. Natrajan, *op. cit.*, pp. 66–67.

22. D. Keer, *Lokamanya Tilak, Father of our Freedom Struggle*, p. 56.
23. "The bhadralok frowned upon popular, traditional songs and recitals within the andarmahal as exposing women to wantonness and vulgarity. Thus, women's education was a way, both of detaching upper-caste women from any contact with 'the vulgar masses', and of curing them of their latent vulgarity." See Radha Kumar, *The History of Doing: An Illustrated Account of Movements for Women's Rights and Feminism in India, 1800–1900*, p. 15.
24. S.J. Singh, *B.M. Malabari—Rambles with the Pilgrim Reformer*, pp. 122–123.
25. R.P. Karkaria, *op. cit.*, p. 118.
26. Hiralal Lallubhai Kaji, *Life and Speeches of Sir Vithaldas Thackersey*, p. 195.
27. V.R. (Karamveer) Shinde, *Renaissance in Western India, 1873–1944*, p. 141.
28. *Ibid.*, p. 141.
29. Aparna Basu, "A century's journey: women's education in Western India 1820–1920", in Karuna Chanana (ed.), *Socialization, Education and Women—Explorations in Gender Identity*, NMML, New Delhi, 1988.
30. *Ibid.*
31. Ganesh L. Chandavarkar, *Maharishi Karve*, p. 80.
32. S.K. Nehru (ed.), *Our Cause*, pp. 8–9.
33. Ganesh L. Chandavarkar, *op. cit.*, p. 85.
34. D.K. Karve, *op. cit.*, p. 59.
35. S. Natrajan, *op. cit.*, p. 33.
36. Jogesh C. Bagal, *History of the Bethune School and College, 1849–1949*, pp. 12–13.
37. Stanley A. Wolpert, *Tilak and Gokhale: Revolution and Reform in the Making of Modern India*, pp. 6–7; Ganesh L. Chandavarkar, *op. cit.*, p. 54; D. Keer, *Mahatma Jotirao Phule: Father of Our Social Revolution*, p. 83.
38. D. Keer, *op. cit.*, p. 83.
39. A.K. Bhagwat, *op. cit.*, p. 335; Charles H. Heimsath, *op. cit.*, pp. 99–100;
40. Stanley A. Wolpert, *op. cit.*, p. 6; Charles H. Heimsath, *op. cit.*, p. 100.

41. Charles H. Heimsath, *op. cit.*, p. 101.
42. *Ibid.*, p. 101.
43. S. Natrajan, *op. cit.*, pp. 54–55; Charles H. Heimsath, *op. cit.*, p. 100; S. Nurulla and J.P. Naik, *op. cit.*, p. 189; Christine Dobbin, *op. cit.*, pp. 55–56.
44. *Famous Parsis: Biographical and Critical Sketches of Patriots, Philanthropists, Politicians, Reformers, Scholars and Captains of Industry*, pp. 16, 186.
45. D. Keer, *op. cit.*, pp. 62–63.
46. *Ibid.*, pp. 62–63.
47. Charles H. Heimsath, *op. cit.*, pp. 92–95.
48. *Ibid.*, p. 55.
49. *Ibid.*
50. *Ibid.*
51. *Ibid.*, p. 66.
52. Charles H. Heimsath, *op. cit.*, pp. 160–161.
53. Ramabai Saraswati, *The High-Caste Hindu Woman*, pp. 8–11.
54. Husain B. Tyabji, *Badruddin Tyabji, a Biography*, pp. 71–79.
55. F.H. Bana, *History of Institutions Supported by Parsi Philanthropy and Enterprise in Education*, p. 150.
56. Helen S. Dyer, *Pandita Ramabai: The Story of Her Life*, p. 10.
57. Kusumvati Deshpande, *Ranade—His Wife's Reminiscences*, pp. 3–7.
58. J. Joshi, *op. cit.*, pp. 49–50.
59. *Ibid.*, pp. 123–124.
60. Sarojini Vaid, *Shrimati Kashibai Kanitkar Atmacharit ani Charit*, p. 74.
61. Jyotiba Phule Samagrah Granth, p. 294.
62. Agarkar's letter, Poona, dated 25 November 1890, NMML.
63. Mahadev Patwardhan, *Autobiography and Character of D.D. Karve*, pp. 187–188.

Gandhi and the National Education Movement

B.M. SANKHDHER

Gandhi had a unique understanding of human nature. He was among the few Indian leaders able to look clearly at the working of the British mind. He understood the psychology of British colonialism, and used it to defeat them. He knew the British were using education for their own political purposes. They had imposed their own ideas and institutions despite the total non-applicability of most of them. Gandhi attacked the colonial system at its base. He described it as "sinful, with a tendency to dwarf the Indians, body, mind and soul."

Gandhi's educational philosophy was evolved with the help of stalwarts like Zakir Husain, Kakasaheb Kalelkar, K.T. Shah, Jamnalal Bajaj and K.G. Saiyidain. To his mind, his scheme was better suited to the needs and aspirations of the Indian people. It came to be called the Wardha scheme of education.[1] Gandhi wanted education to be an effective instrument for the realization of India's independence, besides achieving social justice and the eradication of illiteracy and poverty. By contrast, India had suffered incalculably because of the introduction of the British system of education.[2] He was particularly incensed at the replacement of the Indian languages by English as the medium of instruction. He felt that elementary and mass education should be through the vernacular or mother tongue.[3] He described the colonial system of primary education as a "snare and a delusion."[4] He said:

> The present system of education does not meet the requirements of the country. English has created a permanent bar between the highly educated few and the uneducated many. It has prevented knowledge from percolating to the masses. The excessive importance given to English has cast ... a burden which has maimed them mentally and made them strangers in their own land.[5]

Colonial Exploitation through Education

To many Indian leaders, British education was founded on multiple fallacies. According to Annie Besant, the primary fallacy was the British conviction that a foreign system of education would best promote the interests of the Indian people. She also felt it denied Indians the knowledge of their own past, which "conduces to patriotism and enables the formation of a sound judgement."[6] Other Indian educationists and political leaders were also astonished why the system should emphasize British studies while neglecting Indian philosophy, science and religion. A large number of them were not impressed by British advances in the fields of science or technology. At one time, the British India Association had even submitted a detailed memorandum to the government in this regard.[7]

The system also kept the Indian languages undeveloped, so that science and other subjects could not be taught in them. Many Indian educationists protested this treatment of their languages,[8] as did Sir William Jones and many members of the Asiatic Society, who were convinced that Sanskrit was among the most scientific languages of the world. But the British, with all the arrogance of a colonial power, did not yield. They had remained unmoved even earlier, in the first half of the nineteenth century, when Robert Macnaghten made a powerful appeal in favour of Indian languages, saying "impart ideas not words." Among the nineteenth-century educationists who protested the use of English as the medium of instruction were Radhakant Dev, Jagannath Shankarseth, Bankimchandra Chatterjee, B.D. Basu, Mahendranath Banerjee, Srinivasa Shastri, R.G. Bhandarkar and Madan Mohan Malviya. Gandhi agreed with them.[9]

The protestations continued into the twentieth century. Lala Hardayal said in 1922, "This British educational policy diminishes Indians' love for Rama, Krishna and Guru Govind. The British system of education throws our social life out of gear." Lala Lajpatrai added that the system was "calculated to prolong indefinitely our political bondage." Gandhi claimed that the British used their education for religious and political purposes.[10] The system was un-Indian, and it ignored the religious sentiments and moral values of the people.[11]

In the wake of Bengal's partition in 1905, some Indians established a National Council of Education and a network of "national" educational institutions all over the country. A growing number of Indian leaders now agreed that the British system only perpetuated India's political bondage. Gandhi called the British system of education sinful, discriminatory and racist.[12] Whenever possible, it even injected the venom of communalism into Indian society and politics.[13]

Many Indians resented having to learn British history and undertake, in some Christian institutions, compulsory Bible study. They had no choice because, wherever there were large Christian educational institutions, the government was reluctant to open its own.[14] As for the indigenous institutions, a large majority of them found it extremely difficult to receive any aid or financial support from the government.[15]

The racism Gandhi spoke about was evident when it came to appointments, promotions, scholarships, study abroad, training and other monetary incentives. British teachers were paid much more than their Indian counterparts, as were those who taught English rather than Indian languages.

Statistics show that the number of Christians increased yearly.[16] It was this conversion through education that Gandhi and many other Indian leaders called "sinful".[17] They also felt the government was high-handed in closing down women's educational institutions because they refused the entry of British male officials for examinations and inspections.[18]

Gandhi thought that race differences would vanish if the vernaculars became the medium of instruction.[19] The system discouraged manual work; the people were "weaned away from the plough, the axe and the loom," as Radhakant Dev said in 1835.[20] The system did not create opportunities for industrial growth through science and technology, and it hardly cared about medical care, education for all, and the removal of poverty and social injustice.[21] It had a tendency to dwarf the people and produce social parasites. It was expensive without being self-supporting or related to employment opportunities. It did not meet the expectations of those who wanted education to create excellent, economically viable units or individuals.[22]

Colonialism cannot survive except when a sense of inferiority is injected into the minds of the subject people. The British, therefore, tried their utmost to do this through a sometimes subtle, sometimes blatant policy of debasement, denunciation and destruction towards the inheritors of a great civilization and culture.[23] The British pushed the idea of the "white man's burden". They never tired of reiterating the "superiority" of the British people, British civilization and Christianity.[24]

Gandhi's educational ideas were a radical departure. Since the establishment of British rule, others had condemned British education as unreal, inadequate, rootless, shallow, alien, demoralizing, even denationalizing. It was also called bastard, communal, and a road to "imminent national death."[25] But no one, before Gandhi, condemned it in moral terms like "conceived and born in error, nurtured in sin." Nor had anyone else castigated British colonialism for being so ignorant of Indian ideas and aspirations and yet forcing its educational system on the country.[26] Others had pointed out the shortcomings and drawbacks of the British educational system, but no one had yet called it positively harmful.[27] Sir Surendranath Bannerji and Annie Besant did talk about the "emasculation" of the Indian people by British rule, but it was Gandhi who traced the cause to British education. He insisted it was a handicap, and had made Indians strangers in their own land.[28]

Impact on the Struggle for Freedom

The ideas described above culminated as follows.

1. In quick succession, some educationists renounced their government honours, titles and awards.
2. There were country-wide boycotts of government-controlled and government-aided institutions by some students and teachers.[29] This coincided, around 1920, with the establishment of the Jamia Millia Islamia and Kashi Vidyapith universities, and a network of national schools and colleges at Poona, Ahmedabad, Lahore and Patna.
3. Some students decided they would stop paying their fees and other dues.

In response to Gandhi's call, many teachers and students also organized massive political meetings and took out prabhat pheris (processions). They set fire to British-made clothes and goods, wore khadi, and refused to cooperate with the British in every possible manner.[30] They openly defied colonial laws and regulations.[31] They felt, with Bipin Chandra Pal that education could wait but swarajya could not. Thus they courted arrest, faced bullets and suffered tortures and humiliations.[32] Although most of these activities were peaceful, following Gandhi's concept of satyagraha, there were also students, teachers and even principals who adopted terrorist methods.

Gandhi's educational thought, as his entire political and economic philosophy, continued to evolve with the passage of time. But he remained steadfast to some ideas, among them the following.

1. British rule in India was "satanic" and India could therefore have "no respect or affection" for the British government.[33]

2. The British system of education was a trap; it had done irreparable loss to the country.
3. Learning without earning could never succeed in India; hence the use of devices like the charkha (the spinning wheel).

Like the charkha, Gandhi's national education scheme operated quickly, and both horizontally and vertically. It drew in countless millions, including women and children, and also those who had no direct involvement in education. The charkha was a powerful, almost mystical symbol of his entire philosophy. The rest of the world could not understand its significance, and yet it did wonders. It created a bloodless revolution, and its impact on education was clearly discernible. It produced cords of unity linking the countless numbers involved in India's struggle for national education, emancipation and enlightenment. The charkha provided a unique monetary mooring to Indian society and, to extend the metaphor, the threads it spun roped off the ruinous fabrics imported from Lancashire and Manchester.

Gandhi's Radical Approach to Education

As noted earlier, Gandhi was the first to proclaim that British education was destructive and a trap. Thus, it could be suspended or even given up for the achievement of a higher national ideal: swarajya.[34] He borrowed openly from but gave a new orientation to the educational ideas of others: Radhakant Dev, Dayanand Saraswati, Ramakrishna, Vivekananda, Dadabhai Naoroji, Syed Ahmed Khan, Gopalkrishna Gokhale, Balgangadhar Tilak, Aurobindo and Madanmohan Malaviya. Also radical was the way he managed to involve almost everyone he came in contact with in the stupendous task of enlightenment and nation building.

Gandhi felt that students and teachers should not keep themselves aloof from politics or the struggle for India's independence. Their participation was imperative not merely because of political expediency; it was also their inescapable moral obligation.[35] They should feel no ambiguity or timidity about this. They should prepare themselves to face police batons, tear gas and bullets, and be ready to undergo solitary confinement, physical torture or even death.

Gandhi's was a movement for all: the rich and the poor, the young and the old, the employed and the unemployed. It was an everyday programme involving spinning, weaving, knitting and earning as well as learning.[36] It was a total movement because it was not confined to education alone, but involved politics, society, economy, religion and culture.

Gandhi was absolutely sure of his movement's success, even in the initial stages. This was why he had no hesitation in asking students and teachers to join it whole-heartedly and in great numbers. In a historic address at a huge public meeting at Calcutta on October 16, 1920, he shocked the British Empire by promising the people of India swarajya within a year.

Gandhi did not claim that his movement was a panacea for all the educational and social ills of India. What he wanted was to make the Indian take a rational, realistic attitude towards the problems of their own enlightenment and freedom. They should develop the courage and conviction to throw overboard their worn-out traditions as well as the effects of British colonialism, which had dwarfed them body, mind and soul. Gandhi's replacement of the colonial system of education by his Wardha scheme was a part of his total philosophy for the upliftment of his people. It was a philosophy for political emancipation, social justice, economic progress, communal harmony and religious tolerance through truth, peace and non-violence.

Notes

1. For details, see C.J. Verkey, *The Wardha Scheme of Education*, London, 1940, and K.L. Shrimali, *The Wardha Scheme*, Udaipur, 1949.
2. On the contrary, Dadabhai Naoroji wrote in his well-known book, *Poverty and Un-British Rule in India*: "If there is one thing more than another for which the Indian people are ...

deeply grateful to the British nation ... it is the blessing of education, which Britain has bestowed upon India."

3. Even in the nineteenth century, many Indian educationists and thinkers had stressed the need for instruction in the vernaculars. Gurudas Bannerjee, the first Indian vice-chancellor of the University of Calcutta, had emphasized in an 1892 convocation speech the need for introducing the mother tongue as the medium of instruction. Similar views were expressed by the great poet-philosopher, Rabindranath Tagore, in 1893. For details, see Uma and Haridas Mukherjee, *The Origins of the National Education Movement: 1905–10*, Calcutta, 1957.
4. *The Harijan*, September 18, 1937.
5. *The Young India*, April 27, 1921.
6. For the views of Srinivasa Sastri, Annie Besant, the Lord Bishop of Madras and Gandhi on using the vernaculars as the medium of instruction, see *Government of India, Home Department, Education A: Proceedings*, No. 1, September, 1919.
7. This was submitted to Sir John Lawrence, Viceroy and Governor-General of India, on August 1, 1867. The prominent signatories were Raja Jaikishan Das, Syed Ahmed Khan, Badri Prasad and Ishwarchandra Mukherjee. See *Government of India, Home Department, Education A: Proceedings*, No. 19, September, 1867.
8. Manindranath Banerjee explained in 1915 how using Sanskrit scientific terminology would not in any way be a handicap.
9. Mahatma Gandhi likened British antagonism to the vernaculars to a sandcastle. In a speech on February 17, 1916, only a year after he returned from South Africa, he boldly remarked that the objections against the introduction of the vernaculars were all baseless. See *Government of India, Education A: Proceedings*, No. 1, September 1919.
10. Thomas Macaulay wrote that if the British system of education continued, there would not be any idolaters. Other British educationists and politicians were sure it could bring benefits because Indians taught this way would demand British goods. See B.M. Sankhdher, *Press, Politics and Public Opinion in India: Dynamics of Modernization and Social Transformation*, New Delhi, 1984.
11. In the first half of the nineteenth century, James Buckingham pleaded for adult education in India, and Thomas Munro submitted plans for mass education. A Bombay society for the

education of the poor wanted rapid expansion of education among the underprivileged sections of society, and Gopalkrishna Gokhale started a powerful movement for free, compulsory, elementary education. However, the British government was interested only in a limited education to suit the exigencies of their rule.

12. It was morally indefensible because, till 1877, women were not allowed to appear even in the matriculation examinations of Indian universities.
13. For example, the government encouraged the establishment of such purely Muslim institutions as the Calcutta Madrasa, the Bethune School and Dacca University.
14. In Assam, for example, there was no government educational institution for women, even till the last quarter of the nineteenth century.
15. As early as 1843, the British tried to introduce the Bible as a textbook in government schools. Gazulu Chetty (1806–1868), the founder-president of the Madras Native Association, was one who opposed this move.
16. The number of Christians in India increased at an average rate of about 100,000 every year from 1891 to 1947: from 100,000 in 1891, the total number went up to 10,000,000 in 1947.
17. As early as the first half of the nineteenth century, many Indians condemned the use of education or educational institutions to spread Christianity by converting the poor and the needy. Balshastri Jambhekar condemned the practice in the columns of his paper, *Bombay Darpan*. Later on, Dayananda Saraswati, the founder of the Arya Samaj, described such forcible conversions as sinful.
18. For details, see *Oudh Education Reports* for 1872–73.
19. *The Young India*, 1922.
20. Radhakant Dev described the British system of education in India as "insensible". See William Adam, *Report on Vernacular Education in Bengal and Bihar*, submitted to the government in 1835.
21. Kristodas Pal condemned the British system of education because it did not encourage the development of science or the establishment of large industries. Thus India had to import "pins and matchboxes", even after 100 years of British rule. Later, R.L. Madholkar condemned the whole system for reducing industrial India into an agricultural country.

22. This was stated by S. Rajagopalchari of the Council of Indian Education, Madras, on May 24, 1915. For details, see *Government of India, Education Department A: Proceedings*, No. 1, September, 1919.
23. B.M. Sankhdher, *op. cit.*
24. The idea of the white man's burden was a cover to propagate Christianity.
25. These expressions were among those used by Indian educationists and national leaders such as Chittaranjan Das, Keshavchandra Sen, Dadabhai Naoroji, Bipinchandra Pal, Satishchandra Mukherjee, Lala Lajpatrai, Lala Hardayal, Hans Mehta, Subodhkant Mallick, Surendranath Banerjee and Aurobindo.
26. *The Harijan*, September 10, 1937.
27. Valentine Chirol wanted a complete change in the British system of education in India because, to her mind, it was responsible for the production of "unemployables".
28. R.N. Gilchrist, *Indian Nationality*, 1920. He says here, "It was pathetic to see students mentally searching for nouns and conjugating verbs before speaking or writing. The student flounders among his ideas. The progress is backward."
29. Much of this began earlier, after the partition of Bengal in 1905. But with the coming of Gandhi onto the political scene, the whole movement underwent a radical transformation. Even those Indians not directly involved now joined the movement for national education as a part of India's struggle for freedom.
30. The participation of students, teachers and other educationists in politics was hitherto considered taboo, both by the government and by society. It was now patronized by some political leaders as a sign of heroism. Prominent were Lala Lajpatrai and Subashchandra Bose, who appealed to the academic community to make the struggle for freedom a success through active, fearless and wholehearted cooperation.
31. Gopalkrishna Gokhale, whom Mahatma Gandhi regarded as his political mentor, considered student participation in politics completely unjustifiable. He said, "The active participation of students in political agitation really tends to lower the dignity and responsible character of public life, and impairs its true effectiveness." Quoted by Srinivasa Sastri in "Students and politics", *The Indian Review*, Madras, September, 1930, p. 612.
32. To cite only one example, Sampurananand (1890–1969)

resigned the principalship of Dungar College, Bikaner in 1921 and joined the Non-Cooperation movement. He was imprisoned by the British government.

33. In his well-known letter of March 4, 1930, written to the British viceroy before starting his Civil Disobedience movement, Gandhi wrote, "I hold British rule to be a curse ... It has impoverished the dumb millions, reduced us politically to serfdom, sapped the foundations of our culture and degraded us spiritually."
34. Gandhi was condemned for this by many, who said he had no business destroying the careers of young men and women. Openly opposed were Asutosh Mukherjee, Rabindranath Tagore and Madanmohan Malaviya. Even Annie Besant and Srinivasa Sastri were not prepared to support him because they did not want education to be suspended for a single day.
35. Many of Gandhi's followers and friends also advocated active participation by students in politics, among them Lala Lajpatrai, called the "Lion of Punjab". Presiding over an all-India conference of students in Nagpur in 1920, Lajpatrai said, "I am not one of those who believe that students, particularly university students, ought not 'meddle' in politics ... It is a most stupid theory."
36. These activities started at sunrise and continued even after sunset.

SECTION IV: SCIENTIFIC AND TECHNICAL EDUCATION

Educational Ideas of Bengali Scientists from 1850 to 1920

DEEPAK KUMAR

We shall begin by citing the views of scientists from the two ends of the time period of the title. In a June 1855, lecture at Calcutta on the appointment of "natives of India" to the Indian Covenanted Services, S.C. Chuckerbutty says:

> Education, in its intellectual sense, means the drawing out, disciplining, strengthening, and refining the powers of the understanding; and no language is more calculated for this work in the present state of our country than English ... It has made us all independent thinkers, and some of us independent actors.

A different perspective is given by P.C. Ray seventy years later. In September, 1923, he addressed the convocation at Jamia Millia Islamia, Aligarh, as follows:

> Oxford and Cambridge, with their costly appurtenances, will not do for us; in the rage for forms, furniture and machinery, we must not lose the substance ... Let us not give merely a purely theoretic and literary education that has unfitted us for the affairs of the world, and made us service hunters, thus inviting to our schools the appellation of golam-khanas. Let us, along with the humanistic studies, which are by no means too neglected, arrange for scientific and technical studies which will enable our boys to earn an independent livelihood.

S.C. Chuckerbutty (1824–74) was one of the first Indians to receive higher education in Western medicine, and the first to compete successfully for admission to the Indian Medical Service (IMS). It is natural that he should talk glowingly of Western education, language and method. Exposure to the new education definitely turned some Indians into "independent thinkers" and, to some extent, "independent actors" as well. But as the years rolled by, the complexities and benefits of this encounter with the West were intensely debated. P.C. Ray (1861–1944), a fine chemist and teacher, appears more cautious, even despondent. He shifts the focus from independent thinking to "independent livelihood." How did this shift occur? How did the new men of science view colonial education, and what did they think of national education? What makes education national? Is it the medium of instruction, the structures of control, or books and ideas? The present paper seeks to probe into the way the first generation of Indian scientists coped with the tensions of the new but alien system of education, and what alternatives they had in mind.

Early Stirrings

After becoming the first Indian to top the list of successful candidates at the IMS examination in 1855, Chuckerbutty went on to become professor of *materia medica* and clinical medicine at Calcutta Medical College. Between 1854 and 1870, he delivered a series of lectures on subjects like "native" education, "national" education, the medical profession and sanitary conditions.[1] He defined education as "the cultivation of the mind in relation to the laws of external nature and of our own consciousness," and called it "a result of civilization and the surest sign of human progress."[2] He was forthright enough to admit European superiority, not in racial but in civilizational terms. The finest scientists, laureates and statesmen were to be found "only among the European races," and this he attributed not to their climate or race, but to "the advanced state of their social institutions."[3]

Comparing the social upbringing of an average European with an average Indian, he severely criticized Indian child-rearing methods, the role of gurus, and the fact that the whole learning process ended in clerkdom. As for the subject matter, he found the brahminical system extremely "verbose", leading to no practical results. The Islamic system, with its emphasis on learning by rote, was no less defective. Though he considered the Western system of education "progressive and inevitable," he was aware of its deficiencies in a colonial set-up. He called it "partial" education, "the owner of which may be skillful in special pursuits, but yet remain exposed to the evil influences of designing men who have their own purposes to serve." These "designing men" could be from the new power structure (i.e., colonial government), or from the old, orthodox structures of the brahminical/Islamic variety. The net result in both cases was the same—servility.

In two elaborate public lectures delivered in July, 1861, Chuckerbutty examined native education from a "psychological" point of view. The Hindus could not be faulted on account of perception and reflection, at which they were superb. What they lacked was "watchful observation" and "varied experiments." And what would science be without these two? Along with reflection, one also required ratiocination: "Reflection gives birth to theories and speculation; ratiocination, to accurate and rigid deductions."[4] Knowledge can be acquired through several ways, like instruction, imitation, observation, experiment, induction and abstraction; a good system of education must involve all of them.

This seemed a tall order, especially for a colonial government. So Chuckerbutty wanted it to evolve from within and sought the cooperation of all. He was not alone in this. During 1850–70, an influential section of the emerging middle class continued to ponder different aspects of Indian education, especially the growing demand for science education. Akshay Kumar Dutta, in his famous journal *Tattvabodhini Patrika*, regretted "the lack of coherence and judicious symmetry in the educational system."[5] He published a few elementary books on science in Bengali (e.g., *Padartho Vidya* in 1856), and a number of articles asking for a new techno-scientific education which would enable the students to "earn their livelihood independently and respectfully."

Dutta (as well as several other cultural interlocutors) did try to show that whatever good existed in Western science existed also in ancient India.[6] One does not find this attitude in Chuckerbutty or Mahendralal Sarkar (1833–1904). Both were products of the new medical education. In 1869, Sarkar published a pamphlet "on the desirability of a national institution for the cultivation of the sciences by the natives of India." This was the first attempt to articulate a "national" science. The very next year, Chuckerbutty addressed his students on national education. Earlier, in 1858, he had accused the newly-established Calcutta University of ignoring this aspect. The comprehensive scheme he now proposed would include:

1. vernacular education for the largest diffusion of knowledge;
2. (Oriental) classical education as a complement to the vernacular languages for their improvement and refinement;
3. English education for (a) the highest intellectual and moral development, (b) the most successful pursuit of the physical sciences, and (c) the political education and consolidation of the nation;[7]
4. the union of physical with intellectual education, which would purge the people of their "excessive timidity and sensuality;"[8] and
5. introduction of female education to create a "chastening society of intelligent mothers, virtuous wives, and well-bred sisters."

S.C. Chuckerbutty did not live very long, but he did move a long way from brahmin birth to Christian adulthood, and from an Anglophile stance to nationalistic assertions. His unorthodox views and ways did not endear him to his own people, or even to the government which he served with so much devotion and distinction.[9] He defied his parents and never regretted it. When he embraced Christianity in England, a Calcutta journal called him "an atheist who could not care for any religion."[10] A doctor by training, he remained an educationist to the core, for he considered education not only the best means of ensuring national prosperity, but also "the only means of creating an intellectual commonwealth of all nations." This is precisely what Rabindranath Tagore (1861–1941) was to espouse and epitomize later.

While Chuckerbutty the loner, could not make a big dent, Mahendralal Sarkar was much more active socially, but professionally isolated. In 1865, he helped establish the Bengal branch of the British Medical Association, but only two years later, to the utter disbelief and disgust of his colleagues, he shifted to homoeopathy.[11] Sarkar was unorthodox in one more sense. Sensing that the Indian university system (unlike London University, on which it had been modelled) was not well disposed towards science, he tried to put this subject on the top of the educational agenda. In 1969, he wrote on "the desirability of a national institution for the cultivation of sciences by the natives of India."

Like Chuckerbutty, Sarkar began by blaming the Hindu mind for being more speculative than practical, deficient in observation, and "too prone to hasty generalizations." But unlike Chuckerbutty, Sarkar offered only one remedy: the cultivation of the physical sciences. He asked for the establishment of an institution "which would combine the character, the scope and objects of the Royal Institution in London and the British Association for the Advancement of Science."[12] To inculcate the virtues of self-reliance, he wanted it to be entirely under Indian management and control. His obsession was unique, and this distinguished him from his contemporaries. He came to symbolize dissatisfaction as well as hope. Commending his proposal, a journal wrote, "We confess we are not at all satisfied with the government system of education. Whatever our educated natives have learnt, they have, we may say, learnt in spite of it."[13] Another journal expressed the hope that a new system of education would usher in "a complete reorganization of all our social institutions."[14] This was a far-fetched hope, but surely not misplaced.

Sarkar was very clear about his objective, which he would not allow to be confused with the demand for technical education. This was necessary because, instead of the pure science institution he wanted, the Bengal government, with the help of the Indian League, tried to promote a college of practical sciences for technical and industrial education. This was a subtle attempt to dislodge science from the educational agenda. Even well-meaning friends fell for the ploy. An influential Indian paper wrote of Sarkar: "The word science has misled him. [It is] a word which he jealously guards as his own property."[15] But Sarkar did not budge, and had his association opened in 1876 on his own terms. The debate and its rancour nevertheless had an adverse effect. The new association was granted affiliation by Calcutta University only to the F.A. level; B.Sc. affiliation came only at the end of the century! But his movement for the cultivation of science had an enormous psychological impact. It symbolized the search for a distinct Indian identity in the world of science. Even the British vice-chancellor of Calcutta University called for "the erection of national schools of science [and] the creation of a national literature" to take new knowledge to the masses.[16]

A Cultural Articulation

These stirrings must have deeply influenced students in Calcutta during the 1870s and 1880s. P.N. Bose, J.C. Bose, R.S. Trivedi and P.C. Ray were among those who later made their mark. P.N. Bose recalls that his enthusiasm for "modern culture" was so great that when awarded a fellowship in 1874 to study in England, he chose natural science, not law.[17] He specialized in geology at the University of London, and later joined the Geological Survey of India. In 1886, he wrote a pamphlet on technical and scientific education in Bengal and, a decade later, published three volumes titled *A History of Hindu Civilization*. Fierce nationalism had transformed a geologist into a historian, shifting him from physical mapping to cultural contours.

Like Chuckerbutty and Sarkar before him, P.N. Bose held the brahminical system responsible for seriously neglecting physical science. "Hindu civilization carries the germs of its decay within it," he said, but never agreed with his (geological) chief's perception of Indians as "utterly incapable of any original work in natural science."[18] He saw no reason why, "with an improved system of scientific education, and with just and sympathetic treatment, the young men trained in India, [could not] take a place in the modern scientific world." He pointed to the Japanese: "Instead of being thwarted, discouraged, and set down as incapable, [they] have been aided, encouraged and stimulated by their government to pursue science."[19]

Bose seemed to have forgotten that Japan was not a colony. He did realize, however, that he lived in a colony, and could not always get the "just and sympathetic treatment" he wanted. Every concession had to be literally wrung; it was a struggle in slow-motion but on a high pitch. In 1886, P.N. Bose asked for a science course at the F.A. (intermediate) level to facilitate early specialization, but such a course was not introduced till 1906. He also pointed to defects in the B.Sc. course. For example, it was divided into literary and scientific parts, and Presidency College did not have separate departments for botany, zoology and geology. This last subject was taught by officers of the Geological Survey on a purely temporary basis; he could not imagine any progress coming from such "intermittent lectures." At the Bengal Engineering College in Shibpur, chemistry, physics, geology and metallurgy were all taught by the same teacher.[20]

P.N. Bose wanted science subjects to be taught with an eye to their application to industry. At the same time, he warned against the dark side of European industrialism, namely, the growth of militarism and imperialism.[21] He preferred the cultivation of science and technology "within the limits of intellectual culture." Later, the experience of the first world war made him revert to "the propagation of ancient culture" (as represented by India), which would "rescue humanity from the morass of militarism, malevolence, destitution [and] disease."[22] Thus Bose came to want change and progress but on his own cultural terms and without losing Indian values.

A sharper articulation of the cultural dimensions of techno-scientific education came from Ramendra Sundar Trivedi (1864–1919), a science teacher and, later, principal of Ripon College in Calcutta. He wrote a number of thematically rich yet seemingly popular science articles in Bengali, which were collected together in book form as *Prakriti* (1896) and *Jigyasa* (1904). In 1855, Chuckerbutty had hailed Trivedi as "an independent thinker;" forty-four years later, Trivedi asked, "Is the thinking that we lovingly cherish as our own, truly ours?" He wondered if, despite an English education, the Indians were able to think on their own:

> Have we assimilated scientificity into our system? The very word science throws us into raptures, but what we ultimately imbibe is ... pseudo-science. Having heard that human hair is a non-conductor of electricity, we immediately begin growing pigtails; and as soon as we learn that changes in lunar position cause tides, we take our horoscopes to the astrologer. Can one think of a more piteous situation?[23]

One might be surprised that these questions were asked by a person with a supposedly brahminical, revivalist bias. In fact, they could only have occurred so poignantly to someone with a deep understanding of his traditions, able to relate them to the ideas and requirements of his own time and place.

Trivedi even tried to expand the realm and definition of science:

> Science! science! We all aspire for scientific research. As if science is confined only to physics, chemistry and physiology. As if anthropology is beyond the scope of science; as if historical analysis is outside science's concern.[24]

Such a holistic view may not be appreciated by scientists now, but a century ago it was not so. In fact, scientists like P.N. Bose and P.C. Ray turned into wonderful historians. Like them, Trivedi could see the distorting influence of colonial education and its bureaucracy. The universities had become machines churning out degrees. Even private efforts had come to nought; Sarkar's institution was virtually moribund. Trivedi also criticized the content and quality of education in the tols and chatuspatis, but thought that they, at least, had some "genuine respect for knowledge," which modern educational institutions, with their "mechanized routine," failed to inculcate. P.C. Ray later called them *golam khanas* (slave factories) for the munsifs, clerks, assistant surgeons and overseers needed by the colonial job market.

Trivedi realized that this mechanization could not altogether be avoided; it was part of a global change. That is why he did not follow Gandhi and attack the West with anything he could lay his hands on. Trivedi kept grappling with two different texts: he could accept modernity but not Westernization, and the modern university system of education but not its commercialization. Several Indian thinkers and reformers of his age, like Vivekananda and Aurobindo, held similar views. But Trivedi was a little different because he was deeply aware of the philosophical issues concerning science and scientists, even if (unlike P.C. Ray) he denied modern science any epistemological superiority. He would rather describe Western scientists in Hindu terms: Copernicus as a person with *divyachakkhu* (spiritual vision), Newton as a *rishi* (sage), and Helmholtz as an *avatar* (incarnation).[25]

The Scientists' Perception

In contrast to Trivedi and the others, the two most creative scientists that late nineteenth-century India produced, J.C. Bose (1858–1937) and P.C. Ray (1861–1944), fully accepted the epistemological superiority of modern science. Both of them saw education as the most effective vehicle for the assimilation and gradual diffusion of new ideas. They were well-steeped in Indian history and culture, however, and could discriminate between what was to be taken and what not.

J.C. Bose was a biophysicist who worked on the response of living things to electrical impulses. Borrowing from the technical language of his discipline, he thus described the role of education in the East-West encounter:

> An impulse from the outside reacts on impressionable bodies in two different ways, depending on whether the recipient is inert or fully alive. The inert is fashioned after the pattern of the infinite repetition of one mechanical stamp. But when an organism is fully alive, the answering reaction is often of an altogether different character to the impinging stimulus. The outside shocks stir up the organism to answer feebly or to the utmost in ways as multitudinous and varied as life itself. So the first impetus of Western education impressed itself, on some, in a dead monotony of imitation of things Western; while in others, it awakened all that was greatest in the national memory.[26]

However, unlike P.N. Bose and P.C. Ray, J.C. Bose did not undertake any investigation into "national memory" (i.e., history). But he did try to identify his works with what he considered great in his cultural inheritance. His propositions that life emerges out of non-life, and that there exists an underlying unity between the living and the non-living, were taken as a scientific manifestation of the Samkhya philosophy. J.C. Bose used to quote from the Vedas and had a poetical flavour. He even gave Sanskrit names to his laboratory instruments, and did not see any conflict between science and religion. His contemporaries did not consider him mystical or Oriental; rather, his was hailed as a synthetical mind.[27]

J.C. Bose's works were the first authentic rebuttal of the colonial view that Indians were incapable of original scientific investigations. But his was not an ivory tower projection of education and research. He was convinced of the utilitarian value of science, and wanted its wide-spread diffusion through proper science education. Science must be taught not only for the sake of knowledge but also to harness the economic resources of the country. For example, a science education should enable one to discriminate between industries which can and cannot be profitably carried on under the climatic and other conditions prevailing in India.[28] To achieve this were needed a "satisfactory" science course, good laboratories and scholarships. Bose was particularly perturbed over the science curriculum in Indian universities. At the graduate level in Calcutta University, for example, the vast subjects of acoustics, heat, light, electricity and magnetism got only half an examination paper. To add to the woes of the students, too many textbooks were prescribed, so they looked up help-books. Second-hand knowledge thus took the place of "living science." Even this could not be put to any use because, in the absence of any post-degree scholarship or employment, most students moved to a career in law or administration.

Like his compatriots, Bose excelled in diagnosis, but his solutions were limited and heavily dependent on the government. All through, he remained a devoted researcher, not an activist. P.C. Ray, on the other hand, showed a higher degree of social commitment. He was an educationist, scientist, entrepreneur and Gandhian activist—all rolled into one. He spoke and wrote extensively on educational matters with rare passion, sincerity and clarity. Himself a working scientist and deeply conscious of science's industrial applications, he was one of the earliest to talk about it in terms of social relevance and accountability. He did some original research on India's scientific heritage, attempting a social explanation of what went wrong, when and how.

Unlike Trivedi and others, Ray held the Indian social (caste) structure responsible for the cleavage between mental and manual work, and the resultant stagnation.[29] He wanted modern education to bridge this gulf. In his view, education had to emphasize quality, and aim towards the generation of employment and wealth, not degrees. He called the average graduate "a licensed ignoramus," and the degree itself "a cloak to hide the degree-holder's ignorance." Higher education should be limited to those who feel "an instinctive call in that direction."[30]

The other great defect, in Ray's opinion, was the undue stress on a literary curriculum. In 1930, a Calcutta University student for the M.A. degree had to attend 230 classes in English and only 65 in mathematics. However, he was equally unhappy about the intellectual narrowness of the specialist in science. He visualized a broad "mental culture" in which science, literature, history and philosophy were given almost equal attention. Legal studies, which thrived on colonial requirements, had no place in this scheme. Echoing Gandhi's severe criticism of the legal profession, Ray exclaimed, "If I am made the dictator of the University for one day, I would shut down the law department for at least three years."

Apart from the defective curriculum, what hurt Ray the most was the medium of instruction. He was convinced that learning through a foreign medium killed originality:

> Imagine for a moment what would happen if the English lad were compelled, first of all, to learn Persian or Chinese or, say, German or Russian, and then had to read through the medium of such a tongue ... In India, we have adopted the most unnatural system, and have to pay a heavy penalty for it.[31]

Ray knew that his own forefathers had "gone mad" over English education, but he appreciated why. In the first half of the nineteenth-century, an English education was necessary to acquire new knowledge. Ram Mohan Roy and Vidyasagar had asked for it, although they wrote extensively in Bengali. What Ray resented was that the whole process had degenerated into a "service-seeking mania." He was not against English; he only asked for a late introduction, after the mother tongue had laid the base. J.C. Bose held similar views, and recalled with pride how his father had sent him to a "vernacular" school. This had helped him relate to his surroundings, even if his higher education and research publications had to be in English, the language of the scientific world.[32]

Ray wanted to strengthen the existing institutions of science

Table 1 Calcutta University: Number of graduates

	1858–67	*1868–77*	*1877–87*	*1888–97*	*1898–1907*
Arts: B.A. and M.A. combined	360	1,224	2,717	4,417	5,227
Sciences					
1. B.A. and M.A. combined	72	245	543	883	1,045
2. M.A. alone	11	48	85	133	160
Medicine and surgery: LMS and M.B. combined	101	221	276	20	641
Engineering: all branches combined	33	53	38	70	103

education and research through fellowships, laboratories and private donations. But when J.N. Tata, a leading Bombay merchant, floated the idea of an Indian institute of research, Ray was reticent. He preferred to solicit private munificence for the existing institutions in different parts of the country, rather than create one single island of excellence. He argued, "India is not a compact, homogeneous country like Japan. A central research institute with an imperial university, like that of Tokyo, does not seem to commend itself."[33] Later, in 1931, when the eminent engineer M. Visweswaraya pleaded for a technological university, Ray called it a delusion: "In every country, industrial progress has preceded progress in science and technology."[34] In this industrial progress, he envisaged a greater role for businessmen and workers, rather than graduates in science and the arts. The key to prosperity, he said, lay in the spirit of entrepreneurship, not in mere technical expertise.

As noted, Ray did not advocate higher education for everyone. Primary education was a different matter. As late as 1934, the Bengal government spent just Rs 2.7 million on primary education, less than 1% of the Rs 320 million raised as revenues from the province. Meanwhile, Japan and Denmark spent about 20% of their gross revenue on primary education. Ray cited from the Famine Commission of 1880, the agricultural conference of 1888 and other sources to show how beneficial primary education could be for the peasants. Millions perished in epidemics, and the ignorant masses, steeped in superstition, looked to the goddess Sitala. He said:

> [It is] useless to din Pasteur's researches into their ear ... An ignorant people and a costly machinery of scientific experts go ill together ... It is education, and nothing but education, that can remove social evils, sanitary troubles and economic distress from the country, and can awaken political consciousness and create social solidarity in the people. Self-government without literacy would be nothing but a farce, and might possibly be a tragedy.[35]

The Dichotomies

The fact that science formed the core of modern knowledge and education was recognized very early by Indian cultural interlocutors. Ram Mohan Roy in Bengal and Bal Shastri Jamblekar in Bombay played seminal roles.[36] They began a debate on the context, content and medium of education which continued to engross every succeeding generation. Simply founding educational institutions was not enough, they said; more important was what direction they took and what impact they left.

Ramcomul Sen wrote *Qusadhsamgraha* in 1819; it was the first book on Western medicine in Bengali. When a medical college opened in Calcutta, he guessed that its students would not be the disseminators of any new knowledge, for the lures of private practice would take them away.[37] Later, when some institutions for engineering and technical education were opened, its graduates could see no other avenue than government employment. There were not many of them anyway. B.K. Sarkar, who wrote extensively a century later on education and industrialization, lamented that "engineers, the heroes of the industrial revolution in Euro-America and Japan, were virtually unknown among the leading men of India."

Table 1 summarizes his findings for the period 1858–1907 on the role of Calcutta University in providing scientific education.[38] As late as 1920, Asutosh Mukherjee, a reputed mathematician and twice Vice-Chancellor of Calcutta University, informed his senate:

> I regret to find that the number of students in the department of science has fallen from 174 to 137, whereas the number of students in the department of letters has increased from 1312 to 1380. The number of new admissions in the department of science has remained practically unchanged, but a larger proportion of science students abandoned their studies in the sixth-year class than of those that had selected literary subjects. We have no data to determine whether they left because they could no longer struggle with poverty or because of some other equally potent reason.[39]

Against this background, it is instructive to see how Indian men of science thought about and fought for improvements in education. S.C. Chuckerbutty, one of the first products of Calcutta Medical College, was also one of the earliest to articulate educational imperatives in very definite, "national" terms. Neither an Anglicist nor an Orientalist in the existing sense of the terms, his was an attempt at synthesis, to which he rightly added female education and physical education. Although there is not, unfortunately, a full-length study on him, his views remain as relevant today as they were then.

The "cultivation of science" movement of Mahendralal Sarkar gradually pushed science to the top of the educational agenda. This was, after all, the peak of Comtean influence in Bengal, and several educationists of the time were under the spell of the positivists. Thus science soon became a new deity to the Indians. But for reasons articulated by P.N. Bose, R.S. Trivedi and P.C. Ray, the educational juggernaut remained as it was constructed: the best way for the colonial bureaucracy to secure its survival and continuance. It received indirect but substantial help from the ambivalent attitude of the Indian educationists themselves. They kept arguing about the content and medium of instruction, but they could never reach a consensus or conclusion. Numerous committees and commissions were set up, but none of them could bring about a radical change. In a homogeneous, independent country like Japan, it was possible to take the new knowledge to every section of society.[40] In contrast, the Indians wanted "the light to touch the mountain tops, before it pierced to the levels and depths,"[41] a pious hope that could never become a reality.

All the same, the dilemma faced by Indian educationists was pretty real. Total acceptance of the Western episteme was not thought desirable, while its rejection was almost impossible. There were no clear-cut solutions. The complexities and ambivalences involved make some Indian interlocutors seem to contradict each other. The force with which they argued has been recently interpreted by a critic as "self-consciously paternalistic in the style of English administrators."[42] Were Trivedi or Ray paternalistic? Definitely not. Similarly, Sarkar's perception of science (as a cure for the defects of the Hindu mind) has been compared to that of "every English officer in India."[43] But this similarity is superficial. The diagnosis might be the same, but the motives and methods differed, and the prescriptions differed even more.

Colonialist and nationalist discourses cannot be painted with the same broad brush, although the latter can be criticized as derivative. Both had a cause and effect relationship, and to this was added the problem of the Indians' traditions, their "nativity". The Indian leaders (possibly except Gandhi) could never come out of this dualism. Rabindranath Tagore, the finest laureate and educationalist modern India has produced, was a personal friend of J.C. Bose, R.S. Trivedi and P.C. Ray. He differed with Gandhi on the role of modern science and technology in society. He saw education as the major Indian problem; to solve it, "India must seek the help of European thinkers and scientists in addition to the wisdom of her own seers."[44] Tagore was not alone in thinking this way. The lure of synthesis was too great. The chase continues even now.

Notes

1. S.C. Chuckerbutty, *Popular Lecture on Subjects of Indian Interest*, Calcutta, 1870.
2. S.C. Chuckerbutty, "A defence of native education in India during the sepoy mutinies of 1857–58", lecture delivered on July 8, 1858, *op. cit.*, pp. 74–75.
3. Much before social-Darwinism became fashionable, Chuckerbutty had attacked racialism: "When God made some men dark and other men fair, he had a great purpose to serve. The inhabitants of the colder latitudes are white because the sun is less powerful in them ... In like manner, the proteus, which dwells in caves, when exposed to the sun, becomes coloured, losing its former translucency of surface. The pride of colour, therefore, is as foolish in man as it could be in that humble creature," *op. cit.*, p. 85.
4. S.C. Chuckerbutty, "Native education considered in a psychological point of view", July 18–20, 1861, *op. cit.*, pp. 92–121.
5. Tattvabodhini Patrika, No. 86, 1850, in Benoy Ghosh (ed.), *Samayik Patre Banglar Samajchitra* (in Bengali), Vol. II, Calcutta, 1964, pp. 420–429.
6. B. Bhattacharya, *Banga Sahitye Vijnan* (in Bengali), Calcutta, 1960, pp. 69–80.
7. S.C. Chuckerbutty, "Thirty-sixth introductory address to students of the Calcutta Medical College", June 15, 1870, *op. cit.*, pp. 179–195.
8. S.C. Chuckerbutty, "Physical training as an essential requisite of native education", lecture delivered on March 9, 1854, *op. cit.*, pp. 43–44. Shortly after this lecture, a gymnastic class was formed at Hindu College under a French master. But the experiment failed.
9. In 1867, the government abolished his classes in clinical medicine, and his professorship was merged with the post of medical store-keeper. See *West Bengal State Archive, General, Medical*, Vol. 22–30, June 1867.
10. Samvad Prabhakar, 15-2-1848, in Benoy Ghosh, *op. cit.*, Vol. I, Calcutta, 1962, p. 165.
11. Sarkar brought out the *Calcutta Journal of Medicine* to advocate homoeopathy, and published a *materia medica* for homoeopathic use. See D.G. Crawford, *A History of the Indian*

Medical Service, Vol. II, London, 1914, pp. 454–460; M.L. Sarkar, *The Materia Medica*, Calcutta, 1875.

12. M.L. Sarkar, *On the Desirability of a National Institution for the Cultivation of the Sciences*, Calcutta, 1869, pp. 3–7.
13. *The Hindoo Patriot*, January 10, 1870.
14. *The Bengalee*, June 15, 1870.
15. *Amrita Bazar Patrika*, January 6, 1876.
16. Convocation address by E.C. Bayley, February 26, 1870, and again March 13, 1875, in *Convocation Addresses of the University of Calcutta*, Calcutta, 1914, pp. 231, 330.
17. P.N. Bose, *National Education and Modern Progress*, Calcutta, 1921, p. 52.
18. Note by H.B. Medlicott, Director, GSI, *National Archive of India, Revenue-Agriculture, Surveys*, Proc. No. 25, September, 1880.
19. P.N. Bose, *A History of Hindu Civilization*, Vol. III, Calcutta, 1896, pp. ii–v, 98.
20. P.N. Bose, *Essays and Lectures on the Industrial Development of India*, Calcutta, 1906, pp. 65–85.
21. P.N. Bose wrote prophetically, "The great wars of the future will be fought not for interest in Europe, but for interests outside Europe." *Op. cit.*, pp. 241–258.
22. P.N. Bose, *Swaraj: Cultural and Political*, Calcutta, 1929, pp. 275–76.
23. R.N. Trivedi, quoted in Santanu Chacraverti, *Ramendra Sundar Trivedi and Bengal's Response to Modern Science*, unpublished Ph.D. thesis, Jadavpur University, 1996, pp. 42, 80.
24. *Ibid.*, p. 85.
25. *Ibid.*, p. 183.
26. *Modern Review*, February, 1917, reprinted in D. Sen and A.K. Chakraborty (eds.), *J.C. Bose Speaks*, Calcutta, 1986, pp. 31–32.
27. *The Dacca Review*, Vol. VI, December, 1916, in J.C. Bose Trust Press File No. 2, p. 247.
28. *The Englishman*, May 22, 1897, in J.C. Bose Trust Press File No. 1, p. 58.
29. P.C. Ray, *History of Hindu Chemistry*, II, Calcutta, 1909, p. 195.
30. P.C. Ray, *Life and Experiences of a Bengali Chemist*, Calcutta, 1932, pp. 261, 299.
31. *Ibid.*, p. 289.
32. Those who were not too happy with J.C. Bose (probably Sir

Asutosh Mukherjee) would make fun of his professed love for the mother tongue: "Why does not Sir Jagadish publish his original articles in Bengali? Who knows, there may flock into Bengal thousands of devotees from the remotest corner of the earth to learn the Bengali language only to read the valuable researches published in that language." See *The Century Review*, January, 1918, in J.C. Bose Trust Press File No. F/94.

33. P.C. Ray, "The problem of scientific education in India", *Calcutta Review*, Vol. cviii, 1899, pp. 347–395.
34. P.C. Ray, *Life and Experiences of a Bengali Chemist, op. cit.*, p. 321.
35. *Ibid.*, Vol. II, Calcutta, 1935, pp. 82, 100.
36. Deepak Kumar, "Culture of science and colonial culture: India 1820–1920", *British Journal of History of Science*, June, 1996.
37. Ramcomul Sen's *Qusadhsamgraha* was the first publication on a scientific subject in an Indian language. He picked up words from English, Sanskrit, Persian and Arabic that would convey the exact idea. See P.K. Ray, *Dewan Ramcomul Sen and His Times*, Calcutta, 1990, pp. 162, 176–180.
38. B.K. Sarkar, *Creative India*, Lahore, 1937, pp. 617–619.
39. *Post-Graduate Training in the University of Calcutta*, 1919–20, Calcutta, 1920, pp. 3–4.
40. P.C. Ray cites an interesting encounter. A distinguished Indian lawyer once hosted a party to which a Japanese gentleman was also invited. The host welcomed his guests with a speech delivered in the pure, graceful English for which he was famous. In reply, the Japanese guest acknowledged his inability to emulate his host's knowledge of English, but hoped it would never be the misfortune of the Japanese people to acquire a foreign language with the amount of trouble which his host must have taken! See P.C. Ray, *op. cit.*, Vol. II, p. 66.
41. President of the Madras Educational Board in 1841, quoted in S. Sathianadhan, *History of Education in Madras Presidency*, Madras, 1894, p. 25.
42. Krishna Kumar, "Colonial citizen as an educational ideal", *Economic and Political Weekly*, January 28, 1989, pp. 45–51.
43. Krishna Kumar, *Political Agenda of Education: A Study of Colonialist and Nationalist Ideas*, New Delhi, 1991, p. 42.
44. Humayun Kabir, *Rabindranath Tagore*, London, 1962, p. 50.

Technical Education in Colonial India, 1880–1914: Searching for a 'Suitable Boy'

B.R. TOMLINSON

> The mechanics [at the Praha shoe factory] were pleased to see Haresh ... He was prepared to sit on a stool with them and talk and joke and share experiences, and look inside machines without caring if his hands got soiled with grease ... Through their pleasure in exchanging the expertise of their trade, Haresh himself got interested in the mechanics of machines: how they worked, how they could be kept in good condition, how he might be able to make small innovations to improve their performance.[1]

> A man who has had four years of such training [at Sibpur Engineering College] ... is undoubtedly ... far more useful than the average B.A. or M.A. He has for four years been intimately connected with *things* and not with mere *words*. He has shaken off the trammels of Bengalee thought in such matters as the indignity of honest manual work ... He knows a good deal about physics and the meaning of the ordinary phenomena of nature.[2]

The myth of the "practical Indian" as an exception to racial and cultural norms is wide-reaching and pervasive, featuring in both colonial discourse and post-colonial fiction. Such assumptions about the scarcity of "suitable boys", and the prevalence of the effete, the impractical and the physically timid, coloured many perceptions of Indian receptiveness to technology, and to the "modernizing" virtues that technology was supposed to bring. Thus a study of the history of technical education and diffusion in South Asia during the late nineteenth and early twentieth centuries opens up a number of avenues for the study of colonialism in theory and practice. This paper sets out to explore a number of possible approaches, and to suggest how they may best be followed up in future empirical research.

Educational activity by the state, or by private institutions and individuals, has a number of different purposes in any social and cultural setting. They include the selection and transmission of knowledge, the creation, establishment and maintenance of cultural identity, the implementation of social engineering and control through the manipulation or rationing of knowledge and access to it, and the possibilities of obtaining life-chances through better understanding, or by means of status, power or employment opportunities. Three areas of enquiry have proved especially rewarding within this broad agenda.

Recent work by historians in a wide range of sub-disciplines has identified the diffusion of knowledge as a key element in the history of imperialism and the interaction between Europe and Asia in the nineteenth century.[3] The expansion of British political power in India was accompanied by the control, transmission, production and reproduction of systems of knowledge. These established the main concerns of the British rulers and identified the problems they saw in the construction of educational institutions in India, especially at the tertiary level. They did not always fit a narrow colonial agenda, but colonial officials and others often stressed the written over the oral, the "Western" over the "Eastern", in devising educational systems for primary and secondary education, and propagated a syllabus and educational structure that fit their Orientalist concept of Indian society and culture. Indian intellectuals and educators, who were beginning to construct their own alternative educational system by the early years of the twentieth century, also wanted to divert the diffusion of knowledge into channels defined by their conception of science and technology as a badge of modernity, as well as their political nationalism, which stressed "high" culture over artisan skills.[4]

For economic historians, educational history is crucially important to studies of human capital formation. Many economists concerned with the history of growth, development and comparative rates of innovation have identified the rates of divergence and convergence in the transmission of knowledge, technology and human capital as key elements in explaining rates of economic growth over time. Concepts such as the evolution of patterns of economic choices within a given set of institutions, and the path-dependency of national economies (i.e., future prospects for change being conditioned by the past), have directed attention to educational development as an important element of economic growth through its impact on the transfer of technology, knowledge and skills to generate greater productivity and economic efficiency.[5]

The conventional context within which to study the history of colonial education—especially at the secondary and tertiary levels—has been that of the political, administrative and intellectual history of the British raj and its Indian opponents.[6] The debates over educational institutions and educational policy within the colonial bureaucracy, amongst the nationalist intelligentsia, and between officials and intellectuals, certainly provide a rich source of material on the discourse of colonialism and nationalism in the late nineteenth and early twentieth centuries. Beneath the political debate lurked a series of fundamental development issues—whether technology transfer and absorption could take place without a demand for the technology; whether education could create its own demand for knowledge through linkage and multiplier effects in the economy; and how far educational provision could contribute to social mobility and new life-chances in the absence of investments in other capital items. Such questions, in turn, directed attention to the appropriateness of various types of curriculum and methods of study. Chief among these was the question of what type of technical education would be appropriate for colonial India. Should it be theoretical or practical? Should it aim to develop pure science and generic technologies, or specific areas of "useful" knowledge of direct relevance to industrial production? Should vocational education be run by businessmen or educationalists, by the state sector or the private sector? What sort of industrial training should be given: should it aim at traditional or modern industry; should it build on artisan/craft skills or mechanized techniques? These issues were debated inside and outside the colonial bureaucracy in a discourse that was complicated by colonial concepts of "traditional" Indian craft organization and its capacity to absorb new techniques, and by struggles between "high" and "low" culture within the ranks of Indian educational pioneers. Thus it led to problems in establishing a nationalist curriculum for technical education.

Official British assumptions in the late nineteenth century about educational supply and demand and the diffusion of technology to India were dominated by the identification of a series of supply problems based on culturalist attitudes. These were of three types. First, a number of officials succeeded in convincing themselves that Indian culture was non-material, and, especially, that high culture disdained manual work and practical tasks. As Lockwood Kipling argued in the *Annual Report on Mayo School of Art for 1884–5*, arts and crafts were classified as women's work in the Hindu scriptures:

> The prejudice against manual labour which exists among the upper classes is still stronger than many of us are apt to think; and when we speak of art, its beauties, refining influences, etc., we do not reflect that, for centuries, the most important subjects that our school teaches have been set down in the Kama Shastra among the 64 accomplishments—mostly trivial—in which the public women, or Hetairae of the country, are supposed to be proficient; while philosophy, religion, poetry, *belles lettres*,

> administration, etc., were considered the only pursuits to which a man of position should seriously apply himself.[7]

For this reason, a major commitment to scientific and technical education was deemed inappropriate. One consequence was the early (1850s and 1860s) preference for Eurasians in technical employment, especially on the railways, in the belief that those of mixed race had a more "Western" outlook on mechanical knowledge. Attempts to reverse this policy were met by dire predictions of economic collapse and moral decline. In 1882, for example, the colonial authorities decided that employment opportunities in the subordinate branches of the public works department should be directed towards "natives" (defined as "persons of pure Asiatic origin"), with Europeans and Eurasians being taken on only when Indian candidates were not forthcoming. There was an impassioned response from within the Eurasian community, and a demand for improved technical education for "poor country-born Eurasians and Europeans."[8]

A second set of problems concerned colonial conceptions about the nature of the caste system. It was widely believed that it prevented social or occupational mobility, and linked artisan skills to specific caste groups. Such ideas were fed by missionary concerns with finding employment for converts, who were excluded from caste occupations and had to be trained in a craft. These beliefs implied that the demand for practical education would be low (since caste-based artisans would not wish to teach their skills to outsider apprentices); that the major task for technical education was to provide elementary training in manual crafts to those excluded from the traditional employment structure; and that mechanization would disrupt the established social and ritual structure of Indian society.[9] Officials were further constrained by a political analysis of colonial society that stressed the problems of credentialism (the corruption of educational standards by an obsession with the acquisition of qualifications), and the dangers of creating frustrated expectations among the educated unemployed. In the 1880s, the education department of the government of India did see the need for technical education as providing industrial occupation "for a population rapidly outgrowing the means of support supplied by a too-conservative system of agriculture," and introducing scientific methods "to develop the material resources of India and to improve its agriculture, its products and manufactures." However, officials were also concerned not to go too far, too quickly:

> Technical education proper is the preparation of a man to take part in producing efficiently some special article of commercial demand. It is the cultivation of the intelligence, ingenuity, taste, observation and manipulative skill of those involved in industrial production, so that they may produce more efficiently. And thus technical education ... is an auxiliary of manufacture and industrial capital. In India at the present time, the application of capital to industry has not been developed to the extent which, in European countries, has rendered the establishment of technical schools on a large scale an essential prerequisite of success ... It may be conceded that ... it would be premature to establish technical schools on such a scale as in European countries, and thereby aggravate the present difficulties by adding to the educated unemployed a new class of professional men for whom there is no commercial demand.[10]

Finally, the government of India was unwilling, for the most part, to see education as a way of spreading technical knowledge beyond what was required for existing industries. As a government resolution pointed out in 1894:

> It has for long been accepted that the educational system should comprise a secondary school course which should fit boys for industrial or commercial careers, and the need from a trade point of view of industrial education for developing the resources of India has also been recognized. Technical education is, therefore, supported

> by the government of India as an extension of general education, and industrial education is countenanced in so far as it is of a nature applicable to the service of existing industries.[11]

By 1900, Indian intellectuals had developed a vigorous critique of the colonial discourse on scientific and technical education. In many cases, however, their criticisms were based on a number of equally restrictive assumptions, mirror images of the official ones. Thus the nationalists saw educational deficiencies as a problem of demand, rather than supply, brought about largely by the policies of racial exclusion imposed by the colonial state and its allies in the expatriate business sector. The deliberate policy of training PWD (public works department) officials in Britain, the limited colonial agenda for tertiary education, and the problems of getting Indian labour hired by expatriate capital were all important here. Furthermore, most Indian enthusiasts for technical education linked the issue directly to the larger one of India's industrial backwardness. Both in the activities of the Tatas and other industrialists in western India, and in the swadeshi campaign in Bengal, science and technology were identified as crucial to developing industrialization and self-reliance. All the same, the nationalists, too, had an agenda for the transmission and control of knowledge; they preferred, especially, the theoretical over the practical, the written over the oral, and factory production over artisan techniques. Thus the problem of providing practical education to skilled workmen and factory-floor technicians, which had largely been solved in Britain by 1914, remained unresolved in India.[12]

A brief account of the history of the two higher education institutions founded to further technical education in India during this period will illustrate the complexity of the issues involved, and the intermeshing of colonial and nationalist ideologies with educational practice. The politics of higher education became prominent during the proceedings of the University Commission of 1902. Nationalist opinion mounted a strident campaign against the limits the government was seeking to impose on the spread and scope of higher education, and official proposals for much more stringent controls within universities, and in the relations between universities and government. The Indian Universities Act of 1904 made provision for the creation of industrial, commercial and agricultural educational institutions, and enabled Indian universities to begin postgraduate teaching and research. However, both in Bengal and Bombay, the drive to create the first institutions of this type came from outside the educational establishment.

The upsurge of political, intellectual and cultural activity associated with the swadeshi movement in Bengal in the early 1900s found its educational expression in the formation of the National Council of Education and the Society for Promoting Technical Education in 1906. This led to the formation of two institutions of national education: the Bengal National College and School (BNC) and the Bengal Technical Institute (BTI). Both institutions were broadly dedicated to swadeshi aims, but there were some interesting differences between them. The BNC had ambitions to becoming a full-blown university, with advanced training in arts, science, commerce and technology. The BTI, by contrast, operated at a lower academic level, and was designed to produce properly-trained assistant engineers, draftsmen and mistris (skilled workmen). The difference reflected the fact that the National Council of Education was very advanced in the rhetoric of nationalism and represented one of the cultural pinnacles of the Bengali swadeshi movement, while the Society for Promoting Technical Education had more practical, pragmatic goals, and was prepared to work with the government, if necessary, to achieve them. However, neither institution was able to attract many students, and they merged in 1910 under the management of the National Council of Education. The college part closed soon after in 1917, but the technical part was re-established in the early 1920s as an institute of advanced education. It granted the first engineering degrees in India, and formed the predecessor for the modern-day Jadavpur University.[13]

The early history of the Indian Institute of Science, founded at Bangalore in 1911, shows a similar mixture of political, philanthropic and educational motives. In 1898, Jamsetji Tata, a Parsi businessman with a heavy commitment to both industrial and educational development, offered to donate an annual endowment of Rs 125,000 (£8000) to establish an Indian university of science in Bombay if the government of India would match the funding. He envisaged three faculties: scientific and technical, medical and philosophical, and educational. The last included education, ethics, psychology, Indian history and archaeology, statistics, economics and comparative philology. The scheme was presented to Lord Curzon on his arrival as viceroy. Sceptical of the need for so ambitious a project, Curzon commissioned Sir William Ramsay, professor of chemistry at University College, London, to examine the possibilities and report back. Ramsay visited India in 1900 and, after a lengthy tour, recommended that a scientific research institute be founded at Bangalore, where the local resources, infrastructure and political climate were supportive. However, Ramsay was concerned about the weakness of basic scientific research and availability of laboratory facilities in India. He proposed that the new college should feed into a broader technical environment by stimulating the process of industrial development:

> Members of staff [should] each take up some question of the development of some industry, and the utilization of some natural product; each will associate with him some students as assistants; and they will develop the processes as far as laboratory work can do it ... There are really no industries in India: [but there is] any amount of raw material, easily got and cheaply worked; and there is no opening for any young men scientifically trained, unless openings are made.

The staff was to consist of professors in chemistry, engineering technology and industrial bacteriology; a lecturer in physics; a sewage specialist (chemist); an electrician with works experience; and an assistant to the professor of bacteriology.

One of the staff was to hold the office of director. Industrial development would be in the hands of assistant professors, who would ultimately become managers when their industries were developed on a commercial basis.[14]

Ramsay's scheme, which he submitted in 1901 as *The Indian University of Research: A Report*, pleased nobody, neither the government of India, which thought it too ambitious and expensive, nor J.N. Tata and his chief advisor, J.B. Padshah, who envisaged an institute with a much wider syllabus of national education incorporating history, philosophy and social science. The government now commissioned D.A. Masson, a professor from Melbourne and former assistant and friend of Ramsay, and Colonel J. Clibborn, the principal of Roorkee Engineering College, to provide an alternative plan. Masson and Clibborn duly reported in favour of a pure research institute; it would teach the principles of scientific investigation, be led by professors of experimental chemistry, physics and biology, and have no direct links to industry.

Eventually, Morris W. Travers, an ex-student of Ramsay and assistant professor of chemistry at University College, was appointed director of the new Indian Institute of Science, which opened in 1911 with departments for chemistry, physics, engineering science and biological science. According to Travers, "the ultimate object was to establish a single-faculty university ... providing for postgraduate study in pure and applied science," modelled on Imperial College in Britain and M.I.T. in the United States. Travers clung to this vision during his period as director (to 1914), fighting off attempts to dilute the pure research role of the institute in favour of the social sciences or practical applications that might benefit local industries.[15] Subsequently, the institute did become much more orientated towards practical work, especially as senior staff positions were taken over by Indians during the inter-war years.

Another, very limited, experiment in providing technical higher education was initiated at the 1901 education conference at Simla, which led to the establishment of an

Indian government scholarship scheme, specifically for technical education, to enable ten students a year to undertake study at British universities. The amount of the scholarships was fixed at £150 plus fees and travel (based on the experience of an existing state scholarship scheme, and the examples of technical schemes implemented by Japan and Siam). It was agreed between Calcutta and London that the scheme should concentrate on the textile and mining industries, with civil engineering excluded since adequate provision for this was thought to exist at the government of India's engineering college at Coopers Hill in Surrey, and at the various Indian engineering colleges.[16]

The first students under this scheme were sent to British universities in 1904 (the year that Coopers Hill was closed down as impossibly uneconomic and academically inadequate). In 1913, a wide-ranging official committee was appointed to report on the progress of the scheme.[17] This committee concluded that the scheme had been successful academically, demonstrating that Indian students with a B.Sc. or appropriate B.A. degree were well able to keep up with British university courses. Practical experience had caused more difficulties, with Indian students having some problems in securing work experience while in Britain, but no more so than other foreign students. Such experience was arranged through personal contacts between academic staff and local manufacturers, but many businessmen were unwilling to admit any outsider into their works, especially one who would be returning to another country once their course was over. The two largest groups of students were in textiles (24) and mining (19), and the main finding of the committee was that their success depended very much on prior experience of the industry with which they were associated. The textile students were usually of a very high standard. Many were sponsored by companies, and had spent some time working in mills in Bombay. Some had passed through the Victoria Technical Institute, established in Bombay in 1887 by private Indian initiative, which provided a good range of instruction in cotton-textile technology. By contrast, the Indian mining students were the weakest in the scheme, largely because very few had any prior training or worked in a mine before coming to Britain, or had worked in small mines that did not provide an appropriate introduction to mining engineering as taught in U.K. universities.[18]

Engineering education in Britain at this time stressed the importance of practical experience, and many engineering students at British universities came from families with a firm to run. Few of the Indians who took up technical scholarships came from this background, although their success-rate in finding relevant employment on their return to India was quite high. Of the 66 students who had come to Britain since 1904 through the technical scholarship scheme, only 31 had returned to India by 1913. Of these, 26 had obtained employment within "relevant" areas: 18 in industries, 7 in government service (including two in the Geological Survey of India), and one in the service of Mysore state. A further six graduates had stayed on in Europe or the United States to do research, or had found employment abroad. Data are also available for a parallel, non-official scheme run by the Association for the Advancement of Scientific and Industrial Education for Indians, which was a swadeshi-inspired Calcutta agency that sent Indians abroad to study. By 1913, the association had sent 80 students to Japan, Germany and the United States, as well as Britain. Of these, 56 had found employment (most of the rest having only recently returned): 28 in established industrial firms, 9 by starting their own businesses, and 19 in public service or teaching.[19]

One serious drawback of the technical scholarship scheme was that educational agencies in India found it hard to develop high-level technical skills in industries that were not already established, or in which Indian employees did not have access to skills-training and promotion. This is demonstrated by the differing competencies of Indian textile and mining students in Britain. It is also borne out by a comparative perspective based on the experience of Meiji Japan.[20] For roughly a hundred years following the Meiji restoration in 1868, manpower strategy in Japan depended on developing skills within specific industries rather than throughout the economy as a whole. Government policy sought to train students for particular sectors of the economy, with little concern for the creation of an open market or the teaching of transferable skills. Large-scale enterprises in the private sector then built up these skills in-house. The skills were utilized flexibly, but only inside the organization. Open markets existed only for unskilled labour.

During the late nineteenth and early twentieth centuries, the Japanese government sought to implement an ambitious programme of technical education, but with only partial success. By far the greatest success was in the public sector, notably railways and telecommunications, which developed well before large-scale industrialization had taken place, and were subject to centralized state control. They used foreign capital and foreign experts to start up, but then quickly switched to indigenous sources and efficient training schemes developed through enterprise-based schools and training programmes for all levels. Both the Telephone and Telegraph Corporation and the National Railways had virtual civil-service status; those who had graduated from the government's enterprise schools got formal, graded training within the bureaucratic structure, employment security and welfare benefits. This led skilled personnel to identify their future career narrowly with the national corporation, and resulted in very few linkage or leakage benefits being created for the private sector.

The traditional private-sector industries of textiles and mining had to undergo considerable changes in form following the opening up of Japanese domestic markets to foreign competition in the 1870s, but the creation of a technically-skilled workforce played little part in this. The cotton-textile industry relied throughout the Meiji period on cheap, low-skilled workers from the labour market to operate increasingly sophisticated machinery. It was eventually forced to develop its own training programmes, even for short-term female workers at the lowest skill levels, but not until the labour shortages caused by the wartime boom of 1914–18.

Engineering skills were needed in some parts of the textile industry during our period, and these were supplied from the higher education sector at home or abroad. Similarly, the mining industry depended on higher-education institutions for the limited numbers of highly skilled workers it employed, but ignored skill training for the manual workforce for even longer than the textile industry. Both textile and mining firms were subject to intense internal and international competition, and operated in markets given to wide fluctuations in demand and price. They also used very similar machinery and techniques that required a low level of skill on the part of the bulk of the workforce. They depended, for the most part, on paternalistic, often despotic, labour recruitment and employment agencies that gathered marginal members of the labour force together in tight-knit groups under authoritarian control. In these circumstances, skill training within firms was unlikely to flourish.

The "basic" industries of steel and shipbuilding showed a somewhat similar pattern of events. Foreign technicians and managers were used in the first instance, followed by conscious effort to replace them with native-trained personnel as quickly as possible. As the technology used became more complex, major firms found it necessary to establish their own training schools, since the educational system could not supply suitable graduates. After 1918, most firms began to shift away from established patron-client relations in labour recruitment; internal training of staff became widespread in the 1920s and 1930s in large-scale enterprises. For the capital-intensive industries that developed out of the new technology of the "second industrial revolution" (heavy machinery, electrical equipment and chemicals) in the late nineteenth century, internalized skills-training was even more important. Again, this developed mainly after 1918, and largely because it had become clear that neither the existing labour market, nor the school and university systems, nor patron-client relationships could provide the educational and learning opportunities required.

Once training-within-enterprise schemes developed in these

industries, they started hiring new school graduates (rather than those with existing manual skills), fostered the careers of key workmen, and provided lifetime employment guarantees, annual wage increments based on length of service, welfare benefits and so on. These devices, which make up the popular image of Japanese corporate employment culture, were developed to meet a specific and novel set of economic requirements. In particular, the large corporations that suddenly emerged after 1914 needed an immediate supply of specifically-trained labour to work under the direct control of their engineers and administrators. This workforce had to have skills that were complex, unpredictable and ever-changing, so the large corporations sought to attract the most educable and adaptable, and then hold on to them by building rewards for loyalty. Within the machinery industry, much of the old manual-skill based workforce did not cross the divide to the new large-scale industry.

Historians of tertiary education in India have been concerned chiefly with the history of educational administration, or of those institutions that propagated education as a way of establishing cultural, religious or political identity.[21] Such work has been valuable and there is still more to be done here. But we also need to broaden the research agenda to include groups in colonial society who sought to secure social mobility, increase human capital, and establish their own criteria in the reproduction of knowledge. There are a number of possibilities to investigate: the history of professions such as engineers and research scientists; the creation of human capital by the provision of "learning on the job" through staff training within factories and industrial firms; the issues of social mobility, which would involve tracing students from family origins to job destinations as graduates. We also need to look at the history of curricula and the process by which technical information has become institutionalized, so that we can address issues concerning the control and transmission of knowledge and its cultural attachments. Such work has been done elsewhere. In Britain, for example, university archives have provided a rich source of information on social mobility (or the lack of it) and the development of the curriculum. Research on the professions has been carried out by constructing mass biographies of entrants' cohorts, adding significantly to our knowledge of medical history. The acquisition and diffusion of specialized knowledge within firms has also been recognized as an important part of the process of technical change.[22] For India, such issues provide a new agenda for research, requiring a search for new sources of information, especially within educational establishments themselves. The task is large, but the rewards will be larger yet.

Notes

1. Vikram Seth, *A Suitable Boy*, London, 1993, p. 1213.
2. "Note on the Seebpore Engineering College course of training" by F.J. Spring, 24 July 1887, reprinted in Government of India, *Papers Relating to Technical Education in India, 1886–1904*, Calcutta, 1906, p. 45.
3. For a convenient collection of recent work that explores these issues, see Nigel Crook (ed.), *The Transmission of Knowledge in South Asia: Essays on Education, Religion, History and Politics*, OUP, Delhi, 1996. See, especially, the essays by Crook, Harrison and Bayly.
4. On the cultural and intellectual background to Indian initiatives in scientific research and education during the colonial period, see Sureschandra Shukla, "Indian educational thought and experiments: A review", *Comparative Education*, **19**, 1, 1983, pp. 59–71; Deepak Kumar, "The 'culture' of science and colonial culture, India 1820–1920", *British Journal of the History of Science*, **29**, 1996, pp. 195–209.
5. Recent work in this area includes G. Psacharopoulos and M. Woodhall, *Education for Development: An Analysis of Investment Choices*, World Bank, OUP, 1985; Howard Park, "Endogenous growth theory", *Journal of Economic Perspectives*, **8**, 2, 1994; Richard R. Nelson and Gavin Wright, "The rise and fall of American technological leadership: The postwar era in historical perspective", *Journal of Economic Literature*, 1992, pp. 1931–64. On education and development in a historical context (for both developed and developing economies), see

Hermann van der Wee and Erik Aerts (eds.), *Debates and Controversies in Economic History: Proceedings of the Tenth International Economic History Congress*, Leuven, August, 1990, pp. 213–46.

6. Official policy and attitudes can be investigated from a number of important sets of published documents, notably, Government of India, *Papers Relating to Technical Education in India: Report of the Indian Industrial Commission, 1916–18*, London, 1932; Government of India, Bureau of Education, *Post-War Educational Development in India: Report by the Central Advisory Board of Education*, Delhi, 1944. On Indian activities and opinions, see Amitabha Mukherjee, *Fifty Years of National Education: The Story of an Experiment*, National Council of Education, Calcutta, 1992; Kim P. Sebaly, "Tata Steel and higher technical education in India: The Padshah plan, 1916–21", *History of Education*, 17, 4, 1988, pp. 309–20; B.V. Subbarayappa, *In Pursuit of Excellence: A History of the Indian Institute of Science*, New Delhi, 1991; Roy Macleod and Deepak Kumar (eds.), *Technology and the Raj: Western Technology and Technical Transfers to India, 1700–1947*, Delhi, 1995.
7. "Report on Mayo School of Art for 1884–1885", quoted in *Papers Relating to Technical Education*, p. 32.
8. W.A. Symonds, late honorary secretary Friend-in-Need Society, to Chief Secretary, Government of Madras 11-8-1884, reprinted in *Papers Relating to Education*, pp. 102–3.
9. In optimistic moments, some officials disputed this view. The final paragraph of Sir A.P. MacDonnell's "Memorandum on technical education in India prior to 1886" of 23 July 1886, for example, noted: "It may be observed that, although among the higher-caste natives of India, the obligations of caste still give a quasi-religious sanction to the distinction between the employments deemed menial and those deemed honourable, there are, nevertheless, indications that this sanction is losing something of its force, and that natives of all castes are, in increasing numbers, looking to technical education as affording an honourable livelihood and career in life." (Reprinted in *Papers Relating to Technical Education*, pp. 36–6.) But when the government of India produced plans for technical training in handicrafts in 1904, officials were careful to stress that skills-training in particular trades would only be open to those of the

specified caste: see "Resolution of the government of India on the report of the committee on industrial schools in India", 14 January 1904, reprinted in *Papers Relating to Technical Education*, p. 260.

10. "Resolution of the government of India upon Sir A. Croft's review of education in India in 1886", 18 June 1886, reprinted in *Papers Relating to Technical Education*, p. 36. MacDonnell, on the other hand, hinted that technical education might provide a solution to the problems created by "the crowd of young men whom our system of education has rendered discontented with the sphere of life to which they were born, without fitting them for another" (*ibid.*, p. 2).
11. Government of India resolution, 7 September 1894; reprinted in *Papers Relating to Technical Education*, p. 246.
12. For a convenient summary of the progress of British technical education in a comparative perspective, see Sidney Pollard, *Britain's Prime and Britain's Decline*, London, 1989, chapter 3.
13. On the history of swadeshi-inspired further education in Bengal, see Amitabh Mukherjee, *National Education, op. cit.*
14. The Mysore government had promised help to establish such industrial undertakings. See "Ramsay to G.F. Fitzgerald", 19-2-01, University College, London, *Ramsay Papers*, XI. Extracts from this letter are reproduced in Sir W.A. Tilden, *Sir William Ramsay*, London, 1918, pp. 256–8. On the early history of the Tata Institute, see also B.V. Subbarayappa, *Pursuit of Excellence, op. cit.*
15. This is Travers' own assessment of his achievement. See "Draft summary of my work in India" by Morris Travers (unpaginated), University College London, *Ramsay Papers*, Vol. 97.
16. The relevant documents are reprinted in *Papers Relating to Technical Education*, pp. 249–57. By this date, there were four Indian engineering colleges in the university sector (Roorkee, Sibpur, Pune and Girni) and four government engineering schools (Dacca, Lahore, Patna and Jabalpur), all created to supply candidates for the subordinate posts of the PWD.
17. Report of a Committee appointed by the Secretary of State for India to inquire into the system of State Technical Scholarships established by the Government of India in 1904 (1913).
18. A further complication over mining was the clash of views within British universities over the most appropriate form of

education for mining engineers. Sir Thomas Holland (ex-director of the Geological Survey of India, future chairman of the Indian Industrial Commission, and currently professor of mining at Manchester University) argued that any mining engineer required a long practical apprenticeship below ground: "A mine manager, like a master mariner, is made only by a long and often painful practical experience." Others disagreed because this meant that university education was largely irrelevant. Thus, Professor Cadman of Birmingham University argued that "sound principles of science are as necessary to the successful management and development of a mine as they are to the efficient geological survey of a country." He found the Indian students weak, but only because of their lack of practical experience, not their inability to absorb scientific knowledge. *Committee to inquire into the System of State Technical Scholarships*, Appendix VII.

19. *Committee to inquire into the System of State Technical Scholarships*, Appendix V and VI.
20. This account of Japanese educational history is based on Soloman B. Levine and Hisashi Kawada, *Human Resources in Japanese Economic Development*, Princeton, 1980. On the range of official activity, see Japan National Commission for UNESCO, *History of Industrial Education in Japan, 1868–1900*, n.p., 1959. Serious weaknesses in the much-vaunted German system of technical education have also been exposed by recent research, with a greater stress now placed on the effectiveness of training within firms. See Pollard, *Britain's Prime and Britain's Decline*, chapter 3, and Wolfgang König, "Science-based industry or industry-based science? Electrical engineering in Germany before World War I", *Technology and Culture*, **37**, 1, 1996, pp. 36–69.
21. Conventional accounts on the history of technical education at secondary and tertiary levels will be found in Robert I. Crane, "Technical education and economic development in India before World War I", in C. Arnold Anderson and Mary Jean Bowman (eds.), *Education and Economic Development*, London, 1966, pp. 167–201; Aparna Basu, *Essays in the History of Education*, New Delhi, 1976, pp. 39–59; Daniel R. Headrick, *The Tentacles of Progress: Technology Transfer in the Age of Imperialism, 1850–1940*, OUP, 1988, pp. 315–351; Roy Macleod and Deepak Kumar (eds.), *Technology and the Raj, op. cit.*

22. For a convenient recent introduction to some of this work, see R.D. Anderson, *Universities and Elites in Britain since 1800*, Economic History Society, *New Studies in Economic and Social History*, Cambridge, 1992; David Edgerton, *Science, Technology and the British Industrial 'Decline'*, Economic History Society, *New Studies in Economic and Social History*, Cambridge, 1996.

Teaching Science through the Local Language: An Aborted Pedagogical Project

S. IRFAN HABIB

> The constant use of English, even from our childhood, so that we begin to express our thoughts in it instead of in our mother tongue, will go far to denationalize us. If we wish to remain an Eastern people, we must not neglect the language which we learnt at our mother's knee ... To forget it or to despise it, is to lose one of the strongest factors in the building up of national character. (Munshi Zakaullah)

In nineteenth-century India, modern science was introduced as part of the colonial educational package, conforming assiduously to the diffusionist model. This model was patently passive, as it did not involve any participatory element from the local population, which was supposed to receive the scientific wisdom from above. Knowledge was supposed to descend from the higher or educated classes and spread gradually through their example. The post-Macaulay phase extended the scope of the model further by introducing English as the medium of learning, which led to modern science education being increasingly conducted in a separate enclave. To counter this, some vernacular projects of the nineteenth century tried to enlarge the scope of science education through translations as well as original writing in various Indian languages. I will try to deal with one of these projects in north India, which tried to push Urdu as a medium of learning.

In earlier work, I have tried, within the framework developed for the sociology of scientific knowledge, to grapple with the issue of the popular perception of science in the process of cultural redefinition. This led to a three-phase model of adaptation in institutional and cultural terms.[1] The first phase was one in which auto-didacts had a crucial role to play; it is with this phase that we are concerned in this short paper.[2] The auto-didact is placed in the indigenous system of knowledge and pedagogically exposed to modernity. He or she then decides to intervene at the level of translation, i.e., rendering modern science textbooks into the vernaculars. This, in turn, would require "the production of a cultural lexicon of metaphors and images that renders the world epistemologically refigurable."[3] It would also mean domesticating this knowledge through the definition of a grammar, and replicating it.[4]

The efforts of Ramchandra, Syed Ahmad Khan, Munshi Zakaullah and others exemplify this tradition. All these intellectuals from Delhi and the area around it, and a large number of auto-didacts and school teachers elsewhere, went on to sensitize vernacular Indian cultures to modern science. Most of these intellectuals were the pillars of a "Delhi renaissance", which shared common concerns regarding education, religious reform and the status of women with the contemporaneous Bengal renaissance. Since the Delhi renaissance stressed the role of the vernacular and had more indigenous sources of inspiration, it has been unfavourably compared with its counterpart in Bengal and ignored by most scholars.[5]

Delhi College (now Zakir Husain College) was at the centre of the Delhi renaissance, and most of its teachers and students got involved in promoting the cause of education through the local language. I will be referring to some of this work, particularly the role of Ramchandra and his favourite student, Munshi Zakaullah. Ramchandra was a student of Delhi College, and later a science and mathematics teacher there. He is well known to scholars as one of the pioneers of modern Urdu journalism, who introduced *haqeeqat nigari* (realist writing). I have described elsewhere his contributions to the pedagogy of mathematics and his popular science writings in Urdu.[6] In general, Ramchandra was an enthusiastic promoter of science education through the local language, laying particular emphasis on the role of translation. He himself translated into Urdu, but in the later years of his life he worked in Punjabi.

The attempts by Ramchandra and others to teach science in the vernacular were motivated by politics. They were critics of Macaulay's education policy.[7] They felt that they were looking beyond the colonial era, while the Anglicists supporting Macaulay's policy had the more practical objective of producing administrative clones. There are references to science education as well the vernaculars in Macaulay's document, but for all practical purposes, they were rhetorical. Rather, the lack of science in the Indian tradition compared to its strong presence in the European one was a hinge that allowed the smooth introduction of English language and learning in the curriculum of Indian education.[8]

In practice, however, colonial education was heavily tilted towards literary rather than scientific education. With increasing demand for trained manpower, some courses in science were introduced, but only "to provide training in various branches, rather than creating an appreciation of science as a tool of intellectual and social transformation."[9] From the start, these courses were in English, so one was first required to master a new language—a long, tedious and often difficult process for some students. There was hardly any possibility of awakening much original thinking if the students were taught in a foreign language so different from their own.

Moreover, as the nineteenth century intellectuals had stressed, the vernacular languages were part of the national-cultural perspective.[10] That is, there were cultural implications of colonial education in English. This was Ramchandra's rationale for demanding education in the local languages. It would not only facilitate the task of communicating precious knowledge, but also enable Indians to make the achievements of science their own, and thereby contribute to its development.[11] He was convinced that learning in the mother tongue was more instinctive and natural.[12] Sharing Ramchandra's conviction was Imdad Ali, who founded the Bihar Scientific Society in 1868. He, too, felt that Indian students could not properly acquire knowledge of science and technology through a foreign language. Even if they did, they were unable to transmit the same to their countrymen for want of suitable expressions in the Indian languages.[13]

Soon after joining Delhi College as a student, Ramchandra got involved in translating a number of English textbooks on science and mathematics into Urdu. Felix Boutros, the French principal of the college, had established a Vernacular Translation Society in 1843, and all these translations were carried out under its auspices.[14] The translated books were introduced as course books in the Oriental section of the college, where Urdu was the medium of learning. Ramchandra wrote about this experience in these words:

> These translations were undertaken to produce textbooks for the Oriental department. So, within two or three years, the students of the Arabic and Persian departments became, to some extent, aware of European knowledge. The ideas based on ancient philosophy, imparted through Arabic, were overshadowed by modern science, based on reason and experiment.[15]

The translated course books also introduced the more general Urdu-reading population to the world of modern science and philosophy, for Ramchandra's commitment was not limited to teaching in the college. In another attempt to acquaint the people with modern science, Ramchandra launched an Urdu fortrightly in 1845. It was called *Fawaid-ul-Nazrin*, and was devoted to science and education. A representative list of the articles he wrote in this journal appears at the end of this paper.

After retiring from the college, he joined Delhi Society in 1865. This had most of the leading cultural figures of Delhi as its members—men like Mirza Ghalib, Syed Ahmad Khan, Pyare Lal Ashob and many others, including some civil servants. The society discussed topical issues at its meetings, and sent its criticisms to the colonial government for consideration. During one of these meetings, Ramchandra entered into debate with a Christian missionary, who was dismissive of translation as a meaningful way of acquiring knowledge. Ramchandra put forth an argument which was pregnant with historical consciousness, unusual for the period:

> It is not that only Muslims gained through the translation of Greek works, but Europe also acquired knowledge through translations only. The Muslims got it from the Greeks, which they later transmitted to the Europeans. This is how the knowledge spread in Europe.[16]

This way, Ramchandra not only defended translation, but also gave his own perception of the past. He showed that he could visualize the growth of knowledge in a cross-cultural perspective, thereby countering all those missionaries and colonial administrators who disparaged the East as uncivilized. He saw that the growth of modern scientific knowledge had been a cumulative process in which all cultures had a role to play; no one civilization could lay exclusive claims over it.[17] Imdad Ali expressed a similar sentiment:

> England, France and Germany would never have attained that exalted degree of civilization which they now enjoy if the works of science originally imported from Rome and Greece were not disseminated among the people by means of their own vernacular.[18]

Even in Europe, according to Merz, the vernacularization of science and literature in the 17th and 18th centuries had produced national "spirits" or intellectual climates.[19] Latin and Greek were rejected as the languages of learning in favour of local languages. This enabled ordinary people to participate in and identify with the development of knowledge.

Munshi Zakaullah was another prominent Delhi

educationist trying to reverse the process of Anglicization by committing himself to vernacular education. He felt that education through a foreign language meant sapping the mental capabilities of the students.[20] He had himself learnt his science and mathematics from Ramchandra through the medium of Urdu, and he did not see any reason why the younger generation should not do the same. Following Ramchandra, he taught in the local language, and was also actively involved in producing books on science, mathematics and other subjects through translations as well as original writings. As a colonial subject, he was conscious of the weakness of Urdu as a medium for modern education, and that proficiency in English would ensure employment and social prestige. However, even Syed Ahmad's shift to English in the 1870s did not deter Zakaullah from his commitment to the local language, although his passion for modern education, particularly science, kept him involved with the former's Aligarh movement.

Like his teacher, Ramchandra, Zakaullah is well known to scholars of Urdu literature and journalism for his efforts to introduce modern scientific and social ideas. All the same, his popular writings on science have not received as much attention. They were carried in various contemporary journals: *Tahzib-ul-akhlaq, Scientific Gazette, Aligarh Institute Gazette, Al-Nazir, Mohsin-ul-Akhlaq, Shams* and many others. He began writing very early in life, his first piece appearing in 1849. Unlike Ramchandra, Zakaullah did not write anything in English, though he had acquired some proficiency in it. On average, he wrote around 1,000 pages per year and, by 1901, he had produced 146 books on science, mathematics, history and literature.

His first book on mathematics, called *Tuhfat-ul-Hisab*, appeared in 1852; it is considered one of the first books in any Indian language on modern Western mathematics. Zakaullah himself wrote about the book in these words:

> I may not be wrong if I claim that I wrote the first book of its kind in 1852 which had few hundred questions on

mathematics. It became very popular and was published 15 to 20 times in different parts of the country.[21]

Zakaullah went on to produce a historical account in Urdu of the development of mathematics from the earliest times to his day. Called *Ajaib-ul-Hisab*, it was again one of the first of its kind. It dealt with the contributions of the Greeks, Romans, Iranians and Hindus.

Zakaullah worked hard to produce as many books as possible to prove that a local language could be an effective medium for teaching and communicating modern scientific and social ideas. His writings contributed to widening the range of Urdu and its vitality as a language. It began to contain the flavour of modern ideas and philosophies and, for a short while, it flowered as a language for the teaching of science and socially relevant issues. This was a significant transformation for a language associated till then with "decadent" Mughal court culture, better known for poetry and rhetoric.

Unfortunately, the post-Orientalist phase of the latter half of the nineteenth century in India found no place for the educational ideas of men like Ramchandra and Zakaullah. Moreover, the dependence of these men on the colonial state to implement their programme made it a self-defeating exercise. It was too different in its assumptions and purposes from colonial education policy.[22] In his last days, Zakaullah himself used to point to the books he had written lying idle on the shelves with no one to take them. The tide had gone against him, he said, and he had not been able to turn it back.[23]

Ramchandra's Popular Science Writings

Ramchandra published a large number of articles on popular science in his newspapers. Listed below are some of his articles (with brief translations of the Urdu titles) which appeared in *Fawaid-ul-Nazrin* between 1845 and 1852.

1. "Bayan pan chakki ka" (water mills), October 6, 1845.
2. "Hal Suqrat ka" (Socrates), November 3, 1845.
3. "Risala paimaish compass ka" (the compass), December 1, 1845.

4. "Hal Arastu ka" (Aristotle), December 1, 1845.
5. "Usul ilm-i-hisab juziyat-o-kuliyat" (maxima and minima), December 29, 1845.
6. "Hal tarbiyat larkiyon ka" (the education of girls), December 29, 1845.
7. "Telegraph", August 24, 1846.
8. "Dar bab dahkani kashti ke" (steam boats), October 4, 1846.
9. "Charkhi ka bayan" (pulleys), October 19, 1846.
10. "Hal ilm hiyat ka" (astronomy), November 15, 1846.
11. "Hal gardish zamin ka" (the roundness of the Earth), November 30, 1846.
12. "Bayan balloon" (balloons), December 14, 1846.
13. "Bayan sarak ahni ka" (railways), April 25, 1847.
14. "Jadu hikmati ke bayan mein" (the science behind magic), May 31, 1847.
15. "Firangistan mein rahne walon ko ilam aur aql hasil hone ke bayan mein" (the acquisition of knowledge and wisdom by the Europeans), June 14, 1847.
16. "Hal doorbeen ka" (telescopes), September 6, 1847.
17. "Hal dumdar sitaron ka" (comets), September 6, 1847.
18. "Chhape ke ijad ka bayan" (the invention of printing), February 21, 1848.
19. "Daurah-i-khoon ke bayan mein" (blood circulation), March 6, 1848.
20. "Hal tabdeel fasal ka" (crop rotation), June 26, 1848.
21. "Galileo sahab ka hal" (Galileo), July 10, 1848.
22. "Dar bab mirage" (mirages), April, 1850.
23. "Hal barometer" (barometers), September 5, 1850.
24. "Hal shahanshah-al-hukmah aur fauzola Sir Isaac Newton ka" (Sir Isaac Newton, king among scientists and scholars), November 30, 1850.

Some Publications of Zakaullah

Zakaullah was a prolific writer. He wrote and translated around 150 books. Given below is a sample of some of his original writings.

Mathematics

1. *Tuhfat-ul-Hisab*, Delhi, 1852. His first book, published at the age of nineteen. It dealt with modern mathematics using a

question-and-answer format. The book was highly appreciated, and the first edition was sold out in three days.

2. *Risala Masahat Mubtadiyon ke Liye* (Mensuration for Beginners), Delhi, 1881. This 160-page book included a field book, questions, figures, and a number of illustrations.
3. *Risala Ilm-i-Masahat* (Mensuration), Delhi, 1871. Another book on mensuration, written at the behest of the Aligarh Scientific Society and also for the students of the Thomson Civil Engineering College, Roorkee.
4. *Sharah Jabr-o-Muqabla* (Algebra), Delhi, 1873. A 150-page book with a number of problems and examples.
5. *Risala Masail Ma-adlat* (Treatise on the Problems of Matter), Delhi, 1871. This book dealt with problems in mechanics and dynamics as propounded by Newton, Descartes and others. Zakaullah himself called this work a "strange publication."
6. *Ilm-i-Musallas* (Trigonometry), Delhi, 1871.
7. *Risala Ilm-i-Jabr-o-Muqabla* (Algebra), Delhi, 1871.
8. *Ajaib-ul-Hisab* (History of Mathematics), Delhi, n.d. Mathematics from the beginning till the author's time. It included the work of the Greeks, Arabs, Romans and Hindus.
9. *Zabani Hisab* (Mental Mathematics), Meerut, 1870. A 221-page book emphasizing the skill of the Hindus in the subject.

HISTORY

10. *Tarikh-i-Hind* (A History of India). A voluminous work beginning from the ancient times to the British takeover in the 19th century. Probably the first detailed historical account of India available in Urdu. The whole work was spread over 10 volumes, the first appearing in 1873 and the last in 1898, all published in Delhi.
11. *Tarikh-i-Uruj-i-Sultanat-i-Englishia* (History of the Rise of the British Empire). A five-volume work, the first appearing in 1904 in Delhi.
12. *Muharbat-i-Azim* (History of Great Battles), Delhi, 1904.
13. *Curzon Nama*, Delhi, 1907. A 461-page book covering the period Curzon was viceroy.

GEOGRAPHY

14. *Ilm-i-Geographia* (Geography), 1875. General and Indian geography.

15. *Geographia-i-Tabai* (Physical Geography), Delhi, 1876. A 132-page book with an 18-page introduction, it covered the change of seasons, the phenomena of day and night, clouds, rain, snowfall, etc.
16. *Geographia-i-Riyaziya* (Mathematical Geography), Delhi, 1884. Describes the moon, the rotation of the earth, cartography, etc.

Morals and Culture

17. *Tahzib-ul-Akhlaq Arya Hind* (Morals and Culture of the Hindus), Delhi, 1890.
18. *Muhasin-ul-Akhlaq* (Good Morals), Delhi, 1891. A 720-page book based on borrowings from various European works on morals and conduct. Included non-European writing, such as Persian couplets from Rumi and Nizami.
19. *Mukarram-ul-Akhlaq* (Traditional Morals), Delhi, 1891. A 356-page book on morality and conduct as specified in the Koran and Hadith.
20. *Ta-alim-ul-Akhlaq* (Moral Education), Delhi, 1892.

General

21. *Sahifa-i-Fitrat* (Nature), Delhi, 1894. A 640-page publication with more than 300 figures to explain various natural phenomena.
22. *Hikmat-ul-Mizan* (Physical Sciences of the Muslims), Allahabad, n.d.
23. *Char Ansar* (The Four Elements), Delhi, 1879. A book on chemistry dealing with the characteristics of air, water, fire and earth.
24. *Falsafa-i-Amsal-o-Muntakhab-ul-Misal* (Selected Aphorisms and Proverbs), Delhi, 1898. A 304-page book drawing from 27 Asian, European and African languages. Around 4,365 proverbs were included.
25. *Gharbi Sharqi Tabiyat ki Abjadon par Mahakmat* (Beginnings of the Physical Sciences in the East and the West), Delhi, 1900.
26. *Uloom-i-Tabiya ki Tarikh* (History of the Physical Sciences), Delhi, 1901.
27. *Uloom-i-Tabiya Sharqi ki Abjad* (Beginnings of Eastern Physical Sciences), Delhi, 1900.
28. *Musalmanon ke Uloom-i-Tarbiya ki Tarikh* (History of the Physical Sciences of the Muslims), Delhi, 1900.

29. *Science aur Mazhab ki Razm-o-Bazm* (Science and Religion), Delhi, 1901.
30. *Taqwim-ul-San* (The Development of Language), Delhi, 1893.
31. *Risala Ta-alim Zamana-i-Hal* (The State of Education Today), Delhi, 1892.

TRANSLATION

Zakaullah translated over 100 books, mostly on mathematics and science. The majority were textbooks for schools. The authors Zakaullah chose to translate were often Irishmen such as Bernard Smith, I. Todhunter, Galbraith, Snow Harris and Tate.

Notes

1. Dhruv Raina, "The early years of P.C. Ray: The inauguration of the school of chemistry and the social history of science (1885–1907)," in *Science in Context*, 1994.
2. In the second phase of the model, the scientist-cum-renaissance mind occupies centre stage. It includes intellectuals like M.L. Sarkar who founded the Indian Association for the Cultivation of Sciences in 1876, several other university figures such as J.C. Bose, Ramendra Trivedi, P.C. Ray, and even "traditional" scholars like Hakim Ajmal Khan. The third phase is reached in 1914 with the founding of the Indian Science Congress. Through the efforts made in the earlier two phases, modern scientific research now comes into its own.
3. Raina, *op. cit.*, 1994.
4. Dhruv Raina, "Lamenting the past, anticipating the figure: A chronology of popular science writing in India (1850–1914)", paper presented at the seminar on science popularisation in pre-independence India, April 21, 1995.
5. R.E. Frykenberg, Gail Minault, Syed Ahmad Dehlvi and the "Delhi renaissance", in *Delhi Through the Ages*, New Delhi, pp. 289–290.
6. For details, see S. Irfan Habib and Dhruv Raina, "The introduction of scientific rationality into India: A study of Master Ramchandra—Urdu journalist, mathematician and educationalist", *Annals of Science*, **46**, 1989; Dhruv Raina and S. Irfan Habib, "Ramchandra's treatise through the haze of

golden sunset: An aborted pedagogy", *Social Studies of Science*, **20**, 1990.

7. Habib and Raina, *op. cit.*, 1989, p. 349.
8. Krishna Kumar, "Colonial citizen as an educational ideal", *Economic and Political Weekly*, January 28, 1989, p. PE-50.
9. Irfan Habib, "Institutional Efforts: Popularization of science in the mid-19th century", *Fundamenta scientiae*, Vol. 6, No. 4, pp. 299–312.
10. K.N. Panikkar, "Culture and ideology: Contradictions in intellectual transformation of colonial society in India", *Economic and Political Weekly*, December 5, 1987, p. 2119.
11. S.R. Kidwai, *Master Ramchandra* (in Urdu), Delhi, 1963, p. 105.
12. *Ibid.*
13. B.K. Sinha, "Syed Imdad Ali—an eminent educationist of 19th century Bihar", *Journal of Historical Research*, Vol. XIII, No. 1, August 15, 1970, p. 2.
14. "Khutbaat Garcin de Tassy", in *Anjuman Taraqi-Urdu*, Delhi, 1935, p. 274.
15. Ramchandra, *A Treatise on the Problems of Maxima and Minima*, London, 1859, p. xv.
16. S.R. Kidwai, *op. cit.*
17. S. Irfan Habib, "Beyond the transmission model: Master Ramchandra—pioneer among science popularizers in 19th century India", to appear soon in the *Journal of the Asiatic Society of Bengal.*
18. Irfan Habib, *op. cit.*, p. 302.
19. John Theodore Merz, *History of European Thought in the Nineteenth Century*, 4 volumes, 1896. Quoted in Lewis Pyenson, "Prerogatives of European intellect: Historians of science and the promotion of European civilization", *History of Science*, Vol. 31, Part 1, No. 93, September, 1993.
20. "Fanoos-i-Adab", in *Delhi College Magazine*, 1953, p. 145.
21. Zakaullah, *Intikhab-Manahi-ul-Hisab*, Delhi, 1880. However, Zakaullah's own teacher, Ramchandra, wrote a book on mathematics in Urdu called the *Sari-ul-Fahm* in 1849.
22. K.N. Panikkar, presidential address at the Indian History Congress, 36th session, Aligarh, 1975, p. 13.
23. C.F. Andrews, *Zakaullah of Delhi*, London, 1929, p. 99.

SECTION V: COMPARATIVE PERSPECTIVES

Going Back to the Educational Future: Using Indigenous Ideas to Meet the Challenge of the 21st Century

JOSEPH DI BONA

Introduction

World educational practices seem to be headed in two contrary directions at the same time. On the one hand, we increasingly see universal features of finance, administration and curricula everywhere; at the same time, we recognize that there is great diversity in literacy, achievement, resources and goals. As the world becomes more closely integrated financially, industrially, and in terms of communications and media, there appears to be a greater need for national systems of education to reflect that global tendency and to write curricula that will be pretty much the same in Caracas or Calcutta. Computers, satellites, fax machines, the World Wide Web and CNN are but the most visible portions of the universalization that is taking place. The end of the cold war has brought greater cooperation among nation states, and this, too, facilitates the transmission and acceptance of ideas which, in turn, produce a kind of global culture. OECD, the United Nations and other international organizations help create a community of educational ideas that are as much at home in Bosnia as in Bolivia.

There is equal pressure to ensure that the roots of the past are preserved in all cultures. The traditions of the past form a strong bond within nations, and serve as a powerful vehicle for learning when they can be effectively harnessed. Moreover, culture and identity help to create a sense of who we are, where we come from and where we are headed, and to this extent, serve as powerful mediums of instruction. In the United States, for example, African-American children are deeply drawn to do well in school when they see learning in the context of an African past that is neither neglected nor put down. The same is true of children in Israel, where the past is very much a part of the present and serves to create a talented, dedicated citizenry. This tendency is clearly apparent in many other countries of the world.

These two tendencies, while not mutually exclusive, indicate an ambivalence in the minds of intellectuals concerning which direction is the more appropriate one to pursue. This is not an abstract debate, since the right direction will lead to the most effective integration with the future world of work. Computers may well be the wave of the future, but in reality, the most opportunities could well be in such mundane occupations as cashier and home-care provider.[1] When we evaluate the benefits of a more nationally oriented education, we need to base our considerations on occupational projections such as those above. In this way, we can avoid the ideological pressure to be carried away with enthusiasms that are sometimes politically inspired.

This occurred not long ago when President Bush said in a speech that America should become more like the Waltons than the Simpsons. What he meant by reference to these two popular television programs was that he endorsed the traditional values exemplified by the Waltons, an early 20th century family working hard to earn a dignified living from the Virginia mountains where they lived in near pristine isolation. Hard work, honesty, diligence and individuality characterized this close-knit cooperative family, which was able to overcome all obstacles through their own efforts and a firm belief in God. It didn't matter that America's rural past was irrevocably gone, and that America had long been an urban, industrial nation. What the President recognized was that such myths evoke a nostalgic warmth in the hearts of many, and create a popularity on which more relevant issues can advance. The Simpsons, on the other hand, are a more smart-aleck, sophisticated, shrewd family made up of strangely exotic individuals who are critical, irreverent, often hostile and even violent but who, nevertheless, have a contemporary quality that endears them, especially to the youth of the country.

The same debate occurred between President Clinton and Bob Dole in the 1996 U.S. presidential campaign. For political advantage, the President was urged to abandon liberal ideas for "traditional" values. This included welfare reform (get the lazy poor off the dole and into work), school uniforms (more rigour in the classroom), curfew (don't trust young people to be out at night after 11 p.m.), and V chips, which enable parents to censor what their children watch on television. This traditional-values approach also endorses more police on the streets, the death penalty for serious criminals, and victim rights (Mayer, 1996).

Reorienting education so as to include a more nationalist or indigenous orientation can be a great benefit when it is linked closely to existing job opportunities, and is broadly supported by opposing political factions in society. In the American case alluded to above, there is already opposition to the Clinton strategy from the Black community, one of his staunchest support groups. This group regards all of his proposals here mentioned as retrogressive, unneeded and discriminatory. Therefore we must consider the implications of change in the larger political context in which those changes are to operate.

More potentially divisive still is the use of religious symbols to aid learning and achievement. In Israel and Algeria, we see the strength of religious zealots violently seeking to impress their views on the larger society. Geoffrey Hawthorn mentions the same problem in the Babri Masjid incident at Ayodhya.[2] In America, this use of religion has taken the form of a call for prayer in the school—something barred by constitutional mandate but which continually reasserts itself in debate and local elections when the virtues of a Christian upbringing are extolled. But religion is not always troublesome; it can serve positive ends as well. Recently, some scholarly attention has indicated that religion can have a powerful effect on learning. One could therefore justify its use in the schools. Looking at the examinations system of East Asia, Zeng found that the students used prayer and sacred talismans as a way to get potential benefit from reliance on more than their own efforts (Zeng, 1996).

Each country will have its own manner of addressing this question of how tradition or values can best be infused into the regular curriculum. India is unique in many ways; not the least is its long association with British models in language, organization and content. At the same time, there exists an old and successful indigenous system of education which can support valuable ideas that enhance national learning. It is important to explore how these various strands can be harnessed for the benefit of future generations. The only caveats I can offer are, first, that the debate should be as free as possible of political rhetoric; second, that change should relate directly to the job market of the future; and third, that any innovation should recognize the nature of today's youth—sometimes sceptical, often frustrated, occasionally hostile, but for all their faults, our only hope for progress.

The Demands of Global Learning

There is no way to avoid the future demands of global competition on educational practice. To ignore the clear indications of what is anticipated would not serve the needs of either the individual or the nation. Instead, our efforts must be to discover how best to blend the legitimate aspirations of a nation's culture and history with the learning requirements of the 21st century. While any attempt to do this must be cautious, we have, nevertheless, a number of international documents which can help predict what to expect.

We begin with the notion of globalization: the concept that

the world is becoming more and more integrated, interdependent and, in many ways, a generator of its own unique culture—the idea of the Global Village. While globalization is easily accepted in entertainment, industry and finance, it also applies to educational goals and structure as one moves from one capital to the next (Ramirez and Boli, 1987). Scientific reports, videos, films and music, all move freely via satellite, with or without the benefit of government sanction. The result is a homogenization of educational ideas, practices, certificates and achievement criteria that obscures national efforts to forge a unique system of learning designed to meet national needs. Already, financial transactions worldwide dwarf the activities of any national trading centre, and promise to frustrate efforts to control either capital or information.[3]

Two implications flow from this simple concept. The first is that, at the highest levels, our educational systems increasingly serve a new ultra-national constituency as never before. Instead of analyzing educational inputs and outcomes in terms of national planning needs and priorities, we must now look at our system of education in larger, more inclusive terms. We see this among guest workers in Germany and France, and also among South Asians in America and elsewhere; they have received an education in their own countries, often technical or scientific, and have gone on to successful careers in the industrialized world. In the United States, for example, the South Asians, thanks to their superior preparation, form the minority with the highest family income in the country.

The second implication is that, if this globalization is indeed inevitable, we will need to adjust our thinking concerning whose educational system we are trying to reform. Is it "ours", or is it in the larger world context that our mission lies? The British legacy can be seen as an early aspect of this globalization, in which case, the process of world integration has been going on for a long time. Globalization means that each nation state may have only a limited ability to redirect education in a world-wide context. Noel McGinn of Harvard

University makes the same point when he writes that national universities are becoming more susceptible to the influence of multinational corporations than to that of governments (McGinn, 1995). He further suggests that this is one way that global needs, rather than parochial learning, will be the focus of future attention.

But doesn't such a debate affect only a small number of trained and mobile scientists, technicians and other workers? Since most people will never travel outside their native land, doesn't globalization affect only a few? What is happening is that the nature of work has been altered by the impact of world trade and commerce. From the macro-farms of Colombia to the smallest villages and towns of Nigeria and North Carolina, workers are fired, hired, trained or ruined by the movement of goods and services around the world. As a result, efforts are made to eliminate illiteracy, to reform education, and to prepare workers for future opportunities. Due to this, more and more students are enrolled in schools each year. Agencies such as UNESCO and the conference on Education for All convened a few years ago, called for making education a universal reality (UNESCO, 1993). Because of the accepted idea that an educated population is a more productive population, efforts are now directed more to the neglected area of primary schooling. So crucial is this sector now considered, that the World Bank has altered its priorities to emphasize basic training at the primary level, rather than at the college or university levels. Women and girls are especially likely to be shut out of any improvements in education, and need to be provided with special consideration if they are to succeed.

Of course, despite our best efforts, considerable disparity exists in the world-wide provision of schooling. If we compare sub-Saharan Africa with Korea or Canada,[4] we see how great is the difference that currently exists. But efforts to improve the situation by added provision are also augmented by changing the curriculum to reflect non-traditional priorities. Instead of a narrow focus on reading and math, the curriculum is now expected to consider how to promote sustainable development, protect the environment, halt runaway population growth, combat the spread of disease, and further democracy, respect for human rights, tolerance and understanding. Any changes in the direction of a national curriculum today cannot avoid looking carefully at such priorities, which are now part of our common concern.

Reform and change, while dictated by expert opinion, are also subject to local democratic control. All over the world, there is a new awareness that education should respond to people's needs, and, increasingly, students, teachers, parents and citizens agitate to influence the nature of schooling. People everywhere are reluctant to place their lives and children in the hands of organizations over which they have little control. Hence we have seen a rise in the need for greater choice to enable parents and children to select the kind of education or school they feel best suits their needs. While there have traditionally been several options available—vocational, academic, scientific—the notion of choice is a broader concept; it ensures that, even without local catchment areas, parents will be able to have several options. Despite a school's democratic nature, parents often find it unresponsive to their wishes. Also, in the expectation that selecting schools will promote the good and punish the bad, school choice has become a watchword for change.[5] Choice is more than a gesture to give parents the illusion of control. It is sometimes endorsed by government as a device for placing more of the financial burden on the student's family. A number of educators also recognize that, with limited budgets, it is unlikely that adequate funds will be forthcoming to provide properly for what has been called equal educational opportunity. Such opportunity calls for some cost sharing in which those who benefit from the new arrangement will share more of the costs with the government and, in this way, lessen the burden on the general fund. The 1993 UNESCO education report says on this point:

> The general idea of requiring the beneficiaries of education and training to bear a much larger share of the real costs of providing the services was consistent with a

broader policy—widely stressed in other sectors such as public utilities—of applying realistic "user charges".

One outcome of this choice proposition is the expectation that government involvement in education in the 21st century will be less, not more. Particularly, government will play a smaller part in the education of children. This idea may conflict with international covenants which endorse "free and universal" schooling, and with our best efforts to nationalize schooling.

When we consider change in our educational systems, we may also want to look closely at what we mean by schooling. The image of a room, a person in charge in front, and a group of young people in seats—this whole picture may change with the increasing presence of powerful technological innovations that affect the consciousness of youth. More and more learning will be individualized through computer programs and disks that are available everywhere. More and more work is performed at home with computers and satellites and, in the future, we can expect this practice to proliferate in schools as well. This "third channel" will use television and the World Wide Web instead of chalk, books and blackboard. It will be a move away from formal learning as well as informal learning, and will depend on technological innovation exclusively. It suggests a new level of freedom from the constraints of state mandated texts and syllabi, and promises each student the opportunity and perhaps the right to make up his or her own curriculum. Such developments are seen as more humane and child-centered, and are welcomed as a needed departure from the drab tradition of discipline, tests, certificates and authoritarian organization.

Would this new-found freedom be consistent with the demands of commerce and industry world-wide? Will giving parents and students more choice really prepare them for global careers? Certainly, as was stated in the conference on Education for All, there is a continuing need for literacy, numeracy and oral expression. But while the old fashioned 3 Rs (reading, 'riting and 'rithmetic) are still important, the notion of values is now part of the planner's horizon. Workers who are test-smart but street-wise dull are not as likely to succeed as was the case previously. These values are not a part of regular school objectives. They include problem solving, working in groups, and entrepreneurial skills that bring people together. In a way, the regular school does not train leaders but followers, while the demands of the future call for much more initiative on the part of students. Robert Reich, the current U.S. Secretary of labour, outlines in his book, *The Work of Nations*, what he anticipates will be required of future workers in the industrialized countries. His emphasis is not on the hard sciences but rather, on attitudes and values which contribute to problem solving. He calls for the capacity to see relationships in unique ways, whether they refer to molecules, semiconductors, movie scripts, pension funds or information. Second, we need people to help others understand their needs and how those needs can be met with customized products. This is very different from training sales people to take orders and write receipts. It calls for understanding, sensitivity, and a host of other skills that are alien to the standard course of study. Last, Reich wants students who can bring people and products together to create new opportunities. Instead of waiting for a few talented individuals to come forward, he wants all students to consider themselves capable of seizing opportunities as they arise (Reich, 1994). Our work is a whole lot more than we expected when we began. It calls for great skill in blending the old concept of nationalist education with the new vision of 21st century needs.

Indigenous Learning

Can we look to past practices in pedagogy for guidelines that will be useful in the future? Are there, in fact, traditional ideas that represent a kind of cultural icon around which we can organize a new approach to learning that will enable us better to face the challenges of the 21st century? Throughout the world today, there are efforts to recapture elements of tradition for contemporary use. One of the most successful efforts has been the development of Hebrew as the national language of

Israel. This long-lost and near-dead language has been modernized to serve the commercial, industrial, scientific and security concerns of the modern state—something sceptics long doubted would succeed when the state of Israel was founded after WW II. So, too, much of the Islamic world has used the Koran to bring elements of ancient tradition into modern life. Iran, Malaysia and Sudan are all attempting to use Koranic principles to enhance development. Nor are all such efforts founded on religion. Secular efforts among the African-American minorities in the United States have found that including African dance, stories and history can heighten students' awareness, learning and motivation.

In India, the secular tradition since independence has formed a barrier to using overtly religious ideas as aids to learning. But there is a long and honorable tradition of secular learning that existed in India prior to the coming of the British, a tradition which served as a training ground for all the professionals in society. The small schools that existed in Bengal and Bihar as well as elsewhere are carefully documented in the Adam reports of the early 19th century (Adam, 1835–1838).[6] They turned out the accountants, lawyers, doctors, priests, logicians and bureaucrats that were required. There were Persian schools that taught not only the language but also law, literature, administration and court protocol. There were Sanskrit academies which gave brahmins the essentials of specialized knowledge in the literature, law, logic and language of the epics that provided a useful career. There were also more vocational places that taught commerce and trade as special subjects. All of these were practical places where students were able to relate what they studied to what they could use. There was no dichotomy between learning and living, and no cause for alienation.

While nationalist ideas drew most heavily from the thinking of the late 19th and early 20th centuries, a number of ideas had their origin in the more distant past, prior to British occupation. It seems appropriate to look carefully at this storehouse of experience, so reflective today of contemporary and future needs. While much of the nationalist educational philosophy grew out of a reaction to what the British represented, the indigenous schools drew their strength from an older tradition. Here, we had choice; we had the fostering of nearly individualized learning and useful careers. In Nattore thana of Rajshahi district, for example, practically each school had its own curriculum. Grammar was the first subject taught: Panini was used in six of the schools, Kalapa in two, the Mughabodha in three, and Rannamala in two. In another 19 schools, Hindu law was taught. Students entered after they had completed study in grammar and literature. There were two schools of logic forming a level higher than law. There were vedantic, pauranic, tantric and medical schools and, again, each catered to a social need. The pauranic taught the Mahabharata for recital at festivals and in private homes; from this knowledge the student expected to and did earn his livelihood.

The schools of Nattore in Bengal were very different from the Sanskrit academies. Here, learning was largely oral, since there were no printed texts. Instruction was often conducted outdoors or wherever a room could be provided, and teachers worked hard for what little pay was available. Commercial and agricultural accounts were taught to children of parents already in those professions and, as was usual, when the study ended, the students could begin working. More students, it turned out, were instructed at home than in formal schools, and it was here that the majority of women learned to read and write and conduct accounts. What is surprising is that these rather extensive efforts in education were attained without any state subsidy. There were lands devoted to education, there were fees paid, and there were generous and altruistic teachers, but the entire and very extensive record of education came about through the efforts of various communities working for their own good. In Culna thana, a remarkable 16% of children were enrolled in school—a record that could not be duplicated in some areas of the United States a century later.[7]

Modern values are sometimes suggested as ways to overcome barriers to development. Saving, achievement, planning, individuality and secularism were assumed to be absent from pre-colonial society. The value of the Adam reports is that they reflect accurately how misguided such distinctions are. The student in a Persian school working six hours each day to perfect his calligraphy is nothing if not the epitome of deferred gratification, planning and individual effort. And all this without the need for certificates of any kind. Many of these same promising features of education were also evident in the Gandhian basic education system. At Sevagram[8] in the 1950s, the students' industriousness was demonstrated by their efforts to spin enough cotton for their personal use. At the same time they were taught horticulture, chemistry and economics, and all this through the practical application of what they knew intimately already. There were, of course, many other crafts that were taught in addition to cotton spinning: weaving, paper making, gardening, bee keeping, and a host of others as well. In each case, the effort was to integrate a student's personality with the type of curriculum that appealed to him. In this way, it was hoped that he could be successful. The effort, of course, proved most beneficial. There was another way in which this nationalist innovation proved superior to modern practice, and that was in the area of personal attention or monitoring. In smaller schools, it is possible to know and understand students in personal ways in order to guide them to make wise choices. Where enrollments are massive, there is little choice but to process students like so much cord wood and let the chips fall where they may. In both the schools that Adam studied and in Sevagram, students were known and appreciated in a way that created a family atmosphere. It was a close, nurturing environment that was at once domestic and institutional—each enhancing the other for a stronger bond.[9]

In both Nattore and Sevagram we find a decentralized system of local control and finance. The curriculum was practical, by which we mean it provided a training which led to a livelihood. If a student did not spin enough cotton on his charkha—well, no harm was done with a shorter dhoti. The choices provided fostered a harmony between heart and mind, and avoided the alienation so evident in schools today. The self-supporting aspect gave students pride in their work, and by not granting diplomas, the system made it clear that one's talents or accomplishments must be evident rather than obscured behind some scrap of paper.

But there were other ways in which indigenous and nationalist concepts met future needs. They taught team work and cooperation, rather than competition and suspicion. They were also characterized by a sense of service to mankind. The great principle of sarvodaya still beckons us to meet the needs of the poor, whether there is government provision or not. The idea of service, so much a part of Indian life, is often neglected in the modern race for personal advantage. It looms large in the work of Vinoba Bhave and his bhoodhan movement. The same sense of selfless service is evident at the Aurobindo ashram in Pondicherry, at Dakshineshwar, and in myriad other places.

Today, the rest of the world recognizes the importance of service as an aid to learning as well as to personal growth. We recognize this need increasingly in industrial society. A recent annual survey of education in America by the Phi Delta Kappa/Gallup organization found that 66% of Americans favored a community-service requirement for high school graduation (*Herald-Sun*, August 29, 1996). Some colleges and universities have already introduced this idea as a requirement. North Carolina Central University is one such institution. Their requirement for service-learning is endorsed by the American Association of University Professors, the American Association of Higher Education, and others.[10] While a great deal more can be said concerning the nature of traditional education, as well as those nationalist changes brought about by political leaders in the 19th and 20th centuries, it is only our purpose to suggest how past practices are consonant with values and needs that can serve the future.

What the British Brought to India

Over the centuries of British control in India, numerous innovations and changes reflected the different requirements of the colonial government and the private, profit-making East India Company. The Orientalist controversy extolled indigenous culture and sought to prevent missionary intrusions into the subcontinent. But with Macaulay and after, we hear speeches about the evils of Hinduism and the disparagement of indigenous society. This led inevitably to the introduction of English and Western learning, which have proved resilient forces in Indian society.

The language, culture and organization brought by the British was a source of power. P.J. Marshall, in his *Cambridge History of the British Empire,* makes the point that the men who mapped the empire, who photographed and named its various people, plants and animals, who imprisoned hitherto free-floating local dialects between the covers of neat, printed dictionaries, knew that ordering things could consolidate political power. Using the printed word, the British spread their language and religion, fuelled their bureaucracy, and set the stage for the neglect of indigenous leadership and learning.

The Japanese suffered the same hostility towards their culture in the 19th century, when it was claimed that the Japanese language was just too awkward to support the subtleties of Western science and learning. Today, we see research pursued in many national languages, both with alphabets and with other writing forms, and no one claims that progress is dependent on language. Nevertheless, English persists in India as the *lingua franca* of politics, education and commerce. What this has meant is that the country continues to suffer the malignant effect of a schism between the successful and the marginalized. To know English well today is to be a part of the country's elite; not to know that language is to be relegated to the parochial margins of intellectual life.

While attention has long been directed to this unfortunate dichotomy, there is no easy road to change. As Nehru said, English is a window on the world, and it is also a source of great benefit to Indian society, so its elimination cannot be expected by the stroke of a pen. At the same time, no really acceptable, democratic system of education can continue the use of a foreign tongue as the premier medium of expression.

Nonetheless, with English came a host of other changes that must be viewed today in the context of how they will serve the needs of tomorrow. The British also introduced an examination system which has evoked general condemnation over the years. The notion that paper and pencil tests of rote-learned facts can somehow represent understanding, sensitivity, creativity or talent is a point made again and again. Then we have the reliance on textbooks, class schedules and hours to determine when a student has been educated and when he needs another course or two before he is granted evidence of success. All such ideas, now accepted and incorporated as normal for the existing system of education, can be considered for elimination by reference to the criteria of future needs.

Combining the Best of the Past with the Present to Create a New Future

The hardest part of combining the past with the future needs of society is to acknowledge the dead hand of the present restraining what initiatives we may propose. Let us begin with finance. How can schools be financed in the future to better prepare students with less government dependence? We saw that, in both the 19th century schools of Bengal and in Buniyadi Talim, there was, of necessity, a close link between the educational establishment and the sources of community wealth, whether that was land or trade or power. Today, the movement around the world is towards less government control and intervention and more support by local industry. In a recent article in the newsletter of the International Institute for Educational Planning in Paris entitled "University-industry collaboration still a difficult process", the benefits as well as the problems of school/industry cooperation were spelled out. In countries where industry is more modernized due to its research and marketing, technological innovation will be more accessible to the classroom. Part of the benefit also encompasses employment, if it is assumed that having industry positively involved in the curriculum makes it more likely that students coming out of the educational process will be better able to work in available jobs than would otherwise be the case. An additional benefit was recently highlighted in *Forbes Magazine*, in an article entitled "Good schools, good business". Most parents turn out to be more dedicated, productive workers when companies subsidize superior schools. In a case cited from Dade County, Florida, American bankers gave the school $146,000 in support annually, but estimated a benefit from the investment of $475,000, due to the lower worker turnover that could be directly attributed to the enthusiastic reception the subsidized school received.

One of the fears often mentioned of allowing business interests into schools is that they would then abandon their role in training for citizenship, and become subject to "the bottom line". The only source of independent intellectual development would be gone, and with no countervailing force, the arrangement would lead to a complete domination of schools by individuals whose main interest was profit. While certainly an important concern, there is a great deal of evidence from the 19th and 20th centuries that, although the British colonial government controlled schools, curricula, examinations and texts, independent thinkers were still able to exert a sometimes radical critique of current practice. A more serious issue concerns how young people will be absorbed into the work force if their numbers already far exceed the number of job places in the modern sector. What is called the educated unemployed is always a frustrated, unhappy lot, both for individuals and society at large. If each individual who goes into a course of study could look forward to rewarding employment, everyone would benefit. Near guaranteed employment would call for a radical shift in the kinds of courses offered throughout the system. And yet, isn't this what we mean by a new nationalist education—one in which there will be a closer fit between people and opportunity? And if it does not exist now, it is a challenge to propose ways by which that very goal can be met.

As government becomes less able to adequately finance

education—and this is already clear in many countries—there will be only two possibilities for support. It will either have to be generated locally, or it will come from outside government. Government can fight this tendency, or work to promote positive relations between local resources and schools. There is no reason that agricultural cooperatives, religious orders, or labour unions cannot conduct schools of their own creation. This, indeed, will lead to a diversity that is certainly not apparent today, but is more like the indigenous system prior to the British incursion. Further, government can be in the lead in removing legal obstacles to the creation of such innovative efforts. There are already many examples of such private initiatives. The Aurobindo ashram in Pondicherry, the school at Shantiniketan and the Gujarat Vidyapith in Ahmedabad, all are examples of thoughtful departures that work and can be duplicated on a larger scale but with the proviso that support should come locally.

One problem that can be anticipated from such an initiative is that experienced educational managers will resist any erosion of their usual prerogatives. It would undermine the clear financial arrangement between the centre, the states, and other sources of existing support. But present managers can be trained to supervise the new arrangement. A second obstacle is due to most educational institutions being unable to accept autonomy. They may cry for more but are ill disposed to go out and find their own resources, even if it is for a good cause. Educators are taught to think along disciplinary lines—they know what is math or science—but to think interdisciplinarily about cotton and exports and jobs and happiness, that defies logic.

Another important departure from current practice, which would serve both a contemporary need as well as meet the future requirements of the 21st century, is in the area of cooperative learning. What British examinations really brought to India was not a love of achievement but competition, and while that is still an accepted value, so, increasingly, is the idea that we can accomplish more by team work and cooperation than we can by ourselves. In most large organizations, there is nothing comparable to the student working diligently on his own to prove his individual accomplishments. Most activities, whether in the emergency room of a medical trauma centre, a TV production studio, or a Japanese commercial boardroom, call for people to work together, to help one another, and to magnify their individual efforts by group activities. This was traditionally the case in India's past, when the superior accomplishments of a school were enjoyed by all concerned, and the reciting of a long epic poem could be shared by several voices, either in union or in sequence. Needless to say, schools today do not try to create or reward group work. In fact, just the opposite is true; if two or more students work together, it is called cheating and is severely punished. Not long ago, *Newsweek* magazine published an article detailing the 10 best school practices, and in all of them, the element of group work was featured, whether it was the teaching of reading in Lake Tekapo, New Zealand, where children not only chose their own texts but shared their experiences with their classmates and thus stimulated others to read as well, or the Diana school in Reggio Emilia, Italy, where youngsters and their parents worked with teachers in the same room for a wonderfully exciting learning environment. The basic idea in the Diana school was that youngsters are different, they are individuals and should not be subjected to a rigid discipline. That is why the early schools of Nattore were successful: children studied at their own pace; some took longer to master the material, and some were very swift, but that was not the key. The main Diana feature was the cooperation of teachers, parents and peers. It began after the devastation of World War II, when parents gathered rubble and sand to physically build their school. It is an inspiring story, but no more so than countless examples around India that have not yet been told.

Since 1989, Japan has been improving its education despite an enviable record of academic success. It is moving from pure science to applied science, where students work together to repair VCRs and toaster ovens in an effort to break through the cult of obedience and develop a creative mentality. Instead of the stereotype of automatons, the new Japanese students are noisy and active; they move around, ask questions, shout answers, try ideas, and generally have a good time. This is what the future will reward; not the sit-in-your-place-and-listen-to-me syndrome. In the modern Dutch school where language is taught, 95% of the children learn a foreign language not by listening but by speaking. We have spoken of English as a divisive force in Indian society, but it need not be if a majority of students learned English. Can it be done? Of course it can be done. If Israelis can learn Hebrew, South Africans Afrikaans, and Dutch children English, there is nothing less to be anticipated in India.

One feature of the new learning that has not been touched upon is the idea of life-long learning, in which parents and other members of the community take part in the educational process along with their children. If learning is related to the material conditions in which children live and learn, it is only natural for them to use the accumulated knowledge of parents and community leaders to enhance their own learning. This calls for bringing the classroom more closely into the community and sharing that learning with all. These are but a few ways that nationalist ideas can work for future growth.

Conclusion

Giving Indian education a more nationalist slant can be justified only if the benefits outweigh the problems that may be created. Any departure from tradition implies a critique of the people who have nurtured the very structures that are to be changed. This was the case in Japan, when the Meiji restoration brought an end to the privileges of the feudal lords and ushered in a more class-oriented society. Currently, Japan has been trying to bring about a similar change in the educational system through liberalization. This has meant, among other things, a decentralization from the control of education by Tokyo. Japan's outstanding record of scholastic achievement has been the envy of all other countries, so it is understandable that the central control of education was considered a chief cause of that success.[11] Nevertheless, it was widely accepted in Japan that the dependence on book learning, examinations and authoritarian control was not suited to the future challenges that would have to be met. The new emphasis called for more choice in what students studied and more flexible curricula, so that different combinations were available to excite student involvement and individualize school practice to meet the challenge of the 21st century.

One more element that needs to be considered in educational modernization concerns the nature of the student psyche. Any change towards a national system of education must take into account the nature of present student consciousness. Amano Ikuo saw the trauma that ensued from the recognition that the well-behaved, loyal, patriotic, dedicated young student also exhibited a dark side that had not previously been suspected. Young people were turning towards drugs, violence, anti-school behaviour and disrespect for tradition. He says:

> ... schools and teachers control students' lives through strict rules covering everything from hair style to details of dress. What is more, everyone must go through the tough examination competition in order to go to high school and university. These realities of education are powerful forces working to weaken the children's motivation and enthusiasm (Ikuo, 1992).

So it is not only the nature of the culture that must be considered but also the nature of the occupational structure into which the educated youth must fit. On top of that, we must be cognizant of the changes taking place in world youth culture. A successful plan must take all three facets of change into account.

In 1937, the Zakir Husain Committee was charged with the development of a truly national system of education. It began with a condemnation of the development of Western education: the curriculum, practice and goals. This old system, they said, "had no conception of the new cooperative social order which education must help to bring into existence to replace the present competitive and inhuman regime based on exploitation and violent force." Their recommendation was to return to an education founded on crafts and useful work and, most significantly, taught in the mother tongue rather than English. In his endorsement of the committee's work, Gandhi said, "... the scheme is a revolution in the education of village children. It is in no sense an importation from the West." Many of the ideas already mentioned are consistent with the meaning of what was so ably said more than a half century ago. We have, then, a strong base to build on, and giants to help us realize these important goals. Let us pray we can rise to the challenge.

Notes

1. These occupational categories are drawn from American government statistics contained in J. Michael Farr's compilation, *50 Fastest Growing Jobs*, which show that the next decade will see the largest growth in home health aides, human services workers, and computer engineers and scientists. At the same time, the largest numerical growth in these years (1995–2005) will be in salespersons retail (by 765,000), cashiers (by 670,000), and registered nurses (by 765,000).
2. Geoffrey Hawthorn alludes to the Babri Masjid mosque in Ayodha in "The difficulties of governance now are dauntingly stupendous", *London Review of Books*, 18 July 1996.
3. While a rich literature has documented this trend, two particularly insightful and expert statements are contained in Walter B. Wriston, *The Twilight of Sovereignty* (1992), and Kevin Phillips, *Arrogant Capital* (1995).
4. The school-life experience in Niger and Guinea amount to only 306 days and 449 days, respectively. In the Republic of Korea, it is 2,700 days, and in Canada, over 3,100 days.
5. Economist Milton Friedman of the University of Chicago is often mentioned as the herald of "vouchers" in schooling. He was inspired by the earlier market notions of Adam Smith.
6. These reports serve as a benchmark for indigenous educational practice before the British influence spread inland from their larger administrative centers. The reports were edited in the

19th century by Rev. James Long, in the 1940s by A.N. Basu and, most recently, by J. Di Bona as *One Teacher, One School*, 1983, Biblia Impex, Delhi.

7. H. Leon Prather, Sr. reported that in rural North Carolina, he estimated 100% illiteracy among Blacks in the coastal basin as recently as 1900. The same case can be made for poor Appalachian whites at the same time.
8. During a personal visit to Sevagram in the 1950s, I was part of the debate concerning the virtues of the individual charkha *vs.* the amber charkha. Later, I participated in the Puri sammelan with Vinoba Bhave and, still later, visited the Aurobindo Ashram and the Ramakrishna centre near Calcutta.
9. All my students at Duke University must tutor in local (largely disadvantaged) schools as part of their academic work.
10. All the faculty at the NCCU are asked to integrate service and learning. In one biology course where communicable diseases are studied, students go out to homes and alert citizens about how such diseases are spread.
11. Liberalization in Japan has been delayed due to opposition within the educational establishment. Authorities are just not ready to jettison their successful practices.

References

Di Bona, Joseph, 1983, *One Teacher, One School: The Adam Reports on Indigenous Education in 19th Century India*, New Delhi, Biblia Impex.

Durham Herald-Sun, 28 August 1996 poll.

Farr, J. Michael, 1995, *America's Fastest Growing Jobs*.

IIEP Newsletter, 1996, "University-industry collaboration: still a difficult process", XIV, No. 2, April-June, International Institute for Educational Planning, Paris.

Ikuo, Amano, 1992, "The bright and dark sides of Japanese education", *The Japanese Foundation Newsletter*, XIX, Nos. 5–6, May, Tokyo.

Mayer, Jane, 1996, "The political scene: heart and mind", *New Yorker*, August 12, p. 25.

McGinn, Noel F., 1995, "Options for higher education as Latin America joins the world economy", presented at the 39th annual meeting of the Comparative and International Education Society, Boston, MA, USA.

Marshall, P.J., 1996, *Cambridge Illustrated History of the British Empire*, Cambridge University Press.

Munk, Nina, 1996, "Good schools, good business," *Forbes*, September 9, p. 144.

NCCU Faculty Guide to Service-Learning, 1996 Durham, N.C.

Newsweek, 1992, "The best schools in the world", December 2.

Ramirez, F.O. and J. Boli, 1987, "The political construction of mass schooling: European origins and worldwide institutionalization", *Sociology of Education*, **60**, 1, 2–17.

Reich, Robert B., 1994, *The Work of Nations*.

UNESCO, 1993, *World Education Report*, Paris.

Zeng, Kangmin, 1996, "Prayer, luck and spiritual strength: The desecularization of entrance examination systems in East Asia", *Comparative Education Review*, August, Vol. 40, No. 3.

Education in China Through Indian Eyes

TAN CHUNG

Education in the People's Republic of China (PRC) is a fascinating topic very little known in India. The Chinese civilization, like the Indian is more than 5,000 years old, and yet still young and vigorous because its main icon, Confucius (551–479 B.C.) was a great educator. When Mao Zedong (1893–1976) was asked by foreign writers how he would like to be remembered by history, he expressed his wish to be remembered as a "great teacher". When Deng Xiaoping reviewed student demonstrations in the wake of the Tiananmen episode in the Spring, 1989, he admitted the "mistake" (*shiwu*), and said the mistake was primarily in the field of education.[1]

In May 1985, the Communist Party of China (CPC) made the historic decision of Education Reform which declared the fundamental aim of education as the "improvement of the quality of the Chinese nation, producing more and more and better and better talents". In February, 1993, China issued the "Outline of Reforms and Development of Chinese Education", and in March 1995, the "Education Law of PRC" was enacted. Never before did education occupy such importance in China's socio-political life as it does today. The serious concern for education by Chinese authorities and the ruling elite is testified to by the long incubation period for the creation of the "Education Law" which took ten years of extensive and intensive deliberations and consultations, having referred to similar laws of more than ten other countries. More important is the Chinese determination to use education as the vital instrument to revitalize China in her march into the 21st century. This paper is an attempt to understand the importance of and the problems relating to Chinese education with a historical perspective, looking through the prism of India.

China is not only the inventor of printing and book-making, but has a well established culture with an emphasis on education, particularly book-education. There is a Chinese saying which goes:

"In the books there are houses made of gold;
In the books there are jade-like beauties to behold."

This saying reflects a Chinese psyche which is summarized by one sentence: "*Wanban jie xiaping weiyou dushu gao*" (All vocations are inferior to the only super profession, i.e. reading books). The Chinese term for "studying" is "*dushu*"—reading books. That for "teaching" is "*jiaoshu*"—teaching books. Book-education has been regarded as the best and most important form of education.

Confucius and Gautama Buddha are brilliant examples of educationists. Confucius, after retiring from government service, turned into a teacher, and had more than 3,000 disciples. He said the joy of life was to learn, and to practise what one had learnt. (*Xue er shi xi zhi.*)[2]

Book-education developed side by side with the propagation of Confucian teachings. From the 2nd century B.C. onwards, the imperial government adopted Confucian teachings as the guiding ideology of Chinese government, and prescribed certain compulsory texts of Confucian classics as essential reading materials for the ruling elite. One direct effect of this policy was the emergence of the Kong (Confucius') clan of Shandong (supposed to be the direct descendants of Confucius) as a hereditary ruling elite of China. This Confucian clan dominated Chinese society for several hundred years until the 7th century.

Further expansion of this book-education culture led to the

introduction of the Imperial Examination System (*keju*) from the 7th century onwards. China started recruiting for its imperial services through a three-tier examination. They selected only the best scholars for the top jobs of imperial officialdom. The examination system immediately created a new socio-political phenomenon described as the replacement of the erstwhile monopolist families (of Shandong and other places) by the so-called "*hansu*", i.e. scholars from humble family backgrounds with simple lifestyles. While China continued with this examination-oriented education for nearly one and half millennia, India was the first country outside China to adopt such civil examinations in the 19th century courtesy the Pax-Britannica.

This examination-oriented book-education has had multiple social functions the effect of which is still felt even after China abandoned the Imperial Examination system in the beginning of the 20th century. First, respect for knowledge and the teacher who imparts it has become a lasting Chinese tradition. Confucius said: "*Bu chi xiawen.*" or "I don't feel ashamed in learning from the lowly." He also said: "I am not as good as the farmer."[3] This willingness in Chinese culture to learn from any quarter prompted China's initiative in inviting Indian and other foreign monks to China to preach Buddhism around the time of the Christ. Various Chinese imperial governments honoured such foreign Buddhist monks like Buddhacinga (*Fotuteng*), Kumarajiva (*Jiumoluoshi*), and Amoghavajra (*Bukong*), all from India, as "Guoshi"—the Chinese version of "Rajya guru". The Chinese emperor took the lead by showing deference to the honoured persons so designated.

It is likely that this Chinese practice of appointing "Guoshi" was their adaptation of an ancient Indian tradition. Buddhacinga, Kumarajiva and Amoghavajra, thus, personified the convergence of the ancient Indian and Chinese traditions of respect for knowledge and the teacher.

This examination-oriented book-education has also helped China establish the supremacy of the literati over the military. The genesis of this supremacy can be traced to the time of the first Han emperor in an episode which is well-known as the realization of the importance of "*shishu zhi guo*" (ruling the country by poetry and history books).[4] From that time on, the supermacy of civil authorities over the military has been established till today.

This education has helped to establish in China a tradition of policy-making by consulting the authorities of knowledge. Confucian classics were the major authority. This was similar to the Indian political culture of governing in accordance of the teachings of the *Vedas*, the *Gita*, and other classics. The observance of the classics in letter and spirit was known as "zhengming" (literally "in the name of proper authority"), i.e. sanctity obtained from authoritative classical teachings. If the authoritative classical teachings are observed in the breach it would amount to "*ming buzheng ze yan bushun, yan bushun ze shi bucheng*" (Devoid of sanctity leads to the void of justification; without justification nothing can be accomplished). This has been one of the norms of governance in China for two thousand years.

There is a saying in China's oral literature that the Tang Emperor Taizong (reigning from 629 to 649) who had initiated the Imperial Examination System had "whitewashed the hair" of all the intellectuals of China. As there was no age limit, nor limit for the number of attempts in the Imperial Examinations, and as every male adult, whatever his family background and social status, could appear in the examinations, the system virtually drained the wisdom and energy of all the ambitious Chinese, many of whom could be potential trouble-makers for the establishment. Such a culture has served to bless China with an opposition-free political environment, and helped to uphold Chinese political stability.

Finally, it was this examination-cum-education culture that created a social stratum in China known as the "gentry class". This stratum was initially formed by aspirants, candidates, as well as drop-outs of the Imperial Examinations. These were people who by close association with the ruling elite, had developed a kind of superiority complex in the larger illiterate rural surroundings of their residence. This stratum played an intermediary role between the government and the grass-roots society, rendering social service to both. The cream of this stratum was made up of those who had passed the examinations: some obtaining the title of "*xiucai*" (excellent talent) at the lowest level, few others being admitted to the title of "*juren*" (elevated personality) at the middle level, and a handful every year who were personally picked up by the emperor as "*jinshi*" (literally "entrance to officialdom")—qualifying them for high imperial appointments in the government. The majority of this stratum of gentry played an important role in stabilizing China's socio-political order. However, some members of this stratum who were disillusioned with the government were also active in mobilizing mass peasant wars—a frequent occurrence throughout Chinese history.

Buddhism entered China before Christ, and was a massive educational movement there for two thousand years until the rise of Communism. There is a popular Chinese saying: "All the good words have been uttered by Buddha, while most of the famous hills have been occupied by Buddhist monks." (*Shishang haoyan Fo shuo jin, tianxia mingshan seng zhan duo*). Chinese rulers and the ruling elite found in Buddhism an effective instrument to cultivate peace, harmony, law-abiding temperament as well as loyal citizens. It was they who actively patronized the dissemination of Buddhism. Buddhism in China propagated through wall paintings, stucco and sculptures, performing arts and decorative arts, as well as other forms of oral literature. In this way, its influence among the Chinese masses has surpassed even that of Confucianism and Taoism.

Apart from Buddhist and other religious organizations, the immediate and extended family have played a very important role in education in China. The Chinese family education, till today, has always been moral and pro-establishment. While family education had interacted harmoniously with Confucian and Buddhist indoctrination in the past, it is now a prop for the Chinese brand of a new socialist culture which may be termed as "Marxized Maoistic Buddho-Confucian culture".

Family education has been a long established tradition in

China. Mencius (372?-289 B.C.), who propagated Confucius' teachings just as Vivekananda had done to Ramakrishna, lost his father at a young age, but the strict family education he received from his mother made him a great Chinese.[5] India has a similar tradition. Indian and Chinese parents are the keenest educators of their children. In the one-child families in China today, there is a strong expectation for the son to become a "dragon" and the daughter a "phoenix".

The merit of such a tradition has its modern ramifications. In North America, Asians (particularly Chinese and Indians) are capturing more and more medals in US schools and colleges. The Indian and Chinese communities in USA and Canada are relatively free from juvenile delinquency in comparison with other ethnic groups.

While China has built up a permanent educational infrastructure to facilitate social mobility, it has also confronted the serious challenge of modern times caused by the information explosion in the field of modern science and technology. China's backwardness in this regard invited disaster. She had to bow before the "Gunboat Diplomacy" of Britain and France and other western powers, and take up the humiliating status of "sub-colony" (worse than colony) in the modern world. The realization of the deficiency of modern information and insight made China abandon her Imperial Examinations and adopt the western educational system which because of China's peculiar social milieu did not develop very satisfactorily.

Communism virtually replaced the Buddhist educational infrastructure, and made Chinese family education subordinate to the guiding socio-political culture known as "Mao Zedong Thought"—a kind of sinified Marxism. Mao Zedong, the father-figure of the PRC, was not only familiar with China's fine educational traditions, but also furiously mixed up educational goals with mass revolutionary practice. He arrogated to himself the role of custodian of the nation's moral conscience. This was both a blessing and a disaster for the country. The blessing was that not only was education (i.e. political indoctrination) regarded as a sacred cow, but considerable time and energy were spent on imparting such education across all walks of life. In the words of Mao's detractors, he had converted China into a colossal basin to wash the people's brains—even those of prisoners and criminals. The disaster was that when Mao, the head of state and supreme leader, turned into a hard task master, the entire Chinese nation had to shiver. Mao also created a massive earthquake in China's educational system by launching the "Great Proletarian Cultural Revolution" in 1966.

The Cultural Revolution was conceived with the basic assessment that the school and university education that had prevailed in the PRC from 1949 to 1966 was "reactionary", and polluted with feudal and bourgeois elements. Hence, Mao called upon the youth, particularly the students, to become "Red Guards" to defend revolutionary puritanism. All educational institutions were closed for three years (1966–69), and virtually paralysed for ten. The teachers and administrators of the colleges and schools were sent to the "cow-shed" (a kind of confinement) to write their confessions (of crime) and receive lectures, even insult, from the students. Normalcy in education could be restored only after the death of Chairman Mao in September, 1976, and the downfall of the "Gang of Four" (led by Mao's wife, Madam Jiang Qing) in its wake. It is indeed lamentable that a whole generation in China has suffered without an education because of this "Revolution" in the name of "Culture".

However, the Chinese government under the leadership of the CPC has contributed to the tremendous progress of education in China in the last four and five decades. The achievement in various fields can be spelled out.

Mainstream Education

Despite the aberration of the Cultural Revolution, the PRC has more than upheld the fine Chinese tradition of attracting bright and ambitious youths to educational institutions. Wherever facilities exist, a newborn in the PRC begins his/her tryst with school-going which forms his/her first phase of social life (or struggles in life, if you wish). Modern-minded Chinese (as also their Indian counterparts) conceive two vital phases of life: (1) "*xueye*" (academic career), and (2) "*shiye*" (career). The cream of Chinese youth struggle in the mainstream of Chinese education with the same endeavour as their ancestors did in the Imperial Exams. The mainstream consists of three stages: primary school—six years, middle school—six years, and university—normally, four years.

In 1949, when the PRC was founded, there were only 2.2 students at the university level for every 10,000 Chinese . This figure increased to 16.4 in 1985, and has now exceeded 20. Similarly, while there were, in 1949, only 23 and 450 students studying in the middle and primary schools respectively, the number has increased several tens of times now. According to the statistics of 1994, there were 174,657 kindergartens with 26.3 million children, 682,588 primary schools absorbing 128.226 million students, and 68,116 middle schools accommodating 43.167 million students in the junior middle school section (upto the 9th grade).[6] This is an enormous achievement in comparison to the poor educational facilities in 1949 when only 4.76% of the total population of 500 million attended schools and universities. But, even the total capacity now (which adds up to 197.693 million seats) is still not large enough to enlist all school-waiting children, depriving several tens of million children of a proper education, particularly at the junior middle school level.

Vocational Education

China has a huge population the majority of which fits Chairman Mao's description of "*yi qiong er bai*" meaning "for one thing they are poor, for another, they are blank." This blankness is mainly in terms of modern knowledge in science and technology.

There is a phenomenon which educationists call "*sanji fenliu*" (three levels of side-flows). The mainstream Chinese educational system is like a river flowing from the primary and middle school stages into the university stage. As this is a pyramid with fewer and fewer seats on the way up, the majority of students fall outside of it at the summit, and a large number of students are forced into the side-flow, some after the primary, others after the junior and senior middle school stages. They are regarded as mediocres who have little chances to go far in life. They are thus forced into taking up various vocations, with many of them going back to their villages to join their mediocre parents or being tied up with the soil as another generation of bumpkin farmers.

To remedy this, the Chinese authorities have turned their attention to what is termed "side-flow education". This is a project which targets youths who have been washed to the side-flows, and draws them into a network of vocational education. Out of this project emerges such schemes like "6+1" (adding one year of intensive vocational training to those who cannot continue to study at the middle school stage), and "3+1" (providing the same for those who have to stop their studies after the junior or senior middle school). Other short training schemes, and part-time training programmes are designed to bring the "side-flow" youths back into the mainstream—to let them feel that they too can get ahead in life.

Chinese vocational education has come a long way in its development, particularly with the "specialized secondary schools" designed for "side-flow" youths who have missed their junior or senior middle school stage. In 1984, there were only 3,301 secondary vocational schools with an enrolment of 1,325,000 students. In 1994, the number of such schools increased to 247,048, with an enrolment of 3,197,851 students.[7]

Now, all the provincial governments have realized the importance of expanding secondary vocational education. The Shandong Province has ambitions to enrol 1.3 million students in its secondary vocational schools by the year 2000.

Adult Education

China is concentrating not only on educating the side-flow youths, but on all those who wish to benefit from educational networking. There are various institutions which impart higher education to those who are working, or who are in the side flow. These include:

- Higher educational institutions for the employees run by the large state-owned enterprises: The technical training institution of the Baoshan Iron and Steel Company, Shanghai (the largest and most modern steel enterprise of China) started in 1983 almost at the same time when the factory was being built (in 1981). By 1990, it had enrolled 1,962 students (1,121 who had completed senior middle school, and 841 who had completed junior middle school). From 1985 to 1995, it had trained 1,644 skilled workers for the steel plant.[8]
- Higher education correspondence institutions run by the universities and other higher educational institutions.
- Evening universities run by city municipal governments universities and other higher educational institutions, and state-owned enterprises.
- Institutions that train cadres: This is a well developed system run by the CPC, the Communist Youth League, various ministries of the government, provincial governments, municipal governments, state-owned enterprises etc. An example is the Baoshan Iron and Steel Company, which runs a cadre training institution and a university called "Baoshan Iron and Steel Company Staff University" (*Baogang zhigong daxue*) specially instituted by the Ministry of Metallurgy. It is a prestigious institution training leading cadres for the company. The graduates get a diploma from the ministry, which ensure continuous and good postings all over China in future.
- Peasants' higher educational institutions run by local governments.

Life Education

A new wave emerging in the field of education is "life education". Its aim is to make the entire human life an education course, and have a benign link between education and work. In the USA, it is known as "life study" and involves studying all one's life, and nationally dispensing with "life-long teachers". China is gradually being caught up by the fever of "self study". Bookshops and libraries are crowded, and people buy all kinds of "self study" guide books, dictionaries, and encyclopaedias. This is a healthy trend which deserves commendation.

China's new Education Law reflects this endeavour to "establish a perfect system for life education" (Article 11). It promises to provide every Chinese citizen the facilities for what he/she likes to choose whenever he/she wishes to learn, to provide permanent opportunities for his/her life education. "Life education" is mentioned in other articles (19, 41 etc.) so that Chinese citizens do not lag behind in the rapid advances of modern learning.

Moral Education

Regardless of whatever government has been in power, this has occupied a very important dimension in the life of the PRC. During the Mao Era, there were mass campaigns with heavy moral and ideological doses which no one could escape. Even the Cultural Revolution was kindled by Mao's idealism of rearing "new humans". Today, China still possesses the infrastructure of moral indoctrination which is gradually being revitalized under the rubric of "*zhengzhi gongzuo*" (political work) by the Party and government departments.

Educationists have conceived a three dimensional education in China in modern times. The first is "*deyu*" or moral education which has been reiterated since the time of Confucius. The second is "*zhiyu*" or intellectual education, including normal and vocational education. The third is "*tiyu*" or physical education. In 1978, Deng Xiaoping suggested that these three aspects be incorporated in the qualifications for admission to schools, universities and in job recruitment.[9] Deng further advocated in the early 1980s that there should be a country-wide and all-time endeavour to create new humans who would not only have idealism, but also a good moral character, and be lettered, cultured, and disciplined.

In post-Deng China, moral education receives even more importance for a variety of reasons. It is felt that general moral standards have fallen, and corruption is rampant. A new campaign to enhance "spiritual civilization" (*jingshen wenming*) has been launched in the last couple of years to curb the growing influence of mammonism, hedonism and individualism.[10] The National People's Congress endorsed, in 1996, the "Outline of a Long-term Social and Economic Development towards the Year 2010" which has codified the task of building a spiritual civilization to develop people with the "four qualities" of (*siyou*), idealism, morality, culture, and discipline and "five loves" (*wu'ai*), love for their motherland, the people, labour, science, and socialism.

Women's Education

It is well known that the standard of women's education is the yardstick used to measure the advancement and enlightenment of a society. There is one phenomenon which apparently gladdens international femininists. The Chinese describe it as "Yin seng yang shuai" (flourishing femininity while masculinity decays). This phenomenon was due initially to Chinese female athletes' and sportswomen's who won top honours and Olympic medals in the last couple of decades in contrast to the relatively poor showing of their male counterparts. This is possible only after women, particularly urban women, have been given equal opportunities of education as men.

While urban women in China have reached a level of equality with men in almost all spheres, the women in rural areas are still comparatively less educated and lag behind in other aspects of life. In 1989, the movement of "2 learnings and 2 competitions" was launched which is still being pursued in the countryside. The "2 learnings" relate to learning letters and skills, while the "2 competitions" involve competing (with neighbouring women as well as with men) to achieve results, and contributing (to society). The movement has enlisted the participation of 120 million rural women making it China's largest institution of social educational networking.

In China, there is a symbiosis between China and education. China needs to improve education much as education needs to improve China. The achievements in education do not make a rosy picture. The problems confronting Chinese education are the very woes confronting the country as it marches into the future.

Widening the Education Net

According to statistics of 1992, the populations of the two most populous countries are young, with 94% of people below the age of sixty-five in China, and 96% of them below sixty-five in India.[11] When these young people enter the 21st century and face the age of information technology it will be good and bad news. Good news if a good education is provided to the hundreds of millions of Indians and Chinese at the learning age; bad news that a tremendous amount of money has to be spent to give them an adequate education. Without adequately educating such a young population the two countries will be in peril.

The PRC has made Chinese society a "flying dragon and leaping tiger" (*longteng huyue*) as the Chinese proverb describes. There was unprecedented expansion in almost every aspect of life. This has been even more so during the post-Mao period. The annual expansion of higher education (measured by the number of students) was 8.4% in the 1980s, and 6% in the 1990s. While, at the same time, the expenses on education have gone more and more to the salaries of teachers and supporting staff (40% in the 1980s, and 70% in the 1990s)[12]—leaving little for the development of infrastructure and programmes.

It is estimated that during the Ninth Five-Year Plan period (1996–2000) there will be 54 million young job-seekers, but only about 38 million of them can be accommodated in jobs.

In the year 2000, urban unemployment will reach 7.4% of the total urban population. In the rural area there will be 214 million new youths in search of jobs, and 137 million of them will not be able to find them. Hence, the total unemployment rate of China can go as high as 21.3% by 2000, if corrective measures are not taken.[13] This serious prospect puts great pressure on the Chinese educational system. For one thing, only by imparting adequate necessary education can employment opportunities be sufficiently expanded to meet such a gigantic dimension of demand. For another, more young people in search of jobs means more demand for "side-flow education" as I have discussed earlier.

Providing education to the young population of China will by no means be easy. The cake of the existing educational facilities is not large, as the Chinese say "too little porridge for too many monks". The last Chinese census report (1990) shows that 157.5 million Chinese belonged to the age group 7 to 14, and another 155.5 million were 0 to 6 years old. There has been a substantial increase of these numbers in the last five to six years. However, the existing infrastructure of education in China is too inadequate to meet the increasing demand.

Universal education was the cherished goal of the Mao Era, but Mao passed away (in 1976) without meeting the deadline of introducing a nine year compulsory education. In 1986, only 50%, i.e. 1,152 counties of China had realized universal education. Great efforts have been made to introduce compulsory education in recent years, and 91% of the counties realized it in 1995. However, even today there are still a large number of illiterates in China. Mr. Li Ruihuan, one of the top leaders of China (Member of the Standing Committee of the Politburo and also the Chairman of the Chinese People's Political Consultative Conference which is China's equivalent of the Rajya Sabha), spoke in the All China Education Conference in Beijing in January, 1995, and revealed that on an average, a Chinese was exposed to only 5.4 years of systematic education. He also revealed that the per capita share of the government education budget was only

US$12.92 a year as against the average allocation of $42 among all the developing countries of the world.[14]

The purpose of enacting the "Education Law" is to mobilize the resources of the entire country to create educational facilities while, at the same time, preventing profiteering from eating into the vitals of the educational edifice. The Education Law prescribed that there should be "3 increases" in the funds for education: (1) The allotment for education should be higher than the increase of government finances; (2) the educational funds per student should increase every year; and (3) the teachers' salaries and the public utility part of funds per student should increase every year.

For some time, education was regarded as the state's responsibility only. But, the state treasury of China has too lean a purse to cater to so large a population. Society has to lend a hand in creating educational facilities. Right now, the wealthy section of the Chinese population is indulging in lavish spending and precocious consumption. Government organizations, particularly those at the lower levels, are also less concerned with investment in human resources than in economic constructions.

Improving the Standard of Education

Apart from the shortage of seats, the existing quality of education also needs enormous improvement. Like in India, most Chinese schools are in the countryside without proper buildings, adequate text books, and recreation facilities, let alone good playing grounds. The teacher-student ratio in the rural schools is extremely low—too low for a teacher to provide enough attention to the many who need to be taught. There are many rural schools that have combined classes with one teacher teaching pupils of various standards. Teaching methods are outdated, and the quality of teachers much below standard.

One serious handicap to the improvement of educational standard is the utilitarian orientation among educators and parents. Like India, China's educational institutions are becoming increasingly marks-oriented. Marks are the proverbial damocles sword hanging before every teacher whose teaching ability is only judged by the marks her students score. It is this mark-score that is the sole criterion for the worth and reputation of a school.

Even after the 1985 reforms, the Chinese educational system remains a virtual exogenous exercise, not an endogenous learning process of the learner. But, even when the push is exogenous there can be two approaches. The better approach aims at stimulating the learner to programme his/her own learning process so that he/she knows how to take his/her own initiative, and enlarge his/her vision of information and knowledge according to his/her own talent and capacity. Another approach also known as "feeding the Beijing duck" (*tianyazi*). The "Beijing duck" is a young, tender and fat bird reared through forcible feeding—literally forcing the food into the mouth of the duck by holding its throat. Like in India, the latter approach is very prominent in China.

A Chinese expert on education describes this system:

> "...[I]t treats students as the basket into which knowledge is thrown, and makes them the instruments of exams. Thus, the students are mistakenly led to treat exams as the goal of learning. Exams are conducted for exams' sake. The result is that the students dread exams, hate studies and are in an all-controlled disorder."[15]

Education through such exams produces a great number of feeble-minded high-scoring persons who have lost much of their initiative and creativity, and who cannot learn further once they are out of the educational institutions and away from their teachers. This, in a way, confirms what Chairman Mao had said during the Cultural Revolution that universities and schools made pupils stupid rather than enlightened.

Parents are also responsible for degenerating education to the level of manipulation of marks. An incident in Tianjin, the major city next to the Chinese capital, Beijing, reveals the shocking obsession of Chinese parents with their child's performance in examinations, not caring at all for the child's natural development of personality. A twelve-year old girl who could not perform to the expectation of her parents tried to commit suicide by swallowing sleeping pills. Before she did this she even asked her mother about the quantity of sleeping pills that could kill. (Even this did not register an alarm in the mother's mind.) She admitted later that every time she walked away from the examination hall she was reluctant to return home—that "execution ground" where the only thing to look forward to was her parents' mental and physical torture.[16]

This incident typifies the unhealthy and irrational elements in parents' expectations of their children. First, there is selfishness in such a demand—to get material returns from the children by forcing them to do well in studies, or to add glory to themselves without the least consideration for the healthy growth of the children's personality and character.

The incident is also a sad reflection on the degeneration of family education in China. Despite China's excellent tradition of family education, many parents in China today, particularly those who work in the government, and in responsible positions, do not devote time to educating their children. These children deprived of a strict family education are being pampered, are subject to bad influences, because of the high positions of their parents. In the 1970s and 1980s, the authorities were alarmed by the high ratio of crime among the children of the high-ranking cadres. Since then a greater stress is being laid on family education.

Family education is now facing a crisis in China as a result of the contradiction between the fast changing times and out-dated educational approaches and parental attitudes. One out-dated method is to punish the children who are not sincere in studies. When competitions become tougher, the parents' pressure on children becomes greater—even excessive and repressive.

The degeneration of family education in China is compounded by an entirely new sociological phenomenon. Neither society, nor the government authorities anticipated this unprecedented development which is peculiar to China.

Because of the stringent birth control measures by the

government and the vigorous implementation of incentives and disincentives (for the one-child family and against the violation of this norm), China has succeeded in slowing down population growth, but has also become a country of 50 million one-child families. There are 50 million brotherless and sisterless children in China. These children are alternately nicknamed "small emperors" (*xiao huangdi*) or "little suns" (*xiao taiyang*). There is an abnormal social relationship known as the "4-2-1" syndrome. This syndrome presents an inverted pyramid with 4 "grands" (paternal and maternal grand parents) and 2 parents revolving around one little sun. This singular solar centre enjoys a "super-warm" childhood created by two generations of adults who vie with each other to shower affection on the new born (or even the not so new born). The adults struggle to reduce the child's hardship, difficulty, worry, physical and mental labour to the minimum, if not to zero. Thus, we have a generation which grows up but not on their own feet in the arms or laps of adults—a generation that knows to enjoy but not to toil, to receive but not to give, to demand, to order, to throw tantrums and yell, to threaten, to blackmail.

Surveys reveal that this abundant and excessive warmth of parental and grand-parental affection and expectation, the outcome of this "4-2-1" scenario is far from satisfactory. A survey on 2,290 primary school students in Beijing shows that they do family chores for only 0.2 hour on an average, as against that of 1.2 hours by their US counterparts. 87% of the 1,500 school students of Tianjin surveyed don't help their parents at all, 74% of them don't know what to do in the absence of their parents, and 52% of them don't arrange their own things like clothes, school bags and toilet articles. Despite all this, it is surprising that Chinese children are less affectionate to their parents than their counterparts in other countries. According to a survey of some high school students of three countries (1,300 Japanese, 1,000 Americans, and 1,200 Chinese), in response to the question who they most respected mothers and fathers among the figured in the first three positions in the Japanese and American answers, while they came only 10th and 11th among the Chinese answers. In another survey of 1,500 Chinese school students, 76% think their parents don't understand them, 34% don't find their homes attractive, and 16% admit that they don't confide in their parents.[17]

This "4-2-1" syndrome has also fostered a certain greed, and ruthlessness. Children are growing up in this craving for money without other considerations. In 1995, a 12 year old student in Chengdu City, Sichuan Province, committed suicide. He was bullied by a classmate who used to beat him and demand money. The bully forced the boy to give him a ride on bicycle from home to school and back everyday. When the victim was extremely exhausted after returning home, he had to do homework for the bully. One day, the bully demanded 10 yuan (about Rs 40) from him and when he could not produce the money, he was again beaten badly. Depressed and desperate, the boy cut short his life. That such a dark society exists among the youngsters in today's China is shocking. Both the bully and the victim were "little suns". While one "little sun" has turned into a cannibal, the other is reduced to a slave. What is shocking was that the latter didn't even tell his parents or his teachers about what had been happening.[18]

The issue of the social relevance of higher education is not exclusive to any country, developing or developed. If education does not cater to the market then it cannot market its products, and becomes a waste of precious resources, making it out of tune with the socio-economic development of the country. Such a contradiction does crop up in the developed countries like USA and UK. But, in these countries, the enterprises can initiate and organize special training programmes instead of depending on the universities. In India and China, this is being taken up on a smaller scale. But, universities are still the main industry of human resources, and entry to the university (particularly to the prestigious ones) is still a rage in China—so also in India. There is a Chinese saying that "a big ship is slow to change directions." Most Chinese universities, particularly the leading ones, are having difficulty adjusting their curricula to the changing needs of the market which shifts emphasis too often and too rapidly.

The serious dichotomy facing China today is that on the one hand it is trying hard to uphold its civilization status (with educational institutions as important props), while on the other hand it wants all its socio-economic institutions to adapt to the market economy. As educational institutions have to survive the marketization process, they also suffer the market fluctuation of demand and supply. For example, management studies were the hottest cakes in the Chinese market for one and half decades. This stimulated the rapid growth of management studies in Chinese higher educational institutions in the same way there was a huge growth in the TV industry to meet growing market demand. And, like the TV industry, the supply of managerial talents quickly caught up with and surpassed the market demand, resulting in over-production. In 1996, 400,000 highly qualified management students knocked at the doors of enterprises, but only half of them got the right kind of jobs for their training, because the demand-supply ratio came down to 1:2 from 1:1.3 two years ago.

During the "Mao era" (1949–1976), there were no educated unemployed at all. All those who were studying in the universities and other higher educational institutions had their employment reserved well in advance for them by the government. This worry-free university career lasted until 1985 when the government started educational reform and gradually stopped the practice of distributing jobs to university students. In modern parlance, this "marketization", forced university graduates to market themselves as commodities of learning.

Chinese university students used to be described as "the emperor's daughters not worried about getting a good husband". This is no longer so today. The autumn of 1996 was unprecedentedly gloomy for Chinese university graduates after they had collected their prestigious degrees and diplomas. Many of them could not get a job to their liking. Earlier the most difficult gate in life for the Chinese youths was those of the university. After entering a university a Chinese youth entered the enviable situation of romancing with books at ease. Now, the university gate is still a high barrier (if not higher), but a more serious barrier is waiting for the final year university students (900,000 of them in 1996) when they come out of the university gate.[19] Many of them are unemployed.

With the commercialization of the educational system and educated unemployment, school and university graduates have to seek jobs in the open market, the educational curricula have failed to keep pace with the rapid twists and turns of market demand, resulting in a large number of educated youths who do not get jobs immediately after their studies. This educational unemployment, in turn, diminishes the market's reliance on the existing educational institutions to supply human resources (they were trying to train their own resources instead). The more educational institutions become irrelevant to market dynamics the more productive they become in generating educational unemployment.

In China girls have been out-performing boys in many fields. Girl students have also excelled in examinations. As admission to higher educational institutions is related to examination results, girls are squeezing boys out of prestigious universities. In 1996, 1,481 girls figured in the first two admission lists in the universities in Beijing as against 549 boys. And this was announced after efforts were made to balance the male-female ratio. "We can't help! The girls have scored too high." explained the authorities who had made the admission lists.

Is this a good sign? An in-depth study of the phenomenon would give a negative answer. The basic problem lies in the teaching and evaluation schemes that are heavily in favour of memory work and cramming. Chinese boys, like their counterparts in India (and elsewhere), are creative, carefree, and often mischievous. Their potential creativity is what the Chinese educational system frowns upon. Chinese girls are mostly timid, prudent, obedient to teachers, care for details, are capable of endurance and hardship in memory-oriented studies. They thus become the natural favourites of the

Chinese educational system. From the beginning upto the university level this "favouritism" in the Chinese system is vigorously maintained by both teachers and parents, scaring away many boys who could otherwise shine in the pursuits of learning. But, such "favouritism" ultimately harms the favourites themselves as well. Chinese girls grow up with the habit of cramming, leaving their creative faculties underdeveloped. When they enter society they expose their weakness of vision, in potential manifestations, in creative thinking, in adventurous spirit, and even in practical adaptability. In 1995, when China sent 23 competitors for the Science Olympics, only 5 girls qualified after various selections.[20]

Another problem associated with this phenomenon is the rapid decrease of men in the teaching community of China. In 1978, female teachers occupied only 32.5% of the total number of teachers in China (in the primary schools the percentage was 37.8%). In 1994, the percentage rose to 41.2% (and 45.8% in the primary schools).[21] What is more worrying is the new trend of females dominating the normal schools and colleges as well as teacher training institutions. Ten years from now, women teachers will greatly outnumber men in China. China is heading towards a maleless teaching community which will be very unhealthy in many aspects. For one thing, teachers are like deities in China, just as they are in India. When a young unmarried female teacher affectionately guides and helps the growth of a boy who is simultaneously exposed to the seamy side of sex which is churned out every morning and every night from the western media, a dangerous equation is in the offing. There are already a large number of unrequited, one-way love affairs between boy students and their women teachers. Even tragedies happen.[22]

Blurred Morality

Apart from the "obsession with money" (*xiang qian kan*), the Chinese social trend is dominated by such dubious styles termed as "*haoren zhuyi*" (adopting the philosophy of goody-goodiness), and "*haha junzi*" (being the gentleman who laughs away everything). With such social trends in vogue, the standards of social justice and moral values are blurred.

China, like all other developing countries, is opening itself to the influence of developed countries. This includes inhaling their "spiritual pollution" which is unavoidable. China's transforming itself into a market economy is tearing apart its traditional values which creates confusion for moral education. It is felt that every nation at a new juncture of time is in need of an overwhelming guiding morality. Else, a moral crisis may develop. From the micro perspective, Chinese individuality is being diversified into multi-directional and multi-dimensional development which is unstoppable, and desirable. But, such development should be directed to an overwhelming goal conducive to the creation of a healthy ethos of the nation. In pursuing all this there will be a dichotomy between the material life where people vie with each other in making money and getting the better in competitions on the one hand, and the spiritual arena in which such activities are considered selfish and unworthy. It is not clear how such a dichotomy can be reconciled.

Foreigners used to feel that Chinese society was too closed to be receptive to foreign influences. The reality is that when Chinese are under foreign influence, they go overboard and become more royal than the king. In the beginning of the 20th century, when an increasing number of western thinkers were admiring Chinese cultural traditions (much as they felt the weakness of western civilization), the dominant mood among Chinese intellectuals was to discard Chinese traditions totally. This phenomenon is called "*quanpan xihua*" (westernization going the whole hog) which had ignited many radical movements. No sooner had Deng Xiaoping opened China up for rapid modernization, Chinese universities were caught first by the "Nietzche fever" and then by "Freud fever" (influenced by Dr. Sigmund Freud's psychological theories). A six-part TV feature series titled "*Heshang*" (elegy of the Yellow River) vowed to merge China's "yellow earth culture" into the "blue sea culture". There were, and still are, a great number of young

Chinese who would wish to get rid of their yellow skin, black hair, flat nose, and small eyes to gain the physical features of the white race. As there was no possibility of doing it, they cursed their own mother culture and wanted to drown their motherland with the salted sea water, as it were. The acceptance of modernity in China (so also in India) has been entangled with immaturity in cultural thinking. Intellectual idealism is flying like a kite without any root in the soil—easily being blown away by violent winds. This is another dimension of the blurred morality which Chinese educators have to seriously encounter and combat with.

One weakness of "political education" in China today is the absence of saintly priests who can lead by their own exemplary behaviour. Instead, there are too many political priests who fit the description of "a giant in words, and a dwarf in deeds". People laugh at these priests saying: "He talks on the stage, and he is talked of among the audience."

National Minorities

National minorities in China, like those in India, are lagging behind in education because of various reasons. The only exception are the Koreans in Yanbian Country, Liaoning Province, whose per capita education level is the highest among all the counties of China. According to the 1982 Census, the ratio of illiterates among the national minority areas was extremely high. The total illiterates and semi-illiterates of the minority communities in the age group of 12 and above in eight provinces had the following percentage: 73.16% in Tibet, 49.26% in Yunnan, 47.88% in Guizhou, 46.81% in Qinghai, 43.04% in Ningxia, 31.08% in Inner Mongolia, 30.72% in Xinjiang, and 24.96% in Guangxi.[23]

Among the minority communities, women are invariably less educated than men because of male chauvinism. Many of the communities have traditions and customs discouraging women from school going or joining educational institutions. The government which is mostly manned by the officials of the Han majority community is handicapped by the government's cautious policies in pushing women's education among these communities. Hence literacy cannot grow rapidly in the minority areas. In recent years, minority women have increasingly become eager to receive education and better their life prospects. There are instances of their clashing with male members of the family over the issue of education.

"*Shinian shu mu, bainian shu ren.*"

This is an old Chinese saying that means it takes ten years to grow a tree, but a hundred years to rear a Person. This rearing of a perfect personality (a person with a capital "p") is a life-long process. Here, naturally, the "Person" should be the combination of a wise thinker and a sage-like character. I have earlier discussed the "3 in 1" concept of education. It seems what education has been doing in China is only to take care of "*zhiyu*" (intellectual education). Physical education, in particular, faces many constraints such as the acute shortage of land to make playgrounds. Without proper playgrounds, Chinese students cannot improve their physical fitness. But, there is a lack of concern on the part of the educators. It is estimated that 77% of China's university students wear glasses for myopia. The same neglect of physical training is universal among Indian students as well.

Some years ago, the Minister of Education, Mr. Li Tieying, visited India, and gave two talks in New Delhi: one in Jawaharlal Nehru University, and another in the Nehru Museum. I attended both. I remember the slight difficulty some Indian university professors had to impress upon him that apart from creating a competent producer for the socialist construction of China, education should have a higher aim to create a new human being—as Mao Zedong had conceived when he launched the Cultural Revolution in 1966. When leaders don't take a holistic view of education one can't expect new humans to emerge in society.

Like India, China has a long tradition of respecting teachers. While Indians revered their teachers as "gods" (*gurudeva*), the Chinese treated them as "fathers" (*shifu*). But, modern cultural development and lifestyles have diminished this tradition in both countries. During the Cultural Revolution, teachers were denounced by students as "stinking intellectuals" (choulaojiu) and subjected to all kinds of insult and humiliation by the "red guards" among the students. The post-Mao leadership has done its best to reverse this trend and restore the dignity of teachers. Twelve years ago, the government instituted "Teachers' Day". Since then, a series of laws, including a "Teacher Law" have been enacted to enhance the status of the teachers. However, many teachers, particularly those who serve in rural China, are still among the lowest paid employees in China. Such a situation discourages bright youngsters, particularly young men, to aspire to be teachers.

Even in post-Mao China, being a teacher was not an enviable position. Teachers were attacked. Their salaries were not paid fully or on time. School buildings were dilapidated, and often occupied by government agencies. Of course, some of these mishaps vis-a-vis teachers have been corrected in the last few years in many places where the government authorities paid serious attention. Still, it will be a long time before China puts its teachers on the altar again.

China has witnessed a phenomenal growth in the number of educational institutions and teachers since 1949. From 1949 to 1980, teachers in higher educational institutions increased 15.4 times from 16,000 to 246,900. During the same period, teachers of the middle schools increased 45 times (from 67,000 to 3,019,700), and those in the primary schools increased 6.6 times (from 836,000 to 5.5 million).[24] Because of such phenomenal growth, many who had insufficient training and inadequate qualifications joined the educational institutions as teachers resulting in substandard teachers, as the Chinese saying goes: "*Wu ren zidi*" (spoiling the careers of others' children). In 1986, only 62.8% of primary school teachers and 27% of junior middle school teachers had the required educational qualifications. The two ratios reached 88.9% and 69.1% respectively in 1995.[25] More efforts have to be made to make the teaching cadre perfectly respectable and competent.

In 1995, the Party and the State Council (China's version of the Cabinet) of the government jointly propounded the strategy of "revitalizing the country by means of science and education" (*ke jiao xingguo*). In implementing this strategy the government is leaving no stone unturned to reinforce education. However, the educators and the teaching community have not responded to the call with full enthusiasm as their living conditions have not been substantially improved, and the respect for teachers has not become universal.

The Education Commission of the central government has asked the universities to frame a "21st century curriculum". But, this is easier said than done. It is a tremendous challenge to Chinese universities to anticipate what would be the best courses for teaching and research that would be relevant to the socio-economic life of the 21st century. On the other hand, if this 21st century curriculum is meant to cut down the academic attention towards such seemingly traditional areas like history, philosophy and even mathematics, then what new disciplines can come up to replace their social functions is still unclear.

Science and education need to be particularly developed and applied in the field of agriculture. Therefore, the Chinese authorities are trying to use "ke jiao xing nong" (using science and education to revitalize agriculture) in the last few years. There is a countrywide movement to disseminate scientific knowledge, economic information, and legal knowledge among the rural masses. The movement is aimed at establishing a new social trend and lifestyle, opposing superstition, extravagance, gambling and other bad habits. The government at various levels is asked to send education, culture, recreation, hygiene and medical care to the remote aras and villages. Right now there is only a strong desire which is yet to be backed by adequate funds and human resources. But things may improve gradually, and where there is a will there is a way.

Li Lanqing, Vice-Premier of China in charge of education, recently wrote that the Chinese government strategy of "using science and education to revitalize the country, and treating education as the foundation" must "give priority to the promotion of teachers' qualities in order to revitalize education" (*zhenxing jiaoyu, shizi xianxing*). He envisaged that the coming two or three decades would usher in a golden period of teachers' training in China.[26]

Li's article quotes Deng Xiaoping who observed that: "Any leader who overlooks education is a leader without far sight, a leader without maturity. Such a leader cannot lead China to modernization."[27] This Deng adage and Vice-Premier Li's reiteration indicate that Chinese leaders are dead serious in promoting education to a new high. Education is no doubt the engine for the onward journey for countries like China and India to walk on the "information super-highway" of the future.

In conclusion, there is great excitement in the Chinese educational scene. Worthy of mention is the text of the Resolution of the 6th Plenum of the 14th Central Committee of the CPC held in Beijing in October 1996. This text is virtually a projection of all the finest traditional values of China dressed in modern Marxist robes. And this traditional value system is what I call Buddho-Confucian culture. The outstanding example is the advocacy of "*zhen shan mei*" as a new socialist idealism. But, these three words are Chinese translations of "*satyam*" "*shivam*", "*sundaram*".[28] It was the ancient Indian Buddhists who had carried these concepts to China to eulogize Buddha dharma (whereas in India today they symbolize the perfection of God). So, once again, here is a convergence of the fine traditions of the two great cultures. This will hearten Indian educationists who, will then join hands with their Chinese counterparts to create a new chapter in history.

Notes

1. *Deng Xiaoping wenxuan* (Selected works of Deng Xiaoping), Vol. 3, Beijing: People's Publishing House, 1993, p. 306.
2. This is the starting sentence of the most important Confucian classic, *Lunyu* (Analects), which was one of the first sentences a Chinese learner had to learn by heart in China for two thousand years until a century ago.

3. *Ibid.*, Chapter 5, 13.
4. The episode occurred in 196 B.C. when Courtier, Lu Jia, talked Han Emperor Gaozu (reigning from 206–195 B.C.) into giving importance to the culture of learning in governance. Initially, the emperor thought military power was the most important thing as he had risen from very humble stations to the supreme position of the "Son of Heaven" on horse back. After hearing the courtier's argument that military power could only seize political power, but would not be able to hold on to it permanently, the emperor began to understand the importance of propagating the classics—poetry and history books.
5. "*Meng mu*" (Mencius' mother) is a household word in Chinese education. She moved her residence several times after discovering that her son was in bad company in the neighbourhood. She was a weaver. One day, she cut off the fabric from the loom to admonish her son that, unless he became diligent in studies, she would stop weaving.
6. *China Statistical Yearbook, 1995*, China Statistical Publishing House, 1996, p. 586–7.
7. For the 1984 figure, see Sun Ruoqiong (ed.), *Zhongguo shaoshuminzu jiaoyuxue gailun* (A general discourse on the education of national minorities in China), Beijing: China Labour Publishing House, 1990, p. 443. For the 1994 figure, see *China Statistical Yearbook 1995*, p. 593.
8. *Baogang zhi* (Gazeteers of the Baoshan Iron and Steel Company), Shanghai: Shanghai Academy of Social Sciences, 1995, p. 392.
9. Deng's address to the National Education Conference on March 28, 1978. See *Deng Xiaoping wenxuan*, Vol. 2, Beijing: People's Publishing House, 1983, p. 103.
10. See Tan Chung, "China Visit-II: Return to Traditional Values", *The Statesman*, December 5, 1996.
11. *China Statistical Yearbook, 1995*, p. 760.
12. Yu Yueqing, "*Gaodeng xuexiao mianlinde yali he xuanze*" (The pressure on higher education and the choices before it), in *Xinhua Wenzhai* (Xinhua Digest), Beijing, No. 11, 1996, p. 153.
13. Feng Lanrui, "*Zhongguo disanci shiye gaofengde qingkuang ji duice*" (The situation of the third unemployment high tide in China and how to tackle it), *Xinhua Wenzhai*, No. 12, 1996, p. 50.
14. *Renmin Ribao* (People's Daily), Beijing, January 10, 1995, p. 5.

15. Tao Tong, "Zikongshi jiaoyu jiqi yu chuantong jiaoyude bijiao" (A comparison between the auto-control education and traditional education), in *Xinhua Wenzhai* (Xinhua digest), No. 7, 1994, p. 156.
16. Yi Ta *et al.*, "Jiating jiaoyo: zai dijie Zhonghua minzude weilai?" (Family education: Creating the future of China?) in *Liaowang* (Outlook), No. 5, January 29, 1996, p. 16.
17. *Ibid.*, pp. 10–20.
18. *Ibid.*, p. 19.
19. This information comes from the director of the division in charge of student affairs, Chen Xi, in the Chinese Commission (i.e., ministry) for Education. See Chen Xi, "Biyesheng jiuye weihe nan?" (Why are the university graduates finding it difficult to get jobs?), in "Education Herald", in *Zhangguo qingnian bao* (Newspaper of Chinese Youths), August 21, 1996, p. 5.
20. These observations about the trend of girl students dominating Chinese education are based on various writings in the Chinese press, particularly the article written by Chen Zhiwen, and others entitled "Nuzhuangyuan duo shi xi shi you?" (Is it good news that girls top the examinations?) in "Education Herald", No. 84, in *Zhouguo Qingnian Bao, ibid.*
21. *China Statistical Yearbook, 1995*, p. 597.
22. Chen Zhiwen *et. al. loc cit.*
23. Sun Ruoqiong, *op. cit.*, p. 471.
24. *China Handbook Series: Education and Science*, Beijing: Foreign Languages Press, 1983, p. 14.
25. Zhao Dongwan, "Ba woguo jiaoyu quanmian naru fazhihua guidao" (Putting China's education entirely on the rail of law), in *Xinhua Wenzhai*, No. 11, 1996, p. 151.
26. Li Lanqing, "Youxian Banhao shifan jiaoyu, wei luoshi ke jiao xingguo zhanlue dahao jichu" (Giving priority to normal education, and lay a good foundation for the strategy of using science and education to revitalize the country), in *Xinhua Wenzhai*, No. 12, 1996, pp. 146–47.
27. *Ibid.*, p. 148.
28. Tan Chung, *loc. cit.*

International Cooperation in Indian Adult Education: Indo-British Scenario (1970–1990)

S.Y. SHAH

Introduction

The role of international cooperation in adult education has been repeatedly discussed by several international agencies during the last two decades.[1] UNESCO, the International Council for Adult Education, the German Foundation for International Development, the Swedish International Development Agency, the Asian South Pacific Bureau of Adult Education, and the Commonwealth Association for the Education and Training of Adults have all been taking active interest in the promotion of collaborative programmes in adult education. The Jomtien conference of 1990, which reiterated the urgency of addressing the basic learning needs of adults and children to achieve the goals of education for all, also generated considerable interest among different bilateral and multilateral agencies in funding basic education projects in developing countries. Today, illiteracy is perceived as a global problem calling for the mobilization of international resources. Hence the earlier tendency on the part

---

This paper forms a part of a research project on "International cooperation in Indian adult education: The role and influence of Britain and Canada", undertaken by the author at the National Institute of Adult Education, New Delhi.

of several donor agencies to view literacy primarily as a national imperative requiring little capital investment or overseas expertise[2] seems to have been replaced by a genuine concern to combat illiteracy; and literacy forms an integral part of their aid packages. Though limited, external assistance in terms of funds and technical cooperation have enabled a number of developing countries to strengthen their adult education programmes and, at the same time, establish professional links with their counterparts in other countries. Notwithstanding the several cooperative endeavours in the field of adult education, there has been hardly any attempt at studying the process and problems of operationalizing international cooperation at the micro-level.[3]

International Cooperation in Indian Adult Education: An Overview

The development of adult education in India has been considerably aided and even influenced by a number of countries, namely, the U.S.A., Denmark, Canada, Britain, Germany, Sweden and the Netherlands. By channeling human and material resources through their respective governmental and non-governmental agencies at various points of time, especially after the 1940s, these countries have not only supported a variety of important but innovative adult education programmes and projects in India, like the Vidyapiths, Functional Literacy, Bay of Bengal and Mahila Samakhya, but also the establishment of institutions like Literacy House at Lucknow and the department of adult education at the University of Rajasthan. Several Indian adult educators as well as adult education organizations have received a variety of resource support from the different inter-governmental bodies of the United Nations, the Commonwealth, and non-governmental organizations such as the International Council for Adult Education, the Asian South Pacific Bureau of Adult Education, the Commonwealth Association for the Education and Training of Adults, Action Aid, Oxfam, and World Literacy of Canada. Undoubtedly, the financial and technical cooperation extended by a host of overseas agencies have enabled India to organize several international conferences and training programmes, produce and publish teaching-learning materials, undertake research studies, and also develop the infrastructure for certain adult education institutions.

International cooperation in Indian adult education has not only brought Indian adult educators and administrators closer to their counterparts in other countries, but also provided better access to overseas literature and programme packages, opening up avenues for the permeation of overseas ideas and programme methodologies into India. While the basic philosophy of certain Indian institutions like the Vidyapiths may be traced to the traditions of the Danish folk schools, the idea behind polyvalent adult education and the farmers' functional literacy programme seems to be linked to the concept of adult education in developed countries. The origins of extramural studies in the Indian university system may be traced to the British tradition of liberal adult education. To a certain extent, the current philosophy and programmes of Indian adult education, which puts emphasis on "conscientization", "each one, teach one", and participatory methodology, owe their origin to the ideas and pioneering works of Paulo Freire, Frank Laubach and Budd Hall.

Unlike Freire, who visited India only for a short while, Laubach spent a great deal of time in this country, and kept up his contacts with its adult educators for thirty-five years from 1935 to 1970. Besides, Indian adult education has been immensely benefited by the active involvement of a number of international adult educators such as Welthy Fisher, Robby Kidd, James Draper, Paul Fordham, Alan Rogers, Asher Deleon and John Oxenham, who, at different points, have spent a considerable amount of time and energy in formulating programme guidelines, doing staff training and developing curricula for various levels of adult education courses. Though a number of overseas adult educators have visited India under various schemes and programmes, a few of them, especially Paul Fordham, Alan Rogers and James Draper, have been maintaining continuous professional links with Indian adult educators through collaborative research studies, institutional networking and participation in a number of international conferences, workshops and training programmes.

Over the years, a clear pattern has evolved in the involvement of international agencies in Indian adult education. During the 1930s, the methodology called "Each One, Teach One," developed by the American missionary, Frank Laubach, found its way to India. The 1940s witnessed the blossoming in India of the philosophy of British liberal adult education and the Danish folk schools. After independence, the involvement of American agencies in Indian adult education increased tremendously, when the community development programme and agricultural extension methods were introduced during the period 1950–60. The late 1960s saw a major involvement by the Canadians, who extended their resources and expertise in establishing the first department of adult education in India at the University of Rajasthan. The British revived significant links with Indian adult education in the 1970s. The 1980s witnessed the beginning of German aid for training and publications in adult education, a Swedish grant for the women's development programme, and the Netherlands' support for the Mahila Samakhya project. This pattern of overseas interest and involvement in Indian adult education is neither accidental nor preconceived; it was dictated by the fluctuating foreign policy of the government of India, India's changing relations with foreign countries, and a host of social, economic and political factors, both within and outside India.

Indo-British Cooperation

India receives a larger share of its development assistance from Britain than any other country. As with other external assistance to India, it is channeled through bilateral, multilateral and non-governmental agencies. Of the official British agencies, the British Council has been playing a significant role in adult education through the implementation of its Higher Education Links Scheme (HELS). In addition, a number of British non-governmental organizations such as Christian Aid, the Catholic Fund for Overseas Development and the Methodist Church Overseas Division have also been supporting a variety of adult education and training programmes in India. British funds are also made available for various developmental programmes, and for training and studies through Commonwealth bodies such as the Commonwealth Foundation, the Commonwealth Secretariat and the Association of Commonwealth Universities. The scope of this paper is confined to the contributions to Indian adult education from the British Council, especially the HELS.

By making use of hitherto untapped primary source materials, especially the unpublished reports of British and Indian adult educators who were associated with several Indo-British programmes during the period 1970–90, and British Council policy documents and annual reports, this paper attempts to answer the following questions. What were the main concerns, channels and strategies of cooperation? What kinds of programmes were supported? What were the experiences of key people associated with Indo-British projects in adult education? Did the cooperation pave the way for any innovation or reform in adult education? Did it generate any conflicts or lead to any crisis? What was the impact of cooperation on the development of adult education in India and Britain? Can the effectiveness of cooperation be enhanced? What insights and learnings can one derive from the past experiences of cooperating for literacy? In the process of answering these questions, this paper points out that, although Indo-British cooperation has been mutually beneficial for the development of adult education in both countries, and professionally rewarding for British as well as Indian adult educators, the success of these educators depended, to a great extent, on their professional competence, commitment to adult education and interpersonal relations. This paper observes that British specialists and bilateral programmes have played a key role in sustaining British influence on Indian university adult education during the last two decades.

The British Council's Partnership Programmes

It was during the 1970s that the British Council started taking special interest in Indian development projects and adult education programmes. It was being argued by a group of policy planners that, for an island trading nation such as Britain, which is dependent upon a widespread network of economic and political interests, the maintenance of international educational and cultural connections was vital.[4] Some of them claimed that Britain had special resources which could be tailored to the needs of developing countries over a number of years,[5] and that such cooperative ventures could gradually stimulate British economy and society. In an article entitled "Idealism and self-interest: Britain's aid programme", Christopher Patten stated, "If we help to build up the economics of poorer countries, we create potential markets for our own products and services."[6] Said another, "helping India will pay a handsome political and economic dividend ... The West's economic interest in making the Indian plans succeed is ... clear cut. A rich customer is, in the long run, a better customer ... A growing country, in the long run, buys more."[7] The commercial connections of aid become evident from the fact that 99.5% of British aid is in the form of loans, and 70% of it is tied to the purchase of British goods and services. Only a small part of aid adopts the welfare approach, i.e., addressed directly to the problems of poverty through basic education, health services and assistance to agriculture. All the same, British policies on educational aid during the 1980s were supportive of broader human resource development strategies; they were based on the principle of bringing British resources in education to bear on the agreed needs of the developing countries so as to "build on, rather than replace, local expertise and other resources."[8] It is in this background that the different partnership programmes of the British Council have been formulated. Since the Council supports the thesis that it is through individuals that bonds of understanding are forged and professional bridges established, it adopts the strategy of identifying and exposing to British influence and thoughts people who are likely one day to be in a position to influence others.[9]

Of the different programmes implemented by the British Council, the Higher Education Links Scheme (HELS) and specialist tours and visitorships have been playing a key role in the field of Indian adult education. It is through these schemes that systematic attempts have been made to establish closer cooperation and links between British and Indian adult educators and adult education organizations.

HELS[10] is just "one element in a larger process of cooperation and development" between institutions in Britain and developing countries. Established by the British Council in 1980 with full financial support from the Overseas Development Administration (ODA), HELS is conceived as a form of cooperation in teaching and research, with specific objectives and duration, between a department or comparable unit of an overseas institution of higher education and one or more in Britain. Aiming at promotion of understanding and cooperation between higher education institutions in Britain and developing countries, HELS strives, *inter alia*, to make the excellence of British higher education known and appreciated overseas, and, simultaneously, informs British institutions of important work which is going on in developing countries. While the scheme may provide an opportunity to British researchers for field work in developing countries, it also exposes scholars from collaborating institutions to advanced developments in the field, and gives them access to the latest literature available in Britain. It is anticipated that HELS will enable collaborating personnel "to derive fresh stimulus from contacts abroad." It is argued that though HELS is "a delicate mechanism," it would, if sustained over a period of time, become one of the best means of developing the personal cooperation and international understanding through intellectual collaboration that is of vital importance for future international relations.[11]

In India, HELS aims at encouraging a high level of professional contact between Indian and British personnel working together in selected high-priority areas. The scheme is intended to benefit, in particular, Indian research departments with a high reputation for applied activities, subject areas that are of high priority to the government of India, and those topics in which Britain has a recognized international reputation. It is expected that India will have an interest in, and an infrastructure to support collaboration in the field with Britain. According to the Guidance Note (1989) prepared by the British Council in India, HELS is "intended to help the development of a department as a whole, rather than that of individual researchers. The emphasis ought to be on the professional enhancement of the younger faculty member, and the orientation should be towards their research, teaching or both." It is specified that the planned link can have the objectives of joint research, joint publication, curriculum and course development, academic/professional/administrative staff exchange, and development. Besides, the Guidance Note states that the links programme should be of 3–5 years duration, and "take place on a scale that is sufficient to make a significant contribution to the knowledge and application of the topic in India and, within which, the British contribution should be substantial and recognizable."[12]

Once the interest has been established and the joint proposal is drafted, it is scrutinized by the British Council in the light of overall policy of the ODA and the particular country, and then the approval is accorded. Financial support is limited to nominal subsistence allowance and 50% of travel costs. Normally, the duration of a visit ranges from 4 to 6 weeks. Although several institutions in Britain and India have established successful links in different subjects,[13] in the field of adult education there were only a few attempts, which were confined to the University of Madras, Mother Teresa University, S.V. University, Jawaharlal Nehru University and South Gujarat University in India, and the universities of Nottingham, Warwick, Edinburgh and Southampton in the U.K.

Under "specialist tours," the British Council sponsors visits by distinguished British experts to overseas countries in order to "establish or renew personal contact with those working in the same subject, and to make British practice and thought better known abroad."[14] The request for a tour generally originates within a ministry, university or other institution in an overseas country, and it is recommended by the local representative of the British Council if it is in accordance with the current policies and priorities of the ODA, and is likely to be of advantage both to the host country and Britain. There are several kinds of tour: advisory work, consultative work, lecturing, teaching, participation in a workshop, etc., or a combination of these. The British Council not only benefits from the assessment made by the specialist of the current status of a particular profession in the host country, but also identifies areas for future cooperation or expansion. It is reported that, over the years, tours by specialists have made important contributions to the work of promoting mutual cooperation and understanding in the educational, scientific and cultural fields.

Operationalization of Programmes

In the late 1970s, the British Council sponsored Paul Fordham (Southampton University) and Alan Rogers (Nottingham University) as experts to a Madras workshop on the "development of adult education as a university discipline". In 1978, under specialist tours, the British Council deputed a team of three British experts, John Oxenham (Institute of Development Studies, Sussex), K.J. Elsdon (Department of Education and Science) and J.W. Spencer (University of Leeds), to participate in two national workshops organized in connection with the National Adult Education Programme.[15] The team hoped to provide academic help in the preparation of guidelines for a training manual for adult education personnel. Besides submitting *ad hoc* papers and sharing in plenary and group discussions, the experts provided "some assistance in drafting the report." The Indian attempt at relating planning as closely as possible to the actual field realities was appreciated by the team. It observed that the experience and understanding which the British may be able to offer in return could include "good field practice in teaching adults and its organisation [and] relating of academic and field levels to one another." However, the team felt that India was not in need of experts, whose influence tends to cause "confusion between practice, on the one hand, and abstract conceptualization, on the other." The confidential report of the team adds: "Nor do we believe that, in this field, Britain has any more knowledge and expertise to offer India than India has to offer Britain. But we do believe that there can be a great deal of mutual learning and sharing of experiences, which could be achieved through exchange."[16] Perhaps because these observations sent certain signals to the British Council, or due to the winding up of the NAEP in 1980, there was a lull in Indo-British cooperation for a short while. Apart from sponsoring a visit by John Foster and Good to study adult education programmes in south India in 1980,[17] the British Council also funded a visit by Alan Rogers in 1983 to help S.V. University (Tirupati) develop an extension education programme.[18] In 1985, when S.N.D.T. University (Bombay) sought the assistance of British experts in developing a curriculum for a certificate course in adult continuing education, the British Council sponsored Alan Rogers (University of Reading), Jennifer Barnes (Sheffield Polytechnic) and Donald Macleans (University of Manchester).[19]

Development of institutional links has been one of the main pursuits of half a dozen British adult educators who visited India between 1979 and 1990. The earliest initiative in this connection was taken by Alan Rogers in 1977, when he made a proposal to the British Council to support a link between the universities of Madras and Nottingham for the exchange of members of staff, and for publications and collaborative research.[20] Since university adult education was at its infancy in India, the link with Nottingham was very beneficial to the University of Madras. Subsequently, in 1979, Fordham explored the possibilities of establishing a link between the universities of Madras and Southampton with the same objectives.[21] These links provided an opportunity to a few members of the staff of the collaborating universities for mutual visits. While the British experts, by virtue of their experience and academic credentials, could participate in teaching and research programmes at the University of Madras, most of the Indian counterparts were found to be lacking in the qualifications required for teaching work at British universities, so their visit to the U.K. was essentially limited to participation in conferences and browsing through libraries. Because of the unequal partnership between Indian and British universities, few significant collaborative research or teaching programmes could be designed. Perhaps the only exception was a research study coordinated by Fordham on "Commonwealth experience in the use of distance teaching for the non-formal education of adults", which was funded by the Commonwealth Foundation and carried out in collaboration with a number of Commonwealth countries, including India.[22] Alan Rogers also carried out a "pilot attitudinal survey of literacy animators in Tamil Nadu" with the collaboration of the department of adult education of the University of Madras.[23]

During 1979–85, two significant reports on Indian adult education were brought out by Paul Fordham and P.J. Sutton. On a study tour funded by the British Council, Fordham visited several universities in India in 1979 with a view to ascertaining the status of university adult education, and exploring the possibilities of developing linkages between British and Indian universities. He brought out a significant report entitled "Indian universities and adult education", which not only discusses the status of adult education in the universities of Rajasthan, Madras, Pune, Andhra and Baroda (M.S. University), but also comments on the work culture in their departments of adult education in a confidential anexure to the report.[24] Commenting on the lack of interest in field programmes among the members of certain departments, Fordham mentions his experience of visiting a village accompanied by a staff member who was supposed to be supervising a student field programme there. When the staff member could not find the way to the village project and had to ask several people about the route, it became apparent that the member might never have visited the village. This report, which is noteworthy for its objective assessment of Indian university adult education in the 1970s, makes interesting reading with a number of anecdotes. The second report, entitled "Adult education in India" by P.J. Sutton, is a detailed study covering the programmes, practices and problems of adult education in four states: Kerala, Karnataka, Rajasthan and Maharashtra. One of its observations is on exaggerated claims of success, and the need to have a sense of proportion in making statistical projections and assessing success. Perhaps Sutton was puzzled by the practice of certain Indian adult educators of supplying inflated figures and making lofty claims of success.

One of the characteristics of the British visitors to India was their keenness to visit the maximum number of university adult education departments, professional organizations and NGOs, and interact with as many leading Indian adult educators as possible. Though most of them gave public lectures and participated in adult education conferences, some like Fordham and Rogers, who were closely associated with the University of Madras, S.V. University, S.N.D.T. University, Andhra University, M.S. University, University of Rajasthan and JNU, also provided academic help, especially in curriculum development, designing extension programmes, staff training, teaching and research. Besides, they also served, and continue to serve, as external Ph.D. examiners for a few Indian universities. Though they have had the professional satisfaction of providing academic support to the development of adult education programmes in a developing country like India and, at the same time, building friendly relations with their counterparts, certain specific academic advantages also accrued to them. Apart from the official reports they submitted to the funding agencies on the various activities they undertook in India, they also gave seminars in the U.K. on Indian adult education and brought out publications.[25]

Impact, Issues and Implications

It is estimated that, over the last two decades, about 47 adult educators—25 British and the rest Indians—availed financial assistance from the British Council, either fully or partly. They did so under three schemes—specialist tours, visitorships and HELS—with three specific purposes: (1) providing academic support to the university departments of adult education, especially in the process of curriculum development, staff training, teaching and research; (2) studying ongoing adult education programmes and visiting adult education institutions and organizations; and (3) participating in conferences and workshops and interacting with fellow professionals. The durations of their visit varied from six days to six months. A number of issues have emerged from the experiences of those who were associated with the implementation of HELS, and its limited success in achieving the objectives of designing and carrying out collaborative research, partnership projects, bringing out collaborative publications, developing innovative models and exchanging publications.

If we subscribe to the view that international cooperation should capacitate and empower the partners, then Indo-British partnership in adult education has been a success, especially from the point of view of the British. This is mainly due to the fact that, over the years, British adult educators have gained considerable professional competence and experience, both as practitioners and researchers, and hence better placed to derive the benefits. When the partnership is between a strong and not-so-strong partner, the chances are that the former reaps maximum benefits. The success of a collaborative programme, however, demands that the strong partner assume a leadership role so as to enable the other to achieve common objectives. In the case of Indo-British cooperation, this did not happen. This may be partly due to the personal idiosyncracies of certain Indian and British adult educators associated with partnership projects, or the tactical decision of British adult educators to remain "absolutely non-interfering."

Indo-British cooperation in adult education has had its impact on the development of the adult education curriculum in some British universities. The experience of studying Indian innovations like the women's cooperatives or income generator programmes seems to have motivated some British professors to incorporate aspects of the programmes and related literature into the curriculum of the masters degree programmes at the universities of Edinburgh, Reading, Southampton and Warwick. T.G. Steward,[26] who took an active interest in establishing links between the University of Edinburgh and S.V. University, observed along with Rogers that, since "much of the interesting developments take place outside England," the opportunity for "creative learning from developing countries" provided through the links scheme was welcome. Vickerstaff, who was associated with the links programme between Kent and Mother Teresa University, considered such a programme an opportunity which provided a "non-Anglo-American perspective" to the British curriculum.[27]

It is rather surprising that, in spite of the longstanding association between British and Indian adult educators, there has been a dearth of collaborative projects. One of the reasons may be the absence of a research culture in some departments of adult education in India, and the lack of interest in research as a key activity among faculty members. The limited number of research articles by Indians in international journals bears testimony to this fact.[28] Some British professors who served as external examiners of Ph.D. theses were dismayed at the quality of research work. Others, who had the chance of working longer in India, were disillusioned with the "total lack of research orientation and work culture" in the departments of adult education in most Indian universities.[29] Perhaps these factors, too, discouraged them from working out collaborative research projects with Indian counterparts. A large number of international adult educators tend to specialize in some area, while Indian adult educators invariably tend to be generalist, so the possibilities of collaboration remain limited.

One of the major irritants in HELS concerned the funding pattern. Participants in HELS receive 50% of their international travel fare and a meagre subsistence allowance ranging from £10 to £20 per day. Few of the British university adult educators who were keen to establish links with Indian universities were able to raise the additional resources to meet their expenses and visit the selected partner institutions for discussions and collaborative projects. For example, although the initiative for the links between S.V. University and Edinburgh and JNU and Warwick came from the British side, the Indian side could not reciprocate. The links scheme provides only half the international fare to the participants, with the other half coming from the parent university or the UGC. The Indian partners were handicapped by the non-supportive attitude of their respective universities and UGC, and hence failed to raise the required resources. UGC policy has recognized extension as the third dimension of higher education in India, and has issued guidelines to the universities to support adult education as a legitimate activity. In practice, however, some key academicians, like the deans and vociferous members of academic bodies, tend to ignore the legitimate claims made by adult educators and do not provide adequate finances. Unless the two collaborating institutions make some preliminary assessment of their strengths and weaknesses and the attitude of key administrators towards adult education, the implementation process is likely to run into trouble. In the light of the experiences of a number of British and Indian adult educators, it is observed that, to be fully productive, the partnership between them needs to be fine-tuned from both personal and professional angles, and all the administrative and financial details of the collaborative programmes need to be meticulously worked out.

Added to this biased attitude of the Indian university community is the unattractive subsistence allowance in the

U.K., which dampens the enthusiasm to initiate any collaborative programmes with British universities. In the absence of a reciprocal response from their Indian counterparts, British attempts at establishing links remain one-sided and, in the long run, may encourage paternalism. Although the links programmes were envisaged with some sharing of expenditure between the two partners, experience shows that adult educators in India rarely get the share that should be contributed by their own universities. In this situation, there could be two alternatives to make the programme reciprocal and productive: (1) the British Council pays the visitor all travel expenses, some research allowance for books, stationery and typing, and a decent *per diem*; or (2) the Indian adult educators seek financial support from professional bodies or research foundations.

One of the handicaps of the links scheme is its over-dependence on institutional leadership. The limited operationalization of the links scheme reveals, however, that its success depends primarily on the ability of key individuals to chalk out a mutually acceptable programme. As long as such individuals remain at the helm of affairs, the programme operates smoothly and successfully. However, there has been high professional mobility among the key individuals. With their departure, the scheme collapses, mainly because of the absence of second-level leadership. This happens when, due to interpersonal problems and professional rivalries, the key persons find it difficult to groom successors. In such a situation, it is utopian to think of strengthening a department as a whole and encouraging younger faculty members to derive benefits from HELS. Since the links scheme is basically an arrangement between institutions, it becomes difficult to transfer the scheme along with the key person to the new institution. Some amount of flexibility in HELS to permit its transfer to a new institution may go a long way in making it more successful.

A review of the implementation of HELS tends to give the impression that the British Council has been operationalizing the scheme in a half-hearted manner. The recipients of British

Council grants invariably submit a report to the Council. Several of these reports contain interesting but important observations and discussions on the problems and prospects of future collaborations. It seems that the reports are examined and filed in a routine manner by the London office of the British Council. They are rarely preserved for more than five years, presumably owing to the shortage of space. Had the British Council preserved the reports for the last two decades, scrutinized them to identify the issues, and perhaps convened a seminar of the recipients, it is possible that ways and means of making the programme more effective could then have been explored. This is all the more important when none of the evaluation studies of ODA-funded projects included HELS.[30]

Although British cooperation was sought by India both to draw on international experience and as an addition to the available resources and expertise within the country, questions have often been raised on the relevance of British experience to the Indian situation. It is a fact that many non-formal education programmes in Britain are far removed from the realities of Indian society. However, with the emergence of Britain as a multicultural society, and growing poverty and unemployment there, special programmes for women and the urban poor are being undertaken which are not much different from the approaches followed in third-world countries. To quote Paul Fordham, the former director of the department of adult education at the University of Southampton: "I was struck by the similarities of efforts being made in Bombay's urban slum areas with those being made by my department ... The great strength of British departments is their wealth of practical teaching experience at a number of different levels ... The British contribution might be offered in terms of adult education training methodology, and on a wider front than just functional literacy."[31] Commenting on the possibilities of developing meaningful cooperation between British and Indian universities, Alan Rogers, who was associated with several Indian universities, observes that adult education methodology being culture-free, there are tremendous possibilities for developing collaborative research, evolving trainer's programmes, and exchanging staff between developed and developing countries.[32] Apart from the deep interest in university adult education, it was the academic challenge of working in such an area in a developing country like India that had motivated some British adult educators. Invariably, most of them seem to have cherished the prospects of developing professional and personal links with the Indians. Those who had the academic competence and third-world experience were acceptable to quite a few leading adult educators of India, who invited them time and again. The closer interaction between Indian and British adult educators not only sensitized them to each other's philosophies, practices and professional ethos, but also generated considerable academic interest in each other's programmes, paving the way for collaborative projects and publications.

A review of the experiences of British experts and discussions with some of them bring out their desire to learn as much as possible from India. Their publications on various aspects of Indian adult education, brought out from time to time, bear testimony to their interest in the subject. While the drawbacks did not escape their notice, they have highlighted several strengths as well. The Indian workers education programme has been identified as worth emulating by Britain.[33] Others have noted that India has one of the most highly developed infrastructures for non-formal and adult education programmes.[34] Emphasizing the need to learn from the experiences of those in economically and technologically less-developed regions, as well as the reverse, Alan Rogers observes, "the West is moving closer to the third-world, and is beginning to seek in that part of the world answers to some of its problems ... In the application of the concepts of development to the West, we have much to learn from the insights and experiences of the third-world countries. The concept of development as applied in the third-world countries might form the basis of the reorientation which is being sought for adult education in the West."[35]

Informal discussions with a few British experts revealed

their disillusionment at not being "properly utilized." Some of them had a feeling that their time and talents were not fully tapped by their local hosts, who considered them "dignitaries", and tried to pack their programmes with public functions and meetings with local luminaries. They mentioned that there was hardly any scope for serious scholarly interaction.[36] Such a situation arises when the local hosts lack international exposure and intellectual orientation to interact with overseas experts. In spite of these limitations, British participation has always been welcomed by Indian adult educators, not only as an addition to Indian expertise but also as a means to enrich Indian programmes by drawing on their international experiences and expertise. On the other hand, British specialists were also keen to visit India, notwithstanding the problems. To quote Lowe, "India is a strange and sometimes irritating country, but ultimately, a rewarding one."[37]

What was the response of the Indian adult educators to British participation? How did the Indian professionals perceive their counterparts? Surprisingly, not many Indians were forthcoming. A questionnaire was mailed to 22 selected Indian adult educators but the response was very disheartening. Unlike in the U.K., it was neither easy nor economic to contact the Indian experts by telephone, since they are scattered all over the country. Only a few could be interviewed personally. Some Indian adult educators rated the leadership qualities of British experts and their contribution to the programme as "very high" on a 3-point scale. The participants at a national workshop held in New Delhi in 1990, in which an eminent British adult educator gave a series of lectures, reported that his lectures were "very scholarly" and "academically stimulating."[38] In view of the vast differences in the academic background and experiences of the British experts, and the large number of programmes in which they participated, it would be misleading to generalize. A more detailed questionnaire, tailored to the role of individual experts in various programmes, will be required to make a realistic assessment. The majority of Indian adult educators who had a chance to interact with British specialists reported that they were "enamored by their academic credentials and ability to cope with Indian conditions." Jayagopal, head of the department of adult education at the University of Madras, who had the chance of working with a number of British experts for more than a decade, categorically stated that his department has greatly benefited by British cooperation. "Apart from the gifts of British books and journals," he said, "the students and staff members of the department also got a chance to interact with British specialists, attend their seminars and even participate in some of their research projects and collaborative publications."[39] The fact that the departments of adult education in the universities of Barkatulla (Bhopal), Kerala (Trivandrum), S.N.D.T. (Bombay), S.V. (Tirupati), M.S. (Baroda) and Madras, which had close contact with British universities, have introduced a variety of short-term adult education courses on the U.K. pattern may be viewed as a manifestation of British influence on Indian adult education. As observed by Styler, "India has shown, however, that she can take models from other countries, give them specific Indian characteristics, and even relate them to her own traditions."[40] A survey of the reading lists of various adult education courses in Indian universities reveals their dependence on British professional literature. It may be concluded that Indian university adult education still follows a British tradition. In perpetuating and promoting this tradition, British experts and various partnership programmes have been playing a key role during the last two decades.

It has been observed that, since 1972, about 22 Indian adult educators have visited the U.K. under various exchange programmes, fellowships, study tours and bursaries. However, only six of them seem to have spent more than 3 months in Britain and made systematic attempts at studying particular aspects of British adult education. While all of them prepared detailed reports about their programmes in the U.K., and disseminated their experiences through presentations and publications, only two of them have brought out comprehensive studies.[41] Those Indian adult educators who had undertaken a study tour to different adult education organizations in the U.K., and whom this researcher could contact, unanimously stated that their U.K. experiences were "academically refreshing and led to the widening of their knowledge, and even helped them to change their attitude and belief on adult education in the Western world." They were also benefitted by access to a wide variety of professional literature on adult education.[42]

Conclusion

A variety of factors have promoted Indo-British cooperation in adult education during the last two decades. If, on the one hand, the continuation of the English language, colonial administrative infrastructure and patterns of education in India brought the two nations closer, it was the growing need for international cooperation between developed and developing countries that paved the way for a number of bilateral and multilateral programmes between India and Britain since the 1950s. The persistent interest of a number of Britons and Indians in maintaining old colonial links due to personal and social reasons cannot be underestimated. Nevertheless, Britain is now a multicultural society with growing unemployment and poverty. These seem to have been the crucial concerns that drew the attention of a number of British development workers and policy planners towards India, which has been tackling such problems on a much larger scale. Since 1980, some British researchers have identified India as a potential field for finding clues to Britain's own developmental issues, such as growing illiteracy and unemployment.

Irrespective of the amount of professional benefit that may have accrued to both the partners, and the immense potentialities of cooperating for literacy, a number of factors are likely to hamper future prospects. With growing regionalism in India, and gradual replacement of English by regional languages as the medium of teaching and research in a number of Indian universities, it will be difficult to pursue collaborative ventures. While the new communication technologies have shortened the distance between India and Britain, postal, fax and telephone charges in India are still far too high to enable the average Indian professor to communicate frequently with his or her counterpart in Britain. The recent budgetary cuts in Indian higher education and increasing international airfares also do not augur well for the development of partnership projects. All the same, the significance of international cooperation in literacy cannot be underestimated, especially because of its role in bringing the two nations closer and thereby enhancing international understanding and friendship. The future challenge lies in exploring the ways and means of enhancing the effectiveness and extent of cooperation in an increasingly interdependent world. What new instrumentalities and methods can be employed? How can the continuing cooperation be strengthened?

Notes

1. Two conferences organized by the International Council for Adult Education and the German Foundation for International Development are noteworthy. See Paul Fordham (ed.), *One Billion Illiterates, One Billion Reasons for Action: Report on the International Seminar on Cooperating for Literacy*, International Council For Adult Education and German Foundation for International Development, Toronto, 1985. See also, "International aid in adult education: working papers from the Kungsalv seminar", *Convergence*, Vol. 19, No. 4, 1986.
2. On this point, see Agneta Lind and Mark Foss, *International Cooperation in Literacy: Two Good Examples*, International Bureau of Education, Geneva, 1990, pp. 5–6.
3. Bhola observes that, although international cooperation in adult education has been handled mostly through UNESCO, not much is available in writing about the pattern and effects of this cooperation from the point of view of UNESCO's member states, perhaps with the exception of a study on Yugoslavia. See N.N. Soljan, "Yugoslavia's international cooperation in the sphere of adult education: policy and practice", in N.N. Soljan,

M. Golubovic, and A. Krajnc (eds.), *Adult Education in Yugoslav Society*, Andragoski Center, Zagreb, Yugoslavia, 1983; H.S. Bhola, *World Trends and Issues in Adult Education*, Jessia Kingsley, London, 1989, pp. 171–173.

4. *Annual Report of the British Council, 1981–82*, p. 22.
5. Overseas Development Administration, *Into the Nineties: An Education Policy for British Aid*, p. 11.
6. See Overseas Development Administration, *Overseas Aid*, 1986, p. 53.
7. Maurice Zinkan, *Why Help India?*, Vol. 2, Pergamon, London, pp. 40–42.
8. Overseas Development Administration, *Into the Nineties, op. cit.*
9. *Annual Report of the British Council for the Year 1981–82*, p. 11.
10. Earlier, the scheme was known as Cooperation Through Links.
11. *Committee for International Cooperation in Higher Education: University Links*, British Council, London, 1987, pp. 7, 10–11.
12. *Higher Education Links Scheme—A Guidance Note*, revised edition, August, 1986, British Council, New Delhi, pp. 1–3.
13. There were successful links in the fields of science and technology. There was a successful link between the universities of Sussex and Rajasthan in chemistry in 1983.
14. See the note on specialist tours, Specialist Tours Department, British Council, January, 1984.
15. *Annual Report of the British Council for the Year 1977–78*, p. 34.
16. See K.T. Elsden, J. Oxenham and J.W. Spencer, *Confidential Report on India's National Adult Education Programme*, Alan Rogers collection, Box No. 3, pp. 10–11.
17. See John Foster and Good, "British Council tour to south India", Documentation Centre, University of Reading.
18. See Alan Rogers collection on India, Box No. 1.
19. *Ibid.*, Box. No. 8 and 9.
20. See Alan Roger's "Report to the British Council on a visit to India", Alan Rogers collection, Box No. 1, January, 1977.
21. See Paul Fordham, "Indian university and adult education: Report of a study visit—2 October–3 November 1979", Paul Fordham collection.
22. For details of this study, see Paul Fordham, "Commonwealth experiences in the use of distance teaching for the non-formal

education of adults", in *Newsletter and Papers*, INCED, Coventry, 1990, pp. 10–36.

23. See Alan Rogers (ed.), *Partners in Literacy: A Pilot Attitudinal Survey of Literacy Animators in Tamil Nadu, India*, Education for Development, Norfolk, 1989.
24. A copy of the report is available at the Documentation Centre, Reading.
25. See, among others: Alan Rogers, *Adults Learning for Development*, Cassell, London, 1992; P.J. Sutton, *Adult Education in India: Literacy, Languages and Social Change*, National Institute of Adult Continuing Education, Leicester, 1984; Paul Fordham, *Commonwealth Experience in the Use of Distance Teaching for the Non-Formal Education of Adults*, 1990; Mal Leceister, "Community development and women's education: The Basti project, Delhi", in *CAETA Newsletter*, January, 1991.
26. Telephonic interview with T.G. Steward on 14-6-1991.
27. Telephonic interview with Vickerstaff on 13-6-1991.
28. A survey of the two leading international journals—*Convergence* and *International Journal of University Adult Education*—shows that there were not many articles by Indians.
29. This was the opinion of most of the British adult educators interviewed by the author.
30. Literacy was outside the purview of the 13 evaluation documents published since 1974. For details, see M. Lipton and J. Toye, *Does Aid Work in India: A Country Study of the Impact of Official Development Assistance*, Routledge, London, 1990.
31. Paul Fordham, "Indian universities and adult education", Fordham collection, 1979.
32. See Alan Rogers, "Report to the British Council on a visit to India, January, 1979", p. 4.
33. See "Report of a six-week visit to India" by Paul Gerhardt, Workers Education Association, Coventry, September-October, 1978, p. 9.
34. See Paul Fordham, "Report on non-formal education", submitted to the Commonwealth Foundation, 1982.
35. Alan Rogers, *Adults Learning for Development*, *op. cit.*, pp. 3–5.
36. Interview with Paul Fordham on 18-6-1991.
37. Letter from John Lowe to Alan Rogers dated 16 September 1975, Alan Rogers collection, Box No. 1.
38. See the participants' evaluation of a six-week all-India

orientation programme of adult education officers held at NIEPA in January, 1990.

39. Interview with R. Jayagopal in New Delhi on 20-3-1992.
40. W.E. Styler, *Adult Education in India*, Oxford University Press, London, 1996, p. 60.
41. S.Y. Shah, "International cooperation in Indian adult education: The role and influence of Britain", unpublished, 1992; K. Sivadasan Pillai, *Non-Formal Education in Britain as an Indian Adult Educator Saw it*, Kalaniketan, Trivandrum, 1984.
42. Ramesh Thanvi, "Twenty weeks in Britain: A brief report", London; Neerja Sharma, "Some observation and experiences: A report of a three-month study tour in the United Kingdom", Commonwealth Relations Trust, 1991. R.S. Mathur observes in a letter to Alan Rogers dated 22 March 1978, "real professional gain accrued to me as a result of my visit to the U.K.," Alan Rogers collection, Box No. 1; see S.Y. Shah, *op. cit.*, pp. 65–73.

Index

Index